World Englishes at the Grassroots

World Englishes at the Grassroots

Edited by Christiane Meierkord and Edgar W. Schneider

Edinburgh University Press is one of the leading university presses in the UK. We publish academic books and journals in our selected subject areas across the humanities and social sciences, combining cutting-edge scholarship with high editorial and production values to produce academic works of lasting importance. For more information visit our website: edinburghuniversitypress.com

© editorial matter and organisation Christiane Meierkord and Edgar W. Schneider, 2021, 2022
© the chapters their several authors, 2021, 2022

Edinburgh University Press Ltd
The Tun – Holyrood Road, 12(2f) Jackson's Entry, Edinburgh EH8 8PJ

First published in hardback by Edinburgh University Press 2021

Typeset in 11.5/13 Monotype Ehrhardt by
Servis Filmsetting Ltd, Stockport, Cheshire

A CIP record for this book is available from the British Library

ISBN 978 1 4744 6755 1 (hardback)
ISBN 978 1 4744 6756 8 (paperback)
ISBN 978 1 4744 6757 5 (webready PDF)
ISBN 978 1 4744 6758 2 (epub)

The right of Christiane Meierkord and Edgar W. Schneider to be identified as the editors of this work has been asserted in accordance with the Copyright, Designs and Patents Act 1988, and the Copyright and Related Rights Regulations 2003 (SI No. 2498).

Contents

List of Figures   vii
List of Tables   viii
List of Contributors   ix

1 Introduction: English Spreading at the Grassroots   1
 Christiane Meierkord and Edgar W. Schneider

2 Grassroots English, Learner English, Second-language English,
 English as a Lingua Franca . . .: What's in a Name?   23
 Sarah Buschfeld

Part I: English at the grassroots in former spheres of British domination

3 The Sociolinguistic Profile of English at the Grassroots Level:
 A Comparison of Northern and Western Uganda   49
 Bebwa Isingoma

4 English Language Learning Trajectories among Zanzibaris Working
 in Tourism   70
 Susanne Mohr

5 Access to English and the Englishes of the Disadvantaged: Examples
 from Uganda and South Africa   91
 Christiane Meierkord

6 Artistic Re-creation of Grassroots English: Ideologies and Structures
 in *English Vinglish*   115
 Edgar W. Schneider

Part II: English in trade and work migration

7 Facets of Intercultural Communication Employed in the Conversations of Local Arab Traders in Bahrain 143
Anthonia Bamidele-Akhidenor

8 The Value of Grassroots English for Bangladeshi Migrants to the Middle East 165
Qumrul Hasan Chowdhury and Elizabeth J. Erling

9 Grassroots Diffusion of English in a 'Blue-collar' Workplace: The Case of a Multilingual Cleaning Company in New Jersey, USA 186
Kellie Gonçalves

Part III: English in forced migration

10 Language Use among Syrian Refugees in Germany 211
Guyanne Wilson

11 Uprooted Speakers' Grassroots English: Metalinguistic Perspectives of Asylum Seekers in Germany 233
Axel Bohmann

12 Onward Migration from Italy to the UK: Reshaped Linguistic Repertoires and the Role of English 255
Francesco Goglia

Index 272

Figures

4.1	Unguja and Pemba islands	73
4.2	Primary school in Jambiani	82
5.1	Selected informants, anonymised	102
6.1	Sapna's smirk	121
6.2	Satish and Sapna exchange glances	123
6.3	Shashi and the café cashier	124
6.4	The language school secretary articulating deliberately carefully	124
6.5	Shashi delivering a public speech in English, with her husband worried and surprised	125
6.6	Distribution of utterance types by acquisition stages	130
6.7	MLUs (mean length of utterances) by speakers and stages	131
6.8	Copula usage by stages	133
7.1	Age range	151
7.2	Gender	151
7.3	Highest educational qualification	152
7.4	Proficiency in speaking English	152
7.5	Mode of acquiring English	153
9.1	Shine's company hierarchy with Magda located at the top	193

Tables

3.1	Level of education of informants	51
3.2	Examples of acrolectal Ugandan English lexical features used by speakers of grassroots English in Uganda	54
3.3	Frequency of the use of English	57
3.4	Interlocutors in the use of English	57
4.1	Socio-demographic background of the participants	76
5.1	Statistics relating to education in South Africa and Uganda	100
5.2	Informants' details	101
5.3	Features across South African and Ugandan speakers	108
6.1	The grassroots learners: origins and motives	128
6.2	The learners' three acquisition stages distinguished	128
9.1	Socio-demographic differences between Newark and Westwood based on 2017 census information (Newark City Data 2017)	192
11.1	Locally relevant sociolinguistic orders at different scale levels	238

Contributors

Anthonia Bamidele-Akhidenor received her master's degree in English Language and Linguistics from the University of Botswana in 2012 and currently teaches English in the Kingdom of Bahrain. Her research interests cover aspects of sociolinguistics, intercultural/cross-cultural communication, migration and diaspora studies, English for academic and specific purposes, and China relations with Africa and the Gulf region. She has published papers in some of these areas, including, most recently, one on 'The roles of online placement tests in English language learning' (2019).

Axel Bohmann holds a PhD (2017) in English from the University of Texas at Austin and currently works as an Assistant Professor at Albert-Ludwigs-Universität Freiburg. He has published on English language contact in German hip hop culture, dialect levelling in Texas English, the role of prescriptivism in written English relativiser choice, ideological debates around hyper-correct language in Jamaica, and innovative forms of *because* in Twitter communication. His book *Variation in English Worldwide: Registers and Global Varieties* (2019, Cambridge University Press) presents a feature-aggregation-based corpus study that develops ten fundamental dimensions of linguistic variation in English worldwide.

Sarah Buschfeld is Full Professor of English Linguistics (Multilingualism) at the Technical University of Dortmund, after previous appointments at the Universities of Regensburg and Cologne. She has worked on postcolonial and non-postcolonial varieties of English (e.g. English in Cyprus, Greece, Namibia and Singapore) and in the fields of bi-/multilingualism and language acquisition. She has written and edited several articles and books on these topics (including *English in Cyprus or Cyprus English: An Empirical Investigation of Variety Status*, 2013, Benjamins, and *Children's English in Singapore: Acquisition, Properties, and*

Use, 2020, Routledge) and she works on the definitions and interconnections of these disciplines and concepts.

Qumrul Hasan Chowdhury is Assistant Professor of English in the Institute of Modern Languages at the University of Dhaka, Bangladesh. He holds an MA in TESOL from University College London's Institute of Education and pursued his PhD in the Centre for Language, Discourse and Communication at King's College London with a Commonwealth Scholarship. His research interests are English and development, language and religion and southern applied linguistics. He has worked in several research projects in Bangladesh on English and development and the internationalisation of higher education. He has published chapters in *The Routledge Handbook of Language and Identity* (2016), *English Across the Fracture Lines* (2017, British Council) and *The Routledge International Handbook of English Language Education in Bangladesh* (2020), and has published articles in the journals *World Englishes*, *Journal of English as a Lingua Franca* and *Multilingua*.

Elizabeth J. Erling is Professor of English Language Teaching Research and Methodology at the University of Graz, Austria. Her research focuses on the perceived impact that the English language has on individuals' lives in terms of social, economic and cultural capital. She led the research project on perceptions of English among migrant workers from Bangladesh and has been involved in many publications on this and related research in *Current Issues in Language Planning*, *Multilingua* and *World Englishes*. She is the editor of *English across the Fracture Lines* (2017, British Council) and *English and Development* (2013, Multilingual Matters).

Francesco Goglia is a Senior Lecturer in Italian in the Department of Modern Languages at the University of Exeter. His research interests are in multilingualism, language maintenance and shift, and language contact in immigrant communities in particular in Italy, the UK, East Timor and Australia. His current research, supported by the Leverhulme Trust, focuses on multilingualism and language maintenance among onward-migrating families from Italy to the UK.

Kellie Gonçalves is currently a Postdoctoral Fellow at the University of Köln, Germany. She has previously held postdoctoral positions at MultiLing, University of Oslo, Norway (2017–20) and the University of Bern, Switzerland (2010–14). She obtained her PhD in Modern English Linguistics from the University of Bern, Switzerland and was a Marie Heim-Vögtlin Grant recipient (2015–17) awarded by the Swiss National Science Foundation. Her research interests include multilingualism, semiotic landscapes, language and workplace studies, tourism discourse, and women and leadership. In addition to her research interests in sociolinguistics, she is an advocate for gender equality and female leadership within academia. She is the author of *Conversations of Intercultural Couples* (2013, De Gruyter), *Labour Policies, Language Use and the 'New' Economy: The Case of Adventure Tourism* (2020, Palgrave Macmillan) and co-author of *Domestic Workers Talk* (forthcoming, Multilingual Matters, with Anne Schluchter). Her articles have appeared in *International Journal of the Sociology of Language*, *Multilingua*, *International Journal of Multilingualism*, *Gender and Language* and *Language Policy*.

Bebwa Isingoma is a Senior Lecturer in English Language and Linguistics and Dean of the Faculty of Education and Humanities at Gulu University (Uganda). He obtained his PhD in English Linguistics (comparative syntax) at the University of Agder in 2013. He is an EU Marie S. Curie FCFP fellow (Freiburg Institute for Advanced Studies, 2018–19) as well as a fellow of the African Humanities Program (American Council of Learned Societies) with a residency at Rhodes University in 2015. His research areas include English linguistics, comparative syntax, sociolinguistics and Bantu linguistics. Recent publications include a co-edited volume with Christiane Meierkord and Saudah Namyalo on *Ugandan English: Its Sociolinguistics, Structure and Uses in a Globalizing Post-Protectorate* (2016, Benjamins) and chapters therein (singly authored and co-authored) as well as a co-authored chapter with Christiane Meierkord 'Capturing the lexicon of Ugandan English: ICE-Uganda – its limitations and effective supplements', in Esimaje, Gut and Antia (eds) *African Englishes and Corpus Linguistics* (2019, Benjamins).

Christiane Meierkord holds the Chair of English Linguistics at the Ruhr-University of Bochum and has previously taught at the Universities of Erfurt, Münster and Stockholm, where she was a visiting professor. She is author of *Interactions across Englishes: Linguistic Choices in Local and International Contact Situations* (2012, Cambridge University Press) and has published extensively on the use of English as a lingua franca, both from a descriptive as well as from a sociolinguistic perspective. She has also co-edited *Ugandan English: Its Sociolinguistics, Structure and Uses in a Globalising Post-Protectorate* (2016, Benjamins), with Bebwa Isingoma and Saudah Namyalo. Her current research focuses on the forms and functions of English in post-protectorates (currently with a focus on African nations, particularly Uganda and Rwanda, and the Maldives) and on the recent spread of English at the grassroots of societies. She regularly serves as a reviewer for publishers, universities and research funding organisations.

Susanne Mohr is Associate Professor of English Sociolinguistics at the Norwegian University of Science and Technology. She spent the 2018/19 academic year at the University of Cape Town, where she worked on her project on language and tourism sponsored by the Alexander von Humboldt Foundation. She recently continued this work with a research fellowship from the cluster of excellence 'Africa Multiple' at the Bayreuth Academy of Advanced African Studies. Susanne obtained her PhD on language contact between Irish Sign Language and English from the University of Cologne and worked on non-standardised plurals and countability in African Englishes for her postdoctoral dissertation at the University of Bonn. She is actively engaged in several interdisciplinary research projects, most notably involving linguistics and anthropology. Her research interests include anthropological linguistics, multilingualism and (cross-modal) language contact, globalisation, tourism studies and intercultural communication.

Edgar W. Schneider is Emeritus Professor of English Linguistics at the University of Regensburg, Germany, after having held the chair there for many years and previous appointments at universities in Bamberg, Georgia (USA) and Berlin. He is an internationally renowned sociolinguist and World Englishes scholar, known widely for his 'Dynamic Model' of the evolution of Postcolonial Englishes. He has lectured on all continents, given many keynote lectures at international conferences and published many articles and books on the dialectology, sociolinguistics, history, semantics and varieties of English, including *American Earlier Black English* (1989, Alabama Press), *Handbook of Varieties of English* (two volumes, 2004, Mouton) and *Postcolonial English* (2007, Cambridge University Press), *English Around the World* (2nd edn 2020, Cambridge University Press) and the *Cambridge Handbook of World Englishes*. For many years he edited the journal *English World-Wide* and its associated book series, *Varieties of English Around the World*, and he is now the editor of Cambridge University Press's new publishing format *Elements: World Englishes*.

Guyanne Wilson is currently a Postdoctoral Researcher at the Ruhr University Bochum. She has worked as a university lecturer since 2009, with previous appointments at the University of the West Indies, Duisburg-Essen and Ghent. She completed her undergraduate study at King's College London and her MPhil in Linguistics at the University of Cambridge, where she received funding from the Cambridge Commonwealth Trust, before pursuing her PhD at the University of Münster. In her doctoral dissertation, she used choral singing data to isolate phonological features of Trinidad Standard English and Trinidad English Creole, and also to examine language attitudes and ideologies in Trinidad. Her current research foci include language use among refugees in Germany, research methods in New Englishes, and variation in agreement in African and Caribbean varieties of English – the topic of her postdoctoral dissertation.

CHAPTER I

Introduction: English Spreading at the Grassroots

Christiane Meierkord and Edgar W. Schneider

1 TIME TO MOVE ON

For centuries, and during the last few decades in particular, the English language has spread vastly beyond its original areas of usage, as a second or foreign language, having produced what are called world Englishes[1] (cf. Schneider 2007, 2011; Mesthrie and Bhatt 2008). While other languages such as Mandarin and Spanish ('super-central languages' after de Swaan 2002) have also been found to be spreading, they do so at more localised levels, that is in the sinophone world and in the Americas. In fact, Sabaté i Dalmau (2014) writes of 'everyone's Spanish' and 'transnational Spanish', and for example Han (2013) observes the use of Mandarin/Putonghua between Chinese and African traders. However, English is said to have emerged as *the* 'hypercentral' language (de Swaan 2002), having more second language speakers than any other and, remarkably, substantially more second and foreign language speakers than native speakers (Crystal 2008). It has become the dominant lingua franca for all kinds of international transactions and communication settings (Meierkord 2012: 132–57), in diplomacy, the business world, the sciences and academic life, sports, the arts, and also various leisure activities with international participation (such as scuba diving; see Schneider 2013).

Typically, the spread of English as a second and foreign language has largely been associated with and analysed as spoken by 'educated' elites in their respective societies. Established as a notion in the 1970s, by scholars such as Quirk (1972), Kachru (1976) and Strevens (1977), the 'educated speaker' in countries in Africa, Asia and on the Indian subcontinent used to be the focus of attention from the early phases of World Englishes research onwards. S/he was held to speak, for example, '[t]he standard variety of Indian English' (Kachru 1976: 10), that is 'Standard English dialect is spoken with a regional accent' (Strevens 1977: 140) ranging on the top end of a 'spectrum of kinds of English, which extends from those most like Pidgin to those most like standard English, with imperceptible gradations the whole way along' (Quirk 1972: 49; reflected also in Mesthrie and Bhatt's (2008: 1–10) notion of an 'English Language Complex').[2] Unfortunately, these are not merely viewpoints that were held in the 1970s, when, arguably, they may have been rooted in the realities that characterised these times. Even recent textbooks and handbooks of World Englishes, and also most publications in the leading journals that deal with world Englishes or English as a lingua franca, predominantly report on the uses of English in academia, business and administration. In fact, over the last decade very little scholarly attention has been devoted to grassroots uses of English (see section 3 below).

Increasingly, however, we have been witnessing radically different contexts and channels of the diffusion of English, outside the worlds of higher education, academia, upper-class orientations, etc. English is rapidly gaining ground 'at the grassroots', as we choose to call this process. English as a second (L2) and foreign (FL) language is also used by individuals from or in disadvantaged backgrounds with often little or no access to formal education and in contexts outside of international organisations, education and academia, and the business world (Meierkord 2012: 147–53), often typically having been learned 'in direct interactions rather than through formal education' (Schneider 2016a: 3). However, these recent developments have not sufficiently been accounted for in research into varieties of English, let alone in theorising and modelling English. It is the increasing spread of English in such situations which is at the centre of the present volume, the first one to explicitly focus on exactly the topic of *World Englishes at the grassroots* and the processes involved, and with this thematic focus it clearly breaks new ground, with important societal implications.

2 WORLD ENGLISHES AND THE GRASSROOTS: A LOOK AT TERMINOLOGY

2.1 World Englishes: A Label and its Development

While the field of World Englishes research has been well-established for a number of decades, '[t]he term "world Englishes" may be understood as having both a narrower and wider application' (Bolton 2013: 230). The former typically refers to the paradigm established by Kachru and a number of scholars following his line of thought and reasoning, as documented for example in Kachru (1982). However, over time, the term has 'been widely used to refer to localised forms of English found throughout the world, particularly in the Caribbean, parts of Africa, and many societies in Asia' (Bolton 2013: 227). As Mesthrie and Bhatt (2008: 3) explain, 'British English is not generally studied within this paradigm'.

One exception is Schneider (2011: 29), who uses the term broadly, as 'denoting all or any of the varieties spoken around the world, including British English, and, of course, forms such as Nigerian, Malaysian, or New Zealand English'. In fact, over the last decades, the scope of the term has grown considerably, following the increasing spread of English around the world, particularly in what Kachru called the Expanding Circle, to include Englishes used in countries where English was not used as an L2 for intranational communication and often had previously not made inroads into the linguistic ecology, such as Vietnam (see section 3.2 below).

Discussions of developments within the Outer and Expanding Circle have traditionally followed a variety-based approach, which typically employs geography and nation states as a frame of reference in talking about world Englishes, such as Indian English or English in Sweden (see Seargeant and Tagg 2011, and Saraceni 2015: 125 ff. for critiques). However, more recent research has questioned the validity of such clear-cut distinctions, highlighted the increasing blurring of boundaries, and proposed a post-variety approach instead (Seargeant and Tagg 2011; Edwards and Seargeant 2020). This line of thinking questions the distinction between postcolonial and non-postcolonial varieties (Buschfeld and Kautzsch 2017), focuses on mobility and what has been called a 'trans-super-poly-metro movement' (Pennycook 2016; see also Bolander 2020), and accommodates uses and users of English that cut across varieties, including uses of English as a lingua franca, both in natural as well as virtual communication contexts (see, for example, Meierkord 2012; Buschfeld et al. 2018; Mair 2020).

2.2 The Grassroots: A Fuzzy Notion

The notion of 'grassroots (movements)' has become quite popular in the recent past in fields such as politics and the business world, though it has been transferred to linguistics only occasionally and marginally. The term itself has, over the last few decades, been used in phrases such as *grassroots movement* or *grassroots democracy*, resulting in a general familiarity with it and a lay understanding of it as referring to local people's activities similar to the definition of *grassroots* offered by the Merriam-Webster Dictionary (2020) as 'the basic level of society or of an organization especially as viewed in relation to higher or more centralised positions of power', 'the ordinary people in a society or organization' and 'the people who do not have a lot of money and power'.

In relation to varieties of English, the term *grassroots* emerged in linguistics around the turn of the millennium. Khubchandani and Hosali (1999: 254) referred to the mixed codes of Hinglish and Tamlish, which are both spoken in India, and in which speakers mix English with Hindi and Tamil respectively, as being examples of 'grassroots English among those who spontaneously acquire certain rudimentary characteristics of the language in plurilingual settings (and not through formal education)' and 'are in a position to handle rudimentary tasks in English' (1999: 255). Similarly, Schneider (2016a: 3) defines *grassroots Englishes* (see 2.3) as Englishes acquired 'in direct interactions rather than through formal education' by individuals of poor backgrounds and with little or no access to formal education.

Besides this narrow use, others have used the term *grassroots* somewhat loosely as ending where 'elites' begin (Blommaert 2008) and employ a broad understanding of grassroots emergence and diffusion. The term has been employed to refer to 'a wide variety of 'non-elite forms'' (Blommaert 2008: 7, when talking about grassroots literacy), or to uses of English beyond contexts of international organisations, education, academia and the formal business world (Meierkord 2012, 2020a).

Han (2013: 84) is equally vague when defining her notion of *grassroots multilingualism* as 'the kind of multilingualism associated with globalization from below, which is characterised by fluid forms, code-switching, and nonstandard linguistic features as a result of uninstructed expansion of multilingual repertoires for localized purposes'. Somewhat differently, Erling et al. (2013) do not explicitly define what they call 'grassroots attitudes', but say that these include 'participants from different socio-economic backgrounds and those living in both urban and rural areas' (2013: 92). Lukač (2018: 5), in her discussion of 'grassroots prescriptivism', uses it to refer to bottom-up prescriptive practices 'of language users from all social backgrounds'. Both, thus, do not restrict the term to particular social classes.

What emerges from these explanations is the fact that *the grassroots* is frequently constructed as a social or socio-economic category vis-à-vis the elite. However, Trimbur (2020) explains that, although located at the edge of metropolitan modernity, the grassroots are influenced by elite conventions, registers and genres. As a result, *grassroots* thus is a fuzzy notion without clear-cut boundaries which would easily allow for individuals to be assigned to either of the two groups. Neither is it clear where 'poor backgrounds' or 'little access to formal education' end, nor do contexts outside of 'international organisations, education, academia, and the business world' clearly exclude societal elites. While socio-economic background, educational level and profession may be factors that allow for an assignment of individuals to lower social classes, similar to the methods employed in early sociolinguistics work, for example by Trudgill (1974), these are not without problems. Neither does a certain level of education assure a particular status in society, nor is wealth and high social status necessarily associated with a high level of formal educational achievement.

As individual contributions to this volume, particularly Mohr, reveal, social class membership, education and English proficiency are in no way clearly correlated. Also, an individual's status may easily change throughout his or her lifespan, as Bohmann's chapter on West African migrants and Wilson's discussion of Syrian refugees indicate. Individuals who found themselves at the upper end of society prior to migration may easily lose that status when migrating into societies that do not acknowledge their educational achievements.

2.3 Histories of World Englishes at the Grassroots: Differences and Similarities

While the earliest uses of English at the grassroots probably occurred in sporadic contacts even before the beginnings of English colonisation, their spread mainly followed the establishment of British colonies in what Kachru (1985) referred to as the Outer Circle.[3] In the late sixteenth and early seventeenth centuries this included West Africa and the Indian subcontinent, and later, starting in the late eighteenth century, Southern Africa, the Far East and East Africa. Despite the fact that the distinction between Outer and Expanding Circle has become increasingly problematic (see section 2.1 above), the fact that English spread to most Expanding Circle countries at a later stage and along different lines has implications for the spread of English at the grassroots.

The countries which Kachru discusses as belonging to the Outer Circle, that is those to which English was introduced as a result of English, and later British, colonialism and where English functions as an L2, used in the domains of administration, politics, education and the media, have often seen the introduction of both non-standard and standard forms of English. Typically, the British did not intend to Anglicise their colonies, and even then access to English was recognised as a precious commodity (Brut-Griffler 2002). Instead, perpetuating class divisions familiar from home, they allowed access to English via a Western education to leading strata of the indigenous rulers in the colonies only. A famous document in the history of education in India epitomises this attitude, namely Macaulay's 'Minute' of 1835, in which the author argued for the formation of 'a class who may be interpreters between us and the millions whom we govern – a class of persons, Indians in blood and colour, but English in taste, in opinion, in morals and in intellect' (quoted from Kachru 1983: 22). In the same vein, Lord Lugard's 'indirect rule' policy, established first in the early twentieth century in Nigeria (where Lugard was the governor) and later in many other colonies of the Empire, called for administering the colonies through a sandwiched indigenous power structure, where a local elite educated in the English spirit would formally hold authority but ultimately act in the interest of the British Crown (Brut-Griffler 2002: 56–7). At the same time, non-standard forms of English came with the settlers and military personnel, which served as input to those grassroots speakers who were in contact with these L1 speakers as slaves, servants and workers.

Towards independence, the British typically aimed to provide formal education to larger parts of the population, often through the medium of English.

However, mostly this involved school fees, restricting access to education and thus to formal acquisition of English. Thus, the attitude expressed above continued in most of the young independent nations: access to English came with access to higher education, and thus was available to wealthy and leading strata of societies only.

To some extent and in some countries this pattern continues in the twenty-first century. Today, the spread of English in the Outer Circle is crucially determined by the countries' language policy and the availability of free education to its citizens (see Meierkord this volume and 2020b). The introduction of the United Nations' Millennium Goals, one of which is the provision of free primary education, has led to increased efforts by the individual member countries and the United Nations, in many countries resulting in higher attendance rates in schools. At the same time, the benefits of mother-tongue education have often, and rightly so, resulted in a mother-tongue-based primary school curriculum, restricting access and exposure to standard English once more (see however, the case of Maldives, discussed in Meierkord 2018 and 2020a). Furthermore, in many Outer Circle countries, there exists a sharp urban-rural divide, with rural areas often seeing little English teaching and less skilled teachers (cf. Michieka 2009 for Kenya, Ssentanda 2016 for Uganda). Nevertheless, English has typically developed into an *intra*national lingua franca in these countries (see Meierkord 2012), allowing for communication across citizens who very often speak L1s that are not mutually intelligible.

By contrast, in Expanding Circle countries, English was normally learnt through formal instruction in schools in the past, initially by the offspring of more affluent parents who were sent to schools that taught a foreign language, often to ensure quality training for a profession in international trade. However, many countries (for example Finland) did not historically teach English as a foreign language in schools. The choice of language was often constrained by the country's major trading partners as, more often than not, the foreign language was learnt to communicate with its L1 speakers. Also, foreign language teaching was not usually offered to the masses, for whom it was not considered necessary. Thus, the spread of English to the grassroots via formal instruction in school is a very recent, twentieth-century development in the Expanding Circle. At the same time, the political outcomes of World War II and the division of the world into communist and non-communist led many countries to ban English teaching (cf. Meierkord 2020a). However, very recently English has also been spreading to the Maghreb, Central and South America, Central and East Asia, and the Middle East.

Uses of English typically do not take place *intra*nationally, across citizens of these states, as opposed to what is the case in Outer Circle countries, but with speakers from other countries. Initially, this involved individuals working in the fields of academia, politics and international businesses, but today users include waiters, tour guides, taxi drivers and bar girls in Vietnam, staff at restaurants, shops and hotels on Mallorca, Filipina nurses, domestic workers and traders in the Gulf states (see, for example, Bamidele-Akhidenor, this volume). Crucially, this is where, also at the grassroots, Outer and Expanding Circle contexts are becoming increasingly similar, as all countries attract traders and tourists from various parts of the world, resulting in new uses of English. Furthermore, citizens of Outer Circle countries engage in work migration just as much as individuals in the Expanding Circle. As a result, uses of English at the grassroots include customers of Chinese traders in Botswana, Ugandan peasants and informal traders dealing at local markets in the north of the country (see Isingoma, this volume) and Filipina and Indonesian nannies working in Hong Kong and Singapore.

Another similarity concerns the link between social status, access to English and tertiary education which exists even in countries in which English is a foreign language (Kachru's Expanding Circle). For instance, in China access to universities is tied to successful scores in English tests of the *gaokao*, the nationwide university entrance examination (although its importance is being reduced in recent reform steps; Rui 2014), and in Korea knowledge of English is a strong class marker, driven by a zeal known as 'English fever' (Rüdiger 2019: 26–7).

2.4 Englishes at the Grassroots and Grassroots Englishes

As a result of the sheer diversity of trajectories of the spread of English at the grassroots, Englishes come in many different forms at the lower end of societies as a result of how English has been acquired by grassroots users. As Meshtrie and Bhatt (2008: 20) explain,

> [w]hether speakers come up with a pidgin, EFL, ESL or ENL [or a jargon or creole, cm] depends on factors such as the following: (a) the relative number of speakers of the different languages, including the TL; (b) the social relations between them; (c) the duration of the contact; and (d) educational opportunities in the TL.

Given these factors, trade scenarios without large-scale settlements typically gave rise to pidgins and jargons, while creoles developed from the involuntary displacement of large segments of a population, mixing speakers of different languages as in the case of the slave trade. When colonisation went beyond trade and resulted in formal government and administration, and when formal instruction in English was involved, foreign language, L2 or L1 varieties evolved in the indigenous populations (cf. Mesthrie and Bhatt 2008: 20). Mufwene (2020: 114) submits that population structure is one crucial factor that determines the emergence of these diverse new varieties of English, but that this interacts with other ecological factors, notably periodisation, demographic proportion of the communities in contact, age differences in the communities, levels of education but also typological differences between the languages in contact with English in the process. Meierkord (2020a) describes the various 'input' Englishes that have historically included non-standard L1 varieties, spoken by missionaries, soldiers and farmers, among others, and standard varieties taught in schools, but over time have come to include pidginised and creolised varieties that spread via the media (cf. Mair 2013) but also through face-to-face interactions. She documents that Englishes which can be observed at the grassroots are extremely heterogeneous, covering various degrees of proximity to 'standardness' and adherence to the grammatical rules of standard Englishes, but also including simplification and transfer from the speakers' L1s. At the same time, the often-multilingual repertoire of the speakers results in processes of translanguaging and the development of hybrid Englishes (Schneider 2016b).

We therefore employ a broad understanding of emergence and diffusion of English at the grassroots and propose the following defining criteria:

- *Non-elite speakers*: Speakers of 'Englishes at the grassroots' typically come from or find themselves at the lower walks of life; they are not wealthy nor powerful, nor are they members of the upper strata of local societies.
- *Heterogeneity*: The trajectories of English acquisition among speakers of 'Englishes at the grassroots', as well as their proficiency in English and the structures that they use, differ considerably.

Located within this heterogenous array are what Schneider (2016a) calls 'grassroots Englishes', which in their prototypical form meet further defining criteria:

- *Natural acquisition*: Typically, 'grassroots Englishes' are acquired in natural communication contexts, outside of contexts of higher or formal education, by interacting with speakers whose performance is observed and copied. This does not mean that speakers of 'grassroots Englishes' have not had any education at all, and probably also not that they have never received any schooling in/on English; but any school training they may have had before is likely to have been poor in quality, delivered under difficult conditions, and did not leave a strong enough imprint to make them fluent, efficient speakers.
- *Instrumental motivation*: Being able to communicate in English is a goal worth striving for and worth investing some energy for grassroots learners, mostly since knowledge of English opens doors to substantially better job and income opportunities than otherwise. For instance, in tourism jobs as drivers, guides or service staff in restaurants or hotels requires the ability to communicate at least minimally and successfully with clients, while the lack of such an ability implies the need to work as porters or manual support staff.
- *Characteristic social settings*: The growth of 'grassroots Englishes' is strong

in developing countries, where one prerequisite, limited access to and poor quality of schooling for the less affluent, appears most widely and characteristically. The instrumental job motivation implies that it occurs most regularly in mid- to low-level functions in service industries, in tourism, in trade, and to some extent in business. Migration also often produces an urgent need to acquire communicative abilities in English with little previous foundation.
- *Characteristic structural patterns*: 'Grassroots Englishes' call for closer structural examination, and certainly variability is to be expected. In principle, however, structural and cognitive products of language contact in bi- and multilingual settings and features associated with early stages of second and possibly also first language acquisition will appear. These may include short or incomplete sentences, missing constituents (e.g. copulas), lack of subordination, and other simplification strategies.

However, as several contributions in this volume document (see for example the chapters by Isingoma, Meierkord, Mohr and Wilson), many other individuals at the grassroots of societies have received secondary education, and some may lack the instrumental motivation to acquire English via informal routes. Also, some degree of variability is to be expected as regards the structural patterns that may characterise uses of 'English at the grassroots', be they 'grassroots Englishes' or not.

One major aim of this volume is to provide initial documentation of the heterogeneity that characterises the forms of English at the grassroots, both in areas where English was introduced through colonialism and those to where it spread through globalisation.

3 RESEARCHING AND THEORISING (FROM) THE GRASSROOTS: TOWARDS AN AGENDA

Despite the fact that there seems to be a huge range of contexts in which English is used at the grassroots by very diverse individuals, there exist only a handful of pieces of research. Meierkord (2020a) reports on studies of Ghanaian artisans and casual workers, local work migrants and Chinese traders in South Africa, jeepney drivers and market vendors in the Philippines' island of Cebu, domestic workers in Hong Kong, refugees in Europe, and construction workers and nurses in the Gulf states. In recent research, Shang and Zhao (2017) have investigated shop signs in Singaporean lower-end consumer markets, Esseili (2017) describes uses of English in Lebanon, and Alomoush (2019) describes the use of English by Jordanian shop owners on their shopfronts. Xu and Tian (2019) discuss uses of English in a variety of public areas in China, while Hillman and Eibenschutz (2018) focus on uses of English in Qatar. From within the English as a lingua franca framework, Iikkanen (2019) examines how nurses communicate with migrants in Finnish family clinics, Orna-Montesinos (2018) presents results of interviews probing into how Spanish soldiers of all ranks use English on international missions, and Seargeant et al. (2017) discuss the role and perceived value of English among economic migrants from Bangladesh. Within the vast field of research in variationist English linguistics and the World Englishes and English as a lingua franca paradigms, these studies remain a minority in comparison to those that place 'elite' speakers in the academic or business worlds at their centre. So there is clearly a need to describe and investigate the spread of English(es) in lower-class environments and to theorise it, that is to establish an empirically based theory of Englishes at the grassroots.

'Non-educated' forms of English observed, albeit not exclusively, at the grassroots have also typically been excluded from models of world Englishes, mainly based on the argument that they are unstable approximations of an imagined target language and therefore lack systematicity,[4] despite the fact that, as Mesthrie and Bhatt (2008: 36) explain, 'there is a large gap between the middle-class varieties of New Englishes and their jargon, pidgin or basilectal counterparts [...]'. Hence, a second desideratum is to go beyond descriptive investigations of the spread of English(es) in lower-class environments and to theorise *from* them, that is to eventually extrapolate common features and patterns from individual descriptions of Englishes at the grassroots towards a fully comprehensive model of world Englishes.

In fact, a few studies have demonstrated how elite and grassroots uses of English do in fact differ. Since grassroots usage strongly correlates with lower-class membership and, often, limited access to education, genuinely sociolinguistic investigations of world Englishes settings outside of native-speaking contexts are closely related to our subject – again, such an approach is relatively rare in world Englishes but noticeable exceptions do exist. For example, Darvin (2017) explicitly compares the experiences of elite and grassroots adolescent Filipino immigrants in Vancouver. Toefy (2017) carefully investigates pronunciation differences between working- and middle-class speakers of Coloured South African English. Ofori and Albakry (2012) attest diversity in lower-, middle- and upper-class uses of and attitudes to English in Ghana. Such studies show that class-based differences in world Englishes settings exist, and they not only need to be acknowledged and described but they also require integration into existing theories and models.[5] The integration of Englishes at the grassroots offers a lot of potential for linguistics, particularly for its variationist and its World Englishes branches, to catch up and draw level with the above-mentioned advances in sociolinguistics. This may also contribute to advancing World Englishes along the lines suggested by Saraceni (2015). As he argues (2015: 6), it is particularly the developments associated with the 'Sociolinguistics of Globalisation' (Blommaert 2010) which the World Englishes paradigm has not sufficiently well integrated.

It is, in fact, mainly within sociolinguistics and linguistic anthropology where the grassroots have featured more prominently. This is particularly true for research which has been conducted at South African universities,[6] particularly at the University of Cape Town (among others, see McCormick 2002; Mesthrie and Hurst 2013; Deumert and Mabandla 2016; Coetzee 2018), at the University of the Western Cape (for example, Stroud and Mpendukana 2012) and at the North-West University (Coetzee-van Rooy 2016). Lower social classes have also been at the centre of research into language and development, such as the papers in Erling et al. (2013). However, the majority of such research does not locate itself within the World Englishes paradigm, and, typically, such studies foreground speakers' multilingual repertoires rather than their use of English(es), so that a unified approach to world Englishes that truly comprises all forms, uses and users of English is missing.

Another, related, aspect that is frequently missing is pidginised varieties,[7] which feature in Mesthrie and Bhatt's (2008) 'English Language Complex' but are later excluded by the authors from their further account of world Englishes on the grounds that they 'are studied as a field in their own right' (2008: 19). In fact, as Schneider (2011: 29) explains, '[e]arly creolist theory vigorously held that creoles are new languages'. As Mufwene (1997: 182) pointed out, pidgins and creoles, that is varieties 'spoken primarily by populations that have not fully descended from Europeans', have frequently been considered the 'illegitimate offspring of English'. Today, in fact, a growing number of English linguists follow Mufwene (1997, 2001) in arguing that English-based pidgins and creoles are varieties of English (although some creolists, for example McWhorter 2018, still posit a categorical distinction between both types of linguistic systems), and, as such, require their integration into existing models and theories, too.

It therefore seems timely to bring these uses and users of English to the foreground and to integrate the various 'non-educated' forms of English, since, although precise figures are not available, such grassroots usage and diffusion of English and other languages appear to be extremely common phenomena these days. As a result of work migration, forced migration, tourism, travel and increasing intercultural contacts in general, speakers of English at the grassroots deserve recognition and need to be investigated also on account of their growing number.

Crucially, then, what are missing and what constitute pressing desiderata for a research agenda are:

- sociolinguistic accounts of grassroots individuals or communities and of grassroots settings and situations in which world Englishes are increasingly used as a second or additional language, at times acquired without the support of formal education;
- investigations of the role and status of world English(es) in such communities;

- descriptions of the structural features characterising the use of world English(es) at the grassroots;
- qualitative data analyses of grassroots uses of world English(es) in specific settings;
- discussions of options for integrating Englishes at the grassroots into existing models of English and its spread;
- theoretical discussions of the relation between notions of hybrid languages, trans- and polylanguaging and world Englishes;
- methodological considerations of best practices for research with informants who may have limited literacy and previous exposure to Western-style modes of data elicitation such as picture-story tasks or Likert scales; and
- discussions of ethical aspects related to pursuing research with communities that are vulnerable.

This collection as a whole[8] thus aims to contribute to an empirical basis for further theorising and modelling of world Englishes. Its goal is to capture a selection of characteristic current societal developments around the world associated with grassroots usage, and the resulting changing realities affecting users, uses and forms of English. As such, it strives to establish *English at the grassroots* as a research focus and to encourage further research in this field. Its individual chapters, outlined in section 5, furthermore allow us to establish similarities and differences between contexts of mobility (as captured in the sociolinguistics of globalisation) and seemingly more 'static', regionally confined ones.

While the contributions to this volume address several of the desiderata mentioned above, they are the tip of an iceberg, and this volume, hopefully, will serve to trigger further research in this exciting and growing area.

4 IMPULSES OFFERED BY THE CONTRIBUTIONS TO THIS VOLUME

Sarah Buschfeld's contribution (Chapter 2) is a theoretically oriented survey paper that points out similarities and differences as regards speakers' language acquisition paths in grassroots usage settings. Using data from countries as diverse as Indonesia, Tanzania, Cyprus, Greece, Italy and Germany, Buschfeld carefully compares existing terminology. She argues that grassroots Englishes and uses of English at the grassroots have their origin in different paths of second language acquisition and that differences between them result from their specific sociolinguistic and/or communicative needs. She challenges established boundaries between English as a second and foreign language and lingua franca communication and argues that Englishes at the grassroots should be conceived of within their speakers' multilingual repertoires and practices.

Thereafter, the volume is organised in three thematic parts that cover the spread of English at the grassroots in three equally prominent contexts: in former areas of British domination in Africa and the Indian subcontinent, in trade and work migration, and in forced migration by refugees.

In 'Part I: English at the grassroots in former spheres of British domination', chapters focus on uses of English in former British colonies and protectorates.

Bebwa Isingoma (Chapter 3) investigates how non-elite speakers (market vendors and *bodaboda* ['motorcycle taxi'] riders in the west and the north of Uganda) use English. Based on participant observation and recorded semi-structured interviews (270 minutes in total) with thirty grassroots users of English, he finds Northern Uganda recording a higher inclination to use English than Western Uganda, as well as displaying more positive attitudes towards its use. He further shows that users of Ugandan English at the grassroots look up to acrolectal users of Ugandan English as their role models, using many of the innovative features that have been attested for these acrolectal speakers. Thus, the acrolectal sub-variety of Ugandan English provides the norms for the grassroots sub-variety and can be said to be both *norm-developing* as well as *norm-providing* (cf. Kachru 1985). His chapter thus provides impetus towards linking acro- and basilectal English(es) in one coherent and cogent perspective.

Susanne Mohr (Chapter 4) describes uses and the acquisition of English on Unguja, the main island of Zanzibar, in Tanzania, where English is an important language in the tourism industry. Based on ethnographic data from interviews and observations, her chapter shows that while English is frequently used with tourists, language competence often does not extend beyond formulaic expressions such as greetings. Most participants feel that Zanzibari English is 'broken', and for individuals from lower socio-economic backgrounds modes of acquisition are highly diverse, ranging from first contact with the language at home over English lessons at school or as part of working towards tourism degrees at university to expensive private tuition and language classes. Mohr shows that on Zanzibar, while interaction in English takes place at the grassroots, far away from academic circles, the trajectories of English acquisition include practices not typically associated with the grassroots level. Thus, her chapter also serves to discuss the fuzzy boundaries of what constitutes the grassroots and their modes of behaviour.

Christiane Meierkord (Chapter 5) compares productions of grassroots speakers of English from South Africa and Uganda and explains the emerging differences with relation to the countries' settlement histories and education policies. She discusses access to formal education and English acquisition as a factor explaining differences between Englishes at the grassroots. This factor has earlier been addressed by Mesthrie and Bhatt (2008: 36), who explain that 'there is a large gap between the middle-class varieties of New Englishes and their jargon, pidgin or basilectal counterparts'. Presenting qualitative analyses of spoken language productions by tradespeople in the Cape Town and Kampala regions, her analyses reveal that, at the grassroots level, productions are highly heterogeneous, showing patterns of stigmatised first language Afrikaans English, informal second language acquisition and pidginisation in older South African speakers, as opposed to features typically discussed as being results of formal foreign language learning in Ugandan and younger South African speakers. Like Mohr's, Meierkord's results document how socio-economic background and opportunities for formal second language acquisition intersect and result in different Englishes.

The section is complemented by Edgar Schneider's contribution (Chapter 6), which investigates representations of early learner English in the 2012 Bollywood movie *English Vinglish* and of the language attitudes and ideologies associated with such low proficiency levels in the movie. In the movie, Shashi, a young Indian mother who speaks hardly any English, when forced to spend some time in New York City to help prepare a family wedding, secretly takes beginners' English lessons in a language school. The first part employs a Critical Discourse Analysis approach to disclose the social implications associated with English (or the lack of ability to speak it) in utterances and gestures made by Shashi's children and husband, other parents, and her daughter's teacher. This is complemented by an analysis of the basic structural patterns employed by Shashi and her classmates in the second part of the chapter. The author finds that attitudes towards the ability to speak English in this movie clearly reflect its character as a piece of entertainment: Despite the occasional critical undertow, in the end they confirm and reinforce rather than problematise conservative language attitudes in society. At the same time, the structural analysis shows a remarkable sensitivity of the movie makers towards the steps and features of early stages of grassroots language learning, largely in line with what is known from the study of pidgins, second language acquisition, or language contact.

The next section of the book, 'Part II: English in trade and work migration', then focuses on scenarios that cover more or less voluntary private migration of individuals pursuing various trades or striving to work abroad.

Anthonia Bamidele-Akhidenor (Chapter 7) investigates interactions between Arab traders and their international clientele in Manama Souq in Bahrain, employing intercultural communication and accommodation theory to explain the communication strategies pursued by the Arab traders to achieve their business goals. Using questionnaires to elicit background details of respondents and recorded informal conversations between local Arab traders and non-Arabic customers and employees, she investigates how non-native speakers cooperate with each other in these conversations, shedding light on the strategies they employ to ensure successful communication. The speakers are shown to be aware of their positions as users of English who are shaped by their different cultural backgrounds and adhere to diverse communicative norms and behaviours, and to be sensitive to one another's need for affirmation.

Qumrul Hasan Chowdhury and Elizabeth J. Erling (Chapter 8) report on their findings in an ongoing research project that follows rural Bangladeshi migrant workers in the Middle East and uncovers the problematic relationship between English language skills and successful migration, which in Bangladesh are often assumed to be linked. Based on analyses of the narratives of four returnee migrant workers from the Middle East, of various ages and professions, they critically explore the value that English had for them. Their results suggest that it is difficult to establish a straightforward relationship between English language skills and successful economic migration. While English does seem to have significant functional value for them, this value is remoulded by domains and contexts of communication and is related to the values of other languages, particularly Arabic, in complex ways. Their contribution integrates a skilful discussion of the limits of the allegedly benefacting role of English proficiency for migrant workers with reflections on the ethical and methodological challenges of conducting research at the grassroots.

Kellie Gonçalves (Chapter 9) presents results from her ethnographic study into the learning and use of English among Portuguese- and Spanish-speaking employees, their multilingual employer and anglophone clients in a 'blue-collar' workplace context, a multilingual cleaning company in New Jersey. Using critical and mobile ethnography comprising in-depth interviews, observations and shadowing of eighteen domestics, four language brokers and twenty-one clients in both 2011 and 2015, she finds that despite the status and value of English on a global, national and regional level, English is not necessarily required in this local workplace setting, for several reasons. Living in a Portuguese-speaking enclave and typically acquiring English informally, the domestic workers successfully draw on their multilingual repertoires and/or the brokering skills of their multilingual employer. Similar to Chowdhury and Ehrling, the author discusses ethical concerns related to conducting research on and with under-documented, vulnerable migrants.

The final section of the book, 'Part III: English in forced migration', is concerned with contexts of refuge. Two contributions deal with newly arrived asylum seekers and the third looks into the effects of onward migration.

Guyanne Wilson's contribution (Chapter 10) focuses on Syrian refugees living in North Rhine Westphalia and the competition between English and German in their interactions in non-official settings, about which little has been known so far. Employing a qualitative approach and reporting on ten hours of interviews with refugees as well as four hours of interviews with state and non-governmental individuals working with refugees, she finds that inhabitants of multilingual refugee camps rarely reported the use of English among the camps' inhabitants; refugees and other stakeholders also explained that bureaucrats and state representatives are reluctant to engage with them in English in official interactions. Conversely, English is important in interpersonal exchanges with

Germans. Particularly among younger, more educated refugees, a high English proficiency seems to result in accelerated acquisition of German. The findings problematise our understanding of the role of English as a lingua franca among immigrants in Europe, particularly in grassroots environments.

Axel Bohmann (Chapter 11) analyses the forms of English used by residents of an initial reception centre for asylum seekers in southwestern Germany and the roles English resources assume in speakers' multilingual communicative repertoires. Using audio-recorded interviews with participants from the Gambia, Cameroon and Nigeria, and taking an interactional sociolinguistic perspective – paying attention to both the discourses participants construct around their linguistic resources and to the contextualised use of individual linguistic features themselves – he discusses how participants negotiate the choice between English and other potential mediums of communication and what kinds of group membership enactment the use of English is claimed to afford. Shifting the focus towards differentiation within English-based repertoires, the chapter also investigates how participants enlist different kinds of English as indexical social categorisation devices in a highly fluid, transient, social configuration.

Francesco Goglia (Chapter 12) focuses on second-generation immigrants who migrate onwards from Italy to the UK, completing this volume. His chapter investigates their use of and attitudes towards their heritage languages and their second languages acquired in migration, Italian and English, and it considers the effects of transit migration or transmigration. In the families of this study, the parents first migrated to Italy from Nigeria, Ghana, India and Bangladesh, and after a long period of life in Italy and obtaining Italian citizenship migrated onward to the UK, where they are now settled. Sociolinguistic surveys and interviews with twenty-four second-generation participants (university students) of onward-migrating families from Italy, both males and females aged between 18 and 23, reveal that second-generation immigrants maintain Italian with same-age peer friendships and older siblings. They view the language as linguistic capital to enhance their future career prospects in the UK or to possibly support a future return to Italy. Italian and Italian dialects are also maintained in conversations with parents, often in the form of code-switching. Parents struggle with English after a long period of residence in Italy, and children are not fluent in the heritage languages. English is considered to be the most important language and, together with a British education to improve their children's life chances, is the main pull factor for families in the decision to migrate onwards.

NOTES

1. As the authors explain, the 'English Language Complex' had been suggested earlier by McArthur (2003).

2. Following recent developments, we capitalise *World Englishes* to refer to the research paradigm, while non-capitalised *world Englishes* refers to the entirety of varieties of English around the world.
3. We adopt Kachru's (1985) categorisation since it is widely established in the field and is still useful for our purposes, although, given rapidly changing realities in many countries and contexts, its validity is becoming increasingly questionable.
4. See Mesthrie and Bhatt (2008: 156ff.) for a comprehensive history of various viewpoints and a discussion of the problematic distinction between learners' errors and the second language speakers' variant; see also van Rooy (2011) and Deshors et al. (2018).
5. The potential of studies of English at the grassroots is, thus, somewhat similar to that of investigations into lesser-known varieties of English, which Schreier (2013: 164) holds to 'represent test sites to test current theories on contact linguistics developed on major varieties'.
6. Research on 'previously disadvantaged communities' has, not surprisingly and rightly so, featured prominently in post-apartheid South Africa.
7. Pidginised and creolised varieties of English, which are often discussed as the 'non-educated' counterparts of standardised or standardising Englishes, for example Nigerian Pidgin English versus Nigerian English or Jamaican Creole ('Patwa') versus Jamaican English are mostly also commanded by many elite speakers of English. Crucially, such varieties are also typically disregarded in most research conducted in the framework of English as a lingua franca, with Guido (2008, 2014, 2016) being a noticeable exception.
8. Originally, this volume dates back to a workshop 'The Spread of English at the Grassroots' which the editors organised at the International Congress of Linguists (ICL20) in Cape Town in July 2018. This backbone has been supplemented by a few papers stemming from a workshop 'English as a Lingua Franca: Focus on Nonstandard Forms and Non-elite Domains' held at the conference of the International Society for the Linguistics of English (ISLE) in London, also in July 2018.

REFERENCES

Alomoush, Omar Ibrahim Salameh (2019), 'English in the linguistic landscape of a northern Jordanian city', *English Today*, 35: 3, 35–41.

Blommaert, Jan (2008), *Grassroots Literacy. Writing, Identity and Voice in Central Africa*, London: Routledge.

Blommaert, Jan (2010), *The Sociolinguistics of Globalization*, Cambridge: Cambridge University Press.

Bolander, Brook (2020), 'World Englishes and transnationalism', in Daniel

Schreier, Marianne Hundt and Edgar W. Schneider (eds), *The Cambridge Handbook of World Englishes*, Cambridge: Cambridge University Press, 676–701.

Bolton, Kingsley (2013), 'World Englishes, globalisation, and language worlds', in Nils-Lennart Johannesson, Gunnel Melchers and Beyza Björkmann (eds), *Of Butterflies and Birds, of Dialects and Genres – Essays in Honor of Philip Shaw*, Stockholm: Stockholm University Press, 227–51.

Brutt-Griffler, Janina (2002), *World English. A Study of its Development*, Clevedon: Multilingual Matters.

Buschfeld, Sarah and Alexander Kautzsch (2017), 'Towards an integrated approach to postcolonial and non-postcolonial Englishes', *World Englishes*, 36: 1, 104–26.

Buschfeld, Sarah, Alexander Kautzsch and Edgar W. Schneider (2018), 'From colonial dynamism to current transnationalism: a unified view on postcolonial and non-postcolonial Englishes', in Sandra C. Deshors (ed.), *Modelling World Englishes in the 21st Century: Assessing the Interplay of Emancipation and Globalization of ESL Varieties*, Amsterdam: John Benjamins, 15–44.

Coetzee, Frieda (2018), 'Hy leer dit nie hier nie' ('He doesn't learn it here'): Talking about children's swearing in extended families in multilingual South Africa', *International Journal of Multilingualism*, 15: 3, 291–305.

Coetzee-van Rooy, Susan (2016), 'The language repertoire of a Venda home language speaker: reflections on methodology', *Language Matters*, 47: 2, 269–96.

Crystal, David (2008), 'Two thousand million? Updates on the statistics of English', *English Today*, 24: 1, 3–6.

Darvin, Ron (2017), 'Social class and the inequality of English speakers in a globalized world', *Journal of English as a Lingua Franca*, 6: 2, 287–311.

Deshors, Sandra C., Sandra Götz and Samantha Laporte (2018), 'Linguistic innovations in EFL and ESL. Rethinking the linguistic creativity of non-native speakers', in Sandra Deshors, Sandra Götz and Samantha Laporte (eds), *Rethinking Linguistic Creativity in Non-native Englishes*, Amsterdam: Benjamins, 1–20.

de Swaan, Abram (2002), *The World Language System: A Political Sociology and Political Economy of Language*, Cambridge: Polity Press.

Deumert, Ana and Nkululeko Mabandla (2016), 'Globalization off the beaten track – Chinese migration to South Africa's rural towns', in Li Wei (ed.), *Multilingualism in the Chinese Diaspora Worldwide*, London: Routledge, 15–31.

Edwards, Alison and Philip Seargeant (2020), 'Beyond English as a second or foreign language: local uses and the cultural politics of identification', in Schreier et al. (2020), 339–59.

Erling, Elizabeth J., M Obaidul Hamid and Philip Seargeant (2013), 'Grassroots attitudes to English as a language for international development in Bangladesh', in Elizabeth J. Erling and Philip Seargeant (eds), *English and Development. Policy, Pedagogy and Globalisation*, Bristol: Multilingual Matters, 88–110.

Esseili, Fatima (2017), 'A sociolinguistic profile of English in Lebanon', *World Englishes*, 36: 4, 684–704.

Guido, Maria Grazia (2008), *English as a Lingua Franca in Cross-Cultural Immigration-Domains*, Bern: Lang.

Guido, Maria Grazia (2014), 'New-Evangelization discourse in ELF immigration encounters: a case study', *Lingue e Linguaggi*, 12, 111–26.

Guido, Maria Grazia (2016), 'ELF in responsible tourism: power relationships in unequal migration', in Marie-Luise Pitzl and Ruth Osimk-Teasdale (eds), *English as a Lingua Franca. Perspectives and Prospects: Contributions in Honour of Barbara Seidlhofer*, Berlin: Walter de Gruyter, 49–56.

Han, Huamei (2013), 'Individual grassroots multilingualism in Africa Town in Guangzhou: the role of states in globalization', *International Multilingual Research Journal*, 7: 1, 83–97.

Hillman, Sara and Emilio Ocampo Eibenschutz (2018), 'English, super-diversity, and identity in the State of Qatar', *World Englishes*, 37: 2, 228–47.

Iikkanen Päivi (2019), 'ELF and migrant categorization at family clinics in Finland', *Journal of English as a Lingua Franca*, 8: 1, 97–123.

Kachru, Braj B. (1976), 'Indian English: a sociolinguistic profile of a transplanted language', *Studies in Language Learning*, 1: 2, 139–89.

Kachru, Braj B. (ed.) (1982), *The Other Tongue. English across Cultures*, Urbana: University of Illinois Press.

Kachru, Braj B. (1983), *The Indianization of English. The English Language in India*, Delhi and Oxford: Oxford University Press.

Kachru, Braj B. (1985), 'Standards, codification and sociolinguistic realism: the English language in the outer circle', in Randolph Quirk and Henry G. Widdowson (eds), *English in the World: Teaching and Learning the Language and Literatures*, Cambridge: Cambridge University Press and The British Council, 11–30.

Khubchandani, Lachman M. and Hosali Priya (1999), 'Grassroots English in a communication paradigm', *Language Problems and Language Planning*, 23: 3, 251–72.

Lukač, Morana (2018), 'Grassroots prescriptivism', *English Today*, 34: 4, 5–12.

McArthur, Tom (2003), 'World English, Euro English, Nordic English?', *English Today*, 18: 1, 54–8.

McCormick, Kay (2002), *Language in Cape Town's District Six*, Oxford: Oxford University Press.

McWhorter, John (2018), *The Creole Debate*, Cambridge: Cambridge University Press.

Mair, Christian (2013), 'The World System of Englishes. Accounting for the transnational importance of mobile and mediated vernaculars', *English World-Wide*, 34: 3, 253–78.

Mair, Christian (2020), 'World Englishes in cyberspace', in Daniel Schreier, Marianne Hundt and Edgar W. Schneider (eds), *The Cambridge Handbook of World Englishes*, Cambridge: Cambridge University Press, 360–83.

Meierkord, Christiane (2012), *Interactions across Englishes. Linguistic Choices in Local and International Contact Situations*, Cambridge: Cambridge University Press.

Meierkord, Christiane (2018), 'English in paradise: the Maldives', *English Today*, 34: 1, 2–11.

Meierkord, Christiane (2020a), 'The global growth of English at the grassroots', in Daniel Schreier, Marianne Hundt and Edgar W. Schneider (eds), *The Cambridge Handbook of World Englishes*, Cambridge: Cambridge University Press, 311–38.

Meierkord, Christiane (2020b), 'Spread of English at the grassroots? Sociolinguistic evidence from two post-protectorates: Maldives and Uganda', in Andy Kirkpatrick (ed.), *The Routledge Handbook of World Englishes*, 2nd edn, Milton Park, NY: Routledge.

Merriam-Webster Dictionary (2020), 'Grassroots', <https://www.merriam-webster.com/dictionary/grassroots> (last accessed 4 May 2020).

Mesthrie, Rajend and Rakesh M. Bhatt (2008), *World Englishes: The Study of New Varieties*, Cambridge: Cambridge University Press.

Mesthrie, Rajend and Ellen Hurst (2013), 'Slang registers, code-switching and restructured urban varieties in South Africa. An analytic overview of tsotsitaals with special reference to the Cape Town variety', *Journal of Pidgin and Creole Languages*, 28: 1, 103–30.

Michieka, Martha M. (2009), 'Expanding circles within the outer circle: the rural Kisii in Kenya', *World Englishes*, 28: 3, 352–64.

Mufwene, Salikoko (1997), 'The legitimate and illegitimate offspring of English', in Larry Smith and Michael L. Forman (eds), *World Englishes 2000*, Honolulu: University of Hawai'i Press, 182–203.

Mufwene, Salikoko (2001), *The Ecology of Language Evolution*, Cambridge: Cambridge University Press.

Mufwene, Salikoko (2020), 'Population structure and the emergence of World Englishes', in Daniel Schreier, Marianne Hundt and Edgar W. Schneider (eds), *The Cambridge Handbook of World Englishes*, Cambridge: Cambridge University Press, 99–119.

Ofori, Dominic Maximilian and Mohammed Albakry (2012), 'I own this language that everybody speaks. Ghanaians' attitude toward the English language', *English World-Wide*, 33: 2, 165–84.

Orna-Montesinos, Concepción (2018), 'Language practices and policies in conflict: and ELF perspective on international military communication', *Journal of English as a Lingua Franca*, 7: 1, 89–111.

Pennycook, Alastair (2016), 'Mobile times, mobile terms: the trans-super-poly-metro movement', in Nikolas Coupland (ed.), *Sociolinguistics: Theoretical Debates*, Cambridge: Cambridge University Press, 201–16.

Quirk, Randolph (1972), *Linguistic Bonds across the Atlantic. The English Languages and Images of Matter*, London: Oxford University Press.

Rüdiger, Sofia (2019), *Morpho-Syntactic Patterns in Spoken Korean English*, Amsterdam: Benjamins.

Rui, Yang (2014), 'China's removal of English from *gaokao*', *International Higher Education*, 75, 12–13.

Sabaté i Dalmau, Maria (2014), *Migrant Communication Enterprises: Regimentation and Resistance*, Bristol: Multilingual Matters.

Saraceni, Mario (2015), *World Englishes. A Critical Analysis*, London: Bloomsbury.

Schneider, Edgar W. (2007), *Postcolonial English. Varieties Around the World*, Cambridge: Cambridge University Press.

Schneider, Edgar W. (2011), *English Around the World. An Introduction*, Cambridge: Cambridge University Press.

Schneider, Edgar W. (2013), 'Leisure-activity ESP as a special kind of ELF: the example of scuba diving English', *English Today*, 29: 3, 47–57.

Schneider, Edgar W. (2016a), 'Grassroots Englishes in tourism interactions', *English Today*, 32: 3, 2–10.

Schneider, Edgar W. (2016b), 'Hybrid Englishes: an exploratory survey', *World Englishes*, 35: 3, 339–54.

Schreier, Daniel (2013), 'English as a contact language: lesser-known varieties', in Daniel Schreier and Marianne Hundt (eds), *English as a Contact Language*, Cambridge: Cambridge University Press, 149–64.

Schreier, Daniel, Marianne Hundt and Edgar W. Schneider (eds) (2020), *The Cambridge Handbook of World Englishes*, Cambridge: Cambridge University Press.

Seargeant, Philip and Caroline Tagg (2011), 'English on the Internet and a "post-varieties" approach to language', *World Englishes*, 30: 4, 496–514.

Seargeant, Philip, Elizabeth J. Erling, Mike Solly and Qumrul Hasan Chowdhury (2017), 'The communicative needs of Bangladeshi economic migrants: the functional values of host country languages versus English as a lingua franca', *Journal of English as a Lingua Franca*, 6: 1, 141–65.

Shang, Guowen and Shouhui Zhao (2017), 'Bottom-up multilingualism in Singapore: code choice on shop signs', *English Today*, 33: 3, 8–14.

Ssentanda, Medadi E. (2016), 'Tensions between English medium and mother tongue education in rural Ugandan primary schools: an ethnographic investigation', in Christiane Meierkord, Bebwa Isingoma and Saudah Namyalo (eds), *Ugandan English: Its Sociolinguistics, Structure and Uses in a Globalising Post-protectorate*, Amsterdam: Benjamins, 95–117.

Strevens, Peter (1977), *New Orientations in the Teaching of English*, Oxford: Oxford University Press.

Stroud, Chris and Sibonile Mpendukana (2012), 'Material ethnographies of multilingualism: linguistic landscapes in the township of Khayelitsha', in Sheena Gardner and Marilyn Martin-Jones (eds), *Multilingualism, Discourse and Ethnography*, London: Routledge, 149–62.

Toefy, Tracey (2017), 'Revisiting the KIT-split in Coloured South African English', *English World-Wide*, 38: 3, 336–63.

Trimbur, John (2020), *Grassroots Literacy and the Written Record: A Textual History of Asbestos Activism in South Africa*, Bristol: Multilingual Matters.

Trudgill, Peter (1974), *The Social Stratification of English in Norwich*, Cambridge: Cambridge University Press.

van Rooy, Bertus (2011), 'A principled distinction between error and conventionalized innovations in African Englishes', in Joybrato Mukherjee and Marianne Hundt (eds), *Exploring Second-Language Varieties of English and Learner Englishes*, Amsterdam: Benjamins, 189–208.

Xu, Mingwu and Chuanmao Tian (2019), '"Open water room" = "hot water room"?', *English Today*, 35: 1, 42–7.

CHAPTER 2

Grassroots English, Learner English, Second-language English, English as a Lingua Franca . . .: What's in a Name?

Sarah Buschfeld[1]

1 INTRODUCTION

Since the early days of World Englishes research, various models, concepts and terms have been devised to capture the complex nature and development of the English language. Most prominently, these approaches describe and distinguish different types and uses of English in a variety of diverse geographical settings. However, conceptions such as the ENL-ESL-EFL distinction (English as native, second, foreign language, respectively) and particularly its clear-cut applications have been called into question in recent times (for example Buschfeld 2013; Edwards 2016; Buschfeld and Kautzsch 2017; Rüdiger 2019). At the same time, new conceptions and labels such as the notion of 'grassroots Englishes' have been introduced. Unlike most of what has been described so far, these performance types have not emerged as the product of elitist diffusion, for example through formal education or in academic circles or business contexts. Instead, the concept aims to capture the ways in which speakers outside of the educated, elite circles use the English language, what characterises these Englishes, and how and why they are acquired (cf. Meierkord 2012; Schneider 2016a). Despite the scholarly and ideological value of this notion, the question arises as to whether we can really draw such clear lines between concepts.

This chapter is a conceptual overview, introducing the topic of grassroots Englishes and related phenomena. To that end, it provides data samples for illustration and some comparative qualitative analyses, drawing on empirical data from what would traditionally be classified as postcolonial ESL and non-postcolonial EFL, lingua franca conversation and grassroots use. The present chapter argues that such traditional clear-cut distinctions between these concepts do not fully depict linguistic realities. I present and discuss spoken data collected by means of informal sociolinguistic interviews and from natural interactions with tourists. The data come from a diverse range of countries including

Indonesia, Tanzania, Cyprus, Greece, Italy, Germany and Spain and thus from different scenarios of acquisition and, most importantly, different usage contexts. I argue that they all have their origin in processes of second language acquisition and that the differences result from the users' specific sociolinguistic and/or communicative needs and, most importantly in the context of 'grassroots communication', from differences in the ways of acquisition.

Furthermore, I broaden the focus to include the notion of 'grassroots multilingualism', namely 'the kind of multilingualism associated with globalisation from below, which is characterised by fluid forms, code-switching, and non-standard linguistic features as a result of uninstructed expansion of multilingual repertoires for localised purposes' (Han 2013: 84). Drawing on observations from Polish-German multilingual conversations and from multilingual language use in the entertainment business at modern holiday resorts, I show how English finds its way into these conversations but is by no means the only important player (see the chapters by Bohmann and Wilson, this volume). On this basis, I argue that 'grassroots Englishes' should be pictured as an important part within a higher-level framework of global, multilingual practices. To conclude, I suggest that different Englishes should better be pictured as nodes in a complex system of Englishes (for example Schneider forthcoming) and, in turn, as parts of a complex system of languages and multilingual practices, in which certain categorical differences can be identified but which, more importantly, overlap and interact in their emergence, existence and uses.

2 ENGLISH AROUND THE WORLD: CONCEPTUALISING ITS DEVELOPMENTS AND MANY FACES

As the result of British (and partly American) colonisation and driven by current forces of globalisation (cf. Blommaert 2010; Coupland 2010), the English language has experienced an unprecedented worldwide spread and entrenchment. As a result, it has developed into an international medium of communication (Meierkord 2012: 1), and it comes in many different forms and guises (concepts and categories mostly created by linguists!). These manifestations are shaped by a variety of factors such as: (1) the historical and sociolinguistic background and entrenchment of English in a country or speech community; (2) the proficiency of its speakers; (3) its usage contexts and communicative intentions; and (4) ways of acquisition, be it that it is mainly acquired as a first or second language, in natural, untutored interactions, or by means of formal instruction. There are certainly further factors operating on the shaping and different manifestations of the English language and these, of course, strongly interact and bring together sociolinguistic issues and aspects and mechanisms of language acquisition. Along these lines, the following labels have been created by linguists to capture the variety of different manifestations of the English language over the last forty years: (1) English as a native, second or foreign language (ENL, ESL, EFL); (2) English based pidgins and creoles; (3) hybrid/mixed Englishes; (4) English as a lingua franca; and (5) English for specific purposes. There are additional, often related, labels (for example Kachru's 1985 classification of Inner, Outer and Expanding Circle Englishes) and models, which cannot all be listed and discussed here.[2] Everything is labelled and categorised, even if the boundaries are often fuzzy as the present chapter will show. This is the result of general cognitive processes at the core of human nature, and it is what we do as linguists. It is – in my opinion – a valid and important approach if we want to describe and understand the complex development and realities of the English language. On the other hand, it is important to keep in mind that these are artificial, man-made constructs, which represent broad categories at best.

Also important for the present chapter is the often-made observation that the majority of interactions in English today are among non-native speakers of the language (for example Graddol 2006). This is also reflected in speaker estimates, according to which approximately 350–380 million speakers are ENL speakers, up to 600 million are ESL speakers, and between 500 million and 1,500 million are EFL speakers of the language (Schneider 2011: 56). All this, namely the emergence and labelling of new forms of English, is reinforced by '[t]he very strong pull of English in globalisation, its "transnational attraction", [which] has increasingly produced novel forms and usage contexts' (Schneider 2016a: 3).

When focusing on the communicative events in which these non-native Englishes are used instead on those labels trying to capture the exact types of English (mostly made on the basis of the historical and socio-political development of the varieties under observation as to be found in the ESL-EFL and Outer and Expanding Circle distinctions), these usage contexts have traditionally been referred to as 'lingua franca communication' (cf. Meierkord 2012: 1).

3 GRASSROOTS ENGLISHES: THE NEW PLAYER IN THE WORLD ENGLISHES PARADIGM

In the following, I briefly define the notion of 'grassroots English' and discuss why we need it as a new player in the World Englishes paradigm. Subsequently, I illustrate and discuss some of the main characteristics of grassroots Englishes. At the same time, this will serve as the basis for arguing that, similar to lingua franca communication, grassroots Englishes are more a mode of communication than an explicit usage type and can best be captured as a non-elitist mode of communication 'from below' (namely the notion of 'grassroots'). The chapter will ultimately conclude that the labels introduced above are to be located in a multidimensional network in which different types of English and ultimately languages manifest themselves depending on their usage contexts, communicative intentions and situations, and their sociolinguistic background. Categories and distinctions between them are fluid and are to be located on a continuum, and, last but not least, everything is related in one way or another (for example the notion of 'Complex Dynamic Systems'; Ellis and Larsen-Freeman 2009; Kretzschmar 2015; Schneider forthcoming). This not only applies to different Englishes but also to languages and multilingual practices in general.

The data come from a range of different countries and usage contexts and were collected through free interaction and by means of sociolinguistic interviews, mostly in the tourism sector between 2014 and 2017 (see the excerpts from Indonesia, Tanzania, Cyprus, Greece and Italy; cf. Extracts (1)–(5)).[3] These data were analysed for local linguistic characteristics, mostly resulting from language contact with the first languages spoken by the informants or universal strategies and mechanisms of second language (L2) acquisition.[4] In section 3.2, the features will be discussed and compared as potential characteristics of grassroots Englishes. In addition to that, I identify and discuss some general trends of grassroots communication on the basis of the five extracts. The data from the German-Polish exchanges come from private conversations between the author and a middle-aged Polish foreign worker in 2018. The observations on grassroots multilingualism and the use of English at holiday resorts are based on an audio-recorded 45-minute conversation between the author and the head of animation at a holiday resort on the Balearic island of Mallorca in 2019. For the purpose of anonymity, only the participant's age, gender, country of origin and linguistic background will be given.

3.1 What it is and Why we Need it

Among the many concepts and labels developed for describing and categorising the worldwide spread of English, the notion of 'grassroots Englishes' has been one of the latest additions to the World Englishes paradigm. In his seminal article on the topic, Schneider (2016a) defines 'grassroots Englishes' as types of English emerging from the grassroots (as opposed to the elitist forms of English). They are acquired in direct interaction between speakers of different languages rather than through formal education (some speakers have never had any formal instruction in English). Grassroots Englishes are often the 'products of strong personal instrumental motivation', for example in search for better job opportunities in the tourism sector (Schneider 2016a: 9). They mostly, although not exclusively, emerge in less affluent societies with limited opportunities for learning English (when approached from a scholastic perspective). The goal of the speakers acquiring such Englishes is to have a communicative ability, rather than earning good grades or the ability to perform according to native speaker standards of language use (Schneider 2016a; see also Görlach 1996 for an early treatment and discussion of similar phenomena). Therefore, the speaker is aiming at communicative effectiveness and not necessarily grammatical correctness. Target variety orientations (and concerns about linguistic correctness) are largely disregarded. To sum up, unlike most of what has been described so far in the World Englishes paradigm, these performance types have not emerged as the product of elitist diffusion. Instead, the concept aims to capture the ways speakers outside of the educated elite use the English language, what characterises these Englishes, and how and why they are acquired (Schneider 2016a).

Earlier frameworks which have dealt with comparable concepts are Blommaert's (2010) 'sociolinguistics of globalization', Meierkord's (2012) 'interactions across Englishes', Canagarajah's (2013) 'translanguaging' and Han's (2013, 2017) 'grassroots multilingualism'. Of these, Han's notion of 'grassroots multilingualism' comes conceptually closest to Schneider's notion of 'grassroots Englishes', as can already be seen in its label. However, it does not exclusively focus on the English language but rather approaches the topic from a wider perspective. '[G]rassroots multilingualism [. . .] describe[s] the kind of multilingualism associated with globalization from below, which is characterized by fluid forms, code-switching, and nonstandard linguistic features as a result of uninstructed expansion of multilingual repertoires for localized purposes' (Han 2013: 84; italics in original). English is often one of the players in these multilingual contexts but is not necessarily the major one (cf. the case studies presented in Han 2013).

In the following, I will illustrate these theoretical observations by means of extracts from the different contexts introduced above and compare and identify some of the major characteristics of the properties and usage conditions of grassroots Englishes. I do not provide a full and detailed analysis of all the linguistic characteristics displayed in the extracts – of course all of them are characterised by a variety of local features, some of them unique to the specific context, some of them shared across contexts – but instead focus on those that are relevant in the context of the present study.

3.2 Its Properties and Use

The first two extracts analysed within the framework of the present study come from Indonesia and Tanzania and illustrate two typical scenarios for the grassroots acquisition and use of English. Extract (1) presents an excerpt from a conversation between a group of German tourists and a driver on the Indonesian island of Bali who acquired English mainly for the purpose of being able to communicate with the ever-growing number of tourists on the island, allowing an increase in business.

Extract (1): middle-aged male driver in Bali, Indonesia[5]
If [de] people going to [de] cem-, if now die, looking for good -, looking eh in Balinese calendar, when I can bring to cemetery, but if we do cemetery, around four o'clock, five o'clock, before [de], uh, sun down, maybe around uh five o'clock, and then, you get in, with many people. If here, if, uh, if I always come when the neighbor co-[?] dead, the neighbor have, uh, something, and then I hel(e)p him, evry[?], evry[?], uh, neighbor dead, yeah, neighbor, I have uh dead, I come. When I die, also come. When me lazy, only my family. There is this difficul' here in, uh, in Bali. Also, I am not from Lovina, when in Lovina I live with uh rented house, yeah, but I'm from the mountain here. If my neighbor in the mountain dead I come with motorbike, broooom. Sometime alone. If I have ceremony, one bike, four people: my daughter, my son, my wife, and suitcase behind. My daughter fourteen years, my son ten years, and small motorbike. But I have only one motorbike. Now I must try another motorbike. (Extract from Schneider 2016a: 7; slightly adapted)

As already accounted for in Schneider (2016a: 7), 'this is an interesting linguistic sample which illustrates a number of phenomena'. The speaker has rather limited proficiency in English, most likely due to the fact that the speaker's motivation is mainly instrumental, that is not guided by the desire to achieve native-like proficiency. Acquisition is mainly informal and natural, that is not the product of a native-speaker oriented school system, but still limited to mainly tourist-based interaction between non-native speakers, who often also have non-native-like and limited proficiency themselves. Most sentences are incomplete, characterised by false starts, repetitions, hesitation markers and self-repairs, and even if these are general characteristics of oral language use, I would argue that they are more prominent in this extract than they would be in other, 'non-grassroots contexts' of higher language proficiency. In addition to that, the excerpt shows a number of non-standard linguistic realisations on the different levels of language organisation. For example, the dental fricatives are often realised as stops, as indicated by the transcription of voiced dental fricative [ð] as [d] in *de* in the extract. The syntax is characterised by many zero elements, such as zero pronouns (*if now die*; *When I die, also come*), missing copulas (*When me lazy, only my family*; *If my neighbor in the mountain dead I come with motorbike, broooom*), zero articles (*when I can bring to cemetery*) or a lack of person/number agreement (*the neighbor have*) (see Schneider 2016a: 7 for similar observations). As already mentioned above, I will not go into detail here and I am not going to discuss potential sources for these errors. Often these lie with the participant's first language (cf. the notion of L1 transfer) or go back to general mechanisms of learning a second language such as simplification, overgeneralisation or incomplete acquisition due to the reduced acquisitional context. The language acquisition paradigm has a lot to offer here but this cannot be discussed in any detail since the focus of the present chapter is mainly on the conceptualisation of the 'final' product.

The next speech samples (Extracts (2) and (3)) come from Tanzania, more precisely from tour guides giving a briefing on an upcoming hike up Mount Kilimanjaro and an explanation on an endemic plant.

> Extracts (2) and (3): middle-aged male tour guides, Tanzania
> After we reaching Saddle we may finding the cooker is already there, we gonna maybe you have a lunch [dere], or we can, we're going to ask him the cooker if you will gonna have a lunch, pocket lunch, on the way, or we're gonna have hot lunch, right? It just depending, with the cooker, how, and we gonna see how you, how you, how, how you fitness you are, right? If you walking very slowly we can decide for all of us, we can make me pocket lunch for you, but if you have a go with the right time, is better for us to go to have a lunch in, in the Saddle Hut, hot lunch, right? Because sometime we will gonna walking slowly, sometime, just depending how our body acclimatisation in that place, all right? Yeah.
>
> And it's among of the leaves, the leaves are growing from 3,500 meters, below that you can't found this tree or this leaves. And this leaves, once their, their leaves are die, can't grow, because, need to cover the body, because the tree inside here, it doesn't have in anything inside you need, because inside it just a hole.(Extracts from Schneider 2016a: 8–9; slightly adapted)

Extracts (2) and (3) appear more fluent in nature and less disrupted by the pragmatic strategies of hesitation, false starts and self-repair when compared to Extract (1). One has to bear in mind, however, that Extracts (2) and (3) might be more rehearsed than Extract (1) because the speaker in Extract (1) spontaneously reacts and interacts with a group of German tourists during a guided drive whereas the speech productions in Extracts (2) and (3) are parts of routine instructions, which the tour guide is not giving for the first time. Still, the speakers in Extracts (2) and (3) seem more proficient for that reason, even though the excerpts show a number of non-standard linguistic features. Again, the voiced dental fricative is replaced by a stop (*[dere]*) and the excerpts are characterised by instances of missing copulas (*we reaching*) and missing number concord (*this leaves*), among other examples. These are in many respects quite similar to those found in Extract (1) despite coming from a totally different country and (socio)linguistic background.

When approaching Extracts (1) through (3) from a traditional World Englishes perspective, the Indonesian sample would be categorised as EFL or Expanding Circle English, while the Tanzanian extracts (Extracts (2) and (3)) would traditionally fall within the category of ESL or Outer Circle due to the country's colonial history.[6] Such strict separation based on only socio-political criteria has repeatedly been criticised in more recent studies (for example Buschfeld 2013; Edwards 2016; Buschfeld and Kautzsch 2017; Rüdiger 2019). We will come back to that in the discussion chapter (section 3.4).

Extracts (4) and (5) come from L1 Greek-speaking backgrounds, Cyprus and Crete, which are very different in their historico-political development and, resulting from that, sociolinguistic setting. Cyprus was under British rule from 1878 through 1960 and reached crown colony status in 1925. Following the traditional ESL-EFL or Outer-Expanding circle distinctions, it would therefore belong to the group of ESL/Outer Circle countries. Crete, as part of Greece, was never under British colonial rule and would therefore be conceptualised as an EFL/Expanding Circle country. Investigations by Buschfeld, however, have shown that things are not as easy and clear-cut (2013, forthcoming) and that due to the shared L1 background, the local characteristics of the English varieties spoken in the two contexts are very similar. Important for the present context and as illustrated in the two extracts, the two excerpts again display features similar to what is illustrated in the first three extracts, that is, for example, lack of agreement (*my husband, and 14 is married*; Extract (4)) or zero sentence elements such as missing subject pronouns (*Yes, is very fresh*) (see Buschfeld forthcoming for further details and a more detailed comparison of the two contexts).

> Extract (4): middle-aged female kindergarten teacher, Cyprus (Greek part)
> S: Okay. [. . .] do you [/] do you remember a very funny experience in your life, when you really laughed?
> I: Yes, we've love uh 13 years, my husband, and 14 is married, he's going to work and going to the school, the night. Because uh everything is work and money to buy my house, to finish my house [. . .]

> Extract (5): middle-aged male waiter, Crete
> I know that in German # it's not possible # for a German # unless he came many times in Greece to go in a restaurant and the waiter tell him 'Today we have very good fish' to do not believe him. The Greeks, the Greek from the other side, some[&] [//] not somebody like me, because I mean general, I try speak, the Greek couple is coming and they go hear 'very fresh fish': 'Show us!' I show them. That's it. Yes, is very fresh.

The last extract in this section was produced by a young female receptionist in her mid-twenties working at one of the hotels in the Lake Garda region of Italy. Again, it is characterised by a number of non-standard characteristics as outlined in the preceding extracts. Most prominently, Extract (6) features incomplete sentences/missing sentence elements (*In the first floor, the elevator on your right; Tomorrow morning, the breakfast straight right; Is also included the outside pool*) and non-standard preposition use (*in the first floor*; *on the breakfast room*) which is also found in the other extracts (although not explicitly mentioned). Apart from that, her speech appears quite fluent (even more so when listening to the recording) but it definitely seems the most rehearsed of all.

> Extract (6): young female receptionist, Italy
> In the first floor, the elevator on your right. Tomorrow morning, the breakfast straight right on the breakfast room, seven o'clock until ten o'clock. Is also included the outside pool from restaurant and from XX, open half past seven until ten in the evening. From the rest, from the left you can go way eh into the pool.

All speech samples discussed (Extracts (1) through (6)) show linguistic characteristics on the different levels of language organisation. There are differences in exact linguistic manifestations between the extracts, some of which are clearly due to cross-linguistic influences from the speaker's first language (as, for example, the Italian-origin morphosyntactic structures in Extract (6)). However, many other of the observed characteristics are shared across the productions (for a short summary of similarities, see the following paragraph) and are not unlikely to be either the results of 'universal laws of ontogenetic second language acquisition and phylogenetic language shift', for example simplification and overgeneralisation (Schneider 2007: 89; see also Williams 1987: 169–70) and/or the result of the grassroots acquisitional context. As it is characterised by the absence of guided instruction, the exact manifestation of the latter, of course, depends on the specific context and is certainly much stronger in African and Indonesian tourism than in Italy, Greece or Cyprus due to differences in the accessibility and quality of schooling.

To sum up, most of the extracts are characterised by non-canonical and/or incomplete syntactic structures, in particular the omissions or repetition of sentence elements, interruptions and false starts, and hesitation phenomena, again to different extents. Some of the extracts (Extracts (2) and (3) and particularly Extract (6)) display rehearsed language use. The speakers tend to 'rattle off' explanations they have repeatedly provided before (but they are still characterised by their specific linguistic characteristics). The extent to which language appears rehearsed decreases with the spontaneity of the conversation.

Apart from the shared characteristics identified earlier in the chapter and the instances of seemingly rehearsed uses that are often of a chunk-like nature, grassroots Englishes are heterogeneous and of a rather transient nature. Normally, grassroots exchanges do not take place in a stable communicative setting, that is at least one, if not both/all, conversational partner/s come from changing linguistic and/or cultural backgrounds (see also Han 2017: 260). Furthermore, speakers bring in their specific learner idiolects, which may share structural similarities if the speakers come from the same linguistic background, but which typically have not developed the systematicities found in nativised second language varieties of English. Grassroots Englishes are spoken in diverse geographical settings, most prominently in marginalised, less-affluent countries or by individuals and speech groups that are structurally marginalised even though living in more affluent societies (see Han 2013: 95 for a similar argument), but not exclusively so (as the above extracts illustrate): Cyprus, for example, is a postcolonial country in which grassroots use of English would normally not be expected since proficiency in English is widespread and supported by formal instruction in English in Cypriot schools (cf. Görlach 1996: 157 for a similar observation in the South African context). In a similar line of thinking, the speakers from Italy and Greece are not marginalised or excluded from education and schooling in English to the same degree as the speakers from Indonesia and Tanzania (see my earlier argument).

What remains to be acknowledged is that, despite what has been described above, all speakers communicate successfully for the purposes required. They all get their messages across according to the situationally given needs and therefore 'qualif[y] as [. . .] successful speaker[s] of English' (Schneider 2016a: 7).

3.3 Discussion

3.3.1 How should these Englishes be conceptualised?

When taking into consideration the above observations and discussion, the following two questions arise:

1. How should these Englishes/performance types be accounted for from a conceptual/theoretical perspective?
2. Where do they fit into our categorisations of Englishes around the world, our existing models and paradigms?

Parts of these questions have already been addressed earlier in the chapter. According to traditional approaches to World Englishes based on the postcolonial/non-postcolonial divide, the extracts from Tanzania and Cyprus (Extracts (2), (3) and (4)) would fall within the category of ESL/Outer Circle English, while the extracts from Indonesia, Crete and Italy (Extracts (1), (5) and (6)) would be categorised as EFL/Expanding Circle Englishes. However, as repeatedly observed, this distinction is not watertight since many hybrid forms, to be located between EFL and ESL, seem to exist, and settings have often been changing in the recent past; postcolonial background is neither a sufficient criterion nor a guarantor for second language (ESL/Outer Circle) variety status (for example Buschfeld on the example of English in Cyprus; Buschfeld and

Kautzsch 2014 on the Namibian context; Edwards 2016 on the Netherlands; Rüdiger 2019 on South Korea). So how should these Englishes be approached from a conceptual perspective?

In a much earlier approach to similar forms of English, Görlach notes that 'adequate methods of description are not readily available' (1996: 155). In his 1996 article 'And is it English?' he aims at such a description. His intentions are noble as he tries to integrate these Englishes/performance types into the existing World Englishes paradigm, to give them a voice. However, he does not call them 'grassroots Englishes' – the term in the sense discussed here is first used and introduced in Schneider (2016a). Throughout his article, Görlach refers to them by a number of rather pejorative labels: 'inadequate English' (156), 'defective English' (158), 'broken English' (153, 155, 158–9), and 'garbled English' (155). He calls them 'messy utterances' (155) and talks about 'dubious "English-ness"' (154), the 'butchering of the King's English' (155) and 'linguistic chambers of horrors' (155).

Such a normative, downright pejorative perspective leaves every variationist linguist speechless and has luckily long been abandoned from the World Englishes research paradigm, even though the term 'broken English' has often been found in the literature, even in the writings of Braj Kachru. It is also still used by many laypeople in countries and societies where English is not spoken in one of its 'pure' forms, namely 'Standard' British or American English, whatever that may be.

Indeed, there is still 'a lack of a suitable theoretical framework to account for grassroots speech forms, no established classification where this kind of performance would fit in neatly' exists as Schneider (2016a: 4) concludes (see Han 2017 for a similar assessment). As Han (2017: 260) points out in relation to grassroots multilingual repertoires as to be found in trading communities,

> traditional theoretical linguistic studies focusing on linguistic products are biased toward standard or national languages [...] The precarious and relatively transient nature of trading communities [and the same is true for many grassroots Englishes contexts] thus means that they are rarely studied because they rarely leave linguistic footprints in the form of languages as stabilised linguistic systems.

And Schneider (2016a: 9) continues his observations by stating that

> [i]t may not be really clear what kinds of sociolinguistic or psycholinguistic entities we are looking at here – with possible linguistic categorizations including anything between 'learners' interlanguages', steps towards 'new varieties', or 'just idiosyncracies'. But as long as this helps people to communicate successfully across cultures – who cares (except for some linguists, perhaps)?

But linguists do care; they strive to explain and categorise the linguistic phenomena they encounter. As we saw earlier in the chapter, Schneider made a first important step in his 2016a article by defining the notion of 'grassroots Englishes'. He identifies some of their potential linguistic manifestations as well as summarises some of their general conceptual characteristics. The extracts discussed in section 3.3 of the present chapter confirm many of his observations but at the same time suggest that we should better refrain from trying to find a conceptual solution that tries to define a handful of characteristics or a common sociolinguistic basis for these types of English. I would not even talk about 'types' of English here as I think that a conceptual definition, similar to those of ESL and EFL, Outer or Expanding Circle (terms that have proven difficult enough for capturing their original, nation-based phenomena), is not a sufficient solution. Grassroots Englishes cannot be conceptualised as a homogeneous category since usage contexts, linguistic manifestations and speaker proficiencies are highly heterogeneous (see Meierkord and Knapp 2002: 10 for a similar argument). Secondly, I think we have to differentiate between types of English/varieties on the one hand and modes of communication/interactions on the other. In this line of thinking, Meierkord (for example 2012) suggests the framework of 'Interactions across Englishes' (IaEs) to approach lingua franca contexts. The core assumption of the IaE concept is 'that the different Englishes potentially merge in these interactions', resulting in 'the development of new emergent varieties' but not 'one stable or even codified variety, but rather a heterogeneous array of new linguistic systems' (Meierkord 2012: 2; italics in original). Whether we want to call these the products (or rather manifestations) of lingua franca communications or grassroots uses is of secondary importance, not least because the dividing line between these two usage contexts is far from clear-cut. As observed above, grassroots uses can be found both in postcolonial and non-postcolonial contexts, in contexts typically characterised as Outer or Expanding Circle (and ESL and EFL respectively), as can lingua franca uses. As the label 'grassroots uses' suggests, I believe we should conceptualise it as a mode of communication, similar to ELF (English as a lingua franca) communication, but exclusively 'from below', that is as characterised by mainly intrinsically motivated, unguided acquisition, leading to self-taught and often rudimentary proficiency. These uses can occur within national boundaries (such as in the tourism and trading sectors) but in principle also across nation states, for example via computer mediated communication. Additionally, grassroots communication can be inter-speaker and thus described as a group or speaker-bound phenomenon because it is also conceivable that a speaker with a 'grassroots competence' of English can communicate with a fully proficient, native-like L2 speaker or even a native speaker of English.

The next, and in many ways related, question I would like to address is the question of what makes grassroots Englishes, which can be both ESLs and EFLs as we have seen, structurally and linguistically discernible from English-based jargons or pidgins and creoles (see Han 2017: 266–8 for a similar question and discussion)? The answer lies in their specific historical, political and sociolinguistic developments and backgrounds, a specific set of partly shared and partly very specific extra- and intra-territorial forces (cf. Buschfeld and Kautzsch 2017 for such a forces-based approach to World Englishes). The linguistic characteristics of these types, however, are often of a similar nature. Han (2017) holds a comparable view in that she states that in traditional accounts of languages and varieties 'the dividing lines between categories and stages seem more *social* than *linguistic*' (Han 2017: 268; italics in original). Naturally, answers to these questions are far from straightforward and have to be approached not only with the background of more detailed, current discussions within the World Englishes paradigm in mind but also from a language acquisition perspective; this general discussion is not actually all that new. A number of researchers have argued that we should conceptualise bilingualism as the exploitation of multilingual repertoires, challenging traditional views of language as bound and clearly delimitable systems. Heller, for example, has argued 'for the notion that speakers draw on linguistic resources which are organized in ways that make sense under specific social conditions' (2007: 1).

So how should grassroots Englishes and the English Language Complex (cf. Mesthrie and Bhatt 2008) be conceptualised in general? As we have seen and as has been argued elsewhere, clear-cut categorisations relying on geographical, historical and socio-political criteria are only useful for sketching out rough tendencies and very general types; in reality, the boundaries between varieties and modes of communication (as well as between the general categorisation types) are fuzzy and they have to be pictured as part of a multidimensional matrix, as part of a Complex Dynamic System (for example Ellis and Larsen-Freeman 2009; Kretzschmar 2015; Schneider forthcoming), taking into consideration a variety of factors, such as

- usage contexts (from individual to societal, from marginal/less affluent to affluent/elitist, from non-postcolonial, to postcolonial, to first language);
- communicative functions and intentions (from getting the message across according to situational needs and requirements to specialised language use in ESP (English for Specific Purposes) and CMC (computer mediated communication), to elitist conversation in academic circles);
- proficiency levels and types (from functional proficiencies, to 'mute Englishes' (for example Wolff 2010), to balanced bilingualism);
- norm orientations (from non-existent norm orientations to exonormative and endonormative orientations).

Moreover, the discussion so far has already suggested that even the Anglocentric perspective exclusively focused on grassroots Englishes may be usefully supplemented by multilingual perspectives, in particular when the overall aim is to depict linguistic realities and communicative practices in the age of globalisation – but, of course, this always depends on the level of granularity and the perspective one wants to take.

3.3.2 The wider perspective: grassroots Englishes and grassroots multilingualism

In the preceding section, I have argued that boundaries between variety types and between varieties and modes of communication are fuzzy. The label 'English Language Complex' (McArthur 2003: 56; Mesthrie and Bhatt 2008) already covers much of the complexity of the phenomenon. Although it is still not a mainstream approach to language but is currently gaining in popularity, the notion of 'Complex Dynamic System' (CDS; for example Ellis and Larsen-Freeman 2009; Kretzschmar 2015; Schneider forthcoming) goes one step further in that 'CDS theory argues strongly against reductionism, categorial and deterministic thinking' (Schneider forthcoming) on the level of language organisation in general. This approach is not necessarily reduced to one specific language. Strictly speaking, a clearly language-based CDS approach such as the one on English taken by Schneider (forthcoming) goes against some of the underlying implications of the approach towards language, namely that no linguistic concept can be completely separated from the other. Admittedly, as Rome was not built in a day, we cannot revolutionise the whole field of linguistics all at once and in some contexts the old feature-based approaches to language and varieties still make sense and are even indispensable, depending on your aims and perspectives – 'they may be heuristically helpful and provide a baseline for more comprehensive perspectives and for understanding interactions between the components of a language' (Schneider forthcoming). But let us take the more fluid, usage-based approach towards language as a complex system and discuss the role of English as part of a higher-level framework of multilingual practices.

In recent times, multilingualism is no longer exclusively defined as the use and mastery of two or more well-defined language systems but as a continuum of linguistic repertoires and resources nearly everyone around the globe has; some, admittedly, to very limited degrees, limited to specific dialects or the use of just a couple of words, phraseologisms/borrowings, or a limited set of simple expressions from another language (for example Horner and Weber 2018). This shows in the extensive mixing of languages (for example the notions of code-switching and, more recently, translanguaging (Canagarajah 2013)) as a part of many people's linguistic routines and the existence of hybrid codes such as Hinglish (spreading in Northern India), Camfranglais (found in Cameroon and also incorporating French components) or Taglish (spoken in the Philippines), to mention just a few (cf. Schneider 2011: 222–3, 2016b). The following extracts (Extracts (7) and (8)) illustrate heavy code-switching (or translanguaging) in the German context. Extract (7) was extracted and put together from Facebook conversations between middle-aged German friends; Extract (8) is an excerpt from a song by a young German hip-hop artist:

Extract (7): bilingual Facebook conversations among German friends
Female, 35: Triple love! The song is really one of the best songs ever (und das Video just super cool ['and the video just super cool']) :) ! :) And Happy Birthday to us, indeed, it's been a great year! :) Dann machen wir doch mal weiter und laden zu einer Runde 'memorable songs' ein [. . .] ['So let's just carry on and invite another round of 'memorable songs'']
Female, 35: Oh yesssss! (More comments later tonight, du hältst mich vom schweren Arbeiten ab ['you're keeping me away from hard work']).
Male, 28: Mensch, da kriegt man so viele schöne Geburtstagsgrüße ['Oh man, you get so many nice birthday greetings'], but this knocks it out of the park [. . .]
Male, 47: Congrats, du Wahnsinniger ['you crazy guy']!!! WOW!! (From Buschfeld et al. 2018; English translations of the German material in single quotation marks and square brackets, slightly modified)

Extract (8): bilingual German-English hip-hop lyrics
Ich bi-bi-bin nicht Drake, doch hab' Love für die Crew, meine Dawgs
['I'm not Drake but I have love for the crew, my dawgs']
Alle Boos sind im Club, but I don't give a fuck
['All the uncool guys are in the club, . . .']
Und alle Babes sagen, ‚Boah, du bist straight hier der Boss.'
['And all babes say, "Wow, you're clearly the boss here."']
Egal wie viele Tapes ich record'
['No matter how many tapes I record']
Und ich sag', ‚Bitch, get off, keine Zeit für dich, Hoe.'
['And I say, "Bitch get off, no time for you, hoe"']
Bin unterwegs mit meinen Doggys, also scheiß mal auf Cro
['I'm on tour with my doggies (a German youth language variant of dawgs, indicating submissiveness), so don't give a shit about Cro']
G-G-Gangsterattitüde, Motherfucker (ah!), life is a hoe
['Ganster attitude, motherfucker . . .']
Und meine Gang ist eigentlich broke, aber immer wieder high von dem Dope, oh, oh
['And my gang is actually broke, but again and again high on dope']
Digga, Digga, meine Gang ist voller Chicks oder Atzen
['Dude, dude, my gang is full of chicks and fellas']
Die bis Mitternacht ratzen, aufsteh'n, obwohl sie noch nicht wach sind
['Who sleep until midnight and get up even though they are not awake yet']

Lieber ficken statt quatschen (ah!), Jimmys lieber spliffen statt klatschen
['Who rather fuck than chat (ah!), Jimmies who rather smoke spliffs than drink (alcohol)']
Kein bisschen erwachsen, but ain't nobody fuckin' with my motherfucking gang
['Not a bit grown-up, but . . .'].
(Excerpt from Cro 2014, *Meine Gang (Bang Bang)*; English translations of the German material in single quotation marks and square brackets)[7]

The Facebook examples in Extract (7) and the song text excerpt Extract (8) are meant to illustrate the fluid transitions between languages. Many, in particular young people in Germany, indeed integrate the English language into their daily language repertoires in similar ways, depending on the context, speakers and intentions. The speakers in Extract (7) are all highly proficient speakers of English, playing with their multilingual identities and repertoires. On the other hand, many young people (in particular the 10- to 20-year-olds) in Germany use the English language in similar ways to Cro (and other German hip-hop artists), even though their general proficiency in English might be limited to the absolute basics, depending on their age and level of formal education. They, too, do not care about grammatical correctness, their motivation is intrinsic and, in many ways, instrumental, yet different from the tourist interaction-oriented extracts discussed earlier in the chapter (in particular Extracts (1) through (3) and (5)). Young Germans often make use of a specific, yet limited, set of words and expressions, sometimes not even truly English in origin but English-sounding, used in their respective circles to express their cool, hip-hop-related and urbane identities. Apart from that, their interest in the English language is rather limited. Whether such uses as illustrated in Extract (8) can be conceptualised as grassroots uses in the strict sense is, of course, debatable. However, as argued earlier, boundaries between variety and usage types are never clear-cut and these uses are certainly closer to the performance types/modes of communication described as ELF or grassroots Englishes than to any other category so far identified in the World Englishes paradigm.

In her 2013 article, Han illustrates a grassroots context proper. She describes the multilingual practices of migrants of African and Chinese backgrounds and how they expand and negotiate their multilingual repertoires in Africa Town in Guangzhou, China. English, of course, plays a key role in these contexts as 'the lingua franca of transnational business' (Han 2013: 83), but not everybody in these multi-ethnic contexts speaks English. She calls the grassroots variety which has emerged Chinglish, which is a mixture of very basic English and vocabulary and syntax from the Chinese languages/dialects spoken in these contexts. Therefore, English clearly plays a role in these contexts, but it is not necessarily the major player in these people's multilingual repertoires; rather, it functions more as an auxiliary language, aiding basic communication. This becomes even clearer when looking into the following exchange between a German and a Polish foreign worker (Extract (9)). The German does not speak any Polish (apart from a few words) but is fully proficient in English, the Polish interlocutor doesn't speak any English, apart from few words and a fixed set of expressions he has acquired as auxiliary expressions in jargon-like interactions with another German in the work context.

> Extract (9): an example of grassroots German
> Ich jetzt in Polen sagen scheiße non-stop.
> Man [English for German ‚Mann'] sagen, im 90er Jahr viele zap za rap Auto, jetzt nein.
> ['I'm saying that in today's Poland many bad things happen non-stop'.]
> ['The man [a specific one] says that in the 1990s many cars were stolen but not anymore.']

As Extract (9) illustrates, this conversational exchange is based on a simplified, grassroots version of German (cf. the early research project on Pidgin-German by Wolfgang Klein and colleagues in Heidelberg; for example Klein 1975).[8] Verbs are not inflected for person and tense (*Ich sagen, Man sagen*) and reduced syntax and missing sentence constituents (*im 90er Jahr viele zap za rap Auto, jetzt nein*), similar to the English extracts presented earlier in the chapter (Extracts (1)–(6)). Still, English and Polish have also found their way into this conversation, mostly as auxiliary languages or to express a certain, culture-related concept (*zap za rap* is a very well-known, iconic expression for stealing something in Polish).

In her 2013 article, Han argues that '[a]ssociated with globalisation from below, grassroots multilingualism is often found among individuals and groups who are structurally marginalised in various societies situated in the global geopolitical order' (2013: 95). This might very well be true and is something we certainly see in many of the extracts above (in particular Extracts (1)–(6)). However, it can also occur in other contexts as Extract (9) illustrates. The conversation took place in Germany and none of the interlocutors is truly socially disadvantaged or marginalised; the speech sample is more a product of communicative necessity between conversational partners who do not share a language, similar, maybe, to incipient pidginisation. Still, the linguistic similarities between Extracts (1) through (6) and (9) are striking.

My last example, also from a not necessarily marginalised context, comes from the tourism sector, more precisely, observations at a Mallorquin holiday resort. An interview between the author and the head of animation of one of the better-situated hotels on the island has yielded interesting insights into the current multilingual practices in today's tourism industry. In an earlier approach to linguistic practices in the tourism sector, Schneider (2013) focuses on the linguistic practices of scuba diving instructors as 'a special case of ELF' (English as a lingua franca). He argues 'that there is one additional, typical context of ELF usage which has been insufficiently recognised so far in the ELF debate, namely using "English for Specific Purposes" (ESP)' (Schneider 2013: 47) and thus takes an important step by establishing a direct relationship between ELF and ESP. He hypothesises that '[t]here is a substantial amount of overlap between ELF and ESP (in specific contexts); both are intrinsically related' (2013: 49). By doing so, Schneider has definitely revealed a valid and important correlation, but again he focuses only on English. Schneider never lays claim to completeness here, but again I would like to argue that ESP communication is just a part of a multilingual greater whole. Returning to the Mallorquin example, it once again shows that English is indeed one of the major players in these contexts. As my informant states in the interview, nobody would get a job as a holiday rep without a sufficient knowledge of English, but any other language they speak would also clearly increase their chances of being hired. Whatever linguistic repertoire the hosts bring with them (at least their native language and English), multilingualism develops automatically, but is often of the grassroots type, since language acquisition is mainly unguided and based upon the communicative needs of the majority of tourists and often takes place through interactions with these groups. My interview partner, Linda,[9] for example, is a young woman from Sweden, speaking Swedish as a first language, who came to Mallorca and started working in the tourism business as an entertainer four years ago; it was her first season as the head of animation at the time of recording. Her English is near-native (more American than British but even here the differences are seldom absolute, in particular in non-native speakers) and therefore definitely not of the grassroots type. Apart from English (and Swedish as her L1) she is fluent in Spanish, Norwegian and Danish, but she came to Mallorca without any knowledge of German. Since she is now working in a hotel that hosts a majority of German tourists who are, on average, not very patient if the host does not speak German and would expect him/her to do so, she is teaching herself a basic knowledge of German through interaction with the guests. As Linda states in the interview (concerning her proficiency in German): 'You heard it [. . .] it's not correct. But I never studied it, that's why as well I never like saw it on paper. I just heard it from the kids [children of the guests] and learned every day [. . .] As well I actually needed to' (and that was when she told me the story about the impatient Germans). Her German is therefore more of the grassroots type and that was confirmed by my observations. Her greetings and common, tourist-related chunks came as rehearsed expressions without much effort and very close to the native standard, but as soon as she had to produce German spontaneously she still had difficulties and her productions were very similar to what was observed in the extracts above for English (namely characterised by the same pragmatic strategies and characteristics, simple, sometimes non-canonical, grammar and incomplete sentences). The 'still' here is important, since following our 45-minute conversation I am convinced that she will improve her German over time. This is another important aspect that should be pointed out when talking about grassroots English, German, multilingualism or whatever type: these concepts are never fixed. As language is in state of constant flux and change, speakers' proficiencies can (and often do) fluctuate. One might want to argue that, particularly in the grassroots context, many speakers' proficiencies 'fossilise' at a comparatively early stage since their linguistic competence is sufficient for the messages they want to or have to bring across (cf. Selinker 1972: 215–17).[10] This, however, not only depends on the context but certainly also on the learner's aim and motivation.

In general, some observations of the moderation practices introducing and concluding the evening shows, together with the information provided by Linda, have revealed that language use and proficiencies in these multilingual contexts are heterogeneous and fluid, depending on the linguistic and ethnic backgrounds of the resort employees, as well as his/her career experiences since most hosts learn the relevant languages and increase their linguistic repertoires over time. The latter, again, depends on the extrinsic pressure put on them by tourists or the hotel management as well as their intrinsic motivation. Once again, it could be observed that language use seems at least partly rehearsed, for example when it comes to the introduction or concluding sequences of the evening shows. Most of the hosts are able to introduce and close the shows in a variety of languages even if, strictly speaking, they don't speak them, by 'rattling off' some more or less target-like salutations and closings, memorised chunks and sequences. Linda, for example, also greets participants in Dutch, a language she does not even mention as part of her linguistic repertoire in the interview and I have never heard her speak it outside of this very limited context.

To sum up, when confronted with the very same languages outside of salutation contexts, user proficiencies are often very limited and productions are rudimentary. They then resemble the extracts presented above, showing non-canonical, reduced syntactic structures and many of the pragmatic strategies and characteristics discussed for Extracts (1) through (3). I would therefore conclude that we are here confronted with highly multilingual contexts characterised by (1) varying proficiency levels; (2) different communicative functions and intentions that can be located on a scale from leading free, fully-fledged conversations to simply paying respect to speakers of other languages through the use of such fixed expressions as, for example, in the salutation contexts described earlier in the chapter; and (3) instances of language mixing, in which English most often plays a central role. Depending on the exact context, the type of English can be more or less ESL or EFL in nature, often of the ESP type (since many phrases and expressions are predetermined and required by the specific communicative context; see also Schneider 2013: 51–6) but interspersed by lexical elements and chunks from other languages. We clearly find characteristics of grassroots communication and lingua franca features as shown in the extracts. However, it is important to keep in mind that all these conceptual boundaries are fuzzy and speaker proficiencies and communicative intentions are fluid in form.

4 CONCLUSION

The present chapter has discussed the notion of 'grassroots Englishes' in relation to existing categories and notions in the World Englishes paradigm. In comparison to these, I have shown and argued that conceptual boundaries between different manifestations of the English language are fuzzy and rough approximations of very general types, at best. Everything should be pictured as a complex network of interacting and fluid forms, types and communicative practices which cannot be fully accounted for when detached from each other. This basically corresponds to what has been suggested by the application of Complex Dynamic System theory to language. In a subsequent step, the chapter has shown and argued that, depending on one's aims and perspectives, even a focus on English as a Complex Dynamic System is, strictly speaking, still a limited approach. If we want to gain a full understanding of the complex realities of linguistic globalisation and the resulting practices worldwide, we have to extend approaches such as Meierkord's (2012) Interactions across Englishes framework and the Complex Dynamic System view as applied to the English language by, for example, Schneider (forthcoming) – which, in principle, both approach the topic from the right angle – to the level of multilingual practices and speaker repertoires. These best depict the complex linguistic realities of today's globalised world. English is a very important, most likely the most important, player in these multilingual complexities, as is the phenomenon of grassroots Englishes within the wider framework of grassroots multilingualism. But since boundaries between languages become increasingly blurred and ever-newer forms of hybrid languages emerge, the best approach is from a multilingual, usage-based perspective. In this line of thinking, any type of human verbal interaction can be conceptualised as parts of a dynamic, complex system of languages, varieties and dialects, different usage contexts and modes of communication in which boundaries are fuzzy and fluent and everything is connected in one way or another. If one wishes to zoom in on particular aspects, such as the notion of 'grassroots Englishes, this is, of course, an equally relevant approach; this clearly remains a question of objectives and perspective.

NOTES

1. I am grateful to Brian Hess, Christiane Meierkord and Edgar Schneider for their helpful comments and suggestions. Any remaining shortcomings are, of course, my own responsibility.
2. For an overview of further potential types, see, for example, Mesthrie and Bhatt 2008 who list and discuss twelve different subtypes of what they call the 'English Language Complex' (for an earlier use of the term, see McArthur 2003: 56). For an overview of the most recent developments in World Englishes model-making, see, for example, Buschfeld et al. 2018; Buschfeld and Schneider 2018; or Buschfeld and Kautzsch 2020, among many others.
3. I would like to thank Alexander Kautzsch and Edgar Schneider for their support in the data collection process. The extracts from Indonesia (Extract (1)) and Tanzania (Extract (2)) were collected by Edgar Schneider in 2014 and 2015. I would like to thank him for making the data available for the present investigation.
4. However, these contact effects or acquisition-based mechanisms and strategies will not be discussed in the context of the present chapter since the focus is a different one.
5. Explanatory notes on the transcription symbols used in the extracts: [?] = best guess/unsure transcription; [/] = retracing of an utterance without correction; [//] = retracing of an utterance with correction; [. . .] = omission of transcribed material; [&] = phonological fragment/incomplete word; XX = unintelligible speech, treated as a single word.
6. Note, however, that Kachru himself conceded that the boundaries between the circles are not clear-cut (Kachru 1985: 13–14, 17), and that '[g]rey areas between the latter two [Outer and Expanding Circles] do exist' (Kachru 1985: 17; my addition). Nevertheless, most ensuing research has treated these categories as absolute until recently.
7. I am grateful to Simon Kautzsch for providing explanations on the youth language related slang terms.
8. I would like to thank Edgar Schneider for pointing this out to me.
9. The informant has explicitly consented to using her real name, Linda.
10. Note, however, that the term 'fossilisation' has been widely and controversially discussed, with some later approaches arguing that since the eventuation of fossilised states cannot be precisely determined, one should rather speak of stabilised forms than of permanent stagnancy of the learning process and should also look into 'the boundlessness of potentiality' in learners (Larsen-Freeman 2006: 189; see also, for example, Long 2003; Birdsong 2006).

REFERENCES

Birdsong, David (2006), 'Why not fossilization', in ZhaoHong Han and Terence Odlin (eds), *Studies of Fossilization in Second Language Acquisition*, Clevedon: Multilingual Matters, 173–88.

Blommaert, Jan (2010), *The Sociolinguistics of Globalization*, Cambridge: Cambridge University Press.

Buschfeld, Sarah (2013), *English in Cyprus or Cyprus English? An Empirical Investigation of Variety Status*, Amsterdam: John Benjamins.

Buschfeld, Sarah (forthcoming), 'What Cyprus and Greece can tell us about the paradigm gap between World Englishes and Second Language Acquisition research'.

Buschfeld, Sarah and Alexander Kautzsch (2014), 'English in Namibia: a first approach', *English World-Wide*, 35: 2, 121–60.

Buschfeld, Sarah and Alexander Kautzsch (2017), 'Towards an integrated approach to postcolonial and non-postcolonial Englishes', *World Englishes*, 36: 1, 104–26.

Buschfeld, Sarah and Alexander Kautzsch (2020), 'Theoretical models of English as a world language', in Daniel Schreier, Marianne Hundt and Edgar W. Schneider (eds), *The Cambridge Handbook of World Englishes*, Cambridge: Cambridge University Press, 51–71.

Buschfeld, Sarah and Edgar W. Schneider (2018), 'World Englishes: postcolonial Englishes and beyond', in Ee Ling Low and Anne Pakir (eds), *World Englishes: Re-Thinking Paradigms*, London: Routledge, 29–46.

Buschfeld, Sarah, Alexander Kautzsch and Edgar W. Schneider (2018), 'From colonial dynamism to current transnationalism: a unified view on postcolonial and non-postcolonial Englishes', in Sandra C. Deshors (ed.), *Modelling World Englishes in the 21st Century: Assessing the Interplay of Emancipation and Globalization of ESL Varieties*, Amsterdam: John Benjamins, 15–44.

Canagarajah, Suresh (2013), *Translingual Practice: Global Englishes and Cosmopolitan Relations*, New York and Abingdon: Routledge.

Coupland, Nikolas (ed.) (2010), *The Handbook of Language and Globalization*, Malden, MA: Wiley-Blackwell.

Cro (feat. Danju) (2014), *Meine Gang (Bang Bang)*. Lyrics available at: <https://genius.com/Cro-meine-gang-bang-bang-lyrics> (last accessed 18 September 2019).

Edwards, Alison (2016), *English in the Netherlands: Functions, Forms and Attitudes*, Amsterdam: John Benjamins.

Ellis, Nick C. and Diane Larsen-Freeman (eds) (2009), *Language as a Complex Adaptive System*, Malden, MA: Wiley and Sons.

Görlach, Manfred (1996), 'And is it English?', *English World-Wide*, 17: 2, 153–74.

Graddol, David (2006), *English Next: Why Global English May Mean the End of 'English as a Foreign Language'*, London: British Council.

Han, Huamei (2013), 'Individual grassroots multilingualism in Africa Town in Guangzhou: the role of states in globalization', *International Multilingual Research Journal*, 7:1, 83–97.

Han, Huamei (2017), 'Trade migration and language', in Suresh Canagarajah (ed.), *The Routledge Handbook of Migration and Language*, London: Routledge, 258–74.

Heller, Monica (2007), 'Bilingualism as ideology and practice', in Monica Heller (ed.), *Bilingualism: A Social Approach*, Houndmills: Palgrave Macmillan, 1–22.

Horner, Kristine and Jean-Jacques Weber (2018), *Introducing Multilingualism. A Social Approach*, 2nd edn, London, New York: Routledge.

Kachru, Braj B. (1985), 'Standards, codification and sociolinguistic realism: the English language in the outer circle', in Randolph Quirk and Henry G. Widdowson (eds), *English in the World: Teaching and Learning the Language and Literatures*, Cambridge: Cambridge University Press and the British Council, 11–30.

Klein, Wolfgang (1975), *Sprache und Kommunikation ausländischer Arbeiter*, Kronberg i.Ts.: Scriptor.

Kretzschmar, William A., Jr (2015), *Language and Complex Systems*, Cambridge: Cambridge University Press.

Larsen-Freeman, Diane (2006), 'Second language acquisition and the issue of fossilization: there is no end, and there is no state', in ZhaoHong Han and Terence Odlin (eds), *Studies of Fossilization in Second Language Acquisition*, Clevedon: Multilingual Matters, 189–200.

Long, Michael H. (2003), 'Stabilization and fossilization in interlanguage development', in Cathrine J. Doughty and Michael H. Long (eds), *The Handbook of Second Language Acquisition*, Malden, MA: Blackwell, 487–535.

McArthur, Tom (2003), 'World English, Euro English, Nordic English?' *English Today* 73, 19: 1, 54–8.

Meierkord, Christiane (2012), *Interactions Across Englishes. Linguistic Choices in Local and International Contact Situations*, Cambridge: Cambridge University Press.

Meierkord, Christiane and Karlfried Knapp (2002), 'Approaching lingua franca communication', in Karlfried Knapp and Christiane Meierkord (eds), *Lingua Franca Communication*, Frankfurt a. M.: Peter Lang, 9–28.

Mesthrie, Rajend and Rakesh M. Bhatt (2008), *World Englishes: The Study of New Varieties*, Cambridge: Cambridge University Press.

Rüdiger, Sofia (2019), *Morpho-Syntactic Patterns in Spoken Korean English*, Amsterdam: John Benjamins.

Schneider, Edgar W. (2007), *Postcolonial English. Varieties Around the World*, Cambridge: Cambridge University Press.

Schneider, Edgar W. (2011), *English Around the World. An Introduction*, Cambridge: Cambridge University Press.

Schneider, Edgar W. (2013), 'Leisure-activity ESP as a special case of ELF: the example of scuba diving English', *English Today*, 29: 3, 47–57.

Schneider, Edgar W. (2016a), 'Grassroots Englishes in tourism interactions', *English Today*, 32: 3, 2–10.

Schneider, Edgar W. (2016b), 'Hybrid Englishes: an exploratory survey', *World Englishes*, 35: 3, 339–54.

Schneider, Edgar W. (forthcoming), '*Calling* Englishes *as* Complex Dynamic Systems: diffusion and restructuring', in Anna Mauranen and Svetlana Vetchinnikova (eds), *ELF and Changing English*, Berlin, New York: Mouton de Gruyter.

Selinker, Larry (1972), 'Interlanguage', *IRAL – International Review of Applied Linguistics in Language Teaching*, 10, 209–31.

Williams, Jessica (1987), 'Non-native varieties of English: a special case of language acquisition', *English World-Wide*, 8: 2, 161–99.

Wolff, Martin (2010), 'China's English mystery – the views of a China "foreign expert"', *English Today*, 104: 26, 53–6.

Part I:
English at the grassroots in former spheres of British interest

CHAPTER 3

The Sociolinguistic Profile of English at the Grassroots Level: A Comparison of Northern and Western Uganda

Bebwa Isingoma

1 INTRODUCTION

As a former British protectorate and as is the case with many former British colonies and protectorates, Uganda uses English as (one of) its official language(s) as well as the language of instruction in all upper segments of primary education and all levels of post-primary education. English is therefore used in all domains of public administration, the judiciary and other high domains. In addition, it also finds its way in the media, business and informal domains. Following on from the above and based on Kachru's (1985) taxonomy, English in Uganda belongs to the Outer Circle and as such has started developing its own norms resulting in a nativised variety, which has been termed as Ugandan English. Indeed, it is characterised by heavy lexical borrowing and calquing, semantic extension and phraseological innovations, as well as phonological indexicality and structural variability (see e.g. Fisher 2000; Nassenstein 2016; Isingoma and Meierkord 2019).

The number of speakers of English in Uganda is below 20 per cent of the population in the country, as is the case with other Outer Circle Asian and African countries (see Meierkord 2020). Evidence from census data indicates that around 15.4 per cent of the Ugandan population has attained secondary education, which may translate into such a section of the population being proficient speakers of English (Isingoma and Meierkord 2019). However, usually, such numbers exclude users of English at the grassroots level because they do not meet the exclusionary requirements set by World English scholars (cf. Greenbaum and Nelson 1996), albeit they use English, moreover, sometimes, on a daily basis. Fortunately, there seems to have been a paradigm shift and as a result there is a steady build-up of literature profiling the use of English at the grassroots (cf. Schneider 2016; Meierkord 2020). For a country like Uganda, where there is no national language serving as a lingua franca, English has, to some extent, assumed that role in a de facto manner. Thus, a housemaid in

Gulu, where Acholi is spoken natively, may look for work from a Ugandan working in the area but the latter has only one language that unites him/her with his/her prospective housemaid, i.e. English. While the employer may be an acrolectal speaker of English, the housemaid usually will not be. Yet, the two will use the English resources at their disposal to effectively achieve their communicative needs. For a language that functions as a lingua franca, it is difficult to leave out a section of its users on the grounds that their English falls short of meeting the requirements of sophistication in the name of 'educated English'. This raises the very argument that Kachru (1985) laboured to address, i.e. the failure or reluctance by some scholars of the time to recognise the different forms and manifestations of the English language as the world's lingua franca.

This study is set out to delineate the quotidian linguistic behaviour of grassroots users of English in Uganda, their attitudes towards the use of English, as well as the level of their verbal repertoires. The grassroots users of English under consideration here are *bodaboda* riders and market vendors. *Bodaboda* (also spelt as *boda boda*) is a term used in Uganda (or East Africa) to refer to a bicycle or motorcycle taxi (*OED*). The taxis belong to an informal sector of transport and are very popular since they can easily navigate traffic in Kampala, where traffic jams are routine, and they also take the passengers directly to their destinations (cf. Raynor 2014). In addition, they are inexpensive in terms of fares and are readily available everywhere in the country (including in remote villages) and at any time. Moreover, the riders know all the places within their areas of operation. Thus, one does not need a map (which is a rare occurrence in Uganda) to find one's way as long as one uses a *bodaboda*. Market vendors, on the other hand, are people (many of them women) involved in informal economic activities in markets, selling food or manufactured goods including clothing and electronics, and providing services such as sewing, repairs, hairdressing, etc. (Young 2018). Usually, both categories are school drop-outs or people who did not go to school at all (Raynor 2014: 25; Young 2018: 139). As mentioned above, speaking English in Uganda (or in any other Outer Circle country) is associated with advanced schooling. Yet, by virtue of their trade, these categories of people may volitionally or incidentally have to speak English, as their trade requires them to interact with their customers who may not speak their L_1 or an indigenous language of wider communication, given that Uganda does not have a national language that serves as a lingua franca. It is against this background that this chapter sets out to profile the use of English by these categories of people in Uganda.

2 METHODOLOGY

This study used mainly semi-structured interviews involving thirty grassroots speakers of English in Uganda, who were asked to speak in English about issues of general concern regarding their trade and daily life in Uganda, as I recorded the conversations. The recording lasted for 270 minutes in total. The informants were also required to fill in a short questionnaire. For *bobaboda* riders, all the informants were male; as the trade is typically a male enterprise, finding a female rider is extremely rare. On the other hand, market vendors were predominantly female, with only four male informants, since the enterprise is dominated by women. Nonetheless, gender was not considered as a variable in the study. The thirty informants were drawn from two geographical regions in Uganda, i.e. fifteen from the Northern Region and fifteen from the Western Region. Linguistically, the two regions are characterised by the fact that the Northern Region is inhabited by speakers of Nilotic and Central Sudanic languages, while the Western Region is inhabited by Bantu. However, in the Northern Region, the study considers only the Nilotics, who, together with the Bantu, are the predominant speech communities in Uganda, with the Bantu constituting 66.4 per cent of the total population of the country, while the Nilotics constitute 27.2 per cent of the population (Namyalo et al. 2016: 27; Eberhard et al. 2019). For Western Uganda, the informants came from Fort Portal and Bundibugyo towns, while for Northern Uganda, they came from Gulu town.

The informants, who were aged between eighteen and fifty years, were selected purposively and the requirement to participate in the interviews was that one should not have gone beyond the fourth grade of secondary education, as that would make such informants (more or less) acrolectal speakers of English. However, the proviso was that one should be able to speak English. Table 3.1 summarises the level of education of the informants:

As can be seen, the majority of the informants only attended primary school, with four having studied for between one and four years of primary education and fifteen reaching between the 5th and the 7th grade of primary schooling. Those who attained secondary education were eleven in total, with six dropping out either in the first or second year, while five reached either the 3rd or the 4th year. Note that none of the informants attended nursery school or studied in an urban boarding school, where improved proficiency in English in Uganda

Table 3.1 Level of education of informants

Level of education[a]	Number of informants
P1–P4	4
P5–P7	15
S1–S2	6
S3–S4	5

Note: [a] Primary education in Uganda takes seven years, i.e. from the first grade (locally known as Primary One or P1) to the seventh grade (locally known as Primary Seven or P7), while secondary education takes six years, that is from S1 to S6.

has been attested (Namyalo et al. 2016). All the informants said that they had wanted to study further than that but could not due to lack of fees. As noted by Schneider (2016: 4), many speakers of English at the grassroots are often from a 'relatively poor background'. Although, in the 1990s, the Government of Uganda introduced universal primary education and subsequently universal secondary education (in 2007), many of the informants had already dropped out of school. In addition, despite the universalisation of education in the country, implementation has been problematic, because of insufficient funding from the government, which makes many schools charge parents some money (Huylebroeck and Titeca 2015). As Namyalo et al. (2016) report, the levels of education shown in the table only allow for basic and intermediate levels of proficiency in English if one completes the seven years of the primary cycle and the four years of the secondary cycle, respectively. Crucially, some of the informants revealed that they did not really acquire English at school but in the neighbourhood (see section 4).

In addition to the interviews, the study used a short questionnaire (see the Appendix at the end of this chapter) in order to find out the opinion of acrolectal speakers of English hailing from the two regions in relation to the fervour about and knack for speaking English at the grassroots level in the two regions. Forty people were involved, twenty from each region. They were all adults and were selected deliberately as regards their level of education, i.e. all had at least thirteen years of English education so as to qualify as acrolectal speakers of English (cf. Greenbaum and Nelson 1996). The variable of gender was deemed orthogonal for the current purpose of the study. These acrolectal speakers were involved because they had the capacity to provide opinions with respect to a comparative assessment in terms of enthusiasm, propensity and verbal repertoires as regards the use and users of English at the grassroots. These opinions were meant to provide a triangulation measure for my own assessment based on the recordings and daily observations.

3 LINGUISTIC FEATURES OF ENGLISH AT THE GRASSROOTS IN UGANDA

Schneider (2016) has shown that grassroots Englishes may characteristically have heavy simplification as well as restructuring. While it is hard to produce a unified characterisation of the features, some general observations can be made, as shown below ((1), (2), (3) and (4)). Note that these do not blur comprehension and, as Schneider (2016: 6) observes, some of the occurrences could be due to speakers' insecurity.

(1) Lack of concord
   (a) Few ladies who has come . . .
   (b) Few customer/many customer/two year/all category
   (c) We makes money.
   (d) It depend/your child come from . . .
(2) Verb usage
   (a) We get suffered.
   (b) I was wanted to study . . .
   (c) I am stop at P7.
   (d) I am studied from P1 up to S3.
   (e) We appreciate you for what you have did.
   (f) Our shelter is builted . . .
   (g) Because we born here . . .
(3) Preposition usage
   (a) After entering to her home
   (b) They talked to that issue, but . . .
   (c) It depends to the time.
   (d) My brother started getting annoyed on me.
(4) Others
   (a) When something good is in front . . .
   (b) There is a different in . . .
   (c) For I, the problem was money.

The picture depicted among the informants in this study is that some display patterns that are closer to the country's standards, while others deviate substantially from the standards (see discussion on the causes in section 4). In addition to the above specific features, many forms of acrolectal Ugandan English are used by speakers of English at the grassroots, as the latter look up to speakers of acrolectal Uganda English as their role models (see section 5). Abstracting away from the more evident phonological features, the indexical features of acrolectal Ugandan English below (Table 3.2) were observed among speakers of grassroots English in Uganda. Further, we notice the same expressions in the speech of speakers of grassroots and in Web-UG (see Table 3.2), a collection of web-based acrolectal Ugandan English compiled by Isingoma and Meierkord (2019).

While many of the lexical items are borrowings, there are also cases of semantic extension and calquing as well as some phraseological innovations. The calqued expression *slowly slowly*, while anecdotally heard among acrolectal speakers of Ugandan English (and reported to occur in Ghanaian English by Blench 2006: 35), may be said to occur more among the speakers of English at the grassroots than the acrolectal speakers, as evidenced by its absence in Web-UG. But since Web-UG is written English, it evidently does not capture what takes place in acrolectal spoken discourse; hence, we may not rule out the ubiquitous usage of

Table 3.2 Examples of acrolectal Ugandan English lexical features used by speakers of grassroots English in Uganda

Expression	Meaning	Attestation in Web-UG (normalised frequency per one million words)
according to me	'in my opinion'/'as far as I'm concerned'	09 (0.75)
askari	'security guard'	17 (1.41)
be on demand	'be in demand'/wanted by a lot of people'	12 (1.00)
be on X's neck	'pressurise X/breathe down X's neck'	03 (0.25)
bodaboba/boda boda	'motorcycle/bicycle taxi'	363 (30.25)
branch	'to branch off', 'turn'	03 (0.25)
drunko	'wino', 'drunkard'	01 (0.08)
garden	'field', 'garden'	200 (16.66)
good enough	'luckily'	11 (0.91)
kumbe	'yet', 'actually'	08 (0.66)
mairungi	'khat'	12 (1.00)
muyaaye/bayaye[a]	'vagabond', 'rogue'	09 (0.75)
muzungu/mzungu/bazungu	'white person/people'	95 (7.91)
posho	'cornmeal'	76 (6.58)
reduce on something	'reduce something'	54 (4.5)
saloon	'salon'	19 (1.58)
shamba	'field', 'garden'	07 (0.58)
simsim/sim(-)sim	'sesame'	35 (2.91)
slowly slowly	'bit by bit'	00 (0.00)
stage	'taxi rank'	13 (1.08)
turnboy/turn-boy	'assistant to a driver'	12 (1.00)

Note: [a] The prefix *ba-* is a plural marker for noun class 1 in Ugandan Bantu languages.

the expression among the acrolectal speakers as well. On the other hand, while *drunko* has only one hit in Web-UG, one cannot say that it is not a salient lexical item among the acrolectal speakers of Ugandan English, as a search in national newspapers in the country gives us twelve entries.[1] However, it has a lower frequency of usage than its synonym-cum-unclipped form, namely Standard English *drunkard*, which occurs in Web-UG twenty-two times. Crucially, it is not evident from the grassroots English data whether the speakers prefer *drunko* to *drunkard*, as the latter did not occur in the conversations.

Speakers of English at the grassroots in Uganda also share many structural properties with their acrolectal counterparts: the examples in (5) are taken from speakers of grassroots English, and, as we will see shortly, acrolectal speakers of Ugandan English also use similar patterns:

(5) (a) I *am having* one garden.
   (b) *My space*, it is small.
   (c) *Me*, I have one thousand shillings.
   (d) We have a problem of riding *gears*.
   (e) ... to run away with customers' *properties*.

The use of the progressive aspect in (5a) is akin to what Ssempuuma et al. (2016) describe in their paper on the extended use of the progressive in acrolectal Ugandan English. In (5b) and (5c), we have cases of topicalisation or left dislocation, a feature that Nassenstein (2016: 413) and Ssempuuma (2019: 53–102) analyse and about which they state that it occurs more in acrolectal Ugandan English than in British English. In Ugandan English, the left dislocated NP in (5b) and (5c) is not necessarily given information, as would be the case in British English. Finally, sentences (5d) and (5e) have non-count nouns that are pluralisable in Ugandan English, whether used by acrolectal speakers or speakers at the grassroots, similar to what Fisher (2000: 60–1) lists, such as *equipments*, *sceneries* and *beddings*. The examples in (6) below illustrate the acrolectal use of *gears*, on a par with the speakers of English at the grassroots in (5d) above:

(6) (a) ... when confiscated *gears* were allegedly resold to other fishers. (Web-UG)
   (b) ... reducing on the use of illegal fishing *gears*. (Web-UG)
   (c) ... provide workers with protective *gears*. (Web-UG)

While above I have shown sentences of the type in (1a) as a feature of English at the grassroots in Uganda, there are two important points to note here: (1) this feature is also common among the acrolectal speakers in the Northern Region; (2) consequently, in relation to this feature, it may be difficult to draw a borderline between the speakers of English at the grassroots and their acrolectal counterparts in the Northern Region. Compare the sentences in (7) from speakers at the grassroots and the sample sentences in (8) from acrolectal speakers in the Northern Region, i.e. my students of English (whose mother tongue is Acholi or Lango, i.e. Nilotic languages) both at bachelor's and master's level:[2]

(7) (a) Sometime we recruit when some of our colleagues *has* left.
   (b) Many guys *has* left.
   (c) We have few ladies who *has* come.
   (d) The customers *comes* but ...
   (e) Many people *does* not want ...

(8) (a) The verbs *agrees* with the subjects.
   (b) Affixes are morphemes that *occurs* before or after a base.

(c) Other loanwords *appears* to have their origin . . .
(d) Coinage phrases emanating from native language *has* a different semantics.
(e) The words on their way out *includes* the following . . .

It is not very clear why the patterns in (8) occur among the speakers of Lango and Acholi but not among Bantu speakers (a separate study is required in order to pin this down). However, one preliminary conjecture may be the fact that verb forms in Acholi and Lango are not formally distinguished in terms of singularity and plurality. In addition, in English, regular number inflection of nouns requires adding <s> for plurality. These two cases seem to cause an interlanguage scenario, whereby distinguishing plural forms from singular forms in English verbs is problematic. On the other hand, Bantu verbs are complex morphological units with noun class concordial markers, where the dichotomy singular vs. plural is crucial. Nonetheless, what this state of affairs highlights is what Meierkord (2012) refers to as interactions across Englishes; namely, Ugandan English is not homogeneous due to different types and levels of substrate influence. A study that looks at regional/ethnic differences at all linguistic levels in relation to Ugandan English is therefore envisioned. Thus, from the data in (7), we see that the speakers of English at the grassroots in the Northern Region share the feature of verb concord with many of the acrolectal speakers of English in the region (as shown in (8)). This usually involves those who have studied in the region throughout. Crucially, this feature is typically non-existent among the acrolectal speakers in the Western Region.

4 A SOCIOLINGUISTIC ACCOUNT OF ENGLISH AT THE GRASSROOTS IN UGANDA

One question that was posed to every informant participating in this study was to state whether they used English at all in their day-to-day communication and, if yes, how often and with whom. To achieve this, a short questionnaire was distributed to the informants and they were required to tick where appropriate. And where relevant, they could tick more than one alternative. The answers of the informants are presented in Tables 3.3 and 3.4:

As is the case in Schneider's (2016) study, the informants in this study need English primarily because of the nature of their work. As Table 3.4 shows, they typically need English to communicate with their customers. Most of them also indicated that they used English regularly, while two informants said that they used English on a daily basis. However, eight respondents said that while they used English with their customers, this was not something that occurred regularly. Interestingly, six of these were from the Western Region,

Table 3.3 Frequency of the use of English

Frequency of English use	Number of informants
Daily	2
Regularly (but not daily)	20
Rarely	8

Table 3.4 Interlocutors in the use of English

Type of interlocutors	Frequency counts
Customers	30
Friends	11
Relatives	2

while only two were from the Northern Region. This is understandable, as, for example, the informants from the Western Region said that in addition to using English with some of their customers, they also had at their disposal Luganda (or sometimes Kiswahili), which they use with customers who cannot speak Runyoro, Rutooro, Runyankole, Rukiga, Lukhonzo or Lubwisi, which are the major languages spoken in the Western Region, with the first four being highly mutually intelligible, while speakers of the latter two are also fluent L2 (second language) speakers of at least one of the first four languages. The informants from the Western Region stated that they only used English when dealing with people from the Northern Region (because they cannot generally speak Luganda) and *bazungu* (a Ugandan English word for 'whites'). They said that the language they preferred to use when speaking to an African stranger/ visitor was Luganda. If this fails, then they have recourse to Kiswahili, while English is the last resort. Sometimes, it is the stranger/visitor who initiates the conversation in one of these languages. Luganda is the most spoken L2 indigenous language in Uganda, while Kiswahili is the most spoken L2 endogenous language in Uganda (Namyalo et al. 2016: 43). In contrast, in the Northern Region, where Sudanic and Nilotic languages are spoken, the languages used to communicate with people who are not from their areas are Kiswahili and English (cf. Kaji 2013: 4), and Luganda is used only very sporadically (cf. Namyalo et al. 2016: 43), especially in some urban areas. Namyalo et al. (2016: 43) present results from a survey they conducted in three of the regions in Uganda, namely the Central, Western and Northern Regions and found out that overall English was more spoken in the Northern Region than in any other part of the country. Anecdotally, on my first visits to markets in Gulu (one of the large towns in the Northern Region), I could use Kiswahili while transacting with the market vendors, but most of them would reply in English. I thus stopped using Kiswahili when communicating to them.

In addition to using English with their customers, some informants said that they used it to communicate to friends and even relatives. Two important observations can be made here: (1) while for Schneider (2016), the use of English at the grassroots is motivated by the need to secure a job for which speaking English is a prerequisite, in Uganda and specifically in the Northern part, it is more than just securing a job, as English is also used in casual communication with friends and relatives; (2) this situation is not surprising in a country in which English is revered as a language of prestige and high status (cf. Nakayiza 2016). Just as is the case in Ghana (Dako and Quarcoo 2017: 24), some families in Uganda use English only in their homes (Ssentanda and Nakayiza 2017: 113), sometimes because the spouses' L1s (first languages) are mutually unintelligible but, other times, because parents believe that an early exposure of their children to English will make them more proficient in it. In addition, some people simply think since they are educated, the language they should speak is therefore English so as to maintain their high status in society. Along these lines, Nakayiza (2016: 85) reports that in Uganda 'there is a general feeling that in order to be listened to or in order to be taken seriously one has to be able to speak English fluently'. Thus, if the users of English at the grassroots are relatives to such families, they may have to speak English as well. We are well aware that African families are of the extended type (i.e. families that include not only parents and children, but also uncles, aunts, grandparents, cousins, etc.) and it is possible for a *bodaboda* rider or a market vendor to live at the home of his/her exclusively Anglophonic family. Likewise, when one needs to communicate to the English-only-speaking children of one's relatives, the only option is to use English. But also since speaking English translates into social superiority, it might be the case that a speaker of English at the grassroots will also want to flaunt his/her linguistic credentials in respect of the 'language of the educated', despite his/her low level of education, thereby showcasing his/her ability to penetrate what is seen as a territory of the elite. Importantly, some of the informants factually shared the perception that speaking English does not necessarily mean being (highly) educated. In her narrative, one of the informants said:

Extract (1)
For me, P1, I jumped, P2, I jumped because during war eh, so I was deep in the village. So when they brought me in centre, they thought I am just very tall; I cannot start P1. Then I jumped up to P3. Yeah, P1, P2 I never. So P3 I studied only two terms because when landmine started killing people, they put even what? on the school road so that we cannot move. So from that time maybe all my what . . . study, ah, if I mix it together, maybe four term only, four term only in my life. I started learning writing at home. So slowly, slowly, slowly. To talk English sincerely speaking, I start learning English from home where our friends come from Madi side.

> They come to my uncle. They talk English. Then for me I am quiet at home; I just listen. From that time when I got saved, then I feel the spirit of God would lead my prayer in English. That is why I just move into this level.

Despite the fact that there are several non-standard features (e.g. omission of the article 'the' in *during war* and *brought me in centre*, as well as the use of the preposition 'in' instead of 'to' in the latter example), the message in the narrative is fully comprehensible (cf. Schneider 2016: 4), depicting a somewhat (pre-) intermediate level in English. As can be discerned from this testimony, this informant studied for only four terms of elementary education, cumulatively translating into roughly one and a half years, which, by all standards, is quite an insignificant period of time as regards the acquisition of English in a primary school in rural Uganda (where at this level English is only taught as a subject, while the medium of instruction is the local language). More importantly, she reveals that she owes her proficiency in English to her friends, who could only speak English. In addition, she says when she became a Pentecostalist, she realised that God wanted her to pray in English. The situation here echoes Schneider's (2016: 3) revelation about speakers of English at the grassroots who have learnt English via 'direct interactions rather than through formal education'. Although this informant only associated her use of English in relation to her church practices to the Holy Spirit (an issue that we cannot evidently pursue here), we are aware that Pentecostal churches in Uganda (and in other parts of Anglophone Africa) use English (usually alongside an indigenous language) in their sermons and other liturgical activities (cf. Bremmer 2013: 210), with pastors striving to imitate the American accent.[3] As Adams and Beukes (2019) found out in South Africa, members of the Pentecostal churches highly espouse this practice. Therefore, this is not only another avenue for the acquisition of English in non-formal domains of learning in Uganda, but also a place where English is widely used at the grassroots level. Bremmer (2013) reports on how a man she met at a Pentecostal church in Kampala was able to ameliorate his proficiency in English during her one year of ethnographic fieldwork at the church. Bremmer (2013: 170–1) thus writes:

> In the early days of the research, Matthew was a peripheral figure in the cell group. Shy about his lack of proficiency in Luganda and English, he rarely spoke unless his opinion was specifically sought. Towards the end of our time visiting the cell group, however, he sometimes chaired the whole discussion, and with vastly improved spoken English.

Moreover, many of the pastors of the Pentecostal churches also acquire or improve their English on the job, as a number of them usually start pastoring with little or no education at all (cf. Fresh Revival Fire Ministries, undated)[4]. Therefore, the above informant has in effect had two main loci for her acquisition of English, i.e. the home (where she interacted with her friends in English as a child) and the church, where she has always used English in her prayers and other church activities. In addition, since she lives in the Northern Region, where the use of English is more pervasive, the language has become part and parcel of her life.

From the above, we now know that Ugandans in the Northern Region speak English at the grassroots more than those in the Western Region. While speaking English in the Western Region is not voluntary, in the Northern Region it is sometimes voluntary. This points to the fact that there is generally a positive attitude or inclination towards the use of English at the grassroots in the Northern Region compared to the Western Region, where using English at the grassroots is only conditionally motivated. Nakayiza (2016: 89) observes that an informant from the north-eastern part of Uganda told her that 'in my home area, people value English, even those who did not go far in school, you can think they work in offices'. Consequently, it is not surprising that the verbal repertoires of the speakers from the Northern Region appear to be richer than those of the speakers from the Western Region, especially for the informants who did not go beyond primary education.[5] For example, let us compare two informants from the Northern Region and their counterparts from the Western Region (cf. (9) and (10)), all of whom had the same level of education (i.e. seven years of primary education in rural settings):

(9) Northern Region
Extract (2)
First when you want to join our stage, we have some part payment; you must pay. The limit is four hundred and fifty thousand shillings to join the stage. You know our stage is big and there is a lot of customers and there is some rule and regulation we give you to work on our stage: not to abuse customers, to run away with customers' properties, to ride when you are drunk, or to behave badly . . . We don't allow a rider to do bad thing. If you continue, we fine you and you must pay or we chase you.

Extract (3)
For me, I just stopped in Primary seven at Panyikwal, that side of Bungatira in 2015. So I stop in . . . that 2015, 2016, I was home due to lack of money. 2017, I went to Saint Janan Vocational Training Centre and from there I was there for one year. After my mum now bought for me the, the machine now. So I am now using it. Now, I can even support my sister or even my mother, personally, I can help her.

(10) Western Region
Extract (4)
The problem what I have is that the, the, those ones the customers. You may be, you may buy there fish; you may buy one fish for five thousand but the customer come to your . . . when you say that this fish is for five hundred, eh, five thousand, they want to give you three thousand. That a problem what we have, what I have. And two, the problem, other problem what I have . . . is our shelter are not builted well; we have some place their shelter builted by cement but for us we have shelter builted by this wood. Others we have problem of those one who get tax, small tax, disturb us so much.

Extract (5)
We choosed this market because we born here; we married here; we stay here; the transport and even accommodation, we can sell our things near within us . . . Even me, we have a problem, but, OK by this time we are waiting for tax for our places. That taxi, it, it, it takes us badly because they come, if you have money, if you don't have it, we want our money. If you have refused to pay, we will take your . . . your business away . . . Even if you say to your customer that . . . that . . . my, my, that fish, I, I bought it with ten thousand, I want you to buy for it twelve thousand . . . they can't accept.

Noticeably, while the four extracts contain a number of non-standard linguistic features, the narratives in (10) have more of such features (e.g. 'the problem what I have' for 'the problem (that) I have'; 'our shelter are not builted well' for 'our shelters are not built well'; 'we choosed' for 'we chose'). Moreover, the speakers in (9) spoke with a lot of confidence, while the speakers in (10) felt insecure and had several hesitations. This pattern is observable in the rest of the narratives with a clear demarcation between the Northern Region and the Western Region for the informants who did not attain secondary education.

As pointed out in section 2, in order to verify my observations, forty acrolectal speakers of English in the two regions were also involved in this study so as to provide their reflections on the use of English at the grassroots in the two regions. They were asked to fill in a questionnaire as regards whether both the Northern Region and the Western Region used English at the grassroots at the same level, and, if there were differences, what accounted for those differences. Both groups overwhelmingly (38/40, i.e. 95 per cent) stated that the use of English at the grassroots was more widespread in the Northern Region than in the Western Region, with six informants in the Western Region saying that it was actually non-existent in their area. While the assertion that the use of English at the grassroots is non-existent in the Western Region is evidently an overstatement, it nevertheless corroborates the empirical evidence from the market vendors and *boda boda* riders from the Western Region, who stated that they only used English peripherally.

Most of the reasons that the informants gave as regards the discrepancy between the Northern Region and the Western Region rotate around three factors, namely ethnolinguistic nationalism, the role of Luganda and diffidence. According to the informants, there is a general view that the Bantu prefer to speak their languages more than any other language. And similar to what Nakayiza (2016: 90) reports, some informants in the Western Region stated that for the Bantu, speaking English 'unnecessarily' is tantamount to showing off and to effusiveness. This means that speaking English outside official domains with people with whom one shares the same (or mutually intelligible) language(s) is not generally seen as a necessary enterprise. Crucially, Nakayiza (2016) states that ethnolinguistic nationalism is more prevalent among the Luganda speech community (in the Central Region), where speaking Luganda is associated with supporting the kingdom of Buganda (a traditional cultural entity for the Baganda, i.e. the ethnic group that speaks Luganda natively). Isingoma (2016) notes that ethnolinguistic nationalism is also somewhat strong in the Western Region, and as a corollary it saw the clustering of four mutually intelligible languages (Runyoro, Rutooro, Rukiga and Runyankole) into what is known as Runyakitara in the 1990s, so that the four languages could be taught at Makerere University (the premier university in Uganda) on a par with Luganda, which had been introduced way back as an academic discipline (see also Bernsten 1998). At the same time, it was also necessary to introduce a non-Bantu Ugandan language at Makerere University for purposes of regional balance; whence, Luo, which clusters Acholi, Lango, Alur and Dhopadhola (all spoken in the Northern Region), was introduced. However, there is a clear discrepancy between how Runyakitara and Luo were embraced as disciplines of study by their native speakers, which, in turn, partly speaks to which of the two groups is more inclined to ethnolinguistic nationalism. Reports from Makerere University indicate that for the last five years Luo has only had one student graduate every year, while Runyakitara has had an average of fifteen students graduate every year (Asiimwe p.c. 2019); Luganda, whose speakers exhibit more ethnolinguistic nationalism, as reported by Nakayiza (2016), has had up to an average of eighty graduates per year (Ssentanda p.c. 2020).[6] While there might be other causes for the low number of graduates in Luo, it seems difficult to rule out the fact that since Luo speakers like English (as stated by some of the informants in the north, where Luo is spoken natively), this plays a role in their disposition to study Luo. Nonetheless, overall, studying local languages is generally disparaged by Ugandans (Isingoma 2016; Ssentanda and Nakayiza 2017) but this seems to be more pronounced in the Northern Region.

Relatedly, the role of Luganda in creating the north–west divide should not be underestimated. Some acrolectal informants in the Northern Region affirmed that Ugandan Bantu's preferred L2 is Luganda, while theirs is English. This reiterates what the speakers of English at the grassroots in the Western Region stated, i.e. the first language they use while communicating to visitors/strangers is Luganda. While one could also talk of Bantu nationalism here (i.e. it is better to speak an L2 of Bantu origin than to speak English), it is also a fact that Luganda is far easier to acquire by other Bantu speakers than English and it enables its users to speak to a great number of Ugandans (recall that up to 66.4 per cent of Ugandans are Bantu). Since Luganda also enjoys a certain degree of prestige in Uganda (Ssentanda and Nakayiza 2017), Bantu speakers in Uganda feel that speaking it gives them a social edge of some sort. Luganda's prestigious status started right from colonial times, as it was used as the language of colonial administration in all the Bantu speaking regions of Uganda. It is also the language spoken in Kampala, the capital city of Uganda and the business hub of the country as well as an area with the best schools. Moreover, until three decades ago, it was here that the only university in the country was located (i.e. Makerere University). All the above factors favour the use of Luganda as an L2 (Kaji 2013; Ssentanda and Nakayiza 2017).

The third factor that was cited is the issue of diffidence observable among the Bantu. This may be considered to be a factor which generally prohibits them from speaking English at the grassroots level. While this issue is debatable, we are aware that, right from colonial times, Ugandan Bantu were seen as cowards and weak and therefore could not be recruited into the army, while non-Bantu Ugandans were seen as courageous and daring (Amone 2014). The role of courage in L2 learning has been documented (Wu et al. 2014: 461). Remarkably, speaking English at the grassroots level requires courage, since the level of education of the speakers is indeed low, which means that the level of proficiency in English is also supposed to be low. It thus seems that Bantu speakers of English at the grassroots do not want to risk making mistakes. Conversely, speakers of English at the grassroots in the Northern Region seem to feel that making mistakes is just a process of learning, and they thus determinedly speak English without diffidence. Of course, the prestige associated with speaking English in Uganda is in itself a strong motivating factor, as it makes one acquire a high status. It might be worthwhile to share an anecdote which highlights how the people in the Northern Region view themselves in terms of status. While on fieldwork at Mbarara University of Science and Technology (Western Uganda) in 2018, I was invited to a party for the Mbarara University Luo Speaking Students' Association. I was invited as the guest of honour by my contact person at the university, who was the patron of the Association, partly because I work at a university located in a Luo-speaking area. The members of the Association had a leitmotif they kept on mentioning in chorus, i.e. *we are strong; we penetrate; we dominate*. The thrust of the leitmotif resonates well with the following pronouncement made by a paramount chief of the Acholi – one of the ethnic groups in the Northern Region: 'The Acholi is a proud person . . . [we are] tall people, strong people . . . [brackets in original]' (Davenport 2014: 14). Armed with this kind of amour propre, it therefore behooves the adherents to this credence to seize all available opportunities in their midst to actualise what is embodied in the above statements. Since English in Uganda bestows pride and power on the person who speaks it, the inclination to speak it in the Northern Region could be associated with the above revelation. In addition, the fact that people at the grassroots can succeed in speaking it with a relatively good degree of proficiency is in itself a feat that vindicates the tenor of the above statements. Moreover, some acrolectal speakers of English in the Northern Region stated that the people there not only speak English better than the Bantu, but they speak it just like the British – a claim that is profoundly ingrained in them, as also reported by Adokorach and Isingoma (2020).

5 CONCLUDING REMARKS

What we can finally discern from the above analysis is that users of Ugandan English at the grassroots look up to the acrolectal users of English in Uganda as their role models. Notably, while their English displays a number of differences from the acrolectal speakers of English, it clearly depicts many of the innovative features present among the acrolectal speakers of Ugandan English (e.g. the extended use of the progressive, the ubiquitous use of left dislocation, the pluralisation of some non-count nouns, or lexical items such as *simsim* 'sesame', *turnboy* 'assistant to a driver', *garden* 'field', etc.). In other words, the speakers of English at the grassroots cannot replace the innovative norms developed by the acrolectal speakers with e.g. Standard British English norms. For example, they would not use *assistant to a driver* or *sesame* in place of Ugandan English *turnboy* or *simsim* respectively, even if they were to frequently hear the British English expressions on television or in movies since these media are widely available in Uganda these days. This means that for their target of production, they set for themselves the standards developed by Ugandan acrolectal speakers of English and not L1 speaker standards. Hence, Ugandan English can be said to be both *norm developing* as well as *norm providing* (cf. Kachru 1985), i.e. the acrolectal sub-variety develops its norms and provides them for the grassroots sub-variety.

As researchers have gone ahead to take care of lacunae observable in the current models of World Englishes, it has been stated that it is not only Inner Circle Englishes that provide the norms in contrast to what Kachru (1985) proposes. For example, Mair (2013) has shown that Outer Circle Englishes also provide the norms, with Jamaican English influencing young British English speakers in London. In addition, as Kachru (1985: 17) himself predicts, it has also been shown, e.g. by Schneider (2007: 13), that his Concentric Model should not be treated as containing categorical trichotomic constructs, since sometimes there are overlaps. Indeed, Michieka (2009: 352) has shown how some parts of Kenya behave like an Expanding Circle, while other parts display features of Outer Circle English in terms of the breadth and depth of the use of English in daily life. In the context of this study, indeed we see Ugandan English displaying features of an Outer Circle variety in terms of developing its own norms at the acrolectal level, but it also shows features of Inner Circle Englishes in terms of providing the norms it has developed at the acrolectal level to the grassroots level. As Meierkord (2012) shows, there is a need to always bear in mind the heterogeneous nature of English spoken in one country. The way England has different varieties of English based on regions, social classes, etc., is the same way a country like Uganda has several Englishes based on regions, ethnicity or level of education. Crucially, England (or any other Inner Circle country) has a variety of English spoken by lower social classes and another spoken by upper social classes, i.e. Standard English (Jeffries 1998: 50). English in lower social classes in England has its idiosyncratic features but it also shares (at varying degrees depending on individual varieties) some features with Standard British English (Trudgill 1990: 5–6). Likewise, English at the grassroots in Uganda has its (arguably fluid but generalisable) idiosyncratic features but it also shares some of its features with acrolectal Ugandan English (i.e. educated Ugandan English). However, British English in lower social classes is different from grassroots English in Uganda, as the latter may be categorised as performance English in an Outer Circle country. Like any other performance English, the speakers look up to some other category of speakers (in our case the acrolectal speakers of Ugandan English) for norms despite the fact that they usually do not attain the same level of proficiency with the norm providers (cf. Edwards and Laporte 2015).

APPENDIX: QUESTIONNAIRE FOR ACROLECTAL SPEAKERS OF UGANDAN ENGLISH

Please answer the following questions, bearing in mind the following definition:
Definition: *people at the grassroots* = ordinary people, i.e. those that are not (highly) educated.

Questions:

1. Which group among the following uses English more regularly? Tick where appropriate.
    (a) people at the grassroots in Northern Uganda
    (b) people at the grassroots in Western Uganda

2. Give reasons for your answer in (1) above. (Please feel free to write as much as you can.)

....
....
....
....
....
....
....
....
....
....
....
....
....
....
....
....

NOTES

1. The newspapers are *New Vision*, *Monitor* and *Observer*.
2. The sentences from my students were gleaned from coursework and examination scripts.
3. The association of Pentecostal churches with English could be linked to the fact that they are normally funded by sister churches in the USA (cf. Robbins 2004: 135).
4. This is a church community.
5. This is premised on the fact that the more a person advances with their education, the more proficient in English they become (cf. Namyalo et al. 2016).
6. Allen Asiimwe and Medadi Ssentanda are lecturers at the School of Languages, Literature and Communication, Makerere University.

REFERENCES

Adams, N. Thabisile and Anne-Marie Beukes (2019), 'English as a medium of worship: the experiences of the congregants of a Pentecostal charismatic church in Soweto', *Literator*, 40: 1, 1–9.

Adokorach, Monica and Bebwa Isingoma (2020), 'Homogeneity and heterogeneity in the pronunciation of English among Ugandans: a preliminary study', *English Today*, <https://doi.org/10.1017/S0266078420000152> (last accessed 15 August 2020).

Amone, Charles (2014), 'The creation of Acholi military ethnocracy in Uganda, 1862–1962', *International Journal of Liberal Arts and Social Science*, 2: 3, 141–50.

Bernsten, Jan (1998), 'Runyakitara: Uganda's new language', *Journal of Multilingual Development*, 19: 2, 93–107.

Blench, Roger (2006), 'A dictionary of Ghanaian English', <http://www.rogerblench.info/Language/English/Ghana%20English%20dictionary.pdf> (last accessed 24 April 2020).

Bremmer, E. Sophie (2013), 'Transforming futures? Being Pentecostal in Kampala, Uganda', PhD thesis, University of East Anglia.

Dako, Kari and Millicent A. Quarcoo (2017), 'Attitudes towards English in Ghana', *Legon Journal of the Humanities*, 20–30.

Davenport, L. David (2014), 'Ruptures of war: shame and symbolic violence in post-conflict Acholiland', *The Journal for Undergraduate Ethnography*, 4:2, 1–18.

Eberhard, M. David, Gary F. Simons and Charles D. Fennig (eds) (2019), *Ethnologue: Languages of the World, 18th edn*, Dallas: SIL International.

Edwards, Alison and Samantha Laporte (2015), 'Outer and expanding circle Englishes: the competing roles of norm orientation and proficiency levels', *English World-Wide*, 36: 2, 135–69.

Fisher, E. C. Allestree (2000), 'Assessing the state of Ugandan English', *English Today*, 16, 57–61.

Fresh Revival Fire Ministries (undated), 'Pastors education scholarship fund', <https://frfministries.org/?page_id=1590> (last accessed 27 August 2019).

Greenbaum, Sidney and Gerald Nelson (1996), 'The International Corpus of English (ICE) project', *World Englishes*, 15, 3–15.

Huylebroeck, Lisa and Kristof Titeca (2015), 'Universal secondary education (USE) in Uganda: blessing or curse? The impact of USE on educational attainment and performance', in Filip Reyntjens, Stef Vandeginste and Marijke Verpoorten (eds), *L'Afrique des Grands Lacs: Annuaire 2014–2015*, Antwerp: University Press Antwerp, 349–72.

Isingoma, Bebwa (2016), 'Languages in East Africa: policies, practices and perspectives', *Sociolinguistic Studies*, 10: 3, 433–54.

Isingoma, Bebwa and Christiane Meierkord (2019), 'Capturing the Lexicon of Ugandan English: ICE-Uganda, its limitations and effective complements', in Alexandra U. Esimaje, Ulrike Gut and Bassey E. Antia (eds), *Corpus Linguistics and African Englishes*, Amsterdam: Benjamins, 294–328.

Jeffries, Lesly (1998), *Meaning in English: An Introduction to Language Study*, London: Macmillan.

Kachru, Braj (1985), 'Standards, codification and sociolinguistic realism: the English language in the outer circle', in Randolph Quirk and Henry G.

Widdowson (eds), *English in the World. Teaching and Learning the Language and Literatures*, Cambridge: Cambridge University Press, 11–30.

Kaji, Shigeki (2013), 'Monolingualism via multilingualism: a case study of language use in the west Ugandan town of Hoima', *African Study Monographs*, 34: 1, 1–25.

Mair, Christian (2013), 'The world system of Englishes: accounting for the transnational importance of mobile and mediated vernaculars', *English World-Wide*, 34: 3, 253–78.

Meierkord, Christiane (2012), *Interactions across Englishes: Linguistic Choices in Local and International Contact Situations*, Cambridge: Cambridge University Press.

Meierkord, Christiane (2020), 'The global growth of English at grassroots', in Daniel Schreier, Marianne Hundt and Edgar W. Schneider (eds), *The Cambridge Handbook of World Englishes*, Cambridge: Cambridge University Press, 311–38.

Michieka, M. Martha (2009), 'Expanding circles within outer circles: the rural Kisii in Kenya', *World Englishes*, 28: 3, 352–64.

Monitor, <www.monitor.co.ug> (last accessed 27 August 2019).

Nakayiza, Judith (2016), 'The sociolinguistic situation of English in Uganda: a case of language attitudes and beliefs', in Christiane Meierkord, Bebwa Isingoma and Saudah Namyalo (eds), *Ugandan English: Its Sociolinguistics, Structure and Uses in a Globalizing Post-protectorate*, Amsterdam: Benjamins, 75–94.

Namyalo, Saudah, Bebwa Isingoma and Christiane Meierkord (2016), 'Towards assessing the space of English in Uganda's linguistic ecology: facts and issues', in Christiane Meierkord, Bebwa Isingoma and Saudah Namyalo (eds), *Ugandan English: Its Sociolinguistics, Structure and Uses in a Globalizing Post-protectorate*, Amsterdam: Benjamins, 19–49.

Nassenstein, Nico (2016), 'A preliminary description of Ugandan English', *World Englishes*, 35: 3, 396–420.

New Vision, <www.newvision.co.ug> (last accessed 27 August 2019).

Observer, <https://observer.ug> (last accessed 27 August 2019).

Oxford English Dictionary (OED), <http://www.oed.com/> (last accessed 17 August 2019).

Raynor, Bradley (2014), 'Informal transportation in Uganda: a case study of the boda boda', *Independent Study Project Collection*, SIT Study Abroad.

Robbins, Joel (2004), 'The globalization of Pentecostal and charismatic Christianity', *Annual Review of Anthropology*, 33, 117–43.

Schneider, Edgar W. (2007), *Postcolonial English. Varieties of English Around the World*, Cambridge: Cambridge University Press.

Schneider, Edgar W. (2016), 'Grassroots Englishes in tourism interactions', *English Today*, 32: 3, 2–10.

Ssempuuma, Jude (2019), *Morphological and Syntactic Feature Analysis of*

Ugandan English: Influence from Luganda, Runyankole-Rukiga, and Acholi-Lango, Berlin: Peter Lang.

Ssempuuma, Jude, Bebwa Isingoma and Christiane Meierkord (2016), 'The use of the progressive in Ugandan English', in Christiane Meierkord, Bebwa Isingoma and Saudah Namyalo (eds), *Ugandan English: Its Sociolinguistics, Structure and Uses in a Globalizing Post-protectorate*, Amsterdam: Benjamins, 173–99.

Ssentanda E. Medadi and Judith Nakayiza (2017), '"Without English there is no future": the case of language attitudes and ideologies in Uganda', in Augustin E. Ebongue and Ellen Hurst (eds), *Sociolinguistics in African Contexts*, Cham: Springer, 107–26.

Trudgill, Peter (1990), *The Dialects of England*, Oxford: Blackwell.

Wu, Rui Ting, Van Tai Le and Jin Jin Lu (2014), 'A contrastive analysis of first and second language learning', *Theories and Practices in Language Studies*, 4: 3, 458–65.

Young, G. William (2018), 'Informal vending and the state in Kampala, Uganda', PhD thesis, University of Cambridge.

CHAPTER 4

English Language Learning Trajectories among Zanzibaris Working in Tourism

Susanne Mohr

1 INTRODUCTION

With increasingly mobile people, dynamism in language has become part of our modern globalised world and is increasingly reflected in sociolinguistic theorising (Ebongue and Hurst 2017). One central issue with regard to this mobility is tourism, 'the single largest peaceful movement of people across cultural boundaries' (Lett 1989: 276). The adaptation of language to new cultural contexts in super-diverse spaces created by tourism results in interesting sociolinguistic effects (Vertovec 2007; Jaworski and Thurlow 2010), and this has also been acknowledged for the study of World Englishes (for example Schneider 2016; Buschfeld and Kautzsch 2017; Meierkord 2018). Tourist contexts, where English is often used at the grassroots level by hosts such as guides, hotel staff and tourists alike, provide an important opportunity to investigate English away from traditionally studied academic circles in World Englishes research (Kubota 2018). This *grassroots* language use, as the term is used in this chapter, 'is characterised by fluid forms [. . .] as a result of uninstructed expansion of multilingual repertoires for localised purposes' (Han 2013: 84) and goes back to Blommaert (2004), who used the notion to refer to the concept of grassroots literacy. In this vein, the analysis of English at the grassroots level and through the lens of mobility and globalisation has the potential to contribute importantly to the study of English(es) in multilingual contexts.

This chapter analyses one such context, that is English used in the tourism industry on Unguja island of Zanzibar. In Tanzania, of which Zanzibar forms a part, English is an official language taught as a subject in primary school and employed as medium of instruction in secondary education. Thus, English should be learnt formally, and possibly used in public given its official status. Based on ethnographic data from interviews and observations, this chapter analyses the use and ways of learning English among Zanzibaris, drawing on Blommaert and

Backus's (2011) framework of language learning trajectories in super-diversity. It is shown that, while interaction in English takes place in informal settings that might qualify as 'grassroots', away from academic circles, the trajectories of learning English include practices not typically associated with the grassroots level. This expounds the problem of an easy attribution of individual second language learning paths to particular social groups and reveals the fuzziness of the grassroots concept and its boundaries. Ultimately, the analysis of the Zanzibari data illustrates that grassroots multilingualism is indeed a rather individual phenomenon related to individual language biographies (cf. Han 2013).

2 LANGUAGE LEARNING IN SUPER-DIVERSITY

In an increasingly mobile world, language repertoires reflect mobility as language knowledge becomes ever more dynamic and changeable. In this vein, repertoires do not develop along linear paths but rather unsystematically, 'explosively' or 'gradually' in different phases of life (Blommaert and Backus 2011: 9). Under these circumstances, the trajectories and, with emerging new technologies, means of language learning have become increasingly diverse and polycentric (The Douglas Fir Group 2016). Formal and informal learning often go hand in hand as learners want to acquire communicative competence, that is the knowledge of what means of their linguistic repertoire to employ and how to do that (Blommaert and Backus 2011). From a usage-based point of view (for example Barlow and Kemmer 2000), this communicative competence is built on active use of a language, which is particularly important in informal language learning. In this regard, communicative usefulness and demands of the communicative setting are crucial for assembling the inventory of units making up a language repertoire (Blommaert and Backus 2011: 7).

In a globalised world, communicative usefulness and demands of the communicative setting are strongly influenced by the market and forces of globalisation, which dictate which languages an individual has to learn in order to make sense to others. Thus, language becomes a marketable skill and language repertoires become trajectories of power (Blommaert and Backus 2011; Duchêne and Heller 2012; Muth and Del Percio 2018). In this vein, language repertoires contribute essentially to 'perform[ing] certain social roles, inhabit[ing] certain identities and be[ing] seen in particular ways' (Blommaert and Backus 2011: 22). Especially in tourist spaces, which are characterised by their highly commodified nature[1] (for example Jaworski and Thurlow 2010), language is produced and sold to interlocutors, that is tourist recipients (Schedel 2018), as hosts perform their social roles. English as global lingua franca is central in this regard, as it is the most frequently used language in tourist spaces generally (Maci 2018) and in Zanzibar as well (Mohr forthcoming).

The outlined developments and dynamics, specifically of globalisation, have a significant impact on language learning. Traditionally, language acquisition and language learning were distinguished, specifically in the field of Second Language Acquisition studies (SLA). *Acquisition* referred to a subconscious, naturalistic process encountered for example in child language acquisition, while *learning* is conscious and usually instructed (Krashen 1981). However, in mobile and super-diverse contexts it is difficult to strictly uphold this dichotomy, as these processes become intricately entwined in speakers' language biographies. Thus, in their more recent theory of the dichotomy of language acquisition and learning, Blommaert and Backus (2011) emphasise the entwinement of processes in making a different distinction, one that is related to the effects of these processes and their permanence. While *acquisition* leads to long-term entrenchment of language knowledge, *learning* leads to rather temporary, dynamic entrenchment (Blommaert and Backus 2011: 9–15). Despite its temporary character, they view learning as a crucial part of every speaker's language biography as

> the 'language' we know is never finished [. . .] and learning language as a linguistic *and* a sociolinguistic system is not a cumulative process; it is rather a process of growth, of sequential learning of certain registers, styles, genres and linguistic varieties while shedding or altering previously existing ones. (Blommaert and Backus 2011: 9; emphasis in original)

The varied constituents of language repertoires mentioned above are acquired in many different ways or through many different modes of language learning. Blommaert and Backus (2011: 11–14) suggest at least four:

1. **Comprehensive language learning**, that is full socialisation in a language across the lifespan with access to formal and informal learning environments and leading to a maximal set of linguistic resources.
2. **Specialised language learning**, that is specialised skills and resources in a language used in specific environments and situations, such as academic English for many non-native speakers working in academia, who do not necessarily acquire more colloquial registers of the language.
3. **Encounters with language**, that is learning small bits of language, for instance in age group slang learning, temporary language learning for travel, single word learning of a 'globalised vocabulary', especially of greetings, food and drink or curse words.
4. **Recognising language**, that is recognising but not being able to use certain languages, for example based on their script or sound.

The first two are, according to Blommaert and Backus (2011), enduring and lead to communicative competence in Hymes's (1972) sense, that is the capacity to use language appropriately in a wide range of social contexts. The latter two are ephemeral and restricted. Encounters with language (3 above) are specifically relevant in the tourist context, as has been touched upon by Mohr (forthcoming) for Kiswahili, the local language of Zanzibar. Thus, bits of a language are learned before a holiday, actively or less purposeful, especially with reference to a so-called 'globalised vocabulary', such as *aloha* from Hawaiian or *salud* from Spanish, learnt through pop culture (Blommaert and Backus 2011: 13). Active and purposeful language learning among tourists often takes place informally through the self-study of language guides before a vacation or through interaction with hosts during the holiday (cf. Nassenstein 2019). In a way, it thus takes place 'at the grassroots' and would fall into this chapter's scope. While this issue is interesting, the focus of this chapter is on language learning among *hosts* in the Zanzibari tourist industry, as discussed in the following.

3 ZANZIBAR, TOURISM AND LANGUAGE

Zanzibar is an archipelago situated in the Indian Ocean off the coast of mainland Tanzania and a semi-autonomous region of the country. It consists of two large and several smaller islands, the main ones being Unguja and Pemba (Figure 4.1).

One of the largest economic sectors of Zanzibar is agriculture, catering for

Figure 4.1 Unguja and Pemba islands
Source: Image is public domain from: https://commons.wikimedia.org/wiki/File:Spice_Islands_(Zanzibar_highlighted)_sv.svg)

the spice trade. However, after the end of the Tanzanian socialist era in the 1990s, tourism became the largest economic sector (Keshodkar 2013), employing 50 per cent of the population and accounting for 25 per cent of the islands' GDP (Serikali ya Mapinduzi ya Zanzibar 2013). With the introduction of free markets, many foreign investors settled on the islands, buying land, hotels and other establishments in the hospitality industry, providing for an annual growth of the tourist sector of 16 per cent (Keshodkar 2013: 71). While Zanzibar is not one of the top tourist destinations in Africa (Sarmento and Rink 2016), it has benefited immensely from the popularity of island tourism in the past years. Due to often unregulated and corrupt structures in the tourism industry, 'Zanzibar [has] evolved into a destination for mass tourists in search of sun [and] sand [. . .]' (Keshodkar 2013: 72).

With mostly foreign investors owning businesses in the tourist industry and holding higher positions at managerial level, less than 5 per cent of the jobs in the tourist industry are held by Zanzibaris themselves. These jobs are, largely, low-skill jobs (Chachage 2000). This is due to cultural and, importantly, linguistic reasons. As Zanzibaris are mostly Muslim, women are often prohibited from working in tourism where they come into contact with male strangers, or might have to work without a headscarf, or could be asked to serve alcohol (Keshodkar 2013). Many Zanzibari men are not willing to work in the tourism industry either, at least not in positions where they have to serve tourists, as also mentioned by Mikidadi,[2] one of the participants of my study. Thus, many mainland Tanzanians migrate to Zanzibar to take advantage of the job opportunities in tourism: mainlanders possess the willingness and, importantly, the educational background and linguistic skills to work in tourism (Keshodkar 2013: 62, 74). For instance, managers want to ensure that their staff can interact in foreign languages. Zanzibar is a typical example of a work site in which language is produced for and sold to a specific audience (Schedel 2018: 139).

As mentioned in the previous section, English plays a central role as global lingua franca for the tourist industry worldwide and for Zanzibar as well. This is similar to mainland Tanzania, where English is used for practical reasons in and around tourist hot spots like Mount Kilimanjaro (Schneider 2016) and in the education of tourist guides (Salazar 2006). As part of Tanzania, Zanzibar has to follow the same educational policy as the mainland. The most recent policy is ambiguous, but it is common practice to teach English as a subject in primary education and use it as medium of instruction from secondary level onwards (cf. Mohr and Ochieng 2017). However, this does not usually lead to fluency in English among mainland Tanzanians (Mohr and Ochieng 2017; Mohr 2018) and this situation possibly holds in Zanzibar as well, due to a decline of the educational system on the island (Keshodkar 2013). As is shown in the analysis of the data collected for the present study, only a few Zanzibaris learn English fluently in school.

Besides English, other foreign, usually European languages play an important role in tourism in East Africa. This has been illustrated by studies on the linguistic landscape of tourism in Zanzibar (Storch forthcoming), and by analyses of linguistic interactions in tourist spaces in Kenya (Nassenstein 2016, 2019). In my data set, European languages also form an important part of speakers' language repertoires (Mohr forthcoming). This is briefly touched upon in the analysis of the data presented here as well.

4 METHOD AND DATA

The data set analysed here stems from participatory observation (2.5 months) and sociolinguistic interviews conducted on Unguja island, specifically in Zanzibar City, Nungwi on the north coast and Paje and Jambiani on the east coast. Observations were recorded as field notes and in the fashion of communicative diaries used in the study of multilingualism (cf. for instance Lawson and Sachdev 2000). Sociolinguistic interviews were semi-structured and audio-recorded when participants permitted, some preferred me to take handwritten notes. They were usually conducted at the participants' place of work or another location of their choice where they felt secure and relaxed. All in all, thirteen interviews were conducted, and approximately five hours of these were recorded. Most of these data stem from men, as only few women work in tourism and those who do were generally shy. For the present analysis, only data gathered from participants born and raised in Zanzibar is considered. An overview of these participants and their socio-demographic background is provided in Table 4.1.

All the participants in Table 4.1 are male. Their mean age cannot be determined as half of them did not want to talk about their age or did not know their birthday. The mean age of the four who did is thirty-three. Interestingly, all of them are highly educated, having obtained university degrees of different kinds. Only Hamadi did not finish secondary school and does not possess a degree from an institution of higher education. While this might seem to exclude the participants from a study on English at the grassroots, the analysis and discussion of the results justifies that application of the term 'grassroots' to this participant group. As will become clear, a lot of their language acquisition did not take place within institutionalised contexts. All participants indicated Kiswahili as their home language, Mikidadi reported Kiswahili and English both, which is why English is not reported again under 'other languages' for him. Other results concerning language use and skills are discussed in the following section.

Two other important sources of data for the present chapter are a visit to a primary school in Jambiani including a short interview with its headmaster, as well as several observations during English lessons at an NGO, Kawa Training Center,[3] located in the old town of Zanzibar City, Stone Town. Founded by a

Table 4.1 Socio-demographic background of the participants

Pseudonym	Education	Occupation	Languages apart from native language
Maburuki	University degree in tourism	Tour guide, teacher in madrasa school[i]	English, Arabic, German, Czech
Abdalla	University degree in tourism	Tour guide, university lecturer	English, Italian, Spanish, French
Hamadi	Primary school, part of secondary school	Hotel staff (waiter, assistant manager)	English, Arabic, French, Italian, Spanish
Mikidadi	University degree in computer science	Hotel manager	Arabic, Hindi
Saburi	Degree in education	Hotel staff (receptionist)	English, Arabic, Spanish
Ramadhan	Degree in education	English teacher	English, Arabic, Italian
Suweid	University degree in tourism management	Assistant hotel manager	English[ii]
Hussein	University degree in environmental planning and management	Reservation and reception manager (hotel)	English

Notes: (i) The type of madrasa Maburuki mentioned is a school for Muslim children, where they are acquainted with the Qur'an and the principles of the Muslim faith. (ii) The participant was very shy; he did not comment on further language skills. It is likely that he speaks other languages, as do many highly educated staff in Zanzibari hotels.

Dutch former tourist guide and funded by the TUI Care Foundation, the NGO provides training courses for tour guides including content-related classes on marine biology or the history of Zanzibar, as well as English language classes. These classes are taught by foreign volunteers, former students of the classes and local Zanzibaris. The English classes observed here were taught by a Zanzibari, Ramadhan (cf. Table 4.1), at three different levels, that is foundation, intermediate 1 and intermediate 2. As the foundation classes were largest and took place most frequently, most observations were made during these.

5 ENGLISH IN THE TOURIST SPACE OF ZANZIBAR

As mentioned above, English is one of the most important languages in the tourist space of Zanzibar. Thus, all Zanzibari participants reported English to be the language most frequently used with tourists. This sets the tourist space apart from general public spaces, where all participants reported using Kiswahili most often, except for Maburuki who mentioned both Kiswahili and English. This is in line with Keshodkar's (2013) observation that tourists take over central spaces on Unguja island, from which locals are, albeit informally, banned. This is due to lack of financial resources – and lack of language knowledge, specifically referring to English, is closely related to these financial resources. Public spaces like Forodhani gardens, one of the central meeting points for locals in Stone Town by day, but largely taken over by tourists at night, is one example. In these spaces, Zanzibaris then feel displaced (Keshodkar 2013: 14), a feeling that might also be brought about by the overwhelming frequency of English employed by the tourists.

This exclusion and lack of language knowledge are to a large extent due to the ways that English is learnt at school, making many Zanzibaris resort to other ways of language learning outside of it. Formal ways and informal means of language learning, as well as further details of English use in the tourist space of Zanzibar, are discussed in the following.

5.1 Use of English in Tourist Spaces

The basic issues tackled in the interviews were to determine the participants' home language, the language most frequently used with tourists, the one most frequently used in public and other languages spoken. Apart from that, three of the central questions in the interviews concerned the participants' preferred language, their most useful language and the language they identify with most strongly. Due to the dynamics of the interviews, as well as difficulties with some of the concepts (especially concerning 'language of identity'), not all of the participants answered these questions conclusively and no exact response numbers can be provided. However, with respect to their preferred language, a tendency towards English can be identified. The reasons for this choice are not always clear, even to the participants themselves:

> Extract (1) Interview with Maburuki, tour guide, in Stone Town (Zanzibar City); S1 = interviewer, S2 = Maburuki; minute 08:27–08:47[4]
> <S1> mhm um , and is it different from the preferred language that you have the language that you like most </S1>
> <S2> most </S2>
> <S1> mhm </S1>
> <S2> english </S2>
> <S1> english really </S1>
> <S2> @ yeah </S2>
> <S1> why </S1>
> <S2> @why@ @ </S2>
> <S1> @ @i don't know why@ @ </S1>
> <S2> uh uh i- i- i- don't know but i like english because i have so many books (i can read) books so </S2>

Maburuki's laughter emphasises his uncertainty concerning a preferred language. However, when followed up, he concedes that he likes English because many books are written in it. This demonstrates the association of the language with knowledge and education, a tendency that has also been observed in mainland Tanzania (Bwenge 2012; Mohr 2018). Education, in turn, is a prerequisite for well-paid jobs, so English is also associated with professional opportunities (Bwenge 2012). Thus, English is very much desirable for Zanzibaris in the tourist sector and possibly beyond. Another participant, Abdalla, emphasises this by saying that he knows he needs English 'to go further' although he feels more comfortable speaking Kiswahili:

> Extract (2) Interview with Abdalla, tour guide and part-time lecturer, in Stone Town (Zanzibar City); S1 = interviewer, S2 = Abdalla; minute 13:52–15:11; important passages underlined
> <S1> so but , [. . .] if you had to say what is your most preferred language of all the languages that you speak </S1>
> <S2> aha </S2>
> <S1> is it also swahili or is it </S1>
> <S2> ey this is very technical </S2>
> <S1> @@ </S1>
> <S2> @ technical because i i always proud of myself </S2>
> <S1> mhm </S1>
> <S2> my you know my background my religion [. . .] but i know of [. . .] in life now <u>i know that yeah if you can ask me i can say that i need much more english now</u> [. . .] i i is is okay for me <u>i feel very comfy if i speak uh swahili</u> [. . .] that is uh my my how they it say is my my comfort zone [. . .] yeah so but i know i i need to speak english and that <u>i need to have very good english</u> because of this and that and that [. . .] <u>cause i need to go further</u> [. . .] in my careers [. . .] and everything </S2>

As Abdalla outlines here, he is aware that he needs English to progress professionally. So for him, the matter of preference is not so much linked to liking, in which case Kiswahili would probably take first place, but rather to the demands of the job market. This emphasises the commodified nature of English and its instrumental value (cf. Jaworski and Thurlow 2010). Abdalla mentions the demands of the tourist sector specifically when asked about the language he considers most useful.

> Extract (3) Interview with Abdalla, tour guide and part-time lecturer, in Stone Town (Zanzibar City); S1 = interviewer, S2 = Abdalla; minute 10:03–11:33; important passages underlined
> <S2> uh one thing that i am sure of is like we as zanzibaris, we are prouding

of swahili [. . .] so generally speaking yeah people they are proud of swahili but they <u>they think english is very essential</u> </S2>
<S1> okay </S1>
<S2> <u>because in , most of all official uh gathering and , yeah you find it in english</u> is us- is using so much [. . .] and you need it in [. . .] in that way and i think <u>one of the reason like you cannot see , uh most of zanzibaris in , in a high position maybe in tourisms is because of language</u> </S2>
<S1> okay </S1>
<S2> they can have the the content the understanding knowledge whatever you call it but then they scared with [. . .] the language </S2>

Here, Abdalla emphasises the difference between Kiswahili as a language that he as a Zanzibari is proud of, which is linked to identity as outlined in more detail below, and English, which is needed for official business. However, many Zanzibaris are scared to speak English, which is why many of them cannot get a job in tourism. This requirement is emphasised by Hussein, a receptionist in a large hotel in Stone Town:

Extract (4) Interview with Hussein, reservation and reception manager, at Tanzania Hotel in Stone Town (Zanzibar City); S1 = interviewer, S2 = Hussein; minute 0:31–0:52; important passages underlined
<S2> uh you know uh here [. . .] people from reception <u>the first priority they should know english</u> </S2>
<S1> okay </S1>
<S2> yeah <u>without language in reception is not possible</u> to have [. . .] <u>to get any job in in hotel department</u> [. . .] in hotel company [. . .] soo at reception the department of front office you have to know the language </S2>

The association of English with higher positions does not only associate the language with education and well-paid jobs, but by extension with higher social classes, similar to what is the case in mainland Tanzania (Bwenge 2012; Mohr 2018). Further, Hussein's answers illustrate the commodification of English in the tourist sector once again, where it becomes a required skill produced for tourist recipients as suggested by Schedel (2018). Generally, answers as to which language is considered most useful by participants were mixed; while some of them mentioned English, others mentioned Kiswahili. These answers demonstrate a sharp distinction between personal life and professional opportunities in tourism.

Closely linked to personal life is the participants' language of identity, which was, for all except one, Kiswahili. This one participant constitutes an exception as he emigrated to the UK and lived there for twenty years after finishing school, before returning to Zanzibar to open a hotel. He mentions that for him, English is more than just of instrumental value, 'a tool'. This clearly distinguishes him from the other participants.

> Extract (5) Interview with Mikidadi, hotel manager, at Karibu hotel in Paje; S1 = interviewer, S2 = Mikidadi; minute 02:14–03:09; important passages underlined
> <S2> yeah uuhm it depends uuh , actually i'm at a stage now whereby english language to me <u>if i wanna say something meaningful or if i want to express a feeling uh i actually now have to look at english language</u> that can translate to people exactly what i mean now [. . .] so now uh after all those years in the uk i i feel like uh in <u>english language uh i- uh it's got an emotional ittach- attachment</u> part of me rather than just a tool </S2>
> <S1> okay okay so it's really a language that you identify with </S1>
> <S2> oh yeah oh absolutely [. . .] </S2>

As outlined here, English has acquired a strong emotional attachment for Mikidadi. The lack of identification with English observed among the other participants is probably due to the fact that it remains a foreign language for them, as they might use it in daily interaction with tourists but not in their personal life (except for reading books as mentioned by Maburuki in Extract (1). Mikidadi is in fact married to an Englishwoman and, even back in Zanzibar, he uses English daily for personal interaction. Infrequent usage in personal life seemingly impacts competence in the language, which might add to the lack of identification with it. In (3), Abdalla already mentioned that the fear of speaking English is one reason for many Zanzibaris not being able to obtain a job in the tourist industry. This is also touched upon by Hussein's comment (cf. Extract (4)) that only with sufficient knowledge of English can Zanzibaris be employed in higher positions of the tourist industry. Mikidadi, as a hotel owner, also comments on this, as well as the problems he has finding suitable staff.

> Extract (6) Interview with Mikidadi, hotel manager, at Karibu hotel in Paje; S1 = interviewer, S2 = Mikidadi; minute 26:01–27:33; important passages underlined
> <S1> [. . .] do you have any i mean do you pay attention to how well people speak english when you employ them [. . .] </S1>
> <S2> yeah i mean it is uh it is an achilles heel [. . .] to be honest you know uh hamisi the waiter [. . .] he's good [. . .] and uhm , he uhm , he can communicate and he can speak f- uh french as well [. . .] <u>it is a hardship because uhm . [. . .] people are very reluctant they're they're so shy</u> </S2>
> <S1> mhm </S1>
> <S2> to make mistakes and things like that and i- i- i- <u>they don't wanna look stupid</u> [. . .] and this (and the other) it's more of an insecurity rather

than the willingness [. . .] you know the- the- i mean like <u>hamisi he didn't get any formal english education he just picked up</u> [. . .] maybe watched some couple of movies and stuff like that [. . .] </S2>

Similar to Abdalla, Mikidadi mentions that Zanzibaris are often too shy to speak English and are afraid to make mistakes, which is why they refrain from speaking it at all. Both reluctance to speak and lack of language competence result in Zanzibaris failing to exhibit the desired language skills for tourists (cf. Duchêne and Heller 2012; Schedel 2018). Given that English, according to educational policies, should be acquired in school in Zanzibar, and that it is a frequent language to be found in the tourist space, it is peculiar that many Zanzibaris not (yet) working in tourism apparently do not speak it well. In order to investigate these dynamics further, language learning trajectories of English are discussed in the following section.

5.2 Language Learning Trajectories among Tourism Workers

As shown in the previous section, all participants in this sample are fluent in English as they could participate in an interview and report on different matters of their (work) life and language use. They are hence not those Zanzibaris mentioned in Extracts (3) and (6), who are shy and do not speak enough English to obtain a job in the tourist industry. The question emerges as to why there are such stark differences between Zanzibaris who possess fluent English skills and those who do not. One means of language learning that all Zanzibaris have in common is English instruction at school. This is hence considered here first.

As mentioned previously, English is taught as a subject in primary school and employed as medium of instruction in secondary education and beyond in Zanzibar. Thus, a public primary school in Jambiani (cf. Figure 4.2) was visited and the headmaster, who showed me around, was briefly interviewed. When visiting an English class (Standard 6), the students stood up and greeted me in English. They had apparently learnt the greeting by heart. They also seemed very curious, but when approached and asked about simple topics, such as whether they liked studying English, for instance, they did not actually understand me and could not reply. This was the same among younger children (Standard 1), who also had problems reproducing the greeting they had learnt.

While there are many possible reasons for this lack of language competence, which could ultimately only be determined by long-term observation, one reason did emerge: the school had 702 students at the time, with some classes containing up to fifty-nine students, catered for by a total of eighteen teachers. The student-to-staff ratio was consequently extremely high, which definitely has a considerable influence on the methods that can be applied in teaching, and it is likely that a student who falls behind will not be noticed by the teacher in a class

Figure 4.2 Primary school in Jambiani
Source: Susanne Mohr, personal photograph

such as this. This was also addressed by Abdalla in his interview, who mentioned that he visited schools with 150 students in one class. This is why it is apparently difficult for children to learn (English) in Zanzibari schools, as shown in Extract (7).

> Extract (7) Interview with Abdalla, tour guide and part-time lecturer, in Stone Town (Zanzibar City); S1 = interviewer, S2 = Abdalla; minute 38:06–38:54; important passages underlined
> <S2> uh standard one until six , to take them to secondary we just saying in other way let's rush this to complete our our responsibility </S2>
> <S1> mhm </S1>
> <S2> like we say we give them education let's deal with our issues , <MUMBLING> everything </MUMBLING> because yeah they , <u>until standard six they have even don't know how to write their names</u> [. . .] <u>don't know how to describe uuh you know uh just only few personal details</u> how now eh eh they go to the secondary to deal with a load writing essays doing assignments do that , ah is aaa pity [. . .] </S2>

The same problems related to the conditions in public schools have been reported for mainland Tanzania, and other African countries, for example by researchers involved in the large-scale Language of Instruction in Tanzania and South Africa Project (for example Desai et al. 2010). Large classes and a lack of resources were shown to be important factors influencing the performance of students in all subjects.

Several other participants reported the same problems that Abdalla had with English classes in school. All of them participated in so-called tuition as an extracurricular activity. As it turned out, tuition is very common in Zanzibar, consisting of private lessons taught by teachers on the side or by lay people acquainted with the language and wanting to earn some extra money. When asked where he started learning English, Hamadi does not even mention school first, but rather tuition classes.

> Extract (8) Interview with Hamadi, hotel staff member, at Karibu hotel in Paje; S1 = interviewer, S2 = Hamadi; minute 02:39–03:05, 07:48–08:04; important passages underlined
> <S1> [. . .] where [did you start learning english] was it at home or with other child- or only in [school i don't know] </S1>
> <S2> [@@] @@ [uhh] actually when i was , at uuh , before when i was finishing uh standard seven [. . .] here in zanzibar
> <S1> okay </S1>
> <S2> i go to start eh with eh tuition we call it tuition [. . .] from seven up to nine thirty we come back home [. . .] you know in zanzibar we don't have much this we have [. . .] to go to studying </S2>
> <S1> [yeah] </S1>
> <S2> [always] people they bring some skills so when wey- when they bring [. . .] to us we can ask the- for them they can help us even[5] teaching as well you can go to pay even private if you want </S2>

After mentioning tuition, Hamadi goes on to say that, in Zanzibar, this kind of studying of a language, or rather studying in general, is important. Zanzibaris rely on others who are well versed in a certain subject in order to learn from them. This is interesting in many respects. For one, it shows that a certain kind of informal language learning is taking place in Zanzibar because Zanzibaris rely on friends or acquaintances to learn English.[6] This, however, is paid for, requiring at least moderate financial means to be able to pay for this extracurricular means of language learning. This, once again, emphasises the commodified character of English which has to be invested in as a required skill in the tourist industry (Duchêne and Heller 2012).

Apart from tuition, there are other ways to learn English in Zanzibar, although these also have to be invested in financially. Thus, NGOs like Kawa Training

Center offer language classes in an environment with good resources and usually well-trained or at least enthusiastic teachers. At Kawa, three-month classes cost approximately 320,000 Tanzanian shilling, which is roughly equivalent to US$138, covering payment for the lessons, teaching materials and the final certificate. For the average Zanzibari, this is a lot of money, given that the GDP per capita was US$920 per year in 2017 (UNdata 2017). Several of the students I talked to had saved money for a considerable amount of time or had taken out a loan to be able to pay for the class. This emphasises even more strongly the commodified nature of English in the tourist space of Zanzibar, where educational organisations specifically target (aspiring) workers in the tourist industry in order to provide them with the necessary language skills. Generally, a much higher language competence in English could be observed even among students in the foundation classes, that is beginner's level, as compared to the public schools. While the age and maturity of the students in a primary school as compared to adults certainly needs to be considered, it is remarkable that all students at Kawa were able to communicate with me in some way and even made an effort to learn new words they felt to be important, such as football terminology. The classes were small, that is numbering around ten students, and the teacher could help those students who were struggling with the subject matter. While classes were generally taught in English to create an immersive environment, the teacher sometimes resorted to Kiswahili in order to explain particularly difficult subjects or grammatical rules.

The final and least formal way of language learning reported by the participants, if it can be classified as *one* single way, was learning through interaction. Thus, several of the participants mentioned practising their English with tourists, to continually improve it in this way, as shown in Extract (9). This also, and possibly even more strongly, applies to other foreign languages that are not taught in school, like German, as illustrated in Extract (10).

Extract (9) Interview with Hamadi, hotel staff member, at Karibu hotel in Paje; S1 = interviewer, S2 = Hamadi; minute 04:19–04:52; important passages underlined
<S2> but i couldn't give up , i still continue within the different places where we can find my language good </S2>
<S1> okay </S1>
<S2> <u>i try to go in a different places where i can find the people who are going to speak well even when i find some people who speak english well</u> we talk each other and then sometime i used to go in the forodhani area [. . .] in stone town there are many people there [. . .] <u>so i make a good good practice with them</u> and some- sometime some people they invite me in a groups we stay together i teach them swahili [. . .] and then also me they teach me [. . .] </S2>

Extract (10) Interview with Maburuki, tour guide, in Stone Town (Zanzibar City); S1 = interviewer, S2 = Maburuki; minute 04:39–04:55
<S1> [. . .] okay so how d- how did you learn german @ from the tourists or </S1>
<S2> myself </S2>
<S1> yourself </S1>
<S2> yeah myself </S2>
<S1> oh wow </S1>
<S2> i used my app to learn german [. . .] sometime asked uh tourists uh some [. . .] question if i don't know something just ask them yeah </S2>

Both extracts are interesting: Hamadi clearly states the importance of interaction with tourists for language learning, and Maburuki also mentions this for learning other foreign languages, as well as additional, digital ways of language learning, such as apps. This amply demonstrates the variety of means of language learning in a super-diverse space. Interestingly, these are also the only ways of language learning that do not cost money per se, although one usually needs to sell a service or good in order to come into contact with tourists, thus, indirectly, these ways of language learning are related to financial means as well.

Altogether, it has been shown here that English itself, as well as the ways in which to learn it, are very much commodified and linked to financial capital in Zanzibar. This seems to be necessary because of problems with the formal (public) education system in mainland Tanzania and Zanzibar. Thus, a huge social gap emerges between Zanzibaris with financial means who are able to invest in (language) learning and those without. This adds a further social and economic component to the linguistic super-diversity of the tourist space and enlarges differences between tourists and some of the 'toured', as well as among Zanzibaris themselves.

6 ENGLISH AT THE GRASSROOTS?

The analysis provided here yielded interesting results concerning the use and learning trajectories of English in Zanzibar. It was shown that while English is frequently used by Zanzibaris in tourist spaces, where it could be classified as 'grassroots' in line with Han's (2013) approach, language competence seems to be limited among many of the participants who only know formulaic expressions. This type of language knowledge could be classified as what Blommaert and Backus (2011: 13) have called a 'globalised vocabulary', usually learnt through ephemeral encounters with language. Interestingly, in the Zanzibari case this (small piece of) language knowledge seems to be imparted through formal education. It might however be the case that the children in the primary school visited had in fact learnt the greetings through interaction with tourists, that is through encounters. This is an interesting issue that could be pursued by interviewing children and adults in depth, possibly in Kiswahili.

Most of the study participants, who, in stark contrast to other Zanzibaris they describe, are fluent in English, feel that Zanzibari English is 'broken', and employers interviewed mention English to be one of the main difficulties in finding staff. As language learning in public schools was shown not to be sufficient for acquiring the level of proficiency in English necessary for the job market, English as a required skill has to be invested in financially (cf. Duchêne and Heller 2012). Consequently, Zanzibaris aspiring to a high level of fluency in English resort to a variety of means of language learning. Modes of language learning are equally diverse, ranging from first contact with the language at home, over English lessons at school or as part of tourism degrees at university, to expensive private tuition and language classes. Most of these are closely linked to financial capital and emphasise the commodified nature of English and other foreign language skills in the tourist space. This also illustrates the gap between different social classes in Zanzibari society.

The types of language learning undertaken by Zanzibaris working in the tourism industry probably fall into the category of 'specialised language learning' established by Blommaert and Backus (2011: 11–12), as the competency acquired is used for one particular facet of these participants' lives. The fact that many Zanzibaris learn English only after they have left school and practise it continuously demonstrates the importance of language learning beyond the classroom for acquiring fluency in English. On the other hand, it illustrates that the 'language' they know is indeed never completely finished (Blommaert and Backus 2011: 9).

Overall, it has been shown that while interaction in English takes place in informal settings that might qualify as 'grassroots' (Han 2013) in Zanzibar, the trajectories of learning English include practices not typically associated with the grassroots level. This expounds the problem of an easy attribution of individual second language learning paths to particular social groups and reveals the fuzziness of the 'grassroots' concept. As such, it raises the question as to whether we indeed need to assign English(es) to categories, and to a single one for that matter. The latter has been questioned for categories such as English as a second or foreign language (cf. for instance Bruthiaux 2003). In the case of English spoken by Zanzibaris, and possibly English spoken in multilingual Africa in general, assigning English[7] to a category does not seem reasonable. This also holds true for dynamic spaces such as tourist contexts, where language practices are particularly fluid.

While not easily applicable, concepts such as the grassroots do hold an undisputable value, also for multilingual and dynamic contexts such as the one investigated here. Specifically with reference to English, data are too often collected among highly educated speakers in academic environments (cf. Kubota 2018). The present study, and all the others in this volume, amply illustrates that contexts far away from these spaces present very interesting environments in which English should be studied more in the future.

ACKNOWLEDGEMENTS

I would like to thank all my participants, who took the time to answer my questions. I am deeply indebted to Abdulsatar Ali Mohammed who showed me around Stone Town and introduced me to people on Unguja. Judith Rauland and Sarah Lapacz deserve a mention for their help with transcribing the interview data. I would also like to thank the editors for valuable comments on an earlier version of this chapter and for their support during the revision process. The fieldwork for this project was funded by a research grant from the North Rhine-Westphalian Academy of Sciences, Humanities and the Arts. The project itself was supported by a Feodor-Lynen grant from the Alexander von Humboldt Foundation.

TRANSCRIPTION CONVENTIONS

<Sx>	-	beginning of speaker x's turn
</Sx>	-	end of speaker x's turn
(text)	-	uncertain transcription
@	-	laughter
,	-	brief pause (2–3 sec.)
.	-	longer pause (3–4 sec.)
[text]	-	overlapping speech
[. . .]	-	speech not relevant for the analysis and left out here
<CAPITALS>	-	non-speech related but relevant information, for example background noise, tone of voice etc.

NOTES

1. According to Bourdieu (1982), language becomes a commodity when it adds value to a good or service. Thus, 'the commodity value of languages is the relationship between communicative resources and their potential economic value' (Muth and Del Percio 2018: 130).
2. All participants' names and those of hotels provided in this chapter are pseudonyms.

3. I am thankful to Suzanne Degeling for giving me permission to mention Kawa's name here.
4. The transcription conventions are based on the SELF project guidelines designed at the University of Helsinki. They are outlined above.
5. *Even* is sometimes used in a non-standard way in English spoken by Zanzibaris. It seems to signify 'also', at least in my interview data.
6. In the interview, Hamadi mentioned that his tuition teacher was his friend's mother and most of the other participants also reported that tuition was organised through friends and family.
7. It is questionable whether there is in fact only *one* Zanzibari English.

REFERENCES

Barlow, Michael and Suzanne Kemmer (2000), 'Introduction: a usage-based conception of language', in Michael Barlow and Suzanne Kemmer (eds), *Usage-based Models of Language*, Stanford, CA: CSLI, vii–xxix.

Blommaert, Jan (2004), 'Writing as a problem: African grassroots writing', *Language in Society*, 33, 643–71.

Blommaert, Jan and Ad Backus (2011), 'Repertoires revisited: "knowing language" in superdiversity', *Working Papers in Urban Language and Literacies*, 67, 1–26.

Bourdieu, Pierre (1982), *Ce que parler veut dire: L'économie des échanges linguistiques*, Paris: Fayard.

Bruthiaux, Paul (2003), 'Squaring the circles: issues in modeling English worldwide', *International Journal of Applied Linguistics*, 13: 2, 159–78.

Buschfeld, Sarah and Alexander Kautzsch (2017), 'Towards an integrated approach to postcolonial and non-postcolonial Englishes', *World Englishes*, 36: 1, 104–26.

Bwenge, Charles (2012), 'English in Tanzania: a linguistic cultural perspective', *International Journal of Language, Translation and Intercultural Communication*, 1: 1, 167–82.

Chachage, Seithy L. (2000), *Environment, Aid and Politics in Zanzibar*, Dar es Salaam: Dar es Salaam University Press.

Desai, Zubeida, Martha Qorro and Birgit Brock-Utne (eds) (2010), *Educational Challenges in Multilingual Societies*, Cape Town: African Minds.

The Douglas Fir Group (2016), 'A transdisciplinary framework for SLA in a multilingual world', *Modern Language Journal*, 100: S1, 19–47.

Duchêne, Alexandre and Monica Heller (2012), 'Multilingualism and the new economy', in Marylin Martin-Jones, Adrian Blackledge and Angela Creese (eds), *The Routledge Handbook of Multilingualism*, New York: Routledge, 369–83.

Ebongue, Augustin Emmanuel and Ellen Hurst (2017), 'Dynamic language: sociolinguistic perspectives on African language, ideologies and practices', in Augustin Emmanuel Ebongue and Ellen Hurst (eds), *Sociolinguistics in African Contexts: Perspectives and Challenges*, Cham: Springer, 1–9.

Han, Huamei (2013), 'Individual grassroots multilingualism in Africa Town in Guangzhou: the role of states in globalization', *International Multilingual Research Journal*, 7: 1, 83–97.

Hymes, Dell (1972), 'On communicative competence', in John B. Pride and Janet Holmes (eds), *Sociolinguistics*, London: Penguin, 269–93.

Jaworski, Aadam and Crispin Thurlow (2010), 'Language and the globalizing habitus of tourism: toward a sociolinguistics of fleeting relationships', in Nikolas Coupland (ed.), *The Handbook of Language and Globalization*, Chichester: Wiley-Blackwell, 255–86.

Keshodkar, Akbar (2013), *Tourism and Social Change in Post-socialist Zanzibar*, Lanham, MD: Lexington.

Krashen, Stephen D. (1981), *Second Language Acquisition and Second Language Learning*, Oxford: Pergamon.

Kubota, Ryuko (2018), 'Unpacking research and practice in world Englishes and Second Language Acquisition research', *World Englishes*, 37: 1, 93–105.

Lawson, Sarah and Itesh Sachdev (2000), 'Codeswitching in Tunisia: attitudinal and behavioural dimensions', *Journal of Pragmatics*, 32: 9, 1324–61.

Lett, James (1989), 'Epilogue', in Valene L. Smith (ed.), *Hosts and Guests: The Anthropology of Tourism*, Philadelphia: University of Pennsylvania Press, 275–9.

Maci, Stefania M. (2018), 'An introduction to English in tourism discourse', *Sociolinguistica (A European Yearbook of Sociolinguistics)*, 32: 1, 25–42.

Meierkord, Christiane (2018), 'English in paradise: the Maldives', *English Today*, 34: 1, 2–11.

Mohr, Susanne (2018), 'The changing dynamics of language use and language attitudes in Tanzania', *Language Matters: Studies in the Languages of Africa*, 49: 3, 105–27.

Mohr, Susanne (forthcoming), '"Jambo! I greet them with a smile." Language choices in commodified interactions between tourists and hosts in Zanzibar', to appear in Susanne Mohr, Klaus P. Schneider and Jemima A. Anderson (eds), *Communicative Action and Interaction in Africa*, Amsterdam: John Benjamins.

Mohr, Susanne and Dunlop Ochieng (2017), 'Language usage in everyday life and in education: current attitudes towards English in Tanzania', *English Today*, 33: 4, 12–18.

Muth, Sebastian and Alfonso Del Percio (2018), 'Policing for commodification: turning communicative resources into commodities', *Language Policy*, 17, 129–35.

Nassenstein, Nico (2016), 'Mombasa's Swahili-based "Coasti Slang" in a superdiverse space: languages in contact on the beach', *African Study Monographs*, 37: 3, 117–43.

Nassenstein, Nico (2019), 'The Hakuna Matata Swahili: linguistic souvenirs from the Kenyan coast', in Angelika Mietzner and Anne Storch (eds), *Language and Tourism in Postcolonial Settings*, Bristol: Channel View, 130–56.

Salazar, Noel (2006), 'Touristifying Tanzania. Local guides, global discourse', *Annals of Tourism Research*, 33: 3, 833–52.

Sarmento, João and Bradley Rink (2016), 'Africa', in Jafar Jafari and Honggen Xiao (eds), *Encyclopedia of Tourism (Volume 1)*, Cham: Springer, 14–17.

Schedel, Larissa S. (2018), 'Turning local bilingualism into a touristic experience', *Language Policy*, 17, 137–55.

Schneider, Edgar W. (2016), 'Grassroots Englishes in tourism interactions', *English Today*, 32: 3, 2–10.

Serikali ya Mapinduzi ya Zanzibar (SMZ) (2013), 'Tourism in Zanzibar', <http://www.zanzibar.go.tz/index.php?rgo=tourism> (last accessed 22 January 2019).

Storch, Anne (forthcoming), 'Linguistic landscapes of tourism – a case study from Zanzibar', in Klaus Beyer, Gertrud Boden, Bernhard Köhler and Ulrike Zoch (eds), *40 Jahre Afrikanistik*, Cologne: Köppe.

UNdata (2017), 'Per capita GDP at current prices – US dollars. United Republic of Tanzania: Zanzibar', United Nations Statistics Division, <http://data.un.org/Data.aspx?q=Zanzibarandd=SNAAMAandf=grID%3A101%3BcurrID%3AUSD%3BpcFlag%3A1%3BcrID%3A836> (last accessed 16 April 2019).

Vertovec, Steven (2007), 'Super-diversity and its implications', *Ethnic and Racial Studies*, 30: 6, 1024–54.

CHAPTER 5

Access to English and the Englishes of the Disadvantaged: Examples from Uganda and South Africa

Christiane Meierkord

1 INTRODUCTION

Both South Africa and Uganda are countries in which English is used as a second language (L2) by large parts of the population. While in South Africa the advent of English coincided with the arrival of substantial groups of British settlers (whose descendants today, together with those of the original Dutch settlers, constitute 9.1 per cent of the population, cf. Statistics South Africa 2012), this was not the case in Uganda. In the former British protectorate, a settler strand in the sense of Schneider (2007) was very limited, and English was learnt largely through formal education. Today, whites in Uganda are typically expatriates and constitute a negligible part of the population, so that the sociolinguistic history of English in the two countries has differed considerably (cf. the chapters in de Klerk 1996; Mesthrie 2002; Meierkord et al. 2016).

At the same time, in both nations, formal acquisition of English has often been tied to socio-economic status, which determines access to quality education, disadvantaging individuals of lower social class backgrounds, at the grassroots. In Uganda, primary education has been free from 1996 only. However, low socio-economic status, in principle, typically resulted in a lack of funds to pay school fees and restricts access to secondary education until 2007. In South Africa, access to English-medium education was furthermore restricted due to Apartheid policies. Nevertheless, many individuals in both countries regularly communicate in English despite not having had a chance to complete secondary or even primary education. They rely on the amount of English acquired in primary school or through interaction with other speakers of English.

After an attempt at a definition of the 'disadvantaged', this chapter offers a comparative look at the histories of English in Uganda and South Africa and a concise description of what access to both formal and informal acquisition of English has been like in the two countries, post-independence and in the 2000s.

Against this background, excerpts of data obtained from grassroots speakers in the Cape Town and Kampala regions, whose work and businesses involve the regular use of English, will be presented and discussed qualitatively. I will finish off with an interpretation of the results and a look at how access to English in South Africa and Uganda has shaped the Englishes of those speakers of English who are not as advantaged as others to provide an outlook into how grassroots speakers can (and need to be) integrated in models of world Englishes.

2 THE 'DISADVANTAGED'

While no scientific definition of *disadvantaged* seems to be available, there is a lay understanding of the term as referring to individuals having less favourable positions in terms of the economic and social circumstances of their lives, similar to the definition offered by Webster (2020), namely 'lacking in the basic resources or conditions (such as standard housing, medical and educational facilities, and civil rights) believed to be necessary for an equal position in society', or that offered by the *Oxford English Dictionary*:

> 1. That lacks advantage in some respect; that has been affected adversely or detrimentally in some way; that is or has been placed at a disadvantage relative to another or others. Also: characterized by lack of advantage.
> 2. *spec.* That lacks social or financial advantage; suffering from or characterized by social or economic deprivation.

Mostly, the term is also associated with limited or no access to education. However, in African contexts, this does not necessarily imply poverty but typically a lower socio-economic status and a lower position in society, as the link between level of formal education and wealth is not always as pronounced.

In the South African context, *previously disadvantaged* or *historically disadvantaged* has furthermore assumed a narrower meaning as laid out in the 2001 Preferential Procurement Regulations issued by the Government of South Africa. Here, a 'Historically Disadvantaged Individual (HDI)' is defined as a South African citizen who, prior to the coming into effect of the country's post-Apartheid Interim Constitution,

> due to the apartheid policy that had been in place, had no franchise in national elections prior to the introduction of the Constitution of the Republic of South Africa, 1983 (Act No 110 of 1983) or the Constitution of the Republic of South Africa, 1993 (Act No 200 of 1993) ('the Interim Constitution'). (Government of South Africa 2001: 3)[1]

For the context of this chapter, I use the term *disadvantaged* to refer to individuals whose education, for socio-economic or political reasons, was involuntarily limited to primary school (which is six years in South Africa and seven years in Uganda) and who work outside of formal businesses and academic contexts. Further, I restrict my observations to the black populations of the two countries.[2]

The next section serves to contextualise the data with historical facts as regards the spread of English to the two areas and about how the local black population had access to it, particularly through formal education.

3 INFORMAL AND FORMAL ACCESS TO ENGLISH

Chronologically, the spread of English first reached South Africa, in 1795, and almost a century later, in 1877, Uganda, creating informal and formal ways of L2 acquisition for the indigenous population, albeit in considerably different manners and to very different degrees.

3.1 Informal and Formal Input, Language Acquisition and Outcome Varieties

Research in the field of L2 acquisition has indicated that the outcome of such acquisition processes are, among other factors, constrained by the input that speakers receive. This concerns both quantity and quality of the 'target' language (TL) input as well as the presence or absence of formal instruction, including explicit grammar teaching.

As regards input, researchers have noticed that for successful acquisition of grammar to take place, input must be both quantitatively as well as qualitatively sufficient. Research conducted in the late 1960s and 1970s investigating 'industrial immigrant talk' (Clyne 1978; Heidelberger Forschungsprojekt 1978) revealed that foreign workers were often addressed in ungrammatical foreigner talk, involving omissions, expansion and rearrangement of lexical and grammatical structures. However, '[h]ow TL linguistic input – modified or not – influences SLA is not well understood, nor do researchers agree on its importance' (Bingham Wesche 1994: 248). Since the teaching of target language structures is subject to teachability and learnability, success of instruction seems to hold only for such features 'which are formally easy to acquire and which manifest transparent form-function relationships' (Ellis 2008: 856). Pica (1983, 1985) in fact found that, while plural -*s* benefited from instruction, instructed learners were less accurate in their use of the progressive than naturalistic learners with no instruction (Ellis 2008: 856). Nevertheless, studies such as the OECD's Programme for International Student Assessment (PISA) have found that instruction inhibits (but does not entirely prevent) the use of ungrammatical constructions frequently encountered in pidginised varieties, even if these may be communicatively effective.

From a more descriptive perspective, the acquisition of English, or any other language for that matter, has been demonstrated to result in stable L2 varieties, instable interlanguages, pidginised varieties, mixed codes and translanguaging practices, each characterised by particular characteristics at all structural levels, that is phonology, morphology, syntax and the lexicon.

Mesthrie and Bhatt (2008: 47–89) list the following features: different uses of articles (including omission and insertion), variability in plural and possessive marking, variation as regards gender in pronouns and pronoun deletion, innovative second person plural pronouns, variation as regards tense and aspect distinctions and marking, different semantics of the individual modal verbs, a weaker distinction between stative and non-stative verbs, and variability with conjunctions. At the level of syntax, there are characteristic uses of word order, relative clauses, passives, comparisons, tags, answers to *yes/no* questions and adverb placement.

While L2 Englishes are stable linguistic systems, this is typically not the case with learner Englishes, which are characterised by products that result not only from first language (L1) transfer, overgeneralisation of target language rules and transfer of training, but also from learning and communication strategies (cf. Selinker 1972). The term *learner language* is often associated with instructed L2 acquisition in contexts where English input has traditionally been restricted to the classroom. Crucially, learner Englishes are located at the level of the individual, therefore highly heterogeneous and not varieties. In terms of their features, they display paraphrase, lack of tense and plural marking and developmental patterns (see for example Ellis 2008 for a detailed description of learner Englishes).

As opposed to L2 and learner Englishes, pidginised varieties are typically acquired in a 'natural' setting in the form of either 'partially targeted or non-targeted second language learning' (Mühlhäusler 1986: 5) due to the fact that 'the main aim of speakers is to enable communication, rather than to learn another language' (Mesthrie et al. 2000: 280) and, likely as a result of the latter, reveal a higher degree of restructuring. This is visible in polysemy, circumlocution compounding and reduplication as strategies to make up for a limited vocabulary. At the level of grammar, pidgins have been found to lack standard morphology for tense and aspect marking and plural but to develop their own systems. They all differ as regards their complexity, with jargons (also called pre-pidgins) revealing a more unstable structure and limited vocabulary than stable pidgins and expanded pidgins (see Mühlhäusler 1986; Holm 1988; Velupillai 2015, for details).

Following Weinreich's (1974: 4) position that '[t]he linguist who makes theories about language influence but neglects to account for the socio-cultural setting of the language contact leaves his study suspended, as it were, in mid-air', the following sections contextualise the later data analyses with socio-historical details.

3.2 History of Access to English in South Africa

English came to South Africa in 1795, when the British established a refreshment station for their trading vessels at what today is Cape Town, in an area that had already been settled by the Dutch since 1652. As in most other spheres of their interest,[3] the British made English the official language in their area of control, in 1815, following the Congress of Vienna decisions. To secure their interests and to establish an expedient colony, the British soon also settled people in both the Eastern Cape region, where approximately 4,500 Britons of working-class and lower-middle class origins arrived in 1820, as well as further north in Natal, in 1848 and 1862, where settlers mostly were upper-middle-class retired military personnel (Lanham 1996).

Given the presence of a considerable settler population in the sense of Schneider (2007), for many black South Africans contact with English was through informal interactions, largely at the workplace, for example on the sugar cane plantations, where English served as a lingua franca across individuals of many different L1s, such as Afrikaans, Portuguese, Sotho, Yiddish, Zulu or other European and African languages. However, following the Boer Wars (1880–1 and 1899–1902) and the advancement of the National Party, a number of acts led up to what is known as Apartheid, a system severely restricting interaction between races, leading to separate residential areas, the prohibition of mixed relations and of uses of the same establishments, even toilets, and of course formal education.

In 1923, the Natives (Urban Areas) Act stipulated that separate residential areas for Africans be established. Next, in 1950 the Group Areas Act declared areas reserved for individual population groups, and the Prohibition of Mixed Marriages Act restricted marriages to those with a person of one's own race only. In 1953, the Separate Amenities Act prohibited visits or uses of the same hotels, restaurants, beaches, trains, buses and even toilets by members of different races, and finally in 1956 the Industrial Conciliation Act largely confined blacks to unskilled menial jobs. As a consequence of these measures, contexts for informal language acquisition were severely reduced. At the same time, instructed language acquisition was scarce for the black part of the population, as section 3.2.1 reports next.

3.2.1 English in South Africa – access to education

Education of blacks in the British colony was severely restricted and was largely a mission-run event, from the 1930s, with the government neglecting black education both in the Cape and in the Natal area. This resulted in 'the growth of mission-educated Africans who were beginning to emerge as an identifiable elite' (Cross 1986: 189), while the black working-class that had developed in urban centres as a result of the vibrant mining industry lost out. Government schools had initially used English as a medium of instruction (Hartshorne 1995: 307–8). Following pressure to recognise the mother tongues as medium of instruction, however, by 1935

> the pupil's mother-tongue was to be used for the first six years of schooling in Natal, for the first four years in the Cape and the Free State, and for the first two years in the Transvaal. Thereafter an official language – in practice almost always English – was to be used as medium. (Harshorne 1995: 308)

The coming to power of the Afrikaner-dominated National Party in 1948 and its establishment of the infamous Apartheid system resulted in drastic changes and considerable disadvantages for the black part of South Africa's population. The Apartheid system forced every citizen to register their race and prohibited blacks from visiting the same schools as whites. From this point onwards, Christian National Education stipulated that the mother tongue was to be the basis of education for blacks, and that the official languages of English and Afrikaans were to be taught as subjects. The 1954 Bantu Education Act stipulated that blacks were to receive only six years of schooling, which was neither compulsory nor free, since schooling of blacks should not burden the white taxpayers.

In 1972, this changed, involving the use of mother tongue instruction for the first six years, followed then by either English or Afrikaans as medium of instruction (MOI). In 1974, the 'Afrikaans medium decree' made both English and Afrikaans compulsory in black secondary schools. Ironically, the public examination at the end of Standard 5 (one year after the last primary school year, Standard 4) had to be written in English and Afrikaans, leading to protests that eventually were to culminate in the Soweto uprisings and Hector Pieterson's tragic death on 16 June 1976. The Bantu Education Act was replaced by the Education and Training Act of 1979, which made provisions for the use of English or Afrikaans from Standard 3 (year 5) onwards. By 1989, as Hartshorne (1995: 313) finds, 'the wheel had turned full circle, and language policy was very much what it had been pre-1953'. As during most of this time, education for the black part of South Africa's population was neither compulsory nor free,

> [i]n 1953 only 41% of black children of school-going age were at school. This had risen to just over 70% by 1974. Of concern were the early dropout rates. Of the children who commenced schooling, approximately half

completed four years of schooling, 28% completed their primary education, 7% the Junior Certificate (including those who matriculated) . . . In 1977, parents entering their children into school in Sub A were required to undertake to keep them at school until they completed Standard 2. This gave a measure of compulsory schooling. (Nicholls 1992: 297)

In 1984, the National Policy for General Affairs Act (No. 76) made education compulsory for all racial groups, albeit at different ages. For black children education was compulsory between the ages of seven and sixteen or the equivalent of 7th grade, but this law was not fully enforced, particularly in areas that lacked schools.

In sum, we can clearly say that access to formal instruction in English and exposure to an acrolectal variety of it was severely restricted since (1) many blacks did not attend school and (2) those who did received only limited teaching of English.

Segregation in education ended only with the collapse of the Apartheid system in 1990, and formally with the passage of the South African Schools Act in 1996. Since that year, the South African Constitution has made provisions for the use of the indigenous languages as MOI; and also from that year, very poor families have been exempt from paying school fees, making access to education possible for all, at least theoretically. Since 2009, all schools teach English as a subject from grade 1 and all subjects are taught in English from grade 4. According to the latest figures available from UNESCO (2020a), 80.03 per cent of South Africa's primary school age population was enrolled in primary schools in 2013. The 2011 census found that only 28.9 per cent of the population had completed the full twelve years of secondary education.

3.3 History of Access to English in Uganda

In Uganda, the situation was different from the start in that the area was never a colony but a British protectorate. English came to the area in 1877, when, following an earlier visit of Sir Henry Morton Stanley to King Mutesa I of Buganda in 1874, British missionaries were admitted to the region (Meierkord 2016: 54). Soon thereafter, in 1888, the Imperial British East Africa Company was granted a charter to trade in East Africa and from 1890 treaties were signed with individual kingdoms. Whether English or Kiswahili was used by the traders is unknown, as is their linguistic impact. Following disputes between the *Kabaka* (the Buganda king), the Company and British Protestants and French Catholics, the last two of which had sided with the British and German governments respectively in their attempts to secure their territorial interests and claims, civil war broke out in 1892, leading to the British government declaring a protectorate over the kingdom of Buganda in 1894 and eventually over the area that today makes up

Uganda in 1900. Up until the Second World War, the British deployed personnel, gradually increasing to 521 in 1939. However, as Myers-Scotton (1988: 208) explains, 'the British ... also wanted to use local resources in the civil service and therefore welcomed the idea of a lower level Swahili-speaking cadre'.

As a result, English was made the official language for administration, but due to the fact that land purchases were forbidden, there were hardly any British settlers. The few English-speaking individuals did not only include administrative personnel and missionaries. While the number of traders and settlers in Uganda never came near to that in Kenya, the interest in economic exploitation of the area resulted in the presence of tradespeople, artisans and plantation farmers, which, however, only rose to 2,282 in 1938 (Meierkord 2016: 61). As a result, contact with English was largely restricted to those whom the British wished to train as clerks to work in the administration and it typically came through formal education. For the East African population at large, the British promoted Kiswahili. However, the Baganda as well as the missionaries propagated English, which was also taught at the missionary schools (see section 3.3.1), leading to a strong leaning towards English as a MOI for those who were lucky enough to receive an education.

Given the change of Britain's policy towards its colonies and protectorates when transitioning these to political independence, more emphasis was placed on education following the end of the Second World War. English was now taught as a subject in primary schools and used as a MOI from year 5 onwards. At independence in 1962, English was retained as the sole official language, used in administration and education. The political unrests which then affected the country between 1972, when Amin's decree dispelling all Asians led to mass exodus, and 1978 resulted in the withdrawal of most foreign agencies, including those that had offered teaching support. Only in 2005 was Kiswahili made Uganda's second official language. However, while this is enshrined in the Constitution (Amendment) Act 2005, an enabling law to fully make Kiswahili operational as a co-official language has never been passed by parliament to date.

Uganda has not traditionally had an L1 reference variety, but English is largely a lingua franca to all its speakers, although a limited number of black upper-middle-class families have now shifted to English as their home language.

3.3.1 English in Uganda – access to education

During the times of the protectorate, the British government initially was reluctant to engage in the education sector and largely left education to the missionaries. After the civil wars had ended, the missions greatly expanded their activities in the area, initially in the form of catechumenates (cf. Byabazaire 1979: 64) but soon, from 1893 onwards, in missionary-run formal schools. However, schools and teaching were not, initially, intended for the masses. Rather, they catered for the offspring of chiefs, aristocrats but also pastors and catechists (cf. Byabazaire 1979; Mazrui and Mazrui 1996), 'to educate potential leaders ... with a heavy emphasis on English grammar and the reading of English books' (Scanlon 1964: 9). Also, these schools were primarily located within one part of what today is Uganda, the kingdom of Buganda.

Typically, education was provided in the mother tongue during the first six years, with English being used at advanced levels only. However, the 1924 report of the Phelps-Stokes Commission recommended that the mother tongues be taught in the lower primary classes, followed by a language of wider communication in the middle classes and English in the upper classes. As a result, Kiswahili was promoted in 1926, but dropped again after strong resistance from the Baganda (Ssekamwa 2000). Access to English via formal education was, thus, not only limited regionally and socially but was also constrained by changing policies.

Following the end of the First World War, when trained personnel in all spheres were in high demand, the British eventually established an Education Department in Uganda in 1925. After the end of the Second World War, a new policy stipulated that the mother tongues be used in the first year of primary school only, followed by a language of wider communication or English from the second year onwards. English was introduced as a subject in the third year of primary school and then used as MOI from year four. The increasing engagement of the British government in the education sector after the Second World War affected a small part of the population only. Schools were fee-paying, and Elliot (1953: 3) assumes that at the time of his writing 'the proportion of children attending some kind of school is probably no more than one-third'. In 1963, following the recommendations of the Castle Education Commission Report, English became the sole MOI, with the mother tongues, however, being used at the teachers' discretion (Ssentanda 2016: 98).

It took until 1992 for indigenous languages to be used as MOI during the first three years of primary school. After this period, there is a transitory year 4 during which a switch to English is meant to take place, so that English can become the MOI from year 5 onwards. However, the majority of primary schools have English as their MOI. Primary education (seven years; typically six- to twelve-year-olds) has, theoretically, been free since 1997, following a decision by Uganda's President Yoweri Museveni. Similarly, secondary education has been free since 2007. We shall see from one of the later quotes, however, that 'free' is a label that is interpreted in different ways by different people.

4 SIMILARITIES AND DIFFERENCES IN ACCESS TO EDUCATION AND ENGLISH

As the above sections have revealed, South Africa and Uganda differ crucially as regards access to education for its (black) populations and as regards access to English, both formally through instruction and informally through interaction with British settlers and other speakers of English. Given the social and regional origins of these speakers, English input must have been non-standard, involving lower-class sociolects and various dialects, all with their grammatical, lexical and phonological characteristics. Today, the two countries compare as summarised in Table 5.1.[4]

Table 5.1 Statistics relating to education in South Africa and Uganda

	South Africa	Uganda
Compulsory education	9 years, 7–15; primary and lower secondary	7 years, 6–12; primary
School fees	no fees in poorest primary schools	free primary and secondary education
Net enrolment primary	87.01% in 2017	95.49% in 2013
Survival to the last grade of primary	79.7% in 2015	35.5% in 2016
Expenditure on education	6.16% of GDP in 2018	2.64% of GDP in 2017
Literacy rate	95.32%/87.05%/54.52% in 2017	89.4%/76.53%/42.04% in 2018
Rural population	34%	77%

The following section takes a look at speech recorded from five South African and five Ugandan individuals.[5]

5 REFLECTIONS OF EDUCATIONAL DISADVANTAGE IN THE ENGLISHES OF BLACK SOUTH AFRICANS AND UGANDANS

5.1 Data and Methodology

The data presented below are from recordings of ten semi-structured ethnographic interviews carried out in Cape Town, South Africa, and Kampala and Masaka, Uganda, and at different times. The recordings from South Africa were made in 2006, while those from Uganda are from 2011. While the former do not, thus, reflect language uses in the 2010s, they were chosen for the purpose of this chapter as they capture individuals who grew up in times when access to education was more restricted than today. The individual recordings took place in the

Table 5.2 Informants' details

Pseudonym	Profession	Age at time of recording
Ugandan speakers		
Charles	security person, *askari*	54
Robert	shop attendant	27
Andrew	businessperson	39
Samuel	businessperson	32
Joyce	nursing assistant	23
South African speakers		
Goodwill	handyman	35
Lerato	beadwork artist and entrepreneur	42
Rebecca	waitress	ca. 30
Victoria	room attendant	35
Xolo	wire artist	25

speakers' homes or at their workplace and were between thirty and forty-five minutes long. The speakers, as well as their professions and ages at the time of the recording, are presented in Table 5.2.

Figure 5.1 captures the living conditions of two of our South African informants. Note that, despite the simple dwellings as visible from the plywood in Figure 5.1b, both had dressed up in traditional Xhosa fashion for the occasion of being interviewed.

This section starts with discussions of randomly selected passages from six of the ten interviews, to describe the individual features encountered in the interviewees' speech. This serves to uncover the array and diversity of what uses of English by disadvantaged individuals look like and is followed by a quantitative analysis of a passage of approximately 1,000 words per each of the ten transcripts, in which the features detected in the qualitative passages are examined and compared across all ten speakers.

In combination, the analyses serve to assess whether there are differences between South Africa and Uganda, reflecting the presence of a white, L1, settler community since 1795 versus the lack thereof in Uganda, and whether uses of English vary according to access to education, comparing those who had post-Apartheid or free primary education access to those who did not.

5.2 South African Speakers

The first speaker, Goodwill, aged 35, is a handyman employed at a hotel in Cape Town. He received primary school education during the Apartheid system and acquired a lot of his English on the job.

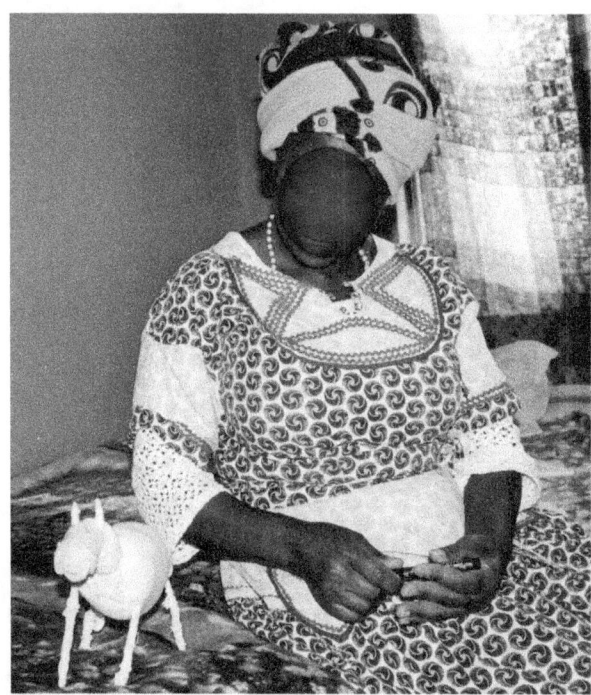
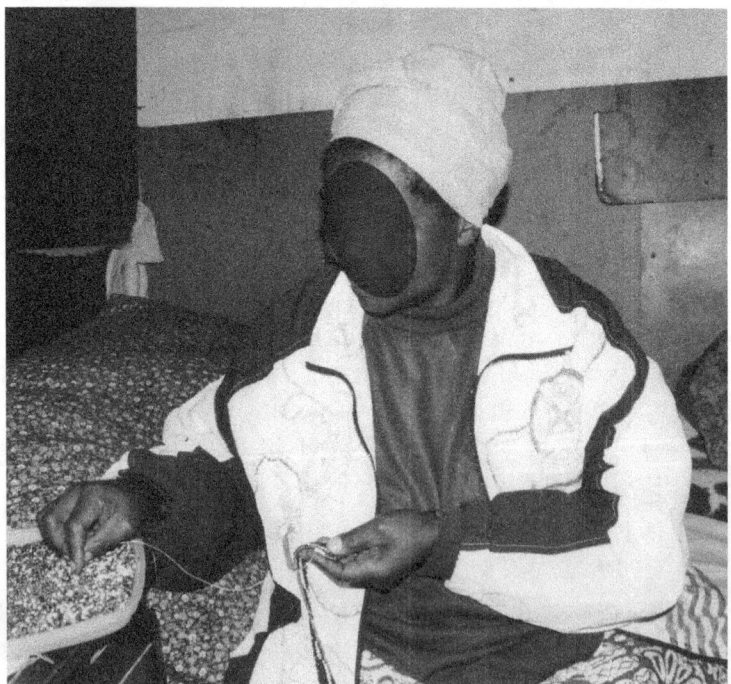

Figure 5.1 Selected informants, anonymized

Extract (1)[6]
Ja, **the o:ne** is doing standard ten, (.) and **the o:ne** standard three, **he's** ten years. **The girl**, is doing standard three. One is eighteen is doing standard ten. And **the one** is still in crèche, three years.
When I'm at home **I'm using** my African language. (.) Yes.
Uh Xhosa. (.) Xhosa. But I/ (..) but sometimes like when uh (.) everybody is happy, like on Sundays when I'm with my family, I like to: (.) to to to to to to to: to to to s+ to <u>speak</u> English with <u>them</u>. Then they can under<u>stand</u> (.) at school. You know? Because (.) sometimes, (..) most of the time they don't uh (1.1 secs) they don't educator/ they don't they don't/ the educator they don't edu<u>cate</u> <u>them</u> (.) uh by uh English. (.) They edu<u>cate</u> them (.) **by** (.) **the African language,** (.) of which that (.) at the end of the day (.) **it cause** (.) a problem. Like (.) like (.) you can find uhm a child from Eastern Cape right there. (.) Maybe **he's uhm (1.4 secs)** she passed the matric.

One of the features which we can observe is his use of *the one* to refer to his three children, used invariably here to replace *one of them, the other one* and *the third one*. The use of *one* as a non-specific determiner, used to 'pick out one of a set' has been described by Bowerman (2004) as a stigmatised feature of Afrikaans English. Most likely, Goodwill picked up the feature from regular interactions with white working-class individuals using it which reveals how face-to-face interaction impacts on the linguistic performance of L2 speakers.

The second noticeable feature is the conflation of the third person singular feminine and masculine pronouns, leading to interchangeable use here, when Goodwill refers to his daughter using *he* in line one but both pronouns in the last sentence. This feature has been found to characterise most pidginised and creolised varieties of English and has also been assessed as being pervasive in a number of L2 Englishes, notably Hong Kong English, basilectal Fiji English and Aboriginal English, for example in Kortmann and Lunkenheimer's (2013) *The Electronic World Atlas of Varieties of English*.

Additionally, there is a use of the progressive for habitual actions in *I'm using my African language*, a use of the preposition *by* that differs from that of standardised Englishes (that would employ *in* or *through*) and zero marking of the third person singular for subject verb agreement in *it cause a problem*. All of these features have been found to characterise L2 Englishes generally but also learner Englishes. At the same time, Bowerman (2004: 952) points out that the preposition *by* 'as in Afrikaans, covers a wide semantic range in White South African English'. Again, this is a stigmatised feature. However, it seems that in White South African English, *by* has a spatial function, while Goodwill seems to further extend its semantics to also cover the instrumental. In sum, Goodwill's English displays evidence of informal acquisition, which is reflected in those features that seem to have their origin in working-class Afrikaans L1 speakers' English. Contact with Afrikaans is also evident from his use of the Afrikaans interjection *ja*, at the very beginning of his first utterance.

The second informant, Lerato, captured in Extract (2), is a 42-year-old lady doing beadwork at a highly artistic level, who also trains other ladies and markets a business. Like Goodwill, she received little formal education during the Apartheid era and acquired most of her English informally.

> Extract (2)
> Yes, like my mum **she do** it. **I learn** from/ actually, s+ started
> on two thousand, ((.h)) and **I <u>learn</u>** the beadwork from my (there/her).
> I didn't know the beadwork from (.) (X). (.) My mum (.) she learned
> the beadwork from her grandmother. (.) For a long time. She said her
> grandmother she (was used to do a) beading, when the beads are falling off,
> she **used to take and take and learn**. (..) So I learn the beadwork from
> my mother. **She's also uhm** (.) **teaching** the well+/ the the ladies at the
> wellness clinic. (.) How to do the beadwork. (.) I also (XX) you/ who can
> do the beadwork and my daughter also. **The one** she's eleven, (.) she know
> how to do the beadwork.
> It's not so difficult (X).
> You can (XX) (..) but you have to be patient. You must have a patient.
> We use like a size (eighty-one). (.) Not **the very very tiny**, but we use the
> very tiny.

Lerato has interesting uses at the lexical level, for example repetition to account for habitual action as in *she used to take and take and learn* and to express superlatives in *the very very tiny*. The feature of reduplication has also been documented as denoting continuation of action or intensification of meaning (as well as plurality and frequency of action, for that matter) for several pidginised varieties of English (Todd 1984; Mühlhäusler 1986). Also, like Goodwill, she uses the non-specific determiner *the one*. Furthermore, we find, again as with Goodwill, inconsistent use of the marking of subject verb agreement, an inconsistent use of past tense marking and an extension of the progressive to habitual actions. This inconsistency is a trait typically associated with learner English.

The third transcript in Extract (3) is quite different from the previous two: Rebecca is a waitress working in the restaurant of a Cape Town hotel. She is several years younger and spent time in the education system after the collapse of the Apartheid system.

> Extract (3)
> From Generations it's just very interesting to me. I just love to learn from
> there. (1.3 secs) And even from The Need, Isidingo. Isidingo, this it's

more/ it's more interesting from there as well. (..) You know at sometimes you know when you get two wives. (.) It's not so easy, it's not easy to (XX) both of them. Ja, that is what I also learnt now, yes. All that **is happening** in Isidingo.
And the wife was very trustful to her husband. Because her husband was never uh uh employed, he was never got a job. And **she was always always helping him**, sending money, giving him money to send to his parents. That's why, on her/ his last day when she was there, (..) the parents **was dema/ they were demanding** eh cars and everything and they/ because they didn't know that he wasn't working.
Everything he had was from his wife.
Wife/ his wife was supporting him a lot.

Her English shows features that have been described for black South African English in general, there is an overuse of the progressive and an indication of a confusion of the pronouns *her* and *his*. Furthermore, there is reduplication of *always* for intensification. Also, there is some insecurity as regards subject verb agreement with regard to the past tense form of BE. Different from Goodwill and Lerato, however, Rebecca seems more conscious of mistakes and corrects herself, making her utterances more similar to those of learners, that is individuals who have acquired English in a formal setting and at the same time reveal limited input from non-standard spoken English.

5.3 Ugandan Security Personnel and Shop Assistants

The individuals who were recorded in Kampala and Masaka[7] are of similar ages to those recorded in the Cape Town region. However, as is evident against the background of the earlier sections, they did not acquire English from L1 speakers but through formal instruction in school, mainly primary school only.[8]

Charles, our first Ugandan informant in Extract (4), acquired English at roughly the same time (in the 1970s and 1980s) as Goodwill from Cape Town, and he also has had limited formal education, but in his case this was through the medium of English.

Extract (4)
The parents (.) have also become a problem (.) to education. They have not taken education to be as (.) something important to a child **(3 secs.)** due to some reasons.
Some of them they might want **take a children uh their children** to school. But (.) **the: what** the necessities of the (..) the school (.) can make them fail.
Yes, if (..) they fulfill it (Universal Education).

They can do eh still have Universal (.) Education. At the end of the day (.) you take your child to school and they demanded the school fees. (..) Would eh that one would be a Universals? (..) Will it be Universal Education?
At the end of the day, they demand the exercise books. At the end of uh the day they say you uh bring some money for coaching. (.) Such things. They will misinterpret the Universal Education. Or let me call it if they would, if those people concerned they would not subcharge it. That is uh I call it subcharging.

What becomes apparent quickly is the absence of most of those features found in the previous extracts, particularly (1) and (2), and identified as being results of informal language acquisition. In Charles's speech, there is self-correction from *take a children* towards *take their children*, which indicates his awareness of standard grammar and the fact that he feels a need to correct himself. Furthermore, in the next line, the long-drawn *the: what* indicates that he very carefully searches for vocabulary items. What we cannot see from the transcript is that his rate of delivery is considerably slower than that of the South African informants, indicating that he takes quite some time to produce his English utterances, most likely as a result of the concentration on reading and rote learning rather than interaction in classrooms.

If we move on to Uganda's younger generation who received primary education in the late 1990s and in the 2000s, like the 23-year-old Joyce, we see that many of them are quite fluent in English and at the same time use grammatical constructions that are close to standard.

Extract (5)
First of all I wanted to be (.) a priest or a lawyer. That was my first priority. But eh (.) I got a problem (.) of school fees. And eh sincerely the marks I scored during my PLE and my S4, I didn't manage to to score good marks that can favour me to join **a law schools or to** (.) **to join a seminaries**. So (.) that's was that's what the problem. And the best eh since I passed (.) sciences, because **in the nursing** when you pass sciences and you got a eighties pass seventy, they they can look they can admit you. (.) You can join any school (.) of nursing. But eh (.) It was easy because I passed those sciences. That's why I decided to (.) join (.) nursing.
The problem? We're overworking because we have no say. Since **we are a student** (.) you have to work (..) everything you have to work uh intensively. From morning **up to**. And we sometimes we (.) we work (.) during midnight eh midnight we work we have no time to sleep (.) because the moment you you refuse to work they can (.) **they can make bad report to you.**

In her utterances, there is, however, some inconsistency in the use of the definite and indefinite article and of plural marking.

Finally, 27-year-old shop attendant Robert from Kampala, who has completed primary school education and also interacts in English on a daily basis, does not show any particular features.

Extract (6)
Well, our clan performed well. Coz I remember it was eh eliminated at eh was it at not even at eh quarter finals. Somewhere in the group stages I think. Yeah. I never followed so (.) so closely.
Well it's a combination of factors. So/ As I said, sometimes it's uh the attitude of the players. Just like at the national level. You know it all begins from the grass root (.) as in in someone interested in playing for for the clan. You know there is this expectation of money, sometimes. Yet in these weaker competitions (.) you hardly find money being given uh given out like allowances. Because it's a it's a tournament which is going to be played for (.) a short period of time. So none is going to pay you an allowance of maybe two-hundred three-hundred. So there are these (fines). If you don't have it, if you don't have the spirit of playing for your team, it means that you're going to be of half service. And it will affect of our performance.

5.4 Quantitative Analyses

In the 1,000-word passages analysed for the ten informants, there are a number of features which are used exclusively by the South African speakers, as Table 5.3 reveals, in which their absence with Ugandan speakers is highlighted by the shading of the cells.[9] These features are unmarked past tense, use of the definite instead of the indefinite article, copula insertion and deletion, preposition insertion, adverb same as adjective, lack of concord with *do*, code-switching, and *the one*. At the same time, self-correction is almost uniquely used by the Ugandan speakers, with one instance also observed with Xolo.

Interestingly, none of the five Ugandan informants reveals any features that have been attested for pidginised or creolised varieties and that would, hence, document manifestations of the result of informal acquisition of English. The differences are, of course, not absolute but matters of preference or frequency. Reduplication occurs in L1 speakers' speech, too, but it is a strategy more often encountered in speakers who acquired English with little or no formal instruction.

The English productions of the South African speakers indicate a much higher degree of structural nativisation, potentially due to endonormative stabilisation, or increasing acceptance of local norms, that has been taking place with Black South African English (see for example Kotze 2019). This is in contrast to the

Table 5.3 Features across South African and Ugandan speakers

	South African informants						Ugandan informants					
	Goodwill	Lerato	Victoria	Rebecca	Xolo	Total	Joyce	Robert	Charles	Andrew	Samuel	Total
Article deletion	2		1	3		6						
Article insertion	1		7	8	1	17		1				1
Definite for indefinite article			3			3						
Copula insertion			3		2	5						
Copula deletion	1	3	3	2	1	10						
Lack of subject verb **concord**		2	2	1		5		1	1			2
Lac of BE concord		2		1		3		1				1
Lack of DO concord		2	1			3						
Noun pronoun concord	1	2				3		1	1			2
Double marking of plural		1				1			2			2
Non-standard **preposition**	3	1	5	8	1	18		1		2		3
Preposition insertion	2	1		1	1	4						
Preposition deletion	1	1				2	1				1	1
Comparative same as superlative			1			1						
Pronoun deletion	1	5	1	1		8	3		1	2	2	8
Pronoun insertion (it)				2		2						
Relative pronoun deletion			2			2		1				1
Personal for reflexive pron.												
Past tense unmarked	1	3	2		3	6						
Extension of progressive	4	3	2	6	1	16	1	1	1		2	5
can be able to express ability			2			2					1	1
Adverb same as adjective			1		2	3						
too for *very* or *much*			1			1						
Comparative = superlative			1			1						
Double negation				1		1						
Reduplication		2				2	1				2	3
Code-switching	11	2		2	1	16						
the one	1	1				2						
Self-correction				1		1	2	1	1		1	5
Inconsistent/variable uses			2			2					1	1
Word order			1			1						
Gerund for infinitive			2			2						
Existential *it's*			2	1		3				1		1
Total						152						36

Ugandan context, where, despite nativisation, attitudes towards English are still very exonormative, with Ugandan English, which Ugandans also label Uglish, looked down on. Potentially in reflection of this, the speech of the Ugandans captured here seems to show a lower degree of structural nativisation.

Importantly, all of the above informants achieve their respective communicative needs. At times, judging from factors such as fluency of delivery and the general tone of the interviews, the South African informants seem to be more at ease when using English than some of the Ugandan informants, despite the fact that the latter display a seemingly higher proficiency level as regards the use of standard English grammar.

6 CONCLUSION: INSTRUCTION AND INTERACTION - STANDARD AND FLUENCY

This chapter started out with a description of grassroots access to English, both through informal interaction with English-speaking settlers and administrators as well as through formal instruction in school, either via the teaching of English as a subject or the use of English as a medium of instruction. From a comparative perspective, South Africa and Uganda differ crucially as regards the options to acquire English available to less fortunate individuals. While in both countries a lack of financial resources typically involves inability to participate in formal education, in the past South Africa's British settler population as well as L2 English speakers with Afrikaans or an Indian language as L1 provided ample contexts for informal acquisition through interaction.

Against this background, excerpts from South African and Ugandan speakers' productions were discussed qualitatively, revealing that, at the grassroots level, productions are highly heterogeneous, but also that there are clear differences between the speakers from the two countries. While the English productions of the South African speakers contain ample examples of influence from working-class White South African English, code-switching with Afrikaans and forms that resemble some of those found with pidginised and creolised varieties of English, the Ugandan speakers lean more towards behaviours typically associated with learners of English. Their productions contain more self-corrections, pausing and hesitators, while at the same time conforming much more to standard varieties of English.

In the South African data, older individuals' utterances reflect their informal acquisition of English through interaction with lower-class whites and their English(es) (in what Meierkord 2012 calls Interactions across Englishes). For example, they use *the one* as a non-specific determiner, to refer to *one of them*, *the other one*, or *the third one*, and they extend the semantics of the preposition *by* to cover an instrumental function. Both patterns have been described by

Bowerman (2004) as stigmatised features of Afrikaans English. Not surprisingly, Black South African English clusters with White South African English as well as Indian South African English in Kortmann and Wolk's (2012) phenogram, which is based on whether individual features had been assessed as either 'pervasive or obligatory' or as 'neither pervasive nor extremely rare' (cf. Kortmann and Lunkenheimer 2012: 5) in the various varieties of English worldwide.

At the same time, utterances are inconsistent in the marking of subject verb agreement and past tense marking, and show an extension of the progressive to habitual actions and reduplication of *always* for intensification, that is features typically associated with learners (Ellis 2008), L2 varieties (cf. Kortmann and Lunkenheimer 2012, 2013) and pidginised forms of English (Mühlhäusler 1986).

Somewhat differently, younger speakers who have attended English-medium schools post-Apartheid seem more conscious of norms and mistakes and tend to correct themselves. Similarly, the Ugandan speakers have a strong tendency towards self-correction, which indicates their awareness of standard grammar. At the same time, they are less fluent and take considerable time to compose their utterances, which seems to be a result of their largely having acquired English in formal instructional settings.

The differences between Black South African English and Ugandan English speakers across generations document that, to a large extent, L2 Englishes at the grassroots are shaped by (1) the presence or absence of a settler population in the history of English in the country, and (2) by access to formal education. While the former explains the presence and absence of features associated with working-class Englishes, the latter is visible in more grammatical but hesitant speech. The results also show that the provision of free education and social engineering (in the case of South Africa) have considerable effects on whether individuals in lower social classes have access to formal education and hence to modes of instructed language acquisition. Since this is reflected in highly heterogeneous L2 Englishes, it is crucial for models of world Englishes to integrate (1) social class, which determines whether access to formal education is possible in the absence of free education, and (2) economic factors, which determine whether and to what extent a nation can provide free education (cf. Meierkord 2020).

NOTES

1. In addition, the same definition includes persons being female or having a disability in the definition of 'Historically Disadvantaged Individual'.
2. Both South Africa and Uganda have citizens, and of course migrant populations, who are white or coloured (in South Africa) or Indian (in both countries).

3. A case in point is Maldives, where no administrative personnel was stationed and hence English was not introduced as an official language (cf. Meierkord 2018, 2020).
4. Data has been taken from the UNESCO Institute of Statistics (2020a, 2020b), available at <uis.unesco.org/en/country/za> and <uis.unesco.org/en/country/ug> (both last accessed 31 January 2020). The figures for the literacy rates refer to the age groups 15–24, older than 15, and older than 65.
5. All names are pseudonyms, to ensure our informants' anonymity.
6. Throughout the extracts, the following transcription conventions have been employed, in addition to regular orthography: (.) = very short pause, (..) = pause below one second, (secs) = pause longer than one second with length mentioned, + = incomplete word, / = cut-off sentence, : = lengthened sound, text = underlining indicates stressed syllables or words, ((.h)) = audible inbreathing, *uhm, uh* = hesitators, (text) = uncertain transcription, (XX) = transcription not possible with each X indicating one syllable, **text** = bold font highlights those words and phrases that are discussed in the sections.
7. I am grateful to Jude Ssempuuma for embarking on collecting data from grassroots speakers in Uganda for the Chair of English Linguistics, as part of a research stay in 2011.
8. We need to acknowledge, however, that the speakers live in a part of the country where attending an English-medium primary school is widespread, due to the multilingual composition of the communities in the region and the resulting inability to decide on a majority indigenous L1 as MOI in the first four primary school years. As explained above, many speakers have considerable proficiency in English after the completion of primary school. Individuals having received their education in rural areas most likely will have very different English productions.
9. Obviously, the figures collected in this table are very low due to the limited data size. However, they serve the purpose of demonstrating how much more restructuring is found in the South African speakers.

REFERENCES

Bingham Wesche, Marjorie (1994), 'Input and interaction in second language acquisition', in Clare Gallaway and Brian J. Richards (eds), *Input and Interaction in Language Acquisition*, Cambridge: Cambridge University Press, 219–49.

Bowerman, Sean (2004), 'White South African English: morphology and syntax', in Bernd Kortmann et al. (eds), *A Handbook of Varieties of English. Vol. 2. Morphology and Syntax*, Berlin: Mouton de Gruyter, 948–61.

Byabazaire, Deogratias M. (1979), *The Contribution of the Christian Churches to the Development of Western Uganda 1894–1974*, Frankfurt a.M.: Lang.

Clyne, Michael (1978), 'Some remarks on foreigner talk', in Norbert Dittmar et al. (eds), *Papers from the 1st Scandinavian–German Symposium on the Language of Immigrant Workers and their Children*, Roskilde: Roskildes Universitetscenter, 155–70.

Cross, Michael (1986), 'A historical review of education in South Africa: towards an assessment', *Comparative Education*, 22: 3, 185–200.

de Klerk, Vivian (ed.) (1996), *Focus on South Africa*, Amsterdam: John Benjamins.

Elliot, A. V. P. (1953), 'The teaching of English in East Africa'. Presented at the International Seminar on the Contribution of the Teaching of Modern Languages towards Education for Living in a World Community, Nuwara Eliya, Ceylon, 3–28 August 1953: United Nations Educational, Scientific and Cultural Organization, <http://unesdoc.unesco.org/images/0014/001445/144532eb.pdf> (last accessed 31 January 2020).

Ellis, Rod (2008), *The Study of Second Language Acquisition*, 2nd edn, Oxford: Oxford University Press.

Government of South Africa (2001), *Preferential Procurement Regulations, 2001 Pertaining to the Preferential Procurement Policy Framework Act: No 5 of 2000*, Pretoria, South Africa: Government of South Africa, Ministry of Finance, National Treasury.

Hartshorne, Ken (1995), 'Language planning and language policy in South Africa: a perspective on the future', in Rajend Mestrie (ed.), *Language and Social History. Studies in South African Sociolinguistics*, Cape Town and Johannesburg: David Philip, 306–18.

Heidelberger Forschungsprojekt 'Pidgin Deutsch' (1978), 'The acquisition of German syntax by foreign migrant workers', in David Sankoff (ed.), *Linguistic Variation: Model and Methods*, New York: Academic Press, 1–22.

Holm, John (1988), *Pidgins and Creoles. Vol.1 Theory and Structure*, Cambridge: Cambridge University Press.

Kortmann, Bernd and Kerstin Lunkenheimer (2012), 'Introduction', in Bernd Kortmann and Kerstin Lunkenheimer (eds), *The Mouton World Atlas of Varieties of English*, Berlin: Mouton de Gruyter, 1–11.

Kortmann, Bernd and Kerstin Lunkenheimer (eds) (2013), *The Electronic World Atlas of Varieties of English*, Leipzig: Max Planck Institute for Evolutionary Anthropology. <http://ewave-atlas.org> (last accessed 31 January 2020).

Kortmann, Bernd and Christof Wolk (2012), 'Morphosyntactic variation in the anglophone world: a global perspective', in Bernd Kortmann and Kerstin Lunkenheimer (eds), *The Mouton World Atlas of Varieties of English*, Berlin: Mouton de Gruyter, 906–36.

Kotze, Haidee (2019), 'Does editing matter? Editorial work, endonormativity and convergence in written Englishes in South Africa', in Raymond Hickey (ed.), *English in Multilingual South Africa. The Linguistics of Contact and Change*, Cambridge: Cambridge University Press, 101–26.

Lanham, Len W. (1996), 'A history of English in South Africa', in Vivian De Klerk (ed.), *Focus on South Africa*, Amsterdam: John Benjamins, 19–34.

Mazrui, Alamin M. and Ali A. Mazrui (1996), 'A tale of two Englishes: the imperial language in post-colonial Kenya and Uganda', in Joshua A. Fishman, Andrew W. Conrad and Alma Rubal-Lopez (eds), *Post-Imperial English. Status Change in Former British and American Colonies, 1940–1990*, Berlin and New York: Mouton de Gruyter, 271–302.

Meierkord, Christiane (2012), *Interactions across Englishes. Linguistic Choices in Local and International Contact Situations*, Cambridge: Cambridge University Press.

Meierkord, Christiane (2016), 'A social history of English(es) in Uganda', in Christiane Meierkord, Bebwa Isingoma and Saudah Namyalo (eds) (2016), *Ugandan English: Its Sociolinguistics, Structure and Uses in a Globalising Post-protectorate*, Amsterdam: John Benjamins, 51–71.

Meierkord, Christiane (2018), 'English in paradise: the Maldives', *English Today*, 34: 1, 2–11.

Meierkord, Christiane (2020), 'Spread of English at the grassroots? Maldives and Uganda', in Andy Kirkpatrick (ed.), *The Routledge Handbook of World Englishes*, London: Routledge.

Meierkord, Christiane, Bebwa Isingoma and Saudah Namyalo (eds) (2016), *Ugandan English: Its Sociolinguistics, Structure and Uses in a Globalising Post-protectorate*, Amsterdam: John Benjamins.

Mesthrie, Rajend et al. (2000), *Introducing Sociolinguistics*, Edinburgh: Edinburgh University Press.

Mesthrie, Rajend (ed.) (2002), *Language in South Africa*, Cambridge: Cambridge University Press.

Mesthrie, Rajend and Rakesh Bhatt (2008), *World Englishes. The Study of New Linguistic Varieties*, Cambridge: Cambridge University Press.

Mühlhäusler, Peter (1986), *Pidgin and Creole Linguistics*, Oxford: Basil Blackwell.

Myers-Scotton, Carol (1988), 'Patterns of bilingualism in East Africa (Uganda, Kenya, and Tanzania)', in C. Bratt Paulston (ed.), *International Handbook of Bilingualism and Bilingual Education*, Westport, CT: Greenwood, 203–24.

Nicholls, Gordon Charles (1992), 'An evaluation of the provision and future development of professional teacher education in South Africa with particular preference to Colleges of Education: a public administration perspective', unpublished PhD dissertation, Durban, South Africa: University of Durban-Westville.

Oxford English Dictionary (*OED*) (2019), 'disadvantaged', adj. <https://www.oed.com/view/Entry/52864857?rskey=2iFpGt&result=2#eid> (last accessed 31 January 2020).

Pica, Teresa (1983), 'Adult acquisition of English as a second language under different conditions of exposure', *Language Learning*, 33: 4, 465–97.

Pica, Teresa (1985), 'The selective impact of classroom instruction on second language acquisition', *Applied Linguistics*, 6: 3, 214–22.

Scanlon, David G. (1964), *Education in Uganda*, (US Department of Health, Education, and Welfare. Office of Education. Bulletin 1964, No. 32.), Washington, DC: US Department of Health, Education, and Welfare (now Health and Human Services).

Schneider, Edgar W. (2007), *Postcolonial English. Varieties around the World*, Cambridge: Cambridge University Press.

Selinker, Larry (1972), 'Interlanguage', *International Review of Applied Linguistics*, 10, 209–31.

Ssekamwa, J. C. (2000), *History and Development in Education in Uganda*, 2nd edn, Kampala: Fountain Publishers.

Ssentanda, Medadi (2016), 'Tensions between English medium and mother tongue education in rural Ugandan primary schools: an ethnographic investigation', in Christiane Meierkord, Bebwa Isingoma and Saudah Namyalo (eds), *Ugandan English: Its Sociolinguistics, Structure and Uses in a Globalising Post-protectorate*, Amsterdam: John Benjamins, 95–117.

Statistics South Africa (2012), *Census 2011: Census in Brief*, Pretoria: Statistics South Africa.

Todd, Loreto (1984), *Modern Englishes: Pidgins and Creoles*, Oxford: Blackwell.

UNESCO Institute of Statistics (2020a), 'South Africa', <http://uis.unesco.org/country/ZA> (last accessed 31 January 2020).

UNESCO Institute of Statistics (2020b), 'Uganda', <http://uis.unesco.org/en/country/ug> (last accessed 31 January 2020).

Velupillai, Viveka (2015), *Pidgins, Creoles and Mixed Languages. An Introduction*, Amsterdam: John Benjamins.

Webster (2020), 'disadvantaged', <https://www.merriam-webster.com/dictionary/disadvantaged> (last accessed 31 January 2020).

Weinreich, Ulriel (1974), *Languages in Contact*, 8th edn, The Hague: Mouton.

CHAPTER 6

Artistic Re-creation of Grassroots English: Ideologies and Structures in *English Vinglish*

Edgar W. Schneider

1 INTRODUCTION

World Englishes appear and have been investigated in a wide variety of settings – in writing, in formal and informal conversations, in electronic discourse, in 'grassroots' emergence (as used in Schneider 2016a; for a wider discussion of the term see Meierkord and Schneider, this volume), on YouTube (Schneider 2016b), and so on. The present chapter looks into a unique intersection of such perspectives: It investigates the artistic portrayal of the use and growth of grassroots English (in India and in an international context) in a Bollywood movie. Among other things, it thus touches upon the question of what level of sensitivity the moviemakers (as non-linguists, perhaps representing a wider non-professional audience) display on issues of linguistic variability, language attitudes and non-standard language use.

The representation of language in works of art constitutes a topic in its own right – this relationship, and earlier approaches at investigating it, will first be addressed, followed by a brief discussion and contextualisation of the notion of 'grassroots' growth of English(es). After introducing the source material, the Bollywood movie *English Vinglish* (2012),[1] the main part of the analysis will then look at language usage in this movie from two quite different angles. Firstly, language ideologies in India on the importance of being able to speak English, hidden in the plot, will be worked out, using broadly a Critical Discourse Analysis approach. Secondly, I analyse the structural properties and the representation of the acquisition progress of the usage of a group of grassroots learners in the movie. Brief sidelines of the analysis work out interesting parallels woven into the plot: the relationships between language proficiency and self-confidence and between language and good food, respectively. Overall, a complex picture of subtle modes of awareness and representation of grassroots usage of English emerges.

2 BACKGROUND

2.1 Artistic Re-creation of Language

In earlier times, prior to modern linguistics, written and especially literary language was imbued with authority: 'great writers' such as Shakespeare were seen as models and constituted sources of the writing of early grammars.[2] One of the main insights of the birth of modern linguistics, following Saussure and others, was then the recognition of the primacy of speech over writing in language, noting that all communities and healthy individuals develop speech but not all command writing systems, since writing is only a 'secondary encoding' of speech. Sociolinguists in particular value vernacular speech as authentic, following Labov's (1972) 'observer's paradox' which shows that the very process of observing (and recording) language, the monitoring of one's speech, transforms it and renders it inauthentic. In a similar vein, this also applies to language employed in works of art and literature, which is always deliberately created and forged, and which in modern linguistics is thus usually sidestepped as inauthentic, not considered suitable data for language representation and analysis.

This widespread attitude calls for some reflection, however. The artistic re-creation of language, in literary dialect, media language, and the like, serves a purpose of its own, being created as it is for a particular effect (to entertain, to inform, and so on – but also just to represent natural speech). Knowing this, and how to do this, is also part of our language capacity and competence – so deliberate language production in works of art and in the public domain constitutes a genre and usage context of its own; it is also worthy of investigation, but needs consideration of factors such as their production context, (artistic) purpose, and so on. Moody (2020) argues that media language is always marked by a tension between 'authenticity' (trying to portray and relate to real-life contexts and usage) and 'authority' (satisfying the demands for formality in public discourse).

Analysing language in arts and media is part of a tradition which I can only sketch out very briefly here. There is a long-standing research strand of investigating literary dialect (Ives 1971), with many applications to individual writers of the Anglo-American canon. An example crossing the bridge to linguistic variability, assessing the authenticity of creole representation and the writer's multilectal competence in the qualitative and quantitative analysis of a Jamaican novel, is Schneider and Wagner (2006). Other examples of deliberate language representation for a public purpose include humorous dialect booklets for tourists and locals – such as *How to Speak Southern*, analysed by Schneider (1986), or fun books on Liverpool Scouse (Honeybone and Watson 2013). Linguistic usage in YouTube clips (Schneider 2016b) can be seen and investigated in a similar perspective. As to ideologies of language representation in film, the best-known study is Lippi-Green (2012), who shows how accent discrimination in Disney movies perpetuates social inequalities via associated attitudes.

Lee (2012) is a paper on a similar topic, analysing how the Korean movie *Please Teach Me English* showcases Koreans' 'metalinguistic discourse on anguish and elation of improving English-speaking skills' (p. 130). She shows that 'popular films provide a valuable window into a society' and have an 'enormous potential as a linguistic and social reservoir' (p. 127).

2.2 Grassroots English

The second important, relatively novel perspective that this chapter brings in is the focus on 'grassroots English'. Schneider (2016a: 3) defines users as 'speakers of forms and varieties of English . . . who come from relatively poor backgrounds but nevertheless have striven and managed successfully to acquire a communicatively effective level of competence' – and this clearly also characterises the main character(s) in *English Vinglish*. This is the topic of the present volume, and Meierkord and Schneider (this volume) define and discuss the notion in greater detail and also comment on earlier and other contributions on this new approach, including Meierkord (2012, 2020), Blommaert (2010), who uses the term slightly differently and looks at language forms as globally fluent resources, Schneider (2016a), or Han's work (for example Han 2013) on grassroots multilingualism involving Chinese and African interlocutors.

One distinctive component in the analysis of grassroots speech and speakers is their very high and usually intrinsic and instrumental motivation: 'In many countries, even limited proficiency levels in English offer relatively attractive job opportunities, often involving interactions with international visitors' (Schneider 2016a: 3). Grassroots English is thus typically acquired 'in direct interactions rather than through formal education' (Schneider 2016a: 3), and its structural properties include reduced, simplified and incomplete utterances. This limitation often results from the speakers' goal of acquisition, which is typically not the full command of the target language but merely a 'domain-specific' level of fluency instead, depending on a speaker's needs in a given communicative context (Grosjean 2008: 14). Many learners display a 'tendency [. . .] to stop learning as soon as they think they have mastered the TL [target language] sufficiently' for their respective purpose (Buschfeld 2013: 58). From an outside perspective, the assessment of such language forms is often one of 'broken English', ideologically negatively assessed, but the acquisition process is purpose-driven, and speakers thus tend to view its result as sufficient for their respective purposes. Language representation in *English Vinglish* shows some of these aspects translated into a fictitious, entertaining movie plot and form.

2.3 *English Vinglish*: The Movie

English Vinglish is a Bollywood comedy-drama directed by Gauri Shinde, released in 2012 in Hindi (with subtitles available) and English. The plot was inspired by autobiographic input, that is the experience of the director's mother (Wikipedia 2019). Originally it generated interest also because of the main actress Sridevi's return to moviemaking after fifteen years. The film was highly successful – it screened at several international festivals, was internationally acclaimed and praised by critics (especially for Sridevi's acting performance),[3] won several prizes, and was shortlisted as India's entry for an Academy Award nomination in the 'Best Foreign Language Film' category. Reportedly, it even had some socio-political impact, motivating girls from the Dalit caste, the socially lowest, repressed stratum of India's society, to work on their (certainly grassroots) English (IANS 2012). The text in Extract (1) summarises the plot.

> Extract (1) *English Vinglish*: the plot[4]
> Shashi, a young Indian wife and mother, speaks hardly any English – a fact which is hugely embarrassing to her; her husband Shatish and her pre-puberty daughter Sapna treat her with disrespect (despite her reputation of being a superb cook and maker of laddoos).
>
> Shashi travels to New York alone to help her sister prepare her niece's wedding. There she discovers and secretly enrols in a language course which promises to teach speaking English in four weeks. Struggling with but gradually mastering her ways through New York City, with a group of other 'grassroots' learners from different countries she gradually picks up some English. After some complications (another course member, the French cook Laurent, confesses to falling in love with her; her family arrives early, which prevents her from further attending and finishing the course; on the wedding day morning the laddoos which she has prepared are crashed to the ground so she has to cook new ones rather than attend the exam), at the wedding to everybody's surprise she delivers a superb speech in English, thus passing the course (since the teacher and the other members have been invited, and her speech is accepted as exam) and, more importantly, gaining her husband's respect.

3 'THE IMPORTANCE OF KNOWING ENGLISH': IDEOLOGY, DISCOURSE AND MULTIMODALITY

3.1 Sociolinguistic and Theoretical Background

The attitudes expressed in the movie become transparent only in the light of the sociolinguistic background and status of English in India. Going back to the early seventeenth century, Indian English is one of the oldest and most deeply rooted World Englishes (Kachru 1983; Schneider 2007: 161–73; Lange 2020). After independence, the Constitution of 1950 retained English for official purposes for a transition period, to be removed after fifteen years; but it has continued to be used indefinitely after resistance against Hindi as the sole official language, as settled in the Official Languages Act (1963, amended 1967). Today English in India is still official and firmly established and widespread, but it is also associated with a symbolic load of education and class, being accessible to (and cherished by) only privileged strata of society. As Lange (2020: 247) states,

> [e]ven though English is mostly no longer framed as a colonial imposition, it sparks ambivalent attitudes: students coming up from rural colleges to metropolitan universities acutely feel the class and caste connotations attached to lingering on the wrong end of the cline of proficiency. English is a highly prized commodity.

This status association motivates the strong underlying ideology to be observed throughout the movie, which will be worked out in the following section. I thereby follow Lee (2012: 148), showing 'how formidable English language ideologies can be and how they affect learners and their lives'. The underlying and unchallenged (but also unpronounced) discourse axiom is the fact that in the social stratum the movie plays in 'RECEIVING RESPECT REQUIRES THE ABILITY TO SPEAK ENGLISH'. I view and mark these ideological notions as 'conceptual metaphor' domains comparable to the ones identified by Lakoff and Johnson (1980), and I employ two methodological approaches to document and create awareness of these 'hidden assumptions'.

Firstly, in the analysis of individual movie scenes I employ Critical Discourse Analysis (CDA) to highlight and connect speakers' behaviour and their camouflaged but persistent attitudes. CDA theory, after Fairclough (2010), makes underlying ideologies, power relationships and asymmetries in discourse visible, often against a given political background, disclosing a hidden agenda. The discipline lacks a coherent, well-defined empirical methodology (Wodak and Meyer 2016: 18–22) and employs various approaches, often using existing data (as is the case here). This section pursues a socio-cognitive approach in its application of CDA. In the movie context, social inequality and consequences as to the status and respect individuals receive is caused by unequal access to English – a 'social wrong' (Fairclough 2010: 235) which, however, is not directly addressed. The purpose of section 3.2 is thus to identify 'underlying ideologies' (Wodak and Meyer 2016: 84) built into the plot, the camouflaged attitudes, views and personal stances which I call 'hidden messages'.

Secondly, given that discourse is understood as 'context-dependent semiotic practices' (Wodak and Meyer 2016: 27), manifestations of these 'messages' are not only or primarily expressed verbally but also via multimodal expressions of attitudes and reactions, that is through gestures or facial expressions (which is relevant here, since these often adopt a subtle, indirect signalling function). In pragmatics, multimodality, the expression of illocutions via various non-verbal channels, constitutes one increasingly important component of theories of social semiotics; pragmatic analysis often thrives on multimodality and increasingly recognises the importance of non-verbal modes (Seaford 1975; Kendon 1990, 2004; Norris 2012; Vigliocco et al. 2014). This was already noted at the beginnings of the discipline, in Austin (1962) who commented on 'tone of voice, cadence, emphasis' (p. 74) as well as 'gestures (winks, pointings, shruggings, frowns, etc.)' and stated that 'their importance is very obvious' (p. 76). Illocutions of speech acts are often signalled by speech tempo, intonation contour, gesture, facial expression, or gaze. In *English Vinglish* facial expressions and gaze are preferred (and highly subtle!) means of implying and expressing personal stance, often functioning as signals of distance and negative attitudes; I will reproduce a few images and comment on these modes to make this point in my discussions.

3.2 English Vinglish: Movie Scenes – and What they Imply

In this section I employ a qualitative documentation, selecting and interpreting some pertinent scenes, including descriptions of the situations, persons and utterances and some short transcripts of conversations. I identify scenes by succinct labels and timestamps referring to the movie. In these scenes selected, important utterances are transcribed (marked by italics), and in addition the plot of the scenes is described, summarised and assessed, again highlighting aspects that are relevant to the current discussion. The consistent purpose of these discussions is to work out the 'hidden messages', the underlying but unpronounced beliefs of the characters.

> Extract (2) Scene 'Jazz' (00:02:30)
> Shashi: . . . [tʃɑːs] *dance.*
> Sapna: (starts laughing) *Dad! I can't control it. It's too funny. . . . Come on, dad, let's do the tshaaas dance. . . .*
> Sagar: *Mom, is no tshaas dance, this is jazz dance.*

Figure 6.1 Sapna's smirk

Shashi's daughter Sapna ridicules Shashi's wrong pronunciation, in an exaggerated fashion. She seeks her father's solidarity in disrespecting her mother.
Sagar, her little son, also finds this funny but pays respect by correcting and informing her.

Sapna's arrogant and disrespectful attitude towards her mother, triggered by her mispronunciation of an English word, is barely controlled and embodied in her smirk, shown in Figure 6.1. The hidden message for Shashi clearly is 'BEING UNABLE TO SPEAK ENGLISH PROPERLY ALLOWS OTHERS TO DISRESPECT YOU'.

> Extract (3) Scene 'PTA meeting' (00:13:20)
> Sapna is upset because Shatish has forced Shashi to go to the PTA (Parent-Teacher Association) meeting instead of him, since he has no time.
> Sapna (on the phone): *No, no, no, dad, how could you do this, please?*
> Shashi is also unwilling and highly insecure, knowing that she will be expected to talk English to the teacher – which she is unable to do.
> Father Vincent, her teacher, praises Sapna's school performance in fluent English, but Shashi is unable to understand, and asks him to talk Hindi.
> Shashi: *Sorry, Father, my English not good.*
> Sapna is hugely embarrassed and angry at her mother.

It turns out that Father Vincent is unable to speak Hindi since he speaks Malayalam, coming from Kottayam, a city in the southern state of Kerala where this language is spoken – but that, in contrast, is no reason to disrespect him. The hidden message for Shashi is 'BEING UNABLE TO SPEAK ENGLISH MAY MEAN BEING UNABLE TO COMMUNICATE ABOUT COMPLEX BUT IMPORTANT THINGS'.

Extract (4) Scene 'Mothers' talk' (00:10:00)
Neelam: *Hello, I'm Neelam, commonly known as Rupals mother these days.*
Shashi: *I'm ahm Sapna mother, Shashi.*
In school Shashi meets another mother who floods her with English words – to which she has nothing to react. Sapna answers to Neelam and pushes her mother away, obviously wanting to avoid her trying to talk and thus disclose her strongly limited ability to speak English.

Sapna's attention is directed to Neelam, who she obviously respects, unlike her mother. Again, her posture and gaze make it clear that she distances herself subtly but clearly from Shashi, backing the hidden message 'WHEN YOU ARE UNABLE TO SPEAK ENGLISH YOU BETTER NOT SPEAK AT ALL'.

Extract (5) Scene 'America is a foreign land' (00:18:00)
Shashi is highly worried about having to go to America on her own and wants to share this concern with Shatish (in Hindi), but he ignores her (and repeatedly talks to her in English himself, disregarding her needs).

Shatish not only ignores his wife's worries but also her plain communicative needs, talking to her in the language that he knows she doesn't command – showing her that 'NOT KNOWING ENGLISH MAKES YOU VULNERABLE'.

Extract (6) Scene 'Hug' (00:21:50)
Shashi observes Satish hugging a young, beautiful colleague, is offended, and blames him.
Satish: *It was a hug, Shashi. . . . Everybody hugs, it's normal.*

Shatish's office colleague is not shown talking, and there is no direct reference to English in this scene, but the implication is clear – she shares his work environment. This scene adds a subtle and tentative but clearly visible gendered, even slightly sexual, dimension in the plot. The body language and gazes are important and straightforwardly suggestive, indicating Shashi's concern, Satish's condescending, annoyed attitude, and the suppressed conflict between them – suggesting that 'BEING SUCCESSFUL MAKES A WOMAN MORE DESIRABLE'.

Extract (7) Scenes 'At the embassy' (00:22:50)
Shashi: *My English . . . weak*
Immigration Officer 1: *Ma'am, how are you manage in our country if you don't know English?*
The officer at the American embassy in India, where Shashi files her visa application, denigrates her.

Figure 6.2 Satish and Sapna exchange glances

It becomes clear that, for Shashi, even entering the United States will constitute a difficult barrier. Shatish and Shashi practise responses to questions an immigration officer might ask; Shashi confuses questions and gives wrong answers. Her husband and daughter, again via multimodal means and behind her back, share their disregard for her (Figure 6.2) – strengthening the hidden message 'NOT KNOWING ENGLISH JUSTIFIES BEING TREATED WITH CONTEMPT' rather than offering real support.

> Extract (8) Scene 'In a café' (00:37:50)
> In Manhattan, Shashi, alone, enters a café. The rude cashier rattles through her series of routine questions, which Shashi does not understand, and abuses her because her slowness causes delay. Shashi starts crying.

This scene thrives by its multimodal encodings: the cashier's monotonous and machine-gun speech and intonation and her aggressive body language and facial expression (see Figure 6.3) against Shashi's growing, clearly visible worries, lack of understanding and increasing insecurity until she physically almost breaks down. She learns the hidden message the rough way: 'IF YOU CANNOT SPEAK ENGLISH YOU ARE UNABLE TO FULFIL BASIC NEEDS'.

Soon thereafter Shashi happens to see the ad announcing a language centre making learners 'Speak English in 4 weeks', that she decides to join – and this changes the direction of the plot decidedly.

> Extract (9) Scene 'Class starts today' (00:42:20)
> When Shashi calls the language centre to enquire about the English course she has seen advertised, the Secretary first speaks very rapid American English but then, realising that she does not understand, repeats the message, pronouncing every word slowly and distinctly.

Figure 6.3 Shashi and the café cashier

This scene presents a straightforward contrast to the previous one, showing how empathetic human behaviour is possible after all, and it marks a turning point in the plot. The secretary at the language school deliberately adjusts her performance (speech tempo, clarity of articulation) to Shashi's comprehension level, thus securing successful communication despite her minimal abilities (see Figure 6.4). The hidden message this time is a positive one: 'PAYING RESPECT TO OTHERS IMPLIES ATTENDING TO THEIR LINGUISTIC NEEDS – WHICH IS POSSIBLE'.

Shashi then enrols in this language class, with other learners. Scene (10), from the end of the movie, showcases her language ability after a few weeks of tuition and intense self-learning.

Figure 6.4 The language school secretary articulating deliberately carefully

Extract (10) Scene 'Wedding speech' (1:55:00)
Manu: *Shashi, please* [talks in Hindi]
Satish: [talks in Hindi] *Sorry. My wife's English is not really good, so* . . .
Shashi: *May I? Meera, Kevin,* [talks in Hindi]. *Oh God, oh God . . . Hindi . . . This marriage is a beautiful thing.* . . .
At the wedding, Shashi is expected to give a speech. Satish tries to prevent that, but she politely claims the floor, playfully starts in Hindi, but then delivers a beautiful, complex (if not flawless) speech in English.
She receives thunderous applause and Satish's admiration; Sapna is embarrassed.

This scene constitutes the fairy tale-like climax of the plot – but despite its brevity it is filled with multimodal implications, a brief power struggle and even some irony. Despite her being explicitly called to the floor, Shatish, in his usual condescending way, claims her right to speak – but she physically pulls him down to sit again, gently but persistently, and starts talking herself – even playing with her putative inability to speak English by starting in Hindi and then ironically distancing herself from that step (see Figure 6.5). Reactions are overwhelmingly positive, from the enthusiastic applause she receives to the obvious embarrassment, with signs of guilt and shame in her glance, on the part of her daughter. The message is perfectly clear: 'IF YOU SPEAK FLUENT ENGLISH EVERYBODY RESPECTS YOU'.

Figure 6.5 Shashi delivering a public speech in English, with her husband worried and surprised

Overall, thus, the plot revolves around different manifestations of consistently the same hidden message: 'IF YOU ARE UNABLE TO SPEAK ENGLISH YOU ARE DESPISED; IF YOU SPEAK ENGLISH WELL YOU ARE RESPECTED'. It is modified, with varying implementations, but never really questioned. The importance of knowing English in this society stratum is paramount.

3.3 Variations of the Core Theme

Two more, related and relevant, ideas and metaphors are built into the storyline: parallelisms between English skills and self-confidence, and between food and language.

3.3.1 Language and personal development

Throughout the movie a recognisable main motif is the parallelism between Shashi's initially lacking, then gaining, self-confidence and her initially lacking, then developing, English skills – a connection that is expressed verbally, factually and also, strongly, visually. In the beginning, as the text examples from Extract (2) to (7) imply, due to her lack of English skills Shashi suffers from a lack of self-confidence and recognition even from her family members; she is often anxious, very reluctant and in some scenes clearly almost depressed. The turning point is the moment when she sees the language school advertisement promising to teach English to beginners in four weeks, which raises hope in her, and also the supportive behaviour of the school's secretary, who provides the necessary information and steers her through the New York City transportation system in a manner that she is able to understand. In the middle part of the film, Shashi is seen fighting her way through the subway interchanges to find the school and to get to classes – insecure but determined, with occasional help from people around her, with her mobility, self-confidence and communicative skills gradually growing. By the end, in the scene 'Wedding speech' Extract (10), she presents herself as self-confident in both factual and linguistic behaviour, claiming the floor from Shatish against his will and starting to speak even when he thinks she is incapable of doing that – to the point of ironically commenting on her faked start in Hindi.

Clearly, there is another hidden message discernible here: 'BEING ABLE TO MASTER ONE'S LIFE GOES HAND IN HAND WITH BEING ABLE TO SPEAK ENGLISH'. Despite and quite unlike her initial, occasional spells of depression Shashi is a strong, determined woman who persistently pursues her goals, against all difficulties and resistance. The movie presents a story of self-development and of gaining self-confidence – in life and language skills! The warmth and sympathetic nature of the central character, embodied in a masterly fashion by Sridevi, and of this story contribute substantially to the appeal and success of the film.

3.3.2 Language and food: a multimodal metaphor?

Another implicit but strong motif recurring throughout the plot is the parallelism between food and language – built into Shashi's character in a concrete fashion in the form of cooking versus English skills, and arguably also to be seen as a more abstract connection of body versus mind. Shashi is a superb cook and prepares outstanding laddoos, an Indian sweet, for which she is praised by other mothers, for example in Extract (4) 'Mothers' talk', but this skill does not earn her respect in her family, and not at all with her husband. This is epitomised in Extract (11), where he cuts her off rudely.

> Extract (11) Scene 'Laddoos vs. business' (00:04:50)
> At a social function Shashi has been praised by other mothers for her superb laddoos. She enthusiastically calls Shatish to share her success with him, also using her minimal English (*'Awesome super hit!'*). But she is slighted and cut off by Shatish, who is in a (in his view much more important) business meeting.

The relationship between these motifs recurs and develops throughout the plot. The teacher in the language school calls Shashi an *entrepreneur* – and she often repeats and practises the word, fondly and proudly, since cooking is credited with being a respectable activity after all. Laurent, her admirer, is also a cook, and calls his crêpe, which he offers her, 'French laddoos' (01:30:00). In the wedding scenes, the plot culminates in a parallel drama: before the wedding Shashi stumbles, and her laddoos fall to the ground and are wasted – and she cannot attend her language exam because she needs to cook new ones. But an equally parallel solution and highlight follows: during the wedding everybody admires Shashi's great speech and great laddoos.

4 *I SHASHI FROM THE INDIA*: STRUCTURAL ANALYSIS OF GRASSROOTS ENGLISH

4.1 Background and Methodological Approach

In this section structural characteristics of grassroots English in the performance of Shashi and her fellow students are analysed. Research questions thus are: Which features occur in the speech portrayed, and how can they be accounted for? Is the learners' language acquisition and development represented adequately? How 'authentic' is the representation of speech?

Admittedly, the speech represented here is 'grassroots' in the sense of a lack of formal higher education with limitations only: speakers attend a language course, so this is not (or only partly) natural acquisition. This is not typical of grassroots usage as defined earlier – but core components of this setting can nevertheless be identified: the learners depicted start from very low initial proficiency levels and lack former formal training in English; their subjective motivation is extremely high, since they need to be able to speak English in their job or some other context; and the teaching context is not elitist secondary education but simply a crash course, targeting quick and incomplete, merely functional, acquisition of English[5] – all of which are characteristics of 'grassroots' acquisition.

Table 6.1 identifies the six learners from different countries who come together in the language school, spend some free time together and provide samples of grassroots speech. In order to analyse this structurally I built a small corpus consisting of all utterances by these speakers, the composition of which is outlined in Table 6.2. I distinguish three learning stages (initial, intermediate and advanced, respectively) – the table shows their respective plot settings, time frames and corpus sizes (number of words produced per stage). The corpus is minimal, of course – but it is sufficient to document some interesting features and developments: as will be shown, the learners go through distinct stages as their proficiency progresses.

Table 6.1 The grassroots learners: origins and motives

Name	Origin	Job	Motivation
Shashi	India	housewife/cook	to gain her family's respect (?)
Eva	Mexico	nanny	employer wants her to speak English, not Spanish, to baby
Salman Khan	Pakistan	cab driver	job; attract Pakistani girls (who only want 'foreigner')
Yu Son	China	hairstylist	job
Ramamurthy	India (Tamil)	software engineer	job, respect from colleagues
Laurent	France	cook	improve 'dirty English' (as he calls it) for work in hotel

Table 6.2 The learners' three acquisition stages distinguished

	Proficiency	Setting in movie plot	Time in movie	Size
Stage 1	initial	Shashi's initial contact with language school – first lessons	44:00–58:00	391 words
Stage 2	intermediate	some time later, until week 3	1.01:00–1.33:30	1107 words
Stage 3	advanced	before exam and during wedding	1.39:33–2.03:40	497 words

4.2 Grassroots Proficiency Replicated: Some Qualitative Observations

I analyse the speakers' performance based on the structure (length, complexity and features) of their individual utterances (with this notion defined by turn, intonation unit and syntactic unit, following Buschfeld 2020: 106 [in greater detail in the 2018 edition: 155]). In terms of these properties the utterances vary considerably. A high proportion of utterances are maximally brief and consist of single words only, shown in Extract (12). Some of these are in fact perfectly fine and acceptable (12a), while others are incomplete and ungrammatical (12b). The same applies to two- or three-word utterances, illustrated in (13a), essentially conventionalised routine formulae, and (13b), respectively.

Extract (12) One-word utterances
(a) acceptable: *Hello! Why? Yes! Okay. Bye!*
(b) incomplete: *Have. Back? Money?* 'How much does it cost?'

Extract (13) Two-/three-word utterances
(a) acceptable: *Very good! Thank you! See you tomorrow.*
(b) incomplete: *Sometimes better.* '. . . it is . . .' *Spicy noodle.* 'She is a . . .' *I come Mexico.* '. . . from . . .' *House me coffee.* 'I will have coffee at home.'

In contrast, there are also a few fairly long utterances. In the early phases these tend to be highly ungrammatical and mostly occur in very emotional contexts, illustrated in (14). At the end point of the acquisition process depicted, after four weeks of the course, at the wedding, several speakers show the ability to produce longer, complex utterances, for example those in Extract (15). This is epitomised, of course, by Shashi's relatively long and fairly elaborate (and reasonably grammatical) speech at the wedding, of which Extract (16) provides a sample. Of course these utterances still contain some errors, and it may be assumed that the progress these learners make in merely four weeks, especially in Shashi's case, is unrealistic – but this is immaterial for an assessment of the movie's artistic intentions and the portrayal of underlying sociolinguistic beliefs.

Extract (14) Long, ungrammatical utterances
The baby mama so worry so worry the baby no speak English. (Eva)
What are doing in the class today, not correct, yah. (Rama)

Extract (15) Long, (largely) grammatical utterances
Thank you very much for calling us to come! (Rama)
Don't call me Rama Bhai. That is name of my servant in India. (Rama)
Oh, may I go help her? (Yu Son)

Extract (16) Shashi's long, elaborate wedding speech
[...] Try to help each other to feel equal. It will be nice. Sometimes, married couple don't even know how the other is feeling. So, how they will help the other, it means marriage is finished? No, that is the time you have to help yourself. Nobody can help you better than you. [...]

4.3 Grassroots English Replicated: Proficiency Advances

Interestingly enough, the distribution of these utterance types is far from random. In this section I document how proficiency advancement is portrayed in the movie, using two different types of measurement: utterance complexity and mean utterance length.

For the first type of analysis utterances have been consistently categorised into the types illustrated in Extract (17), with length and correctness increasing.

Extract (17) Utterance types distinguished systematically in Figure 6.6
(a) One word (for example *Fine. Here? Have.*)
(b) Two words, incomplete (for example *Only girl. Bad day.*)
(c) Three or more words, incomplete (for example *In house only. Me feel sorry. You want ticket? You order correct English.*)
(d) Two or three words, syntactically complete (for example *Thank you. See you tomorrow. I did it?*)
(e) Four or more words, syntactically complete (for example *I like this class. May I go home now? I buy popcorn for you.*)

Figure 6.6 shows the distribution of these utterance types by the three acquisition phases defined in Table 6.2 – which turns out to be very straightforward. At

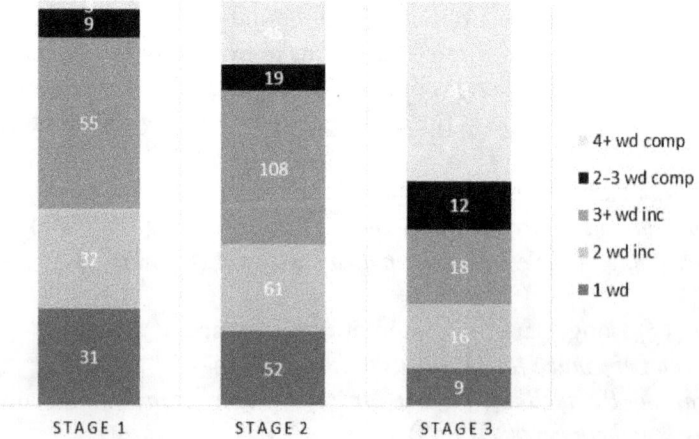

Figure 6.6 Distribution of utterance types by acquisition stages

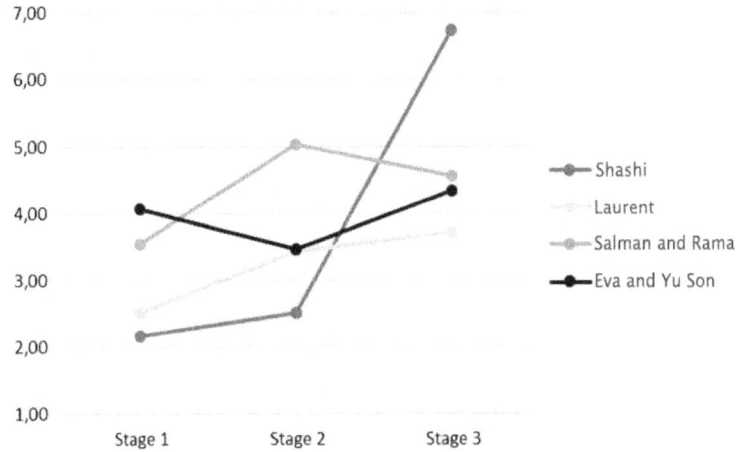

Figure 6.7 MLUs (mean length of utterances) by speakers and stages

the beginning, short and ungrammatical utterances clearly predominate; during the transition phase the balance tips; and in phase 3 the speakers mainly produce long and correct utterances, with the proportion of short and incomplete ones having gone down drastically.

Figure 6.7 presents the growth of utterance length in individual speakers during the three stages. It adopts the 'mean length of utterance' (MLU) measurement, an established technique of measuring utterance length and thus complexity in child language acquisition studies (Brown 1973; for a systematic summary see Buschfeld 2020: 102–9). Specifically, since the words used tend to be morphologically simple I calculated the MLU-word (rather than the MLU-morpheme) value, by speaker and stage, pooled for some sociolinguistically similar speakers with low token frequencies. The results graph displays a steady increase of MLUs in all speakers and thus mirrors their learning progress in complexity of expression. It is prototypically gradual in the case of Laurent, while others show some meaningful special effects. The speakers from India and Pakistan have higher stage 1 values – which may reflect some earlier exposure to English in their home countries where English is a second language. High values for Eva in stage 1 and Rama in stage 2 show the impact of a few very long but highly ungrammatical utterances, quoted in Extract (14). Shashi's stellar increase in stage 3 is caused by her relatively long wedding speech – an outlier effect which implies that in this case artistic intention may override realistic representation.

4.4 Grassroots English Replicated: Structures

This section provides a more specifically grammatical analysis and documentation of the structural types found in the learners' speech. Essentially, as was stated before, the syntax tends to be simple, especially in the early learning stage(s), with very many one-, two- and three-word utterances, often with complex meanings implied but not really encoded due to limited proficiency levels, as illustrated (again) in Extract (18).

> Extract (18) Simple syntax with complex meanings intended (all: Shashi)
> *Late*. ' Sorry I am late.'
> *Have*. 'I have a ticket.'
> *English class?* 'Where can I find the English class?'
> *House me coffee*. 'I will have coffee at home.'

Sentences tend to be paratactic, that is lacking subordination, especially in the early stages. Plain clausal sequences invite conditional, comparative or chronological-causal interpretations, as in Extract (19).

> Extract (19) Lack of subordination
> *You come to parlor, I shave your head.* 'If . . . then . . .' (Yu Son)
> *Italian food, lasun everywhere. French food, not everywhere.* 'While a, not b' (Laurent)
> *I think 'beautiful', I say 'beautiful.'* 'When . . . then . . .' (Laurent)

The examples in Extract (20) imply that there is also a limit to meaningful syntactic analysis – utterances like these could be described using grammatical terminology (some, for instance, also contain missing copulas) but not really interpreted in any generalising perspective. Some speakers simply show several types of reduced constructions, for example in word choices, missing or unorthodox syntactic constituents, or the use of incomplete or unusual sentences, for example:

> Extract (20) Reduced/incomplete constructions
> *I work like nanny.* (Eva)
> *I live on the Queens.* (Salman)
> *I Shashi from the India.* (Shashi)
> *I only say for remembering purpose.* (Rama)
> *Eh, ask question, me?* (Laurent)
> *Man cooking art. Lady cooking daily job, duty.* (Shashi)
> *French Italian not same?* (Shashi)
> *Train back, other side.* (Laurent)
> *But heart pain same same.* (Rama)

A fairly common and interesting construction is the omission of the copula, documented in Extract (21), with instances of lacking forms of *to be* marked by the zero symbol. This construction also offers the potential for a slightly

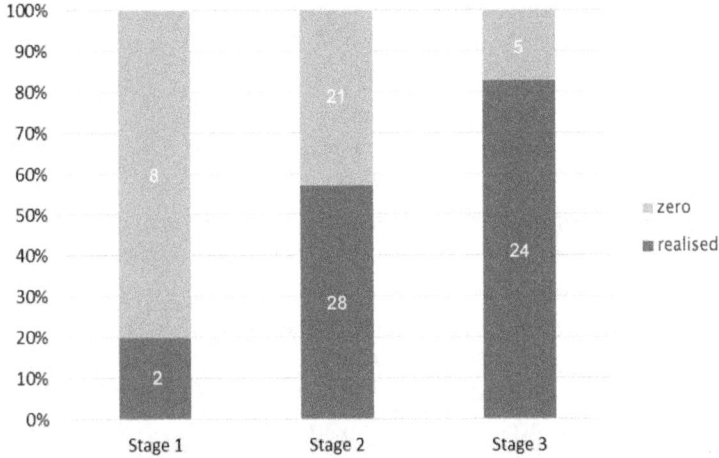

Figure 6.8 Copula usage by stages

more sophisticated analysis of the representation of learners' progress, since the sum total of realised plus zero copulas (easily counted in this small corpus) constitutes a perfect 'envelope of variation' in Labov's (1972) sense. Figure 6.8 shows that the learners' proficiency progress with respect to the acquisition of this feature is depicted quite convincingly: In the beginning, zero copulas predominate by far; in the transition phase the relationship is roughly balanced; and by phase 3 the learners have largely mastered the rules of copula usage in English sentences.

Extract (21) Copula omission
I Ø Shashi . . . . I Ø also cooking. I Ø first from Lahore. My English Ø not clean. You Ø artist. This Ø not your station? Sir David Ø very sad. Eva Ø my white sister. Shashi Ø beautiful, eh?

As the examples in Extract (22) show, copula omission co-occurs quite commonly with the deletion also of subjects, yielding constructions reminiscent of what Quirk et al. (1985: 996–7) call 'verbless clauses', with only bare subject complements realised.

Extract (22) Omission of subject and copula
Dirty. 'My English is . . .'. *Bad day.* 'It was a . . .'. *Spicy noodle.* 'She is a . . .'. *Expert.* 'You are an . . .'. *Correct, nah?* 'This was . . .?'. *Good to talk without understanding.* 'It is . . .' *No, not small, not small.*

Grammatical endings may also be omitted, as in Extract (23), for several word classes. In verbs, the third person singular *-s* suffix for concord is often missing

(23a), or past tense remains unmarked (23b). With nouns, the plural -s can be left out (23c).

> Extract (23) Lack of morphological inflection
> (a) *The baby speak Spanish. She say to me . . . . He say: . . . . But no Pakistani girl marry taxi driver.*
> (b) *You ask, eh, good question! First time I see you in the café . . . You order correct English. 'You ordered in . . .' Sir David and boyfriend break up!*
> (c) *Pakistani girl only marry foreigner.*

Articles and determiners are also repeatedly used differently from standard English habits. Articles can be overused, occurring in unexpected contexts (24a) or underused, missing when they are felt to be obligatory (24b). (24c) suggests a confusion of usage conditions for definite and indefinite articles. There is in fact explicit awareness of this being a problem domain; at one point, Shashi asks in class: '*Sorry. Why "India" not "the India", why "America" "the United States of America"?*'

> Extract (24) Article usage
> (a) *I Shashi from the India. . . . to learn the English.*
> (b) *You ask, eh, Ø good question! Can I ask for Ø telephone number? We will all go watch Ø English movie. You must open Ø restaurant . . . What is Ø good name?*
> (c) *I want to . . . become the better person.*

Finally, the last three example sets illustrate difficulties faced by the learners in the domains of pronoun usage, negation and interrogation.

> Extract (25) Negation with plain preverbal *no* or *not*
> *The baby no speak English. No fine film. Me not forget your face. French Italian not same?*

> Extract (26) Pronoun object form used in subject function
> *Me feel sorry. Me not forget your face. House me coffee.*

> Extract (27) Question formation without auxiliary inversion
> *You want eh water? What you say? I can come in? You bring me sweet laddoos? You want ticket? You okay? You make pasta-shasta?*

4.5 Grassroots English Replicated: Discussion

The question, then, is how to explain the origins and composition of these feature sets in the speech of the grassroots learners as imagined in the film. Comparative investigations show that there are many parallels between the features shown in section 4.4 and typical features observed in other language and usage types.

Quite a number of these features are also considered widespread in and to some extent characteristic of pidgin and creole languages (Holm 1988; Velupillai 2015); namely simple, paratactic syntax, zero copulas, the lack of inflectional endings, the plain preverbal negation with *no/not*, and the functional conflation of pronoun forms, disregarding case and gender distinctions.

World Englishes, notably Asian Englishes, share some of these features, too; the strongest parallel is the variable usage of articles, found widely across Asia. The same applies to many non-standard varieties, including World Englishes, where some non-standard features, so-called 'angloversal', are found widely – such as the use of interrogatives without auxiliary inversion, marked solely by intonation. Some of the learners' features are also strongly reminiscent of what is described for early phases of L1 acquisition (Tomasello 2003), especially the use of one-/two-word utterances, 'holophrases' ('one-word utterances which, however, do not simply refer to individual objects but can normally denote complex events and actions', Meisel 2011: 27) and so-called 'pivot schemas'.

Not surprisingly, many pertinent features are also often found in contexts of second language acquisition (SLA; cf. Saville-Troike 2006; Meisel 2011). The output of SLA settings is difficult to predict, since it is strongly dependent on highly variable parameters including L1 background, contact languages, saliency, or markedness, or individual factors such as learner motivation, learning context, and more. But some structural similarities between learner Englishes and L2 varieties have been worked out (Williams 1987; Mukherjee and Hundt 2011; Percillier 2016; Buschfeld 2020). Compared to the results of the present study, relevant findings in SLA include the lack of morphological endings (for plural or past; Percillier 2016: 68–74), the omission of articles, copulas or subjects (Percillier 2016: 89–95), using *the* with country names (Percillier 2016: 108) and the lack of inversion in interrogatives (Percillier 2016: 114–15).

In SLA research, some work has been conducted on the order of acquisition of specific features, especially morphemes (for example Meisel 2011: 63–70). There is a concept of a 'natural L2 Morpheme Acquisition Order' (Dulay and Burt 1974; cf. Saville-Troike 2006: 43–4; Meisel 2011: chapter 3), where features concerning article and copula usage, or plural, past and third singular *-s* marking rank highly (cf. Meisel 2011: 30). Again, there are some similarities with the observations made here, for example the increase of copula proficiency documented above. As to articles in L2 acquisition, 'determiners continue to be omitted in obligatory contexts for some time' (Meisel 2011: 30), and with respect to negation a shared impact is the fact that 'Neg is initially placed preverbally' (Meisel 2011: 81).

Hence, it can be stated quite broadly that the linguistic features observed in the speech of the grassroots learners in *English Vinglish* show strong parallels with linguistic structures considered typical of pidgins and creoles, World Englishes, non-standard dialects of English and SLA processes. In general, similarities are somewhat superficial – and exact comparisons of constraints or frequencies are hardly possible since the representation of speech in the movie is too limited for a more sophisticated analysis – but the basic causal relationship to these approaches seems well documented and convincing.

5 CONCLUSION

In sum, the replication of grassroots English in *English Vinglish* captures, thematises, develops and applies some essential insights into the usage contexts and structural properties portrayed in the movie, and transforms them artistically.

The first part of the movie, played out in India, and the CDA analysis reveal very clearly that in the culture portrayed there – upper-class Indians – knowledge of English is a prerequisite to gaining respect and happiness, and lack of it is perceived as a huge social problem. Conversely, as the plot implies, acquiring English helps to develop one's personality and self-confidence.

Structurally, grassroots English is characterised by simple, short utterances and some non-standard linguistic features but it gradually increases in complexity, utterance length and correctness – to a certain extent. Grassroots English is not at all linguistically isolated nor unique – it displays some parallels to features of pidgin/creole varieties, to World Englishes and non-standard dialects, and to early stages of L1 and L2 acquisition.

The piece of art investigated in this chapter is an entertaining film, not meant to be an accurate representation of complex realities – so we have to credit a certain light-hearted, perhaps playful component. I agree with Lee (2012: 130), who says that '[m]ovies are not exact replicas of reality . . . [but] often offer some version of reality that resonates with moviegoers'. Analysing this type of artistic product is thus interesting from a linguistic perspective since it shows that outside of linguistics laypeople have a fairly strong intuitive familiarity with attitudes towards and properties of grassroots English. The analysis testifies to the subtle intuitions of the moviemakers on the contexts and properties of language use in the societies portrayed. And it also illustrates the fact that the grassroots growth of English is a topic that has reached general observers' awareness and attention.

NOTES

1. I wish to thank Claudia Lange (Dresden University) for directing my attention to this wonderful film and for pointing me to the *India Today* article (IANS 2012).
2. Baugh and Cable (2002) extensively document how the spirit of early grammar writers was 'firmly grounded [in] reverence for classical literature' (p. 255). Grammarians in the age of prescriptivism believed that reputable use is 'authorised as good by the writings of a great number, if not the majority of celebrated authors' (p. 284, quoting George Campbell 1776), and correct usage is understood as forms 'used by good writers' (p. 285).
3. I dedicate this chapter to the memory of Sridevi (1963–2018), whose outstanding acting performance was decisive in the movie's heartwarming quality and success.
4. This plot summary as well as the later summaries of individual scenes (with characters' utterances transcribed in italics) are mine, highlighting aspects that I consider important for the overall line of argumentation.
5. Shashi's elaborate wedding speech at the end, exemplified in Extracts (10) and (16), is different, showcasing a higher level of proficiency than is implied here. Two possible reasons for this can be speculated on – a linguistic one (she is a dedicated learner, often shown practising phrases or repeating utterances which she hears) or an artistic one (this speech level is in line with the fairy tale-like conclusion of the movie).

REFERENCES

Austin, J. L. (1962), *How to Do Things with Words*, London: Clarendon.

Baugh, Albert C. and Thomas Cable (2002 [1951]), *A History of the English Language*, 5th edn, London: Routledge.

Blommaert, Jan (2010), *The Sociolinguistics of Globalization*, Cambridge: Cambridge University Press.

Brown, Roger (1973), *A First Language: The Early Stages*, London: George Allen and Unwin.

Buschfeld, Sarah (2013), *English in Cyprus or Cyprus English? An Empirical Investigation of Variety Status*, Amsterdam: Benjamins.

Buschfeld, Sarah (2020), *Children's English in Singapore: Acquisition, Properties, and Use*, Singapore and London: Routledge. (Original version 2018, Habilitationsschrift University of Regensburg.)

Dulay, Heidi and Marine Burt (1974), 'Natural sequences in child second language acquisition', *Language Learning*, 24, 37–54.

Fairclough, Norman (2010), *Critical Discourse Analysis. The Critical Study of Language*, 2nd edn, London: Longman.

Grosjean, Francois (2008), *Studying Bilinguals*, Oxford: Oxford University Press.

Han, Huamei (2013), 'Individual grassroots multilingualism in Africa Town in Guangzhou: the role of states in globalization', *International Multilingual Research Journal*, 7, 83–97.

Holm, John (1988), *Pidgins and Creoles*. Vol. I: *Theory and Structure*, Cambridge: Cambridge University Press.

Honeybone, Patrick and Kevin Watson (2013), 'Salience and the sociolinguistics of Scouse spelling: exploring the phonology of the Contemporary Humorous Localised Dialect Literature of Liverpool', *English World-Wide*, 34, 305–40.

IANS (2012), 'English Vinglish encourages Dalit girls in Bihar', *India Today*, 19 October, <http://indiatoday.intoday.in/story/english-vinglish-encourages-dalit-girls-in-bihar/1/225426.html> (last accessed 9 January 2020).

Ives, Sumner (1971), 'A theory of literary dialect', in Juanita Williamson and Virginia Burke (eds), *A Various Language*, New York: Holt, Rinehart and Winston, 145–77.

Kachru, Braj B. (1983), *The Indianization of English: The English Language in India*, Delhi: Oxford University Press.

Kendon, Adam (1990), *Conducting Interaction. Patterns of Behavior in Focused Encounters*, Cambridge: Cambridge University Press.

Kendon, Adam (2004), *Gesture. Visible Action as Utterance*, Cambridge: Cambridge University Press.

Labov, William (1972), *Sociolinguistic Patterns*, Oxford: Blackwell.

Lakoff, George and Mark Johnson (1980), *Metaphors We Live By*, Chicago and London: University of Chicago Press.

Lange, Claudia (2020), 'English in South Asia', in Daniel Schreier, Marianne Hundt and Edgar W. Schneider (eds), *The Cambridge Handbook of World Englishes*, Cambridge: Cambridge University Press, 236–62.

Lee, Jamie Shinhee (2012), '*Please teach me English*: English and metalinguistic discourse in Korean film', in Jamie Shinhee Lee and Andrew Moody (eds), *English in Asian Popular Culture*, Hong Kong: Hong Kong University Press, 127–50.

Lippi-Green, Rosina (2012), *English with an Accent. Language, Ideology and Discrimination in the United States*, London and New York: Routledge.

Meierkord, Christiane (2012), *Interactions across Englishes. Linguistic Choices in Local and International Contact Situations*, Cambridge: Cambridge University Press.

Meierkord, Christiane (2020), 'The global growth of English at the grassroots', in Daniel Schreier, Marianne Hundt and Edgar W. Schneider (eds), *The*

Cambridge Handbook of World Englishes, Cambridge: Cambridge University Press, 311–38.

Meisel, Jürgen M. (2011), *First and Second Language Acquisition. Parallels and Differences*, Cambridge: Cambridge University Press.

Moody, Andrew (2020), 'World Englishes in the media', in Daniel Schreier, Marianne Hundt and Edgar W. Schneider (eds), *The Cambridge Handbook of World Englishes*, Cambridge: Cambridge University Press, 652–75.

Mukherjee, Joybrato and Marianne Hundt (eds) (2011), *Exploring Second-Language Varieties of English and Learner Englishes. Bridging a Paradigm Gap*, Amsterdam: John Benjamins.

Norris, Sigrid (ed.) (2012), *Multimodality in Practice. Investigating Theory-in-Practice-through-Methodology*, New York: Routledge.

Percillier, Michael (2016), *World Englishes and Second Language Acquisition. Insights from Southeast Asian Englishes*, Amsterdam: John Benjamins.

Quirk, Randolph, Sidney Greenbaum, Geoffrey Leech and Jan Svartvik (1985), *A Comprehensive Grammar of the English Language*, London and New York: Longman.

Saville-Troike, Muriel (2006), *Introducing Second Language Acquisition*, Cambridge: Cambridge University Press.

Schneider, Edgar W. (1986), ' "How to Speak Southern" – an American English dialect stereotyped', *Amerikastudien/American Studies*, 31, 425–39.

Schneider, Edgar W. (2007), *Postcolonial English. Varieties Around the World*, Cambridge: Cambridge University Press.

Schneider, Edgar W. (2016a), 'Grassroots Englishes in tourism interactions', *English Today*, 32: 3, 2–10.

Schneider, Edgar W. (2016b), 'World Englishes on YouTube: treasure trove or nightmare?', in Elena Seoane and Cristina Suárez-Gómez (eds), *World Englishes: New Theoretical and Methodological Considerations*, Amsterdam: John Benjamins, 253–81.

Schneider, Edgar W. and Christian Wagner (2006), 'The variability of literary dialect as a reflection of pan-lectal competence: Jamaican Creole in Thelwell's *The Harder They Come*', *Journal of Pidgin and Creole Languages*, 21, 45–95.

Seaford, Henry W. Jr. (1975), 'Facial expression dialect: an example', in Adam Kendon, Richard M. Harris and Mary Ritchie Key (eds), *Organization of Behavior in Face-to-Face Interaction*, The Hague and Paris: Mouton, 151–5.

Tomasello, Michael (2003), *Constructing a Language. A Usage-Based Theory of Language Acquisition*, Cambridge, MA and London: Harvard University Press.

Velupillai, Viveka (2015), *Pidgins, Creoles and Mixed Languages: An Introduction*, Amsterdam: Benjamins.

Vigliocco, Gabriella, Pamela Perniss, Robin L. Thompson and David Vinson (eds) (2014), 'Language as a multimodal phenomenon: implications for language learning, processing and evolution', Theme Issue of *Philosophical Transactions of the Royal Society B*, vol. 369, issue 1651.

Wikipedia (2019), 'English Vinglish', <https://en.wikipedia.org/wiki/English_Vinglish> (last accessed 9 January 2020).

Williams, Jessica (1987), 'Non-native varieties of English: a special case of language acquisition', *English World-Wide*, 8, 161–99.

Wodak, Ruth and Michael Meyer (eds) (2016), *Methods of Critical Discourse Studies*, 3rd edn, London and Thousand Oaks, CA: Sage.

Part II:
English in trade and work migration

CHAPTER 7

Facets of Intercultural Communication Employed in the Conversations of Local Arab Traders in Bahrain

Anthonia Bamidele-Akhidenor

1 INTRODUCTION

English can be used in different new contexts including as a lingua franca (Kachru 1986), as in the case of Bahrain, where Arabic is the official and national language while English is the language for business. This chapter specifically looks at the communication behaviour of Bahraini traders in the souq as 'grassroots English'. Meierkord (2012: 148–9) talks about English at the grassroots, which refers (among other settings) to 'interactions in English between immigrant workers with L2 English background who reside in countries where English is not the majority language'. In other words, her focus was on lower-class speakers of English who engage in small interactions that can be personal or intimate relationships among locals and immigrants 'in the streets'. Furthermore, Schneider (2016) defines grassroots English as the English used by speakers with limited access to formal education and, consequently, rather low proficiency levels. Grassroots English generally implies the interactive way of speaking English by people who are second-language users and have had little or no formal education in the language.

In the present case, the focus is on Bahraini traders, that is locals of the Kingdom of Bahrain who have their own businesses in the traditional market, also known as souq in the Arabic language. The focus of the study is on the interactions between Bahraini traders and other nationals in Bahrain, as employees or potential buyers. The speakers in this context include native speakers (NS) and non-native speakers (NNS) of English who use the English language as a lingua franca to achieve desired business communication results. In line with the fact that World Englishes have spread beyond contexts associated with formal education, this chapter examines how English is used at the grassroots specifically by those Bahraini traders who may not have learnt English through formal education or training but rather informally, typically in most instances from their customers.

The chapter examines two research questions: What communication strategies do local Arab traders employ in their conversations with other non-Arabic speakers and how do they achieve desired business communication goals with other non-Arabic speakers? In order to answer these questions, the chapter draws on the frameworks of intercultural communication (Smith 1983; Meierkord 2000), accommodation strategy (Gallois et al. 2005; Cogo 2009), and negotiation/bargaining strategy (Firth 1995; Ismail et al. 2009).

The study uses mixed methods for data collection: questionnaires to elicit respondents' backgrounds, and recorded informal conversations between local Arab traders and non-Arabic customers and employees. Data were collected at the Manama Souq (market) in the capital city of Bahrain. The data analyses show evidence of accommodation strategies: on the one hand, uses of repetition among NNS to signal their limitation in English through constantly striving for clarity by repeating previous statements; on the other hand, 'imitation', by the Bahraini traders, of the speech patterns of those Western native-speaker customers who rarely adapt their language or speech patterns to suit their Bahraini interlocutors. In addition, the data document strategies of negotiation and bargaining and of the power of persuasion among non-Arabic customers to the point of shaking hands after securing the best possible deals.

Thus, the findings without doubt reveal that Bahraini traders are obligated to communicate in English, as they are aware of their customers' and employees' limitations in speaking Arabic. Also, they have become conversant with some English words through their daily business interactions with customers and employees. The use of English helps Bahraini traders build rapport and establish cordiality with their customers. It is worth noting that NNS cooperate with one another in these conversations. They are aware of their positions as users of English from different cultural backgrounds, communicative norms and behaviours, and they are sensitive to one another's need for affirmation. The results show that the use of English in the business world (in whatever form it is used) makes it a language of interaction even at the grassroots (cf. Kankaanranta and Louhiala-Salminen 2010).

2 ENGLISH IN BAHRAIN

The Kingdom of Bahrain is a part of the GCC (Gulf Cooperation Council) states including Saudi Arabia, Oman, Kuwait, Qatar and the United Arab Emirates. Bahrain is a small island country that nests in the heart of the Arabian Gulf with an estimated population of 1.316 million people in 2014. Most of the foreigners who either come to the country are migrant workers or expatriates. In Bahrain there are mainly nationals from India, Pakistan, Bangladesh, the Philippines,

Africa and other countries (Ministry of Information Affairs 2014; Bamidele-Akhidenor 2019).

It is worth noting that English is Bahrain's second official language, while Arabic is the national and official language, in which most people, especially citizens (Bahrainis) and other Arab nationals, are competent. Bamidele-Akhidenor (2019) observes that due to the high status of English in business, industry, the medical profession and some university colleges, Bahrain considers English a high-status language. In addition, the increase of foreign work migrants from various countries has made many Bahrainis use English as a means of communication with non-Arabic speakers. For instance in Dubai (a state in the United Arab Emirates), one of the most populous and common tourist destinations in the Gulf region, there seems to be a strong dependence on English as its lingua franca rather than the traditional use of Arabic because of the increase in numbers of particularly Southeast Asians and Filipinos. These foreign expatriates work in retail businesses, the construction industry and medical services (Randall and Samimi 2010; Meierkord 2012).

The significance of this study comes from the fact that there is a paucity of research on intercultural communication patterns involving Bahraini traders and other nationals in Bahrain (as well as, in general, trading interactions in souqs in Arabic-speaking countries). Based on the findings, this chapter argues that by deploying specific accommodation, negotiation and bargaining strategies, Bahraini traders improve their knowledge of the English language through their interactions with other nationals that they encounter in the business world either as their employees or as customers. Thus, the study of the Bahraini trading community at the grassroots level in Bahrain seeks to shed new light on intercultural business communication either between NNS of English or between NNS and NS of English.

3 THEORETICAL FRAMEWORKS

3.1 English as a Business Lingua Franca in Bahrain

Ehrenreich (2010: 408–31) asserts that Business English as a Lingua Franca (BELF), which has become a major field of study in recent years, can be defined as 'a language that is nobody's own, but a language that is shared and used in the business discourse community'. However, in this study, the context is on uneducated local traders at the grassroots level, not the professionals and business meetings context.

As Gerritsen and Nickerson (2009: 181) assert, in the past two decades 'English has played an increasingly dominant role in business transactions in general around the globe'. Communicating in English in whatever form appears to be the most viable option which the Bahraini traders have in Bahrain, given the fact that they do not speak Arabic to their customers who are foreign employees and tourists who may not have had the opportunity to learn Arabic prior to their arrival or during their stay in the country. Thus, English serves as a bridge between Arabic speakers and speakers of other languages with whom they do business.

Hence, in line with Roshid et al. (2018)'s paper on communications with non-native English speaking business personnel in Bangladesh, who interact with both NS and NNS, this chapter focuses on grassroots English as used in the marketplace in Bahrain, but involves speakers without formal education, considering the fact that the speakers in this study include both NS and NNS as they interrelate in the business world.

3.2 Intercultural Communication Theory

In the field of intercultural communication, English is used as a means of interaction by people from different countries and cultures in order to communicate with one another (Smith 1983). Bin and Fu-Quan (2007: 77) define intercultural communication as 'communication between people whose cultural perceptions and symbol systems are different enough to alter the communication event'. In other words, when people from different sociolinguistic and cultural backgrounds come together for various purposes (like for business, education and political purposes) such an encounter can be considered an instance of intercultural communication.

Also, intercultural communication, as a process, may involve establishing relationships and understanding between speakers from different cultures and communities who live in the same country. Since the participants in intercultural communication come from different cultural backgrounds, they do not share the same ground rules in interaction. This could result in different interpretations of verbal and non-verbal behaviour, since behavioural conventions are culture specific. It is for this reason that conflict and misunderstandings may ensue, resulting in negative emotions such as anger, frustration or resentment. Therefore, in order for intercultural communication to be effective, participants need to adapt and adjust to one another's culture (Matsumoto et al. 2005: 16). Meierkord (2000) notes that most researchers have focused on intercultural communication between NS and NNS of a language, but have paid little attention to intercultural communication between people who do not have a common language and so have to use a third language as their lingua franca. She asserts that due to the inability of speakers from different cultures to understand one another's first language, they employ imperfect knowledge of the language, that is, English, which they have to use for communication.

Consequently, such speakers rely on what seems a unique set of rules for interaction which is called inter-culture. Meierkord (2000: unpaginated) defines inter-culture as 'a lingua franca culture, which is reflected in specific linguistic characteristics'. That is, participants' choice of words in interaction is determined by the lexical items that are at their disposal. She argues that, in effect, most NNS cooperate with one another in conversations, as they are aware of their positions as learners of English from different cultural backgrounds, communication norms and behaviours. Her analysis of English conversations among NNS is quite relevant to this present study. Meierkord's analysis may also be useful in examining how participants in the study cooperate with one another. However, recent studies have shown keen interest of researchers in the area of intercultural communications within different contexts. These have been studied by several researchers including Jamarani and Sharifian (2013) and Seidlhofer (2005).

3.3 Communication Accommodation Theory

Communication accommodation theory is concerned with the fact that oral communicators adjust their speech styles to meet the needs of the person with whom they are communicating (Street and Giles 1982). According to Gallois et al. (2005:127; and Gallois and Giles 1998: 122), communication accommodation theory 'highlights both intergroup and interpersonal features, recognises the dual importance of both factors in predicting and understanding intergroup interactions ... and recognises the importance of power and macro contextual factors'. This theory has been expanded to incorporate other factors such as the social consequences of the interaction, the intergroup variables and processes within a group, the communication components in everyday settings and language shifts among group members (Giles et al. 1991). As a result, accommodation theory has the potential for a wide range of applications. It is effective and applicable to an understanding of intercultural communication patterns, especially with interactants from different linguistic backgrounds. It builds on two major strategies, namely convergence and divergence.

Gallois and Giles (1998: 123) state that 'convergence is defined as a strategy through which individuals adapt their communicative behavior in such a way as to become more similar to their interlocutor's behavior'. In other words, the convergence strategy in accommodation relates to the way speakers use each other's language to signal acceptance and depict closeness and familiarity. Converging language use can take a range of different forms: repetition, i.e. a speaker repeats the first speaker's words; cooperative turn distributions; the use of similar accent, pronunciations and dialect features; and adjusting one's speech rate.

Gallois and Giles (1998: 123) further state that the strategy of divergence 'leads to an accentuation of differences between self and other. A strategy similar to divergence is maintenance, in which a person persists in his or her original style, regardless of the communication behavior of the interlocutor.' Speakers who aim at divergence usually adjust (or accommodate) their speech styles so as to signal and uphold distinct personal and social identities. Hence, the divergence accommodation strategy highlights differences in speech or in the choice of words between speakers to depict social distance and power relations, and to symbolise exclusion.

In his study, Wilson (2018) focuses on accommodation processes in face-to-face exchanges between speakers in a situation of international tourism. He highlights the importance of English as a linguistic resource through the processes of converging in English as the main language of interaction. Also, his paper explores how speakers accommodate to one another through the use of English. Investigating tourism in France in his study, his attention was on processes of accommodation in the formation of group identities and the development of intergroup relationships. He further looks at code-switching from French to English as well as at the transition from divergent to convergent behaviour in a conversation between a tourist and a tourism officer.

In line with this, the present study builds upon the use of English due to its international and global roles, and it looks into features of divergence and convergence that are prevalent among speakers. However, there was no evidence of code-switching in my data, which in this case would have been between English and Arabic. Interlocutors are aware of the prevailing language disparity by recognising the fact that it is mainly English that is used in the business context in Bahrain in order to avoid communication barriers.

3.4 Negotiation and Bargaining

Negotiating prices and bargaining are essential components of souq culture and hence the kinds of interactions studies here. The principles of negotiation and bargaining are vital in conversations between participants in different business settings. Negotiation is defined by Ismail et al. (2009: 130) 'as the process which involves the meeting of two parties with common or conflicting interests, who try to reach agreement on matters of mutual interest'. Small et al. (2007: 600) state that early studies of negotiation focused on the psychological and social processes related to negotiation strategies and possible effects used by negotiators to make offers and counter-offers. Firth (1995: 3) defines negotiation in relation to business as 'a discourse-based and situated activity which is interactionally constructed in concrete settings'. In other words, Firth's account of negotiation relates to interactions and actions performed by interactants in a business setting or location.

Ismail et al. (2009) explore the linguistic and non-linguistic features which are deployed in business negotiations and which may hinder or promote intercultural communication between Malaysians and Australians. Ismail et al.'s (2009) findings reveal that miscommunication in business negotiations between people from different cultures can be a result of a number of variables: when a negotiator uses his or her own sociolinguistic structure to interpret or convey messages in other languages (especially English); when a negotiator is unable to infer situational cues; and when negotiators are unable to opt for the right speech act to convey their intended action.

The present study seeks to benefit from Ismail et al.'s (2009) analyses and findings on how negotiators from different countries negotiate. In this context the business interaction is mainly between buyers and sellers with the Bahraini traders (as the sellers), and people of other nationalities (as buyers). Using communication events between these two groups as data, the study should unravel the dynamics of power play and persuasion in such business interactions.

Based on the content of the previous passages, this study seeks to answer the following:

1. What intercultural communication strategies do Arabs traders employ in their conversations with other non-Arabic speakers?
2. How do the Bahraini traders achieve desired business communication goals with other non-Arabic speakers?

4 METHODOLOGY AND DATA

4.1 Method of Data Collection

The study used a convenience sampling procedure based on speakers who were available to participate in the study. It used a mixed method for data analysis involving quantitative and qualitative approaches. Qualitatively, the researcher did not use any structured interview but rather acted as a participant observer.

4.2 The Informants

The sample population for the study is the Bahraini traders operating retail shops in Manama Souq, which literally means 'market' in English, in the Kingdom of Bahrain. Although there were other nationalities such as Indians and Bangladeshis with retail shops, they were exempted as the focus was on Bahraini traders. The area itself was used for the study because it attracts a lot of tourists from various countries, mostly Western countries such as the United States of America, the United Kingdom and Europe, who are visiting Bahrain and would like to buy some souvenirs to bring back to their respective countries.

Also, the souq is centrally located as a business area with lots of retail shops selling goods ranging from artefacts, jewellery, fabric tailoring, clothing and various souvenirs. During the data collection period, most of the local Bahraini traders were focused on selling artefacts, handmade crafts and tailoring fabric materials. The buyers present at the time of the recordings were mostly North Americans and also one European from Greece. The topics of conversations focused on the features of specific goods, as the Bahraini traders provided more details on the products that they sell, and on how their potential buyers negotiate prices with them.

Quantitatively, the completed data comprised fifteen survey questionnaires that were filled out by Bahraini traders. However, not all of those who participated in the questionnaires took part in the recordings, as some of them declined to have their voices recorded. The recordings consist of six different conversations in the Manama Souq which involved the traders, customers and employees. The overall set of recordings comprises about two hours. The questionnaires were used to generate information on the demographic profile on the participants such as their genders and age groups, and on how they acquired their knowledge of English. Results will be presented below.

4.3 Transcription

In the present study, the conversations were transcribed orthographically, and the analysis will present some excerpts. Ethical consent was requested from all respondents to receive their approval that their voices would be digitally recorded during their conversations with their employees or customers, and they were duly informed that the recording was for academic research purposes only.

5 ANALYSES OF QUESTIONNAIRE DATA AND RECORDINGS

5.1 Questionnaires

Figures 7.1 to 7.5 summarise the main parameters of the social composition of the survey group.

The data in Figures 7.1 and 7.2 indicate that the majority of the respondents are male and more than fifty years old, which is probably common in the souq. It is noticeable that most local businesses are owned and managed by men, which is culturally and religiously acceptable here. It is also noteworthy that the single female respondent at the time of data collection was there to cover for her father who was occupied elsewhere.

Figures 7.3 and 7.4 indicate that almost all the traders had secondary school certificates, which they mostly finished a very long time ago. However, these secondary qualifications are in Arabic and not in English, as Arabic is the medium

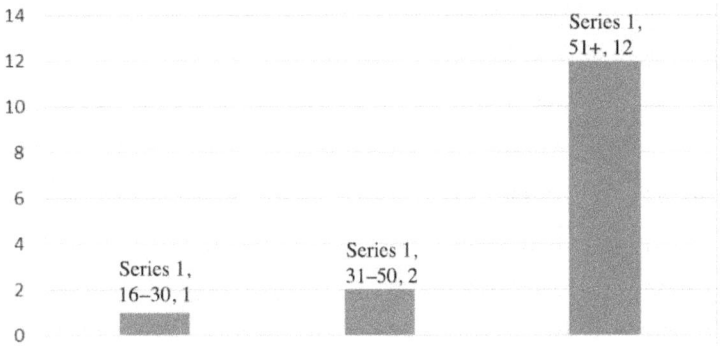

Figure 7.1 Age range

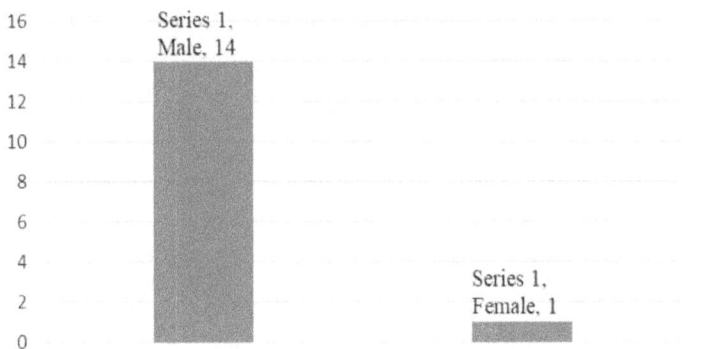

Figure 7.2 Gender

of instruction in government schools. Thus, they rate their proficiency level of English as bad and not 'good enough' to be used for conversations.

The data in Figure 7.5 confirm the presence of grassroots English. The Bahraini traders largely acquire English through their daily interactions with their customers and staff, as they are forced to speak English irrespective of their level of linguistic competence. Due to the nature of their businesses and being fully aware that their buyers are tourists and visitors, they are familiar with the terms that are related to, basically, the products or services that they offer. In addition, their significant efforts to remember basic conversation patterns, terms and prices, and their desire to carry out brief interactions with their customers, are worth noting.

5.2 Analysis of the Recorded Interactions

This section provides answers to the research questions by representing and commenting on conversations that were recorded. For ease of reference,

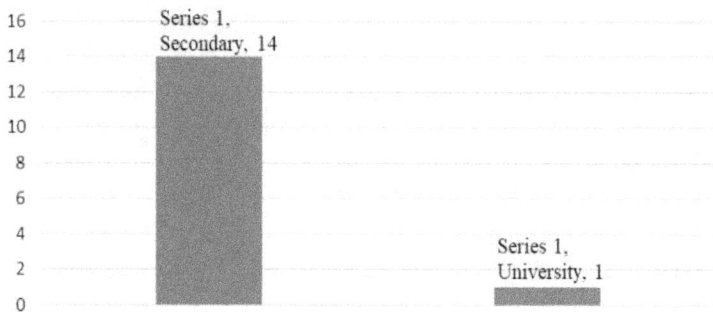

Figure 7.3 Highest educational qualification

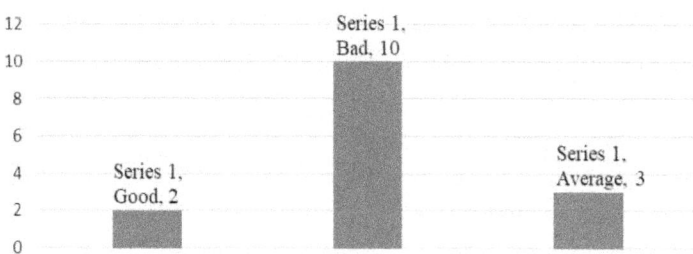

Figure 7.4 Proficiency in speaking English

the following terms are used to identify participants in the recorded conversations:

Bahraini Trader – the local trader
Foreign Employee – employee from another country
Tourist Customer – potential buyer

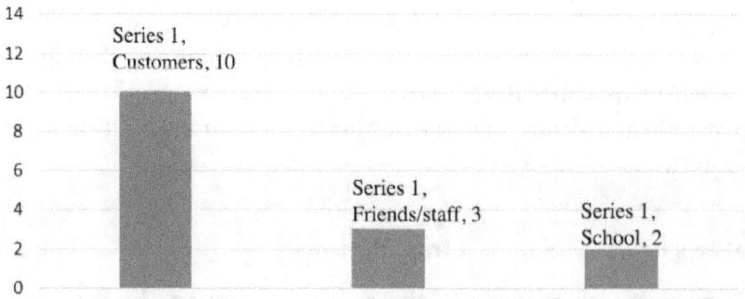

Figure 7.5 Mode of acquiring English

Tourist Friend – someone who accompanies the Tourist Customer
BD – Bahraini dinar
(Comments in Brackets) – Observations from the researcher's field notes

The data exhibit major strategies of accommodation such as convergence and divergence. They also examine negotiation and bargaining, which is relevant to this kind of informal business context. In the following sections, findings representing the major accommodation strategies of convergence and divergence alongside negotiation and bargaining are presented and discussed.

5.2.1 Convergence

The data presented in Extract (1) and (2) show examples of prevalent instances of the repetitions in the interactions between the Bahraini Trader and his female Filipina Employee on the one hand, and between the Bahraini Trader and his Tourist Customer on the other hand.

Extract (1)
1. Bahraini Trader: How are you?
2. Foreign Employee: Fine, thank you.
3. Bahraini Trader: Fine?
4. Foreign Employee: Yeah. This one okay, I will send only the documents by email?
5. Bahraini Trader: Yeah, only this documents use.
6. Foreign Employee: Only this one?
7. Bahraini Trader: Yeah.
8. Foreign Employee: Nothing else eh?
9. Bahraini Trader: Nothing else.
10. Foreign Employee: Okay.
11. Bahraini Trader: Okay.

Extract (2)
1. Tourist Customer: (Looks at some hand wrist bands)[1] Hi, can you tell me how much?
2. Bahraini Trader: One dinar each.
3. Tourist Customer: One dinar? Right. Can you. And this? (looks at another one)
4. Bahraini Trader: One dinar also.
5. Tourist Customer: One dinar? (surprise)
6. Tourist Friend: And something better from beads?
7. Bahraini Trader: This one nice.
8. Tourist Customer: (looks at other items) And how much they cost?

9. Bahraini Trader: This one also three BD,[2] four BD
10. Tourist Customer: This?
11. Bahraini Trader: Three BD.
12. Tourist Customer: Three BD? Have you got a bigger in size?
13. Bahraini Trader: Bigger, no. Bigger also this one.
14. Tourist Customer: Oh this one. Okay, we will have this. (Looks at other items) one (counts the price of the items)
15. Bahraini Trader: One.
16. Tourist Customer: Two. One, two, three (calculates the amount she has to pay)
17. Bahraini Trader: There's no.
18. Tourist Customer: No change? No?
19. Bahraini Trader: Let me check one minute.
20. Tourist Customer: Okay. One, two, three.
21. Bahraini Trader: Three dinar.
22. Tourist Customer: Thank you very much. Okay bye.
23. Bahraini Trader: Okay.

In Extract (1), the Bahraini Trader greets his employee, who is busy at the computer desk. Repetition as a strategy becomes obvious then when the Bahraini Trader repeats the statements made by the Foreign Employee affirmatively as shown in turns 3, 5, 9 and 11. This documents that, in their interactions, Bahraini traders and their employees use reiteration or repetition to ensure clarity and consequently minimise miscommunication and make simple clarifications. However, in Extract (2), the female Tourist Customer from Europe (Greece), keeps repeating the Bahraini Trader's words, especially the prices of the handmade beads she wants to buy, for affirmation and clarity in order to avoid misunderstandings as shown in turns 3, 5, 12 and 18. The repetition of the price in the local Bahraini currency shows that some tourist customers have familiarised themselves with 'Bahraini dinars' during their time in the country. Thus, employing the accommodation strategy of convergence, NNS display awareness of their limitations in English and develop means of overcoming it, due to the need for clarity in employer–employee relationships and seller–buyer relationships. This finding supports Gallois et al.'s (2005: 123) claim that convergence is a 'strategy through which individuals adapt their communicative behavior in such a way as to become more similar to their interlocutor's behavior'.

5.2.2 Divergence

In Extract (3), the Tourist Customer is an American woman, who is interested in buying a dressing table, which, according to the Bahraini Trader, is an artefact worth the desire to make the purchase.

> Extract (3)
> 1. Tourist Customer: So, we're your customers . . . (talks with her friend) one . . . (calls her friend's name), mine's over here, I could give up some of the big ones.
> 2. Bahraini Trader: oh, no.. I have. . . .
> 3. Tourist Customer: (interrupts) . . . I have so many antique stuffs.
> 4. Bahraini Trader: Our changes have, don't worry about it, take it easy.
> 5. Tourist Customer: Okay, we're good, we're good.
> 6. Bahraini Trader: See, you take all things. . . .
> 7. Tourist Customer: I do, I do! I'm taking,.. You need to speak up . . . It's all good.
> 8. Bahraini Trader: No, no, no. I'll bring, I'll bring. Maybe I have some in the storage room.
> 9. Tourist Customer: Okay, okay.
> 10. Bahraini Trader: I'll bring some. I have different colours. Maybe nicer than you.

In the second conversation below (Extract (4), the Tourist Customer is a young American woman. She enters the shop with a friend who accompanies her to purchase a crafted computer mouse pad. Looking around and conversing quietly with each other on the type of designs they prefer they finally select a particular design that appeals to them.

> Extract (4)
> 1. Tourist Customer: (selects some items with her friend) Okay, I like this one. I saw it the last time. It's like a display.
> 2. Bahraini Trader: Yeah.
> 3. Tourist Customer: Okay, these ones. This is nice. Okay, how much?
> 4. Bahraini Trader: Five BD.
> 5. Tourist Customer: Okay. This also five BD?
> 6. Bahraini Trader: Same, same all, you guys choose from there or there no problem. This selling price also nine dinar, eight dinar but you are like a customer.
> 7. Tourist Customer: (laughing) Thank you. Okay, okay, five BD.
> 8. Bahraini Trader: Two pieces?
> 9. Tourist Customer: Yeah. So for ten BD?

10. Bahraini Trader: Ten BD.
11. Tourist Customer: Thank you (leaves smiling)

As shown in the data presented, there is no adjustment in their conversations but there is actually some distancing, as this is strictly a buyer-to-seller business conversation. This also affirms that in their interactions, Bahraini traders and most tourist customers do not converge or change their language/speech patterns to adjust to NNS of English. In this case the Bahraini Trader tries to play along and to show his understanding of the English language to make the customers feel comfortable. Similar to what has been discussed with reference to Extract (2), Extract (4) indicates that the female American tourist had familiarised herself with the local currency and was able to use exchanged currency for her purchase.

5.2.3 *The process of negotiation*

The process of negotiation involves demanding information, naming a price, requesting discounts, making counter-offers, reinforcing the appeal for discounts, building a consensus and closing remarks. Each component of this process is illustrated in the two extracts below. However, not all the individual components are present in both extracts, depending on the decisions of the customer.

In Extract (5) below, the Bahraini Trader tries to persuade his American female customer to buy his product, which in turn reveals the interest of the Tourist Customer as she decides to negotiate the price of the item.

Extract (5)
1. Tourist Customer: Nicer? Yeah. Of course. He's gonna bring me all the nice ones (tells her friend). I'm taking the one he couldn't push. This is a nice piece.
2. Bahraini Trader: That is, don't lose it. If you want it, go ahead for it. It's like a magnificent piece, is. Piece of art.
3. Tourist Customer: Hmm.
4. Bahraini Trader: I'll take more than I ask.
5. Tourist Customer: You'll take more? (both laugh)
6. Bahraini Trader: Alright, do it. Ha . . . how much we say?
7. Tourist Customer: It was One-ninety dollars you asked so, One eighty-five dollars? One-eighty dollars?
8. Bahraini Trader: One hundred and eighty-five dollars. Go ahead . . . One hundred and eighty.
9. Tourist Customer: Done.
10. Bahraini Trader: Sold. (shake hands to seal the deal)

In the conversation below, Extract (6) highlights a more detailed interaction that is filled with a lot of clarifications between the interactants. It focuses on the conversation between the Bahraini Trader, a Tourist Customer and his friend (who had previously bought an item from the shop) as the customer tries to decide on which carpet design he would eventually buy.

Extract (6)
1. Tourist Friend: The Persian carpets ... er different sides and the colour changes ... yeah.
2. Bahraini Trader: Yeah, it depends on the side.
3. Tourist Friend: Yes, the sides. It's a very, very nice carpet.
4. Tourist Customer: Okay, This is eh wool or ...?
5. Bahraini Trader: Wool and silk.
6. Tourist Customer: Wool and silk.
7. Bahraini Trader: This is the best quality for wool and silk. This is more silk one. That's the best quality of silk and then you have wool.
8. Tourist Customer: What's more durable? If you Google it, what lasts longer?
9. Bahraini Trader: Wool and silk for the most people they use. They have all of them like that, same thing like different colours, different design. This is a more comfortable, you know easy to clean, take care of them, wash, water and soap, like that this one no problem.
10. Tourist Friend: Hmm (nods in affirmation), they have several hand-made carpets as well.
11. Tourist Customer: Okay (looks around at some carpets), this (points to a particular design) how much is a typical one?
12. Tourist Friend: They have different styles, I should remember the name of the style.
13. Tourist Customer: That's more natural but they have more pictures in it and you have to do special cleanings.
14. Tourist Friend: Yeah. They have different types, they have even bigger carpets.
15. Tourist Customer: But this size, how much is it? (points to others on display)
16. Bahraini Trader: Like One hundred and fifty dollars, one hundred and eighty dollars depend on the quality.
17. Tourist Customer: But this one? This one is hmm a mixture of wool and silk?
18. Bahraini Trader: Wool and silk, yes.
19. Tourist Customer: This, this particular one (points to the one displayed in front of him)?

20. Bahraini Trader: Selling price like eh two hundred dollars, two hundred and fifty dollars you know eh (smiling) we have love for customers.
21. Tourist Customer: (laughing) Eh so is it in metres or what is it?
22. Bahraini Trader: Two metres by three metres.
23. Tourist Customer: Two, three by three?
24. Bahraini Trader: Two metres by three metres.
25. Tourist Customer: Okay (after a long pause). Yes, thanks.
26. Bahraini Trader: You're welcome.
27. Tourist Customer: We will discuss.
28. Bahraini Trader: No problem.
29. Tourist Customer: And then we will stay a little longer in Bahrain.
30. Bahraini Trader: Anytime.
31. Tourist Customer: And we will come back, yep.
32. Bahraini Trader: Anytime, anytime.

Demanding information
Extract (5), turns 1–5:
1. Tourist Customer: Nicer? Yeah. Of course. He's gonna bring me all the nice ones (tells her friend). I'm taking the one he couldn't push. This is a nice piece.
2. Bahraini Trader: That is, don't lose it. If you want it, go ahead for it. It's like a magnificent piece, is. Piece of art.
3. Tourist Customer: Hmm.
4. Bahraini Trader: I'll take more than I ask.
5. Tourist Customer: You'll take more? (both laugh)

Extract (6), turns 1–14:
1. Tourist Friend: The Persian carpets . . . er different sides and the colour changes . . . yeah.
2. Bahraini Trader: Yeah, it depends on the side.
3. Tourist Friend: Yes, the sides. It's a very, very nice carpet.
4. Tourist Customer: Okay, This is eh wool or . . .?
5. Bahraini Trader: Wool and silk.
6. Tourist Customer: Wool and silk.
7. Bahraini Trader: This is the best quality for wool and silk. This is more silk one. That's the best quality of silk and then you have wool.
8. Tourist Customer: What's more durable? If you Google it, what lasts longer?
9. Bahraini Trader: Wool and silk for the most people they use. They have all of them like that, same thing like different colours, different design. This is a more comfortable, you know easy to clean, take care of them, wash, water and soap, like that this one no problem.

10. Tourist Friend: Hmm (nods in affirmation), they have several hand-made carpets as well.
11. Tourist Customer: Okay (looks around at some carpets), this (points to a particular design) how much is a typical one?
12. Tourist Friend: They have different styles, I should remember the name of the style.
13. Tourist Customer: That's more natural but they have more pictures in it and you have to do special cleanings.
14. Tourist Friend: Yeah. They have different types, they have even bigger carpets.

These passages indicate that customers sometimes examine products or services in order to determine whether or not they are really interested in buying them. This apparent reversal of roles is understandable when they engage in a conversation. In addition, they accommodate to one another by seeking clarification.

Price tag
Extract (5), turn 7:
7. Tourist Customer: It was One-ninety dollars you asked so, One eighty-five dollars? One-eighty dollars?

Extract (6), turns 16 and 20:
16. Bahraini Trader: Like One hundred and fifty dollars, one hundred and eighty dollars depend on the quality.
20. Bahraini Trader: Selling price like eh two hundred dollars, two hundred and fifty dollars you know eh (smiling) we have love for customers.

In response to the demand for price information, Bahraini traders usually name their price in the local currency, Bahraini dinars or foreign currencies. In this case, the quote is made in US dollars, as shown in Extract (5) turns 7 and 8, and in Extract (6) turns 16 and 20 as the trader realises that most tourists may not be familiar with the local currency.

Requesting discounts
Extract (5), turn 7:
7. Tourist Customer: It was One-ninety dollars you asked so, One eighty-five dollars? One-eighty dollars?

The third phase of the bargaining process involves customers asking for discounts. In Extract (5) the Tourist Customer used simple direct prices to request a discount from *one hundred and eighty-five dollars* to *one hundred and eighty dollars*, having acknowledged the initial offer of the selling price at *one hundred and ninety dollars*. It is worth noting that in Extract (6), turn 21, the Tourist Customer did not request a discount, rather he shifted the negotiation to find out more details about the carpet he intended to purchase. This is probably because the initial selling price was between *two hundred dollars* and *two hundred and fifty dollars*, and he was yet to decide on how much discount he could ask for.

Counter-offers
   Extract (5), turn 8:
      8. Bahraini Trader: One hundred and eighty-five dollars. Go ahead . . . One hundred and eighty.

When customers ask for discounts, the Bahraini traders usually make a second or reduced offer, or even go as far as to make a new offer. They are usually willing to come closer to the offer made by the customer, as this is likely to be 'a one-time customer' who they are not willing to lose to another trader. In this data the Bahraini Trader counters the tourist's offer by going from *one hundred and eighty dollars* to *one hundred and eighty-five dollars*. However, this process of making a counter-offer does not occur in Extract (6) as the Tourist Customer did not make an offer at all, as shown in turns 27 and 29.

Reinforcing the appeal for discounts
   Extract (5), turn 7:
      7. Tourist Customer: It was One-ninety dollars you asked so, One eighty-five dollars? One-eighty dollars?

An important component of bargaining in Extract (5) is the customers' reinforcement of their appeal for discounts. In turn 7, the Tourist Customer requests a discount from the initial selling price of *one hundred and ninety dollars* to, firstly, *one hundred and eighty-five dollars* and, later, down to *one hundred and eighty dollars*. Such an appeal is probably not caused by a poor financial situation on the part of the tourist, as tourists are generally considered to be financially stable and to have enough money to spend when visiting other countries. Thus, it can be inferred that independent of their nationality customers in general have a conversational expectation built into the bazaar situation to negotiate and bargain for better deals if they are provided with such opportunities. The reduction or counter-offer from one hundred and ninety dollars to one hundred and eighty-five dollars may seem ridiculous, and just five dollars difference too little to negotiate over, and often one would expect a much lower bargaining point, with the Tourist Customer and the Bahraini Trader meeting somewhere in the middle. However, this real-life counter-offer technique does not apply within the local markets in Bahrain, where as little as just a dollar discount in price – or, in the local currency, one dinar – is valuable to the traders and very much appreciated by the customers.

Building consensus
  Extract (5), turn 8:
    8. Bahraini Trader: One hundred and eighty-five dollars. Go ahead . . . One hundred and eighty.

The next strategy in the bargaining process involves the enactment of agreement by both parties. In the above, Extract (5) indicates that the trader was willing to accept the offer as requested by the customer even though he had initially opted for a higher price, but he could secretly be enthusiastic about the deal as he would still be able to make some profit from the purchase and probably restock the item.

Closing remarks
  Extract (5), turns 9–10:
    9. Tourist Customer: Done.
    10. Bahraini Trader: Sold. (shake hands to seal the deal)

  Extract (6), turns 31–2:
    31. Tourist Customer: And we will come back, yep.
    32. Bahraini Trader: Anytime, anytime.

The closing remarks in the bargaining process involve expressions of appreciation by both parties. In Extract (5) above, the customer acknowledges the offer from the Bahraini in turn 9 with one word, *Done*, rather than using appreciative words like *Thank you*. Also, the Bahraini Trader, in turn 10, further affirms this by uttering the word *Sold*, and by shaking hands to imply that the deal has been concluded. It could be inferred that the Bahraini Trader is accustomed to Western way of conducting business, given that he goes on to shake the customer's hand, which to some Arabs in the region would not be acceptable because of the customer being a woman. However, since in Extract (6) the deal was not concluded, the Tourist Customer made some assurances to the Bahraini Trader that he would come back another day or time – in turn 31: *we will come back*. . . . The trader's response, *Anytime* in turn 32, reveals his strategy of politely maintaining his face needs and not displaying any disappointment despite all his efforts to convince the Tourist Customer to make the purchase, especially as he cannot be completely sure if the Tourist Customer is serious about the purchase nor whether he really will return to the shop again before he leaves Bahrain. Thus, Bahraini traders are willing to accommodate to their customers' face needs and expectations of politeness, too, in order to achieve successful business communication goals.

6 DISCUSSION AND FINDINGS

It can be observed that Bahraini traders often communicate with their customers in English, specifically with those who do not speak Arabic because they are aware that most buyers are tourists who are visiting the country for a few hours or days. Also, most of those who have been in business for a long time have become conversant with some English words through their daily and ongoing business interactions with their employees and customers. The study also supports the assertion that NNS cooperate with one another in conversations, given that they are aware of their positions as learners of English from different cultural backgrounds, shaped by varying norms of communication and behaviour (Meierkord 2000). Thus, Bahraini traders use English to build rapport and cordiality with their employees and customers. Also, as shown in the data, interactants use repetition as a means of signalling affiliation and solidarity with their community (Cogo 2009). In addition, Bahraini traders sometimes shake hands with their customers to signal accommodation and acceptance of one another. Hence Bahraini traders, employees and customers attempt to create and maintain positive personal and social identities through convergence and divergence accommodation or negotiation strategies. This is why the research reported here also illustrates that English serves as a major medium of business transaction in grassroots, face-to-face trading contexts in the bazaar.

7 CONCLUSION

This chapter has provided answers to the two research questions that it set out to investigate. The previous section has attempted to answer these research questions, which deal with the major intercultural communication strategies employed by Arab traders with non-Arabic speakers in their business encounters. The major intercultural communication strategy found in the data was accommodation, specifically in the forms of convergence and divergence. Since bargaining is crucial to the type of language practice observed, the process of negotiating a price as captured in the data was also discussed in some detail. The data have shown that convergence and divergence accommodation strategies are important components used by the interactants in the course of their business conversations. Furthermore, documenting the negotiation and bargaining strategies in the data has shown that different components such as demanding information, negotiating price, requesting discounts, making counter-offers, reinforcing the appeal for discounts, building a consensus and closing remarks were used by interactants for obtaining the best possible deal.

NOTES

1. All extracts in brackets are from my own comments based on my observations and field notes during the time of my data collection.
2. BD is an abbreviation commonly used in Bahrain for the term Bahraini dinar.

REFERENCES

Bamidele-Akhidenor, Anthonia (2019), 'The roles of online placement test in English language teaching', *Knowledge Education Social Sciences*, 3: 24, 1–9.

Bin, Zhou and Cui Fu-Quan (2007), 'On the promotion of intercultural communication competence', *Sino-US English Teaching*, 4: 9, 77–81.

Cogo, Alessia (2009), 'Accommodating difference in ELF conversations: a study of pragmatic strategies', in Anna Mauranen and Elina Ranta (eds), *English as a Lingua Franca: Studies and Findings*, Newcastle: Cambridge Scholars, 254–73.

Ehrenreich, Susanne (2010), 'English as a business lingua franca in a German multinational corporation: meeting the challenge', *The Journal of Business Communication*, 47: 4, 408–31.

Firth, Alan (1995), 'Talking for a change: commodity negotiating by telephone', *The Discourse of Negotiations: Studies in the Workplace*, Oxford: Elsevier, 183–222.

Gallois, Cynthia and Howard Giles (1998), 'Accommodating mutual influence in intergroup encounters', *Progress in Communication Sciences*, 135–62.

Gallois, Cynthia, Tania Ogay and Howard Giles (2005), 'Communication accommodation theory: a look back and a look ahead', in William B. Gudykunst (ed.), *Theorizing about Intercultural Communication*, Thousand Oaks, CA: Sage, 121–48.

Gerritsen, Marinel and Catherine Nickerson (2009), 'BELF: Business English as a lingua franca', in Francesca Bargiela-Chiappini (ed.), *Handbook of Business Discourse*, Edinburgh: Edinburgh University Press, 180–92.

Giles, Howard, Justine Coupland and Nikolas Coupland (1991), 'Accommodation theory: communication, context, and contexts of accommodation', in Howard Giles, Justine Coupland and Nikolas Coupland (eds), *Developments in Applied Sociolinguistics*, Cambridge: Cambridge University Press, 1–68.

Ismail, Jumiati, Michael Azariadis and Kamaruzaman Jusoff (2009), 'An overview of the cross-cultural business negotiation between Malaysia and Australia', *Canadian Social Science*, 5: 4, 129–42.

Jamarani, Maryam and Farzad Sharifian (2013), *Language and Intercultural Communication in the New Era*, London: Routledge.

Kachru, Braj (1986), *The Alchemy of English: The Spread, Functions, and Models of Non-native Englishes*, Urbana: University of Illinois Press.

Kankaanranta, Anne and Leena Louhiala-Salminen (2010), 'English? – oh, it's just work!: a study of BELF users' perceptions', *English for Specific Purposes*, 29: 3, 204–9.

Matsumoto, David, Jeffery Leroux and Seung Yee Yoo (2005), 'Emotion and intercultural communication', *Kwansei Gakuin Sociology Department Studies*, 99, 15–38.

Meierkord, Christiane (2000), 'Interpreting successful lingua franca interaction. An analysis of non-native/non-native small talk conversations in English', *Linguistik Online*, 5, 1.

Meierkord, Christiane (2012), *Interactions across Englishes: Linguistic Choices in Local and International Contact Situations*, Cambridge: Cambridge University Press.

Ministry of Information Affairs (2014), <http://www.msia.gov.bh/en/kingdom-of-bahrain/pages/general-data> (last accessed 25 June 2018).

Randall, Mick and Mohammad Amir Samimi (2010) 'The status of English in Dubai', *English Today 101*, 26: 1, 43–50.

Roshid, Mohammod Monimoor, Susan Webb and Raqib Chowdhury (2018), 'English as a business lingua franca: a discursive analysis of business emails', *International Journal of Business Communication*, 1–21.

Schneider, Edgar W. (2016), 'Grassroots Englishes in tourism interactions', *English Today*, 32: 3, 2–10.

Seidlhofer, Barbara (2005), 'English as a lingua franca', *ELT Journal*, 59: 4, 339–41.

Small, Deborah A., Michele Gelfand, Linda Babcock and Hilary Gettman (2007), 'Who goes to the bargaining table? The influence of gender and framing on the initiation of negotiation', *Journal of Personality and Social Psychology*, 93: 4, 600–13.

Smith, Larry (1983), *Readings in English as an International Language*, Oxford: Pergamon.

Street, Richard L. and Howard Giles (1982), 'Speech accommodation theory: a social cognitive approach to language and speech behavior', *Social Cognition and Communication*, 193–226.

Wilson, Adam (2018), 'International tourism and (linguistic) accommodation: convergence towards and through English in tourist information interactions', *Anglophonia French Journal of English Linguistics*, 25, 1–18.

CHAPTER 8

The Value of Grassroots English for Bangladeshi Migrants to the Middle East

Qumrul Hasan Chowdhury and Elizabeth J. Erling

1 INTRODUCTION

While English has long been recognised as a language of major significance in South Asia as part of the Outer Circle of Kachru's (1986) model of World Englishes, the role and status of the language in the particular context of Bangladesh has been, until recently, relatively unexplored (but see Banu and Sussex 2001). The research that exists has tended to focus on formal domains of language use in Bangladesh, rather than grassroots uses of English, for example in temporary economic migration from the country. Similarly, economic migration has significantly shaped global affairs and economic flows in the last decades but the linguistic implications of this are only starting to receive significant attention in applied linguistics (see for example Canagarajah 2017; Giampapa and Canagarajah 2017). The more routine and temporary migration of non-elite, lower-skilled economic migrants, however, and its consequential impact on individuals and countries in the Global South, have received only little attention. The investigation of the grassroots language skills of these migrants, and the value of these for migration, is only in its infancy (but see Seargeant et al. 2017; Erling et al. 2019)

Low- and semi-skilled economic migration, particularly to the countries in the Middle East, plays a substantial role in sustaining the economies of countries such as Bangladesh, Nepal, India, Pakistan, Indonesia, Sri Lanka and the Philippines. Bangladesh, for example, where this study is based, earned US$17 billion through remittances in 2018, sent mostly by the Bangladeshi labour migrants in the Middle East (Bangladesh Bureau of Manpower and Employment (BMET) 2019). Today, even though the country has concerns for its development in many vital areas, and economic migration may entail significant challenges and adversities for Bangladeshi migrant workers, the steady inflow of remittances has been a major catalyst of the country's economic growth (Siddiqui 2016; Sarker and Islam 2018). With a strong trend of economic migration and relatively low availability of jobs in Bangladesh, labour migration to the Middle East is a major career aspiration and solution for many lower-educated Bangladeshis, despite the risks involved (Sarker and Islam 2018).

With the status of English as a global language, a common view is that better proficiency in English can help people in the Global South to take better advantage of the globalised economy (Erling and Seargeant 2013). Even though a clear relationship between English and economic advancement is difficult to establish, donors and governments in the Global South often align English language skills closely to national development agendas (Erling 2017). Moreover, there is a prevalence of beliefs and assumptions in remittance recipient countries such as Bangladesh linking ability in the English language with profitable economic migration (see also Erling et al. 2019). For example, in a study undertaken in 2011 in two rural Bangladeshi sub-districts to investigate local attitudes to English as a language of economic development, we found that going abroad to foreign countries is a major reason why most of the participants wanted to learn English (see Erling et al. 2013). Despite the strength of such beliefs in Bangladesh, empirical studies investigating their validity are scarce. Because of the globalised nature of its operation and its robust link to global Southern economies, international economic migration seems to be a relevant area for exploring the economic benefits of English. However, whether and how English language skills can be an economically exchangeable resource for migrant workers, including the low- and semi-skilled ones, has seldom been investigated (Coleman 2010, but see Erling et al. 2015).

Seeking to address this gap, we undertook an ethnographically based qualitative study in 2014 exploring perceptions of the relationship between English and economic migration in a rural Bangladeshi village among twenty-seven returnee migrant workers to the Middle East. The study also captured the language skills that were reported by the participants as important for migration, and how most of these skills had been acquired. In this chapter, we analyse the narratives of three participants and critically explore the value of grassroots English for them. We understand 'grassroots Englishes' similarly to Schneider (2016: 3–4), who defines the term as non-elitist varieties spoken by a relatively poorer section of society that learns English informally and through direct interactions, and usually use the language to carry out instrumental goals. While our study did not include a detailed linguistic analysis of participants' uses of English, we find that 'grassroots English' usefully describes our participants' learning and use of the language in the context of low-/semi-skilled economic migration to the Middle East, particularly considering their relatively low educational backgrounds. In examining the value of grassroots English for Bangladeshi economic migrants, we also consider the methodological and ethical challenges faced when conducting this research. These participants' narratives suggest that it is difficult to establish a straightforward relationship between (English) language skills and economic gain in the context of low-skilled temporary migration. While grassroots English does seem to have significant functional value for them, this value is shaped by domains and contexts of communication and is complexly related to the values of other languages, particularly Arabic (see also Seargeant et al. 2017). Moreover, these three narratives reveal the social and psychological costs of economic migration, which also need to be considered when assessing any economic gains (see also Erling et al. 2019). Taking account of these inequalities and costs, we reflect on the methods and ethics that are important to consider when undertaking research about grassroots English in the context of low-skilled temporary migration. Based on our findings, we argue that assumptions and beliefs about English and economic migration should be critically informed by considerations of the structural, geopolitical, social and psychological challenges involved.

2 LANGUAGE IN ECONOMIC MIGRATION

With the increasing importance of human capital in a knowledge- and service-based global economy, the language and communication skills of migrant workers are increasingly valued in host society labour markets (Rassool 2007; Giampapa and Canagarajah 2017). Studies on the value of language skills in economic migration have mostly focused on the economic return of host country language(s) skills for migrant workers in the labour market. Such studies, mostly quantitative in nature, argue that local language competence is an important component of host country-bound human capital, which has a positive impact on the earnings of migrant workers (Dustmann 1994; Chiswick and Miller 1995, 2003). However, such relationships have been argued not to be straightforward, but rather to be affected by factors such as gender, ethnicity, occupation, experience of formal education, age at arrival in the host society, and so on. (Chiswick and Miller 1995; Dustmann and van Soest 2001; Dustmann and Fabbri 2003; Gao and Smyth 2011).

In contrast, the values of different non-local languages, or more particularly English as a lingua franca in migrant work situations, have been investigated less widely (Coleman 2010). Among the studies available, Grenier and Nadeau (2011) examine the economic returns of different languages used in workplaces in Montreal for migrant workers. They argue that the use of English as a lingua franca yields economic returns on earnings compared to the use of French as a second language, allowing them to conclude that English is a 'necessity' to attain economic success in the Canadian labour market whereas French is an 'asset' with inconsequential impact. Elsewhere, Lan (2003) argues that proficiency in English works as cultural capital for Filipina migrant workers in the Taiwanese domestic labour market. The better English proficiency of the Filipina domestic workers positions them well in social class dynamics compared to their Taiwanese newly middle-classed employers who have limited English proficiency, but who acknowledge the value of English, particularly in the context of their children's education and future employment. Despite the low status of domestic service occupations in the transnational labour market, English-proficient Filipina domestic workers consider themselves better positioned in terms of social class and avail socio-economic advantage compared to the less English proficient domestic workers, for example, Indonesian domestic workers (Lan 2003). Elsewhere, in the context of South Korea, Froese et al. (2012) argue that whereas competence in Korean is more useful for cross-cultural adjustments of the migrant workers, English is useful for their workplace-related adjustment and job satisfaction and also lowers their turnover intentions. Deumert et al. (2005) show in the context of rural to urban migration in the multilingual South Africa that proficiency in dominant urban languages (English and Afrikaans) is essential for the rural migrants to Cape Town for their integration to the labour market and the formal economy. However, they also argue that having a social network, both for initial settling down and for mediating access to the labour market, is also necessary for such integration. Guido (2008, 2012) shows in lingua franca contexts of communication between Western immigrant officials and non-Western migrants that asymmetrical power dynamics works as an obstacle for the migrant workers to take any mentionable advantage of English. In the following, we explore particular features of Bangladeshi migration and the potential role of English therein.

3 BANGLADESH AND ECONOMIC MIGRATION

In recent times, Bangladesh has achieved considerable economic growth, being reclassified as a lower-middle-income country in 2015 from its previous position of a low-income country (The World Bank 2018). However, this economic growth should not overshadow the fact that the country ranks 136 in the human development index (United Nations Development Programme 2018) and faces significant challenges regarding poverty, health, good governance, human rights and climate change (Riaz and Rahman 2016).

Large-scale labour migration to the Middle East is a major lifeline of the economic development of Bangladesh. The opportunity for Bangladesh to send its nationals to the Middle East emerged with the discovery of natural resources such as oil in the Middle East in the 1970s, which subsequently resulted in the economic growth of the region, creating demands for skilled and semi-skilled workers. More than 12.5 million workers have left Bangladesh since 1976 for employment in foreign countries, predominantly in the Middle East (BMET

2019), although this number is likely to be considerably higher as it does not include unofficial migration. Some of the most common countries where the Bangladeshis work are Saudi Arabia (30.74 per cent), the United Arab Emirates (UAE) (18.84 per cent), Kuwait (4.95 per cent), Oman (11.69 per cent), Qatar (6.34 per cent) and Malaysia (8.40 per cent) (BMET 2019). Migration from Bangladesh to these countries should be, according to labour policy, temporary and short-term-contract-based, although these contracts can be renewable.

Despite providing a relatively consistent flow of remittances, economic migration from Bangladesh is not without its problems. Some of the common problems include recruiting agencies who charge high intermediary fees to the migrant workers, abuse and exploitation while working abroad, low salaries, inadequate support and rights services and insufficient access to information while abroad and lack of proper training (International Labour Organization 2019; Siddiqui 2016). These problems are particularly relevant for un-/semi-skilled workers, who – due to lower literacy skills – might have particular challenges with the literacy demands of migration and therefore might be more prone to exploitation and abuse. These migrants also tend to have low levels of foreign language skills, especially in English – the global lingua franca. Bangladeshi policy discussions sometimes attribute the economic underachievement of the Bangladeshi economic migrants to this lower level of language skills, particularly when compared to migrant workers from Sri Lanka or the Philippines (see Erling et al. 2019). The majority of migrant workers from Bangladesh are low-/semi-skilled individuals who have limited experience of formal education and language education. According to government statistics, from 1976 to 2018, 47.57 per cent of the Bangladeshi migrant workers were low skilled, 15.27 per cent were semi-skilled and 34.03 per cent were skilled (BMET 2018). Elsewhere, Rahman (2012: 219) finds in a survey among 9,292 Bangladeshi migrant workers that 30 per cent had primary education (levels 1 to 5); 50 per cent had a secondary level of education (levels 6 to 10); 50 per cent of the remaining 20 per cent had no formal schooling and the rest had higher secondary, tertiary and technical education. As a result of the educational and skill profiles as mentioned above, the majority of the language skills of the Bangladeshi migrant workers are learned at the grassroots. In the following study, we present an investigation which seeks insight into the value of these grassroots (English) language skills to the participants' experiences of economic migration.

4 RESEARCH METHODOLOGY

For the study on the value of grassroots English for Bangladeshi migrant workers presented here, data were collected from a group of returnee migrant workers in a village in the middle eastern part of Bangladesh. People in this area have a high tendency of economic migration, particularly to the countries in the Middle East. Data for the study were collected by two Bangladeshi researchers, Qumrul Hasan Chowdhury (a co-author of this chapter) and Sayeedur Rahman. Data collection was conducted in three phases: a pilot study, the main visit, and a follow-up. The researchers accessed the local community with the support of a local guide who played an important role in how the researchers recruited participants through 'snowball sampling'.

Data were collected through an interview-dominant ethnographic approach. The interview schedule designed for the project aimed to elicit narratives of the participants (Pavlenko 2007), guiding them to reflect on their experience of migration and on the role of language in those experiences. The purpose was to gain insight into the value of language skills in economic migration, in relation to the life and migration histories of the participants and their language-learning biographies. The interviews were conducted in Bangla and were transcribed and translated by the researchers. In analysing these narratives, we first constructed a profile of each participant, which included a summary of their biography, as related to us. After an initial reading of the transcripts, we identified common themes that were portrayed as important to the experience of migration, and the transcripts were coded according to these themes. The analysis of participants' narratives provided insight into their experiences, their perceived needs and attitudes to the role of language in migration, and broader ideological patterns relating to the positioning of different languages within society.

In conducting the study, we followed the structured framework of the Open University Human Participants and Material Ethics Committee as well as the British Association for Applied Linguistics Recommendations for Good Practice in Applied Linguistics. All participants are referred to here with pseudonyms. However, we found that additional ethical considerations were required (see further Hultgren et al. 2016), which we discuss further below with regard to the issues of power and inequality among others we experienced during the fieldwork.

In total, twenty-seven people participated in the study, primarily returnee migrant workers; but some migrant workers who were on vacation during that time were also recruited as participants. Twenty-three of them were male and four were female, thus reflecting the male-dominant trend of migration from Bangladesh (Siddiqui 2016). The average duration of their sojourn in foreign countries was ten years and their median age was forty-four. Saudi Arabia (67 per cent) followed by the UAE and Kuwait were the three countries where the participants most commonly had worked. The different professions which the participants were engaged in while abroad included shopkeeper, caterer, domestic worker, mechanic, security worker, driver, construction worker and pipeline worker.

5 FINDINGS: THE THREE PARTICIPANTS

The overall experience of the participants across the different professions in which they were engaged during migration was varied. In another study about economic migration from Bangladesh, Afsar (2009: 44) recounts that the migration experience was found to be positive only for 57 per cent of the participants in that study, while for 21 per cent it was mixed and for 13 per cent it was negative (losses were incurred). Similar results were found in our study, where the majority of the participants reported having profited financially from the migratory experience – and they agreed that they experienced, at least at some level, some enhancement of their capabilities. Sixteen of the participants (59 per cent) had narratives of mostly positive outcomes; seven of them (26 per cent) were more ambivalent about their experience; and four (15 per cent) were very negative about the experience, with two saying they would have been better off not going abroad. All but two of the participants in this study reported being able to remit at least a small amount of money back to Bangladesh, regardless of their educational background and language knowledge, while some had clearly been able to contribute significantly to their own and their family's well-being. In the following, we provide examples from a selected participant who exemplifies each of these perspectives (positive, negative and mixed/ambivalent).

5.1 Migration as 'Contentment' and 'Good Income': The Positive Perspectives of Gofur

Gofur, 58, was one of the oldest participants in our sample, and his experience of economic migration pre-dated the majority of the others. Gofur migrated to the Middle East in the 1980s, in the early phase of Bangladeshi economic migration to the Middle East following the discovery of oil and the resultant opportunities for employment in the region. Most of the other participants, on the other hand, migrated in the 1990s or the 2000s. Gofur's dream as a child was to study and then work in Bangladesh, but he could not continue his education beyond the secondary level because of financial constraints in his family, caused mostly by the sudden death of his father. Seeking a solution to the growing hardships in his family, he decided to go abroad. In the 1980s, he went first to Iraq with the help of an uncle where he was employed as a gardener. When this visa expired, Gofur then went to Kuwait where he worked as a security guard. After this, he went to Saudi Arabia to work as a driver.

Gofur reported that in addition to Bangla, he speaks English, Arabic and Hindi. Although he had only minimal experience of formal education, he was rather proficient in English, and he was able to undertake (part of) the interview in English and chat informally with a foreign researcher who was present. While he had learned English at school, an academic subject that he claimed to be good at, he reported that his English improved while working in the Middle East. Although he had some familiarity with Quranic Arabic prior to migration, his skills in spoken Arabic were also learned on the job, where he also learned Hindi by talking with Indian and Pakistani co-workers.

When reflecting on the value of English for his experience of migration, Gofur reported that the importance of English has grown since the 1980s when he first went abroad. This he attributes to the Gulf War, the influence of Americans, and the increasing incoming flow of non-Arab nationals from China, South Asia and various African countries.

When asked whether he was able to capitalise on the value of English, he thought that a basic proficiency in English was necessary for certain fundamental, routine activities, for example writing one's name or punching one's time cards.

Gofur also viewed English as a particular resource for him, which allowed him access to positions of authority and respect. For example, because of his proficiency in English, he was often assigned the role of interpreter for those of his colleagues who did not speak English or Arabic:

> In my company, there were a few persons who could neither speak Arabic nor English. When they got sick, it was very difficult for the doctors to communicate with them. I was given the responsibility to communicate with the doctors in Arabic and in English on their behalf. I could do that very successfully. There was a Pakistani doctor who told me, 'How could you do this? Have you studied?' I replied, 'a little'. He said, 'You are good'. The engineer of our company was also happy with me. (Gofur, interview)

Gofur also reported that his proficiency in English and Arabic helped him navigate difficult circumstances. For example, when Gofur arrived in Saudi Arabia as part of a group of Bangladeshi migrant workers, there was no one to pick them up and they had to wait helplessly for a long time at the airport. Because of his language skills, he reported that he was able to call to the host company in order to arrange a vehicle to pick them up. He provided a further example of when his ability to communicate in formal written English was useful in overcoming a situation of discomfort, vulnerability and perhaps also discrimination, and also in increasing his level of authority and respect:

> When I used to work at a hotel, our work used to finish at 3.00 pm. But we all had to wait till 5.00 pm because there was no bus before 5.00 pm [. . .] Now since there was no bus, we had to unnecessarily sit down at the basement at this extra time. There were Filipinos and Koreans with us. Then many of the Koreans left the job. The Filipinos used to live in that hotel. So, mostly we the Bangladeshis had the problem. So, I told the authority several times, but the authority did not take our problem seriously. In such

condition, I made a draft of a letter in English where I stated the issue. I sent the letter directly to the Saudi authority. Then they said, 'Come, who wrote this?' I replied that I wrote this. Then they called the transport section in front of me and told 'today from now onwards bus will go at due time so that they can go when they need to go'. Then he put his sign in that letter of mine. And on that day, at lunch, we saw 'transport provided again'. All the people then were very happy on me. (Gofur, interview)

In his opinion, the outcome of migration for Gofur was overly positive. He earned moderately well, although he needed to work very hard and take on extra jobs as his wages from his 'official' jobs were very low. He reported that the criteria for successful migration include having proper work documents, and being humble, hardworking and eager to learn, including languages. He also attributed his success to being lucky enough to have what he considered to be good *maaliks* (employers) and companies, which is not the case for everyone. Not everything about the experience was positive, however, as Gofur also mentioned the particular personal costs of migration. For example, he recounted that he was never able to marry, due to the responsibilities he felt for his uncle's and his brother's families, including supporting the education of their children and later sending some of them abroad. Since returning to Bangladesh, Gofur runs a small pharmacy in the local bazaar, which he, however, does not view as a sustainable means of income. He is an established, active and esteemed member of the community, and is also engaged in community work. Migration has provided him with a desirable socio-economic elevation that he seems to continue to benefit from, despite the personal costs that were incurred.

5.2 'It was good, but . . .": Ambivalent Views about Migration from Afia

Another perspective can be seen in the narrative from Afia who, like 26 per cent of the participants, represents an ambivalent view on migration. Afia is a 42-year-old female migrant worker who has been doing domestic work in six Middle Eastern countries for more than twenty years. She is married with two children. She grew up with financial hardship in the family caused by the early death of her father, which restricted her opportunity to receive any formal education. She got married when she was twelve. Her husband, who is a mason, is unemployed for six months a year during the rainy season. This meant that the family lived under extreme financial constraints, which eventually forced her to seek employment abroad as a domestic worker. In order to raise the money to pay for her visa, the family pawned their house. Afia first worked in Bahrain for eight years, although that did not go very well. Her salary was low and, in addition, she had to work not only in the house of her employer but also in that of his wife's mother, causing excessive demands on her. After she returned from Bahrain, she went to Kuwait and was employed profitably with a family. However, she had to leave that job after two years when her husband became ill, and she returned to Bangladesh to look after him. Afia then went to the UAE but did not stay long as she was pregnant with her second child. Once the child was born, she went back to another job in the UAE, leaving her one-month-old child in the care of her mother. This job was followed by others in Lebanon, Oman and Qatar. At the time of her interview, Afia had just returned from Qatar, utterly discontented with the way she was treated by her employers and the strenuous workload she had faced. In her words:

> I had to do a lot of work. They had big three-storied flats. In the mornings, I had to drop four children to school. I took one of them on my lap, one on my shoulder and dragged the others to their schools. Then I came home and did all the work of the house. Then at 1:00 pm, all those four children came from school and I had to make food for them. It was very, very difficult for me. I could not manage doing all these things. (Afia, interview)

Afia was planning to go to back very soon to another job in Oman, because that is where she had had her best experiences and where there is also a requirement that domestic workers get to rest for one hour in the afternoon.

When asked why she had moved around so much, Afia responded that this was a result of bad luck in terms of the employers she had worked for, combined with her desire to see different countries (although this never really materialised). Afia reflected that she often had to work under unfavourable conditions, with heavy workloads, restrictions on her mobility and verbal and physical abuse being not uncommon.

When asked about her language skills and their role in migration, Afia reported that in addition to Bangla, she spoke Arabic well but spoke very little English. She learned Arabic through her experience of working within families, and she argued that this is the most important language for domestic workers to know, as they rarely communicate with anyone outside of the family. Indeed, Afia argued that knowledge of Arabic is essential, and that difficulties are intensified without it. As an example of this, Afia recounted the following example:

> At the beginning I had lots of problem with language. If they asked for glass, I used to give plate. If they asked for spoons, I gave plates. In the case of such mistakes, they knocked me in my head [smiling]. They knocked me in my head with the thing that they asked for. That's how, I remembered the names of things [. . .] In Bahrain, I was beaten. For example, they asked for tea. I gave tea leaves. I did not make the tea. The madam (house lady) then put her hand on my neck and moved me to say, 'Boil the tea

leaves. Make tea.' They told me things in Arabic, I did not know Arabic. Sometimes, the children said me something, but I didn't understand. Then the children knocked me. (Afia, interview)

With regard to English, Afia reported that because she had no experience of formal education, it had not been possible for her to learn English. Here it is interesting to note her perception that English is out of her reach, though she had been able to learn Arabic. She also recounted that the requirement for English is very low for domestic workers in Arab families who rarely communicate with anyone besides the woman and children of the house.

With regards to her perspective on her financial 'success', despite all of her hard work and experiences of hardship and abuse, Afia was not able to earn a sufficient amount to satisfy her family's financial demands. In reflecting on the reasons for this, Afia explained that since she did not often get a chance to work for one family over a long period of time, she rarely experienced a pay rise. Moreover, since she worked in many different countries, a substantial amount of the money that she earned was spent on travel and visas. She was caught in a vicious circle of having borrowed money to pay for her migration so that she could earn money to support her family, but not being able to earn enough to cover these costs. Yet, overall, she still had more than if she had not worked abroad, as domestic work (the only work she was qualified to do) was not available to her in Bangladesh due to cultural conventions.

Despite having some sense of economic success, Afia recounted certain regrets. First and foremost she regretted that her desire to educate her children – one of the primary reasons that she went abroad in the first place – did not come to fruition. Her daughter, who was eighteen, got married when she was still in secondary school, and her in-laws, much to Afia's regret, did not continue her education. Her son, who was eleven, did not continue onto secondary school and she worried that he was now becoming idle and getting into trouble. Moreover, although she did not ruminate on this, she had been absent for a large part of her children's childhood, and they had been primarily raised by their father and Afia's mother. Moreover, unlike for Gofur, her standing in her family and in the community was in question, as she mentioned that women who work abroad often get a bad reputation and are viewed with suspicion in Bangladesh (Bélanger and Rahman 2013). Still, she was grateful for what she had been able to achieve and willing to continue trying her luck by working abroad.

5.3 Migration as 'waste of money . . . time . . . and energy': The Negative Perspectives of Badol

A third perspective can be seen in the narrative from Badol who, like 15 per cent of the participants, represents a rather negative perspective on migration.

Badol is a 26-year-old, single, ex-migrant worker who worked in the UAE for three years. Having four brothers (three of them older than him) who work(ed) abroad, he too had the ambition to go abroad to earn money. He is one of the most qualified participants in the sample, having completed higher secondary education in Bangladesh and having worked as an electrician at a company near Dhaka before going to the UAE. Badol also claimed to know how to drive and to have some computer skills prior to migration. With regard to language skills, Badol reported that, in addition to Bangla, he speaks English, Arabic and Hindi. He said that he learned English at school and can communicate in the language with 'foreigners and big company officials' if needed. After going abroad, he learned Arabic and Hindi, mostly by communicating with other employees at work.

Overall, Badol's experience of working in Dubai was frustrating. This was in part because he had been required to pay a large amount of money (ca. GBP3,500) to recruiting agents in order to go to the UAE, which he arranged by selling land. These recruiters had promised that he would be given a job as an electrician, which, however, never materialised. Instead, he had to work in construction with varying and unpredictable responsibilities. Moreover, while his pay was low, he was certain that the company was also taking a cut out of his salary. In addition to this, Badol was unhappy with his accommodation and food arrangements. After working for a year in that company and experiencing no improvement, he took the dangerous decision to quit the company and become an illegal worker. Badol then worked as a blacksmith for a year, although not very profitably, until the owner of the shop asked him to quit due to his illegal status. Badol then worked at an Internet shop for nearly a year. It was during that time that he finally decided to return to Bangladesh, as it was becoming increasingly difficult for him to lead such a restricted life and bear the anxiety of being arrested by the police because of his illegal residency status.

When asked about the role of his language skills in his experience of migration, Badol reported that basic proficiency in English can be useful to navigate situations of vulnerability in international domains such as airports. This became apparent to him soon after he embarked on his journey to the UAE.

> I had been told that I would go in a direct flight to Dubai. But that did not happen. I found that there was 7 hours transit in Malaysia. That was problematic. I had problem with eating foods. I asked a woman in the Malaysian airport in English, 'Where can I eat some food? I have some Dirham with me.' The woman replied, 'You can't eat anything with Dirham. You have to change the Dirham into Dollars.' I asked her where I could exchange Dirham into Dollars. She directed me to the place where I could exchange money. I went to that place and asked the person sitting in the counter 'I want to change Dirham into Dollars.' I bought some Dollars and after a long

time, I could eat some food. Then the plane flew to Pakistan. There was three hours transit in Pakistan. Finally, it flew to Dubai. (Badol, interview)

When working with locals in the UAE, Badol reported that proficiency in Arabic is essential, as, according to him, people there often do not speak English:

The Arabs, they even don't understand simple English words like 'water'. If they need water, they can't say that in English. They would say that in Arabic '*ala jibna*' means 'Give me water.' They can't say in English 'Give me water.' They don't even try speaking in English [. . .] In the Internet shop where I used to work, if I said 'sure', they said 'I don't understand what you say.' My friend then told me, 'Look Badol, they don't understand your English *kalam* or language.' (Badol, interview)

However, Badol reported that English was important for communicating with other migrant workers from other countries, although this perceived value of English seemed to be dependent on the various domains of work and the nationalities of the foreign workers. For example, in the Indian construction company where he worked, Hindi was the medium of communication among the Indian-dominant workforce and his proficiency in English was not valued. However, Badol also worked in an engineering company owned by Filipinos and frequently visited by European nationals, where he found his English to be essential:

A lot of German and French people used to visit that power company. There, I needed to read a lot of papers (professional literature). They used to say to me, 'Badol, can you read these?' I read them and then they said, 'OK, you come here to work.' (Badol, interview)

Badol experienced feelings of frustration and resentment over how his long-awaited economic migration unfolded for him. He even failed to earn back the money which he invested in going abroad. He now thinks that he would have been better off not going. This is despite having studied to the higher secondary level, having experience of working as an electrician in Bangladesh before departure, and speaking English, Hindi and Arabic. He now does agricultural work in Bangladesh. As he says:

Now I realise that I can do many things in Bangladesh if I work as hard as I did in foreign country. You can do very well even in Bangladesh if you work hard. This is not true only about me, this is true about all the Bangladeshis. Unfortunately, we don't realise this . . . People say a lot of things, but it's very difficult to change your circumstances at foreign countries. It's indeed very difficult. If situation favours you and you show good performance, you will do well. But things do not work accordingly, and then this is a complete loss. Waste of money, waste of time, waste of your energy and you get old. You do hard work and your body becomes weak. (Badol, interview)

Badol's aspiration of improving his economic circumstances by working abroad having been quashed, he now makes his living in the local village, but his memories are of hardship, worry and having been cheated.

Having presented the diverse experiences of Gofur, Afia and Badol in this section, we now interpret them in relation to grassroots English and economic migration.

6 DISCUSSION

The findings of this study show that grassroots English has certain functional values for these Bangladeshi migrant workers, but these values depend on the context of communication, interlocutors and domain of work among other factors (see also Seargeant et al. 2017). Gofur, for example, who worked as a driver, reported that basic English was essential for accomplishing certain routine tasks in Saudi Arabia, and that having proficiency in the language was an important means of enhancing his power, prestige and voice. Afia, however, found English irrelevant to her job as a domestic worker, where the women and children in the families only used Arabic to communicate with her. The question remains as to whether grassroots English might have helped Afia to navigate some of the difficulties she faced or to find more stable and fair employment. But English did not help Badol either, who knew the language before departure but had no need for it in jobs that he happened to do when he was abroad. English, however, was valuable for him when he worked with Filipinos and Europeans, which shows that the value of language skills varies even within the same country depending on the particular site of employment.

The accounts of the three migrant workers allow us to see that, despite any economic gains (which were not necessarily guaranteed), migration could leave significant social, physical and psychological scars (see also Erling et al. 2019). For Gofur, even though migration provided him with significant economic gain, one significant cost was personal: his long stints abroad meant that he never married. For Badol, the costs of migration were psychological and physical as he was engaged in extremely difficult physical labour with a low salary, and now he regrets the money and physical and emotional energy he wasted. For Afia there were physical but also psychological costs which included her being apart from her family and jeopardising her reputation.

The value of grassroots English in migration for the three participants seems to be significantly enmeshed in structural factors related to Bangladeshi economic migration that they had little control over, making the value of their grassroots English both uncertain and unpredictable (see also Erling et al. 2019). From one perspective, it seems that there is a certain de facto value of grassroots English for the migrant workers in the increasingly globalised Middle East for communication in lingua franca situations. After Arabic, English seems to work as an additional linguistic resource for Bangladeshi migrants, which can be called on at times for specific purposes, for example when communication in Arabic is not possible or when other non-native speakers of Arabic are present. Moreover, English can enhance a speaker's social status, creating an impression of authority and education. However, the extent to which Bangladeshi migrant workers can mobilise grassroots English to influence their economic situation is questionable and seems to depend more on a number of factors beyond their control, including recruiting agencies, employers' whims and personal circumstances. Thus, the question of the value of language skills in economic migration should be understood in relation to macro structural factors including global inequality. For example, with reference to Afia, the harrowing stories of abuse that she experienced in Saudi Arabia are unfortunately not rare (see British Broadcasting Corporation (BBC) 2018). However, in seeking bilateral resolutions to such issues, Bangladesh has limited bargaining power with Saudi Arabia in comparison to countries like Indonesia, the Philippines or Sri Lanka (BBC 2018). This could be seen when, for example, in response to migrant domestic workers' frequent reports of abuse, Indonesia and the Philippines stopped sending domestic workers to Saudi Arabia. During this time Saudi Arabia, the largest provider of employment for migrant Bangladeshi workers, pressured Bangladesh to increase its supply of female domestic workers. Due to Bangladeshis' urgent needs for employment, the country was forced to comply with this demand, agreeing even to low wages for its workers (Wara 2018).

The above discussion of the value of grassroots English for economic migration shows that these values are entangled with global inequality and the social and psychological costs of migration. The participants' narratives were punctuated by tales of hardship, which suggests that some of the methodological aspects of the study require reflection.

7 METHODOLOGICAL CONSIDERATIONS FOR RESEARCHING GRASSROOTS ENGLISH

As can be seen in the narratives recounted above, many of the participants experienced considerable hardships that left substantial social, physical and psychological scars. The recounting of such stories was not planned for in this study's research design, which was primarily focused on the linguistic dimensions of economic migration. We were therefore unprepared when participants like Afia showed us the burn marks on her hands from when her employer pressed a hot iron to her, or when Badol recounted his experiences of living in fear of being arrested and jailed when working illegally. Therefore, we would like to put forward here some particular methodological considerations for researching grassroots English, in order to encourage research practices that promote transparency and fairness but also to not create any false expectations in the research participants. Given the strong trend for economic migration in the village in which the research was undertaken, and the moderate socio-economic circumstances of the participants, it was difficult to avoid creating false hopes among the participants that our research on English and economic migration might provide a potential benefit for them.

We took several measures to make our research appropriate for and comprehensible to the participants, while also aiming to minimise their expectations of the research while still somehow recognising their contributions. We did this by trying to align to local cultural norms and practices during the fieldwork and trying to be sensitive to the experiences and status of the participants (see further Hultgren et al. 2016). The fact that the research team consisted of highly educated, urban, multilingual professionals – whose experiences of migration had been rather privileged in comparison to the migrant workers with relatively low levels of formal education – seemed to evoke a sense of promise. Thus, we were acutely aware of the gap in power created by this and were concerned to minimise the potential influences and possible hopes this had on participants. This was especially important because participants in rural Bangladesh were generally unfamiliar with the process and purpose of research. The idea that researchers would merely want to collect perspectives without any direct impact on them or the local community seemed difficult to convey. Even though we informed the participants about the purpose of our research prior to recruiting them, many of them continued to ask questions to find out what they thought must be the real, underlying 'purpose' of the research.

With regard to the project, we wanted to offer a token of appreciation to participants for the time that they contributed to the research, particularly as this time might have been taken away from people's waged employment, some of whom were living on very limited incomes. We were acutely aware that this token could not be inappropriately generous, as this would enhance the impression that the project would provide participants with direct benefits to them as individuals or their communities. It was therefore decided that a small token of appreciation – a local food item – would be given.

The presence of a white, British, English-speaking male researcher during the pilot study might have spurred hopes further about the research. His presence generated significant interest and curiosity among the local people. Even though we only planned to interview two ex-migrant workers for the pilot, five participants volunteered, seemingly curious about his presence. During the interview, one participant who had returned but was looking for a new job abroad repeatedly offered to show us his passport (perhaps assuming that it would be needed for employment). In order to deflect such perceptions, the foreign researcher made sure to accept any refreshments offered with praise, by showing his familiarity with the context by complying with local customs, and by using some Bangla phrases with the participants.

The enthusiasm about the research, however, lessened considerably during the main fieldwork visit when the foreign researcher was no longer present, in part because of our concerns about the effect of his presence on participants' perceptions. The two Bangladeshi researchers then found recruiting participants more challenging. Moreover, being highly educated and residents of the country's capital, they needed to align with the local cultural expectations in terms of dress, body language and language use. Drawing on experience from previous research in rural Bangladesh (see Erling et al. 2013), they tried to build rapport with people in the local community by visiting the bazaar in the evening and chatting with them over tea. Familiarity with local norms and customs thus seems essential in doing research at the grassroots, though ethical challenges in such contexts are considerable.

8 CONCLUSION

Addressing the scarcity of and need for research on English and low-/semi-skilled economic migration, in this chapter we have explored the value of grassroots English for the Bangladeshi migrant workers. We found that the Bangladeshi economic migrants' grassroots English has some functional values for them in terms of navigating their social and economic lives in the Middle East. However, the enactment of such value depends on the context in which they communicate and who they communicate with along with the languages spoken in the Middle East, primarily Arabic, but also Hindi. Moreover, upon critically analysing the narratives of the participants, sometimes in light of the historical and global issues of economic migration in the region, we found that the structural complexities of Bangladeshi economic migration and global inequality considerably shape the value that grassroots (English) language skills may offer. In addition, given that economic migration, even for those who profit economically, may incur significant visible or invisible social and psychological costs, we found it further problematic to establish any straightforward link between grassroots English and gainful economic migration, particularly when we draw in a more holistic view of development as the 'substantive freedom – of people to lead the lives they have reason to value and to enhance the real choices they have' (Sen 1999: 293). Moreover, taking account of the socio-economic inequality between the researchers and the participants, we also reflected on some relevant methodological issues. Observing the multifaceted entanglements of the issue (that is, grassroots English and economic migration) that we studied, but also to inform research in this area, we found it useful and relevant to reflect on some of our methodological and ethical experiences, in lines of power, hopes and equality. We conclude this chapter by arguing that a critical and holistic approach – informed by individual biographies of migrant workers and structural and contextual factors of migration – and also relevant methodological issues can provide useful direction to scholarship and assumptions on this less explored but increasingly important area of grassroots English and international low-/semi-skilled economic migration.

ACKNOWLEDGEMENTS

The research drawn on in this chapter was funded by a British Council English Language Teaching Research Partnerships Award, for which we remain grateful. We would like to acknowledge the particular contributions of our colleagues Sayeedur Rahman, Mike Solly and Philip Seargeant, who worked with us on this project. We thank the Open University, UK, the University of Dhaka and members of the English in Action project team, who all supported the undertaking of the research. We especially thank our participants, who generously shared with us their thoughts, time and insights.

REFERENCES

Afsar, Rita (2009), 'Unravelling the vicious cycle of recruitment: labour migration from Bangladesh to the Gulf States', International Labour Organization (ILO) Working Paper 63, Geneva: International Labour Office.

Bangladesh Bureau of Manpower and Employment (BMET) (2018), *Category-wise Overseas Employment from 1976 to 2018*, <http://www.old.bmet.gov.bd/BMET/viewStatReport.action?reportnumber=9> (last accessed 7 October 2019).

Bangladesh Bureau of Manpower and Employment (BMET) (2019), *Overseas Employment and Remittances (1976–2019)*, <http://www.old.bmet.gov.bd/BMET/viewStatReport.action?reportnumber=34> (last accessed 7 October 2019).

Banu, Rahela and Roland Sussex (2001), 'English in Bangladesh after independence: dynamics of policy and practice', in Bruce Moore (ed.), *Who's Centric Now? The Present State of Post-Colonial Englishes*, Oxford: Oxford University Press, 123–57.

Bélanger, Danièle and Mahmuda Rahman (2013), 'Migrating against all the odds: international labour migration of Bangladeshi women', *Current Sociology*, 61: 3, 356–73. doi: 10.1177/0011392113484453.
British Broadcasting Corporation (BBC) (2018), 'Ferar por poribareo thai nai: Saudi theke nirjatoner shikar hoye fire asha Bangladeshi nari' [No place in the family upon return: Bangladeshi women returning from Saudi being victim of torture], 4 June, <https://www.bbc.com/bengali/news-44360667> (last accessed 18 January 2020).
Canagarajah, Suresh (ed.) (2017), *The Routledge Handbook of Migration and Language*, London: Routledge.
Chiswick, Barry R. and Paul W. Miller (1995), 'The endogeneity between language and earnings: international analyses', *Journal of Labor Economics*, 13: 2, 246–88.
Chiswick, Barry R. and Paul W. Miller (2003), 'The complementarity of language and other human capital: immigrant earnings in Canada', *Economics of Education Review*, 22: 5, 469–80.
Coleman, Hywel (2010), *The English Language in Development*, London: British Council, <https://www.teachingenglish.org.uk/sites/teacheng/files/UK 011-English-Language-Development.pdf> (last accessed 7 October 2019).
Deumert, Ana, Brett Inder and Pushkar Maitra (2005), 'Language, informal networks and social protection: evidence from a sample of migrants in Cape Town, South Africa', *Global Social Policy*, 5: 3, 303–28.
Dustmann, Christian (1994), 'Speaking fluency, writing fluency and earnings of migrants', *Journal of Population Economics*, 7: 2, 133–56.
Dustmann, Christian and Francesca Fabbri (2003), 'Language proficiency and labour market performance of immigrants in the UK', *Economic Journal*, 113: 489, 695–717.
Dustmann, Christian and Arthur van Soest (2001), 'Language fluency and earnings: estimation with misclassified language indicators', *Review of Economics and Statistics*, 83: 4, 663–74.
Erling, Elizabeth J. (2017), 'Language planning, English language education and development aid in Bangladesh', *Current Issues in Language Planning*, 18: 4, 388–406. doi: 10.1080/14664208.2017.1331496.
Erling, Elizabeth J. and Philip Seargeant (eds) (2013), *English and Development: Policy, Pedagogy and Globalization*, Bristol: Multilingual Matters.
Erling, Elizabeth J., Qumrul Hasan Chowdhury, Mike Solly and Philip Seargeant (2019), '"Successful" migration, (English) language skills and global inequality: the case of Bangladeshi migrants to the Middle East', *Multilingua*, 38: 3, 253–81. doi: 10.1515/multi-2018-0021.
Erling, Elizabeth J., Philip Seargeant, Mike Solly, Qumrul Hasan Chowdhury and Sayeedur Rahman (2013), *Attitudes to English as a Language for International Development in Rural Bangladesh*, British Council ELT Research

Papers, London: British Council, <https://www.teachingenglish.org.uk/sites/teacheng/files/B497%20ELTRP%20Report%20Erling_FINAL.pdf> (last accessed 13 July 2019).

Erling, Elizabeth J., Philip Seargeant, Mike Solly, Qumrul Hasan Chowdhury and Sayeedur Rahman (2015), *English for Economic Development : A Case Study of Migrant Workers from Bangladesh*, London: British Council, <https://www.teachingenglish.org.uk/sites/teacheng/files/pub_2999_BC_OU%20Eltra%20Booklet_05b.pdf> (last accessed 7 October 2019).

Froese, Fabian J., Vesa Peltokorpi and Kyung A. Ko (2012), 'The influence of intercultural communication on cross-cultural adjustment and work attitudes: foreign workers in South Korea', *International Journal of Intercultural Relations*, 36: 3, 331–42.

Gao, Wenshu and Russell Smyth (2011), 'Economic returns to speaking "standard Mandarin" among migrants in China's urban labour market', *Economics of Education Review*, 30: 2, 342–52.

Giampapa, Frances and Suresh Canagarajah (2017), 'Skilled migration and global English', *Globalisation, Societies and Education*, 15: 1, 1–4. doi: 10.1080/14767724.2017.1296658.

Grenier, Gilles and Serge Nadeau (2011), *English as the Lingua Franca and the Economic Value of Other Languages: The Case of Language of Work of Immigrants and Non-immigrants in the Montreal Labour Market*, Department of Economics, University of Ottawa.

Guido, Maria Grazia (2008), *English as a Lingua Franca in Cross-cultural Immigration Domains*, Frankfurt: Peter Lang.

Guido, Maria Grazia (2012), 'ELF authentication and accommodation strategies in crosscultural immigration encounters', *Journal of English as a Lingua Franca*, 1: 2, 219–40.

Hultgren, Anna Kristina, Elizabeth J. Erling and Qumrul Hasan Chowdhury (2016), 'Ethics in language and identity research', in Sian Preece (ed.), *The Routledge Handbook of Language and Identity*, London: Routledge, 257–71.

International Labour Organization (2019), *Labour Migration in Bangladesh*, <https://www.ilo.org/dhaka/Areasofwork/labour-migration/lang--en/index.htm> (last accessed 7 October 2019).

Kachru, Braj (1986), 'The power and politics of English', *World Englishes*, 5: 2–3, 121–40.

Lan, Pei-Chia (2003), '"They have more money but I speak better English!" Transnational encounters between Filipina domestics and Taiwanese employers', *Identities: Global Studies in Culture and Power*, 10: 2, 133–61.

Pavlenko, Aneta (2007), 'Autobiographic narratives as data in applied linguistics', *Applied Linguistics*, 28: 2, 163–188.

Rahman, Md Mizanur (2012), 'Bangladeshi labour migration to the Gulf States:

patterns of recruitment and processes', *Canadian Journal of Development Studies*, 33: 2, 214–30.

Rassool, Naz (2007), *Global Issues in Language, Education and Development: Perspectives from Postcolonial Countries*, Bristol: Multilingual Matters.

Riaz, Ali and Mohammad Sajjadur Rahman (eds) (2016), *Routledge Handbook of Contemporary Bangladesh*, London: Routledge.

Sarker, Masud and Shahidul Islam (2018), 'Impacts of international migration on socio-economic development in Bangladesh', *European Review of Applied Sociology*, 11: 16, 27–35. doi: 10.1515/eras-2018-0003.

Schneider, Edgar W. (2016), 'Grassroots Englishes in tourism interactions', *English Today*, 32: 3, 2–10. doi: 10.1017/S0266078416000183.

Seargeant, Philip, Elizabeth J. Erling, Mike Solly and Qumrul Hasan Chowdhury (2017), 'The communicative needs of Bangladeshi economic migrants: the functional values of host country languages versus English as a lingua franca', *Journal of English as a Lingua Franca*, 6: 1, 141–65. doi: 10.1515/jelf-2017-0008.

Sen, Amartya (1999), *Development as Freedom*, Oxford: Oxford University Press.

Siddiqui, Tasneem (2016), 'International labour migration and remittances', in Ali Riaz and Mohammad Sajjadur Rahman (eds), *Routledge Handbook of Contemporary Bangladesh*, London: Routledge, 197–206.

The World Bank (2018), *Bangladesh*, <https://www.worldbank.org/en/country/Bangladesh> (last accessed 7 October 2019).

United Nations Development Programme (UNDP) (2018), *Human Development Reports*, <http://hdr.undp.org/en/countries/profiles/BGD> (last accessed 2 September 2019).

Wara, Gowhar Noyim (2018), '*Probashi nari sromiker golpota keu shunben?*' [Will you listen to the story of the woman migrant worker?], 4 June, *The Prothom Alo*, <https://www.prothomalo.com/opinion/article/1502416> (last accessed 23 January 2020).

CHAPTER 9

Grassroots Diffusion of English in a 'Blue-collar' Workplace: The Case of a Multilingual Cleaning Company in New Jersey, USA

Kellie Gonçalves

1 INTRODUCTION

There exists a small but growing body of literature within the field of sociolinguistics that investigates language learning, language use and social practices within blue-collar, domestic labour contexts in various parts of the world (cf. Gonçalves and Schluter 2020 for an overview). Despite the variety of contexts in which most of these studies occur, many of them are often one-sided in that they centre either on the experiences of employees or employers, but rarely consider both (cf. Gonçalves and Schluter 2017; Gonçalves 2019, forthcoming). This study addresses grassroots diffusion of English within a domestic labour context and, more specifically, within a multilingual cleaning company in New Jersey, USA. Situated within a broader theoretical framework of globalisation (Blommaert 2010; Coupland 2010) and the 'turbulence of modern migration' (Papastergiadis 2000), this study investigates the complexity of language learning and the use of English at the grassroots level within the twenty-first century (Meierkord 2012) among Portuguese- and Spanish-speaking employees, their multilingual employer and anglophone clients. Investigating a multilingual cleaning company in the US, and accounting for the ways in which an owner, her employees and clients communicate by drawing on diverse linguistic and extra-linguistic resources, sheds light on how languages are being used and acquired from 'below'. Moreover, such a study exemplifies how certain linguistic repertoires are being evaluated and deployed, thus calling scholars to reconsider perhaps the value and status of English and other languages within particular locally situated workplace settings, which may be telling of other language contact situations more generally.

In line with the present volume on English at the grassroots, this chapter has four main aims. Firstly, this study adds to the growing body of literature which investigates blue-collar workplaces, which continues to be unexplored as a result of existing methodological challenges and perhaps even epistemological biases. Secondly, it investigates the ways in which transnational domestic workers within a multilingual cleaning company in the US have learned English from 'below', in other words, informally, and analyses English-language repertoires among employees and clients. Thirdly, it aims to underscore that effective communication for company external purposes (between employees and clients) often relies on creative and improvised, situation-specific deployment of both linguistic and extra-linguistic resources. And, finally, it questions existing literature which promotes English proficiency for reasons of recruitment and social mobility (especially within a US context), suggesting the need to look into more context-specific and local practices between individuals who do not share a first/second language in order for effective communication to be achieved.

1.1 The Role of English Globally

There is a part of the literature which regards English as being the most prestigious language globally as a result of colonialism, and thus continued and recent socio-cultural, political and economic flows within the global economy. As such, it is not surprising that the spread, status and role of English has been investigated worldwide in order to show how it has been contact-derived from its beginnings, and as such presents scholars with an array of potential regarding language contact studies (Schneider 2011; Meierkord 2012; Schreier and Hundt 2013) as in fact one of the 'best-studied languages in the world' (Schreier and Hundt 2013: 5). Indeed, this has led to our understanding of how English is regarded as at once 'globalising' while simultaneously 'nativising' (Schneider 2011: 2). As much as English has international flair, appeal and symbolic capital for its users in different ways and in diverse contexts, it may also serve and fulfil local functions, where users develop specific forms that fit their specific socio-cultural contexts. In nation states where English is the dominant language, like the US (despite its lack of an official language policy on a national level), one might also assume and even argue that English is the language required for employment in terms of recruitment and social mobility (Laitin and Reich 2003). Such is the case, for example, with De Swaan's (2001) model of language hierarchies, which indicates that a high communicative value of a language would transfer directly to the language's high economic value. Within De Swann's model, English in the US is represented as prestigious on multiple levels, globally (*hypercentral*), nationally (*supercentral*) and regionally (*central*). However, a requirement to look into the local contexts in order to better understand situation-specific interaction (Pennycook 2010; Schneider 2016) and the kind of language, languages or bits of language as well as other semiotic resources that are being deployed in order for communication to be carried out among interlocutors of different language backgrounds, needs to be considered. This pertains especially to specific workplace contexts which are largely considered 'language marginal' (McAll 2003; Strömmer 2016), meaning that not much language is actually required or even used within one's job and done by those primarily at the lower end of the socio-economic scale. These are the themes that will be elaborated on and analysed within this chapter.

1.2 Truncated Repertoires, Translanguaging and Grassroots Englishes: Same, Same but Different?

Much sociolinguistic work problematises how a language or languages have been theoretically approached to account for the use of code-mixing, bilingualism and multilingual practices at both the individual and societal level (Heller 2007; Makoni and Pennycook 2006; Auer 2007; Schneider 2016; De Houwer and Ortega 2019). The past two decades have seen a rise in terminology to explain such practices in order to understand how individuals, by drawing on a language, multiple languages or even specific features of a variety, index their socio-cultural and dynamic identities, where meaning emerges, is negotiated and is contingent of social interaction (cf. Pennycook (2016) on the 'trans-super-poly-metro movement' in contemporary studies). This literature, as well as the work on 'truncated repertoires', 'translanguaging' and 'grassroots Englishes', all orient to post-structuralist approaches to language, where notions of fixity and boundedness have been discarded for more favourable and perhaps even more realistic views of individuals' repertoires that are much more flexible and accommodating to interlocutors and their specific spatio-temporal contexts and needs.

In accounting for globalisation processes and their effect on lived sociolinguistic realities and contact situations, Blommaert (2010: 103) refers to the concept of 'truncated repertoires'. Truncated repertoires can be understood to be individuals' partial proficiency levels that are limited to specific skills, that is greetings and salutations or asking for directions. In fact, Blommaert claims that 'no one needs all the resources that a language potentially provides' (2010: 103). In other words, not everyone requires complete mastery in a language since not everyone needs to. Blommaert's notion resonates well with Canagarajah's (2011) discussion of translanguaging, where languages (in the plural) are

> [p]art of a repertoire [. . .] Languages are not discreet [. . .] [but] form an integrated system; multilingual competence emerges out of local practices where multiple languages are negotiated for communication; for these reasons, proficiency for multilinguals is focused on repertoire building i.e. developing abilities in the different functions served by different languages – rather than total mastery of each and every language. (2011: 2)

In a similar vein and in his seminal work on 'grassroots Englishes', Schneider (2016: 3) maintains that

> For many people in very many places, very often speakers with no access to formal higher-level education, there exists an immense instrumental motivation to acquire a form of English which is sufficient for their respective professional purposes. Linguistically talented as they often are, they acquire some English in whatever form and by whatever means available. Rather than having been disseminated, as has been the case traditionally, from above, a process of growth of English from the ground, as it were, can be observed these days – and while this is not a wholly new process in itself, its breadth, regularity and intensity have reached a novel quality in the 21st century. The English language is undergoing a new kind of expansion and transformation, with 'grassroots Englishes' emerging in many countries and contexts. What ultimate linguistic consequences this may have in the long run, if any, is impossible to predict at this point. But the phenomenon as such is worth considering.

What distinguishes the thoughts of Canagarajah from that of Schneider also has to do with questions surrounding social class, status and access. Indeed, much of the work which has emphasised and continues to emphasise the learning or acquisition of English as an L2 or FL has been done within educational settings and thus formal domains (Schneider 2016; Gonçalves 2019). This is perhaps not surprising given the focus of applied linguistics and applied sociolinguistics. However, workplaces and blue-collar settings in particular also present a prime site to investigate language contact and communicative interactions between individuals who do not share an L1 or common 'culture' and who also come from very different socio-economic and thus social class backgrounds (Gonçalves 2019, 2020; Gonçalves and Kelly-Holmes 2021).

Blue-collar is indeed a tricky label and category (Arnold and Bongiovi 2013), generally understood and considered to be working-class labour that is predominately found in both primary and secondary sectors that include manufacturing and agriculture. Service work (including domestic labour) is typically categorised under the tertiary sector; however, it can also be seen to some degree as 'blue-collar' especially if these jobs are by definition temporary and low status and incorporate some type of physical labour that is based on paid hourly wages (Lederer 1979).

It is therefore not surprising that the connotations associated with blue-collar work lead many to perceive it as 'unskilled' and even 'dirty' (Holmes 2012), which has been and remains a peripheral site of research interest for many language scholars (Gonçalves and Schluter 2017; Lønsmann and Kraft 2017; Gonçalves and Kelly-Holmes 2021). While studies of language and the workplace are manifold (see Spolsky 2009; Block 2018; Thurlow 2020; Gonçalves and Kelly-Holmes 2021), many have focused and continue to focus on white-collar domains, a considerable number of which fall under the rubric of the so-called 'new knowledge' economy, an economic system of production and consumption that is primarily based on intellectual capital found within developed countries. Such a focus has continued to neglect what McDowell and Dyson (2011) refer to as the *reproductive economy*, under which care and domestic work (largely considered blue-collar) fall, which is also the subject of the present study.

2 INVESTIGATING SHINE,[1] A MULTILINGUAL CLEANING COMPANY – METHODS AND DATA

This study was carried out together with Anne Schluter and we were able to gain access to this company, which we call 'Shine', through close personal ties of mine. Magda, the owner and main operator of Shine, is a family member of mine and someone I have known since childhood. This close tie and relationship has allowed us relatively unfettered access to Magda and her company, which we have investigated for nearly a decade (2011–20). The methods for data collection were guided by both critical and mobile ethnographic approaches (Madison 2012; Novoa 2015; Gonçalves and Schluter 2017; Heller et al. 2018). Ethnography is considered to be a hermeneutic and thus an interpretative affair (Campbell and Lassiter 2015) which is creative, collaborative and personal requiring us to reach beyond certain methodological approaches by considering its 'histories, philosophies, epistemologies, and ontologies' (p. 3). Drawing on critical ethnography calls for being reflexive about the type of work we are carrying out and acknowledging that as researchers our own positionalities, identities and interests influence our research agenda (Noblit et al. 2004; Gonçalves and Schluter 2017). It also compels us to think about our work and how it contributes to the equality and justice of our informants and our commitment to social change (Martin-Jones and Martin 2016). Mobile ethnography on the other hand sanctions a physical co-presence with participants concerning the proximity of events. It comprises a vast spectrum of activities ranging from shadowing participants' daily lives or workdays (Czarniawska 2007) to engaging with their involvement of 'cross-border mobility' (Novoa 2015: 100). While we did not move with participants across national boundaries, we did shadow them during their work hours and at their workplaces as well as spend time with them 'off the clock'.

Our data methods include document analysis (of Shine's company booklet, emails and notes), participant observations and interviews. The language of the interviews varied according to the interviewees' preferences and, thus, contributed to a multilingual (Spanish, English and Portuguese) corpus of approximately 210,000 words. The interviewees were made up of nineteen clients, eighteen employees and four language brokers of Shine. We acknowledge that our position as both company insiders and outsiders may have compromised our objectivity (Zentella 1997; Lanza 2008); nevertheless, we argue that the quality of the data collected was richer because of this access and that familiarity with the participants likely contributed to more open and intimate accounts of their experiences. Furthermore, these relationships have allowed us to conduct follow-up interviews with both Magda and several of her employees over the years to address themes as they emerge in our ongoing data analysis.

This privileged access to participants has also extended to the location of the interviews. Rather than holding interviews in neutral settings that have little relevance to the workplace context, we were able to conduct the interviews with Magda, her employees and the language brokers directly at Shine's headquarters, which simultaneously serves as Magda's home. Interviews with clients also took place inside their homes, at times that suited their schedules. Spending considerable time at Shine's headquarters as well as physically being inside clients' homes during the interviews allowed us to observe these different environments first-hand.

We engaged in data triangulation of interviews, document analysis and participant observation. The focus of grassroots English within this particular multilingual cleaning company encompasses interlocutors from diverse cultural and linguistic backgrounds with regard to both company-internal (Shine's employees) as well as company-external (Shine's employees and clients) communicative interactions. Analysing interactions, albeit on a meta level, which have emerged within and outside of Shine makes this an especially fitting context in which to both examine the ways in which English is discussed as well as the ways in which the role of English competence is evaluated for effective communicative purposes within this particular workplace context.

2.1 Setting the Scene: Newark and Westwood[2]

Most of Shine's employees reside in the Portuguese ethnic enclave of the Ironbound located in Newark, New Jersey, while a handful live in a Portuguese community located in Elizabeth, New Jersey. In this section, I focus on the sociodemographic differences which exist between Newark and the upper-middle-class suburb of Westwood, New Jersey, where the majority of Shine's clients reside and where Shine's headquarters is based. A look at the participants' home and work environments provides a stark contrast between the relative linguistic, racial, ethnic and class homogeneity in the greater Westwood area as compared to the far more diverse urban context of Newark. Table 9.1 summarises these differences.

As can be readily seen from Table 9.1, the socio-economic, racial, ethnic and

Table 9.1 Socio-demographic differences between Newark and Westwood based on 2017 census information (Newark City Data 2017)

	Newark	Westwood
Population	285,156	30,591
Annual household income	US$35,167	US$159,923
Poverty rate	28.3%	2.66%
Race and ethnicity	Over 40% black followed by 33% 'Hispanic'	Over 90% white
Languages used	70% claim to use Spanish followed by 10% Portuguese	Over 90% claim to speak English

linguistic differences that exist between Newark and Westwood are quite substantial. The twenty-five-minute daily commute from the Ironbound in Newark to Westwood which is provided by Shine takes these female domestic migrant workers to a setting in which the median household income is US$159,923 (in 2017) and exceeds that of their home neighborhoods by roughly four times, highlighting the existing socio-economic and social class differences between these groups of people. Moreover, the racial, ethnic and linguistic differences are also in stark opposition to one another. While the majority of Newark residents, who are racially and ethnically mixed, claim to have Spanish as their main language followed by Portuguese, residents of Westwood are predominately white, monolingual speakers of English.

2.2 Shine: The Cleaning Company

Shine serves the greater Westwood area and was established in the mid-1980s by Magda, a female Brazilian migrant and US citizen, who has a background in bank branch management and strong ties to the local Portuguese community. Magda, a university educated and highly multilingual speaker of English, Spanish and Portuguese, has served as the sole owner and chief operator of the business since its founding, but two of her employees assist her with the administrative load by simultaneously serving as cleaners, assistant managers and drivers. At the time of our first data collection in 2011, Shine served 250 households and employed eighteen full-time cleaners and one American monolingual English speaker, Jill, who was a seasonal driver.

As depicted in Figure 9.1, Shine's workforce is comprised of mainly European Portuguese women despite Magda's own L1 Luso-Brazilian Portuguese linguistic and cultural background. The covert, company-internal language policy that favours European Portuguese does indeed stem from these numbers and reflects Magda's preference for European Portuguese employees, who she considers to be diligent workers, obedient and more submissive than her Luso-Brazilian

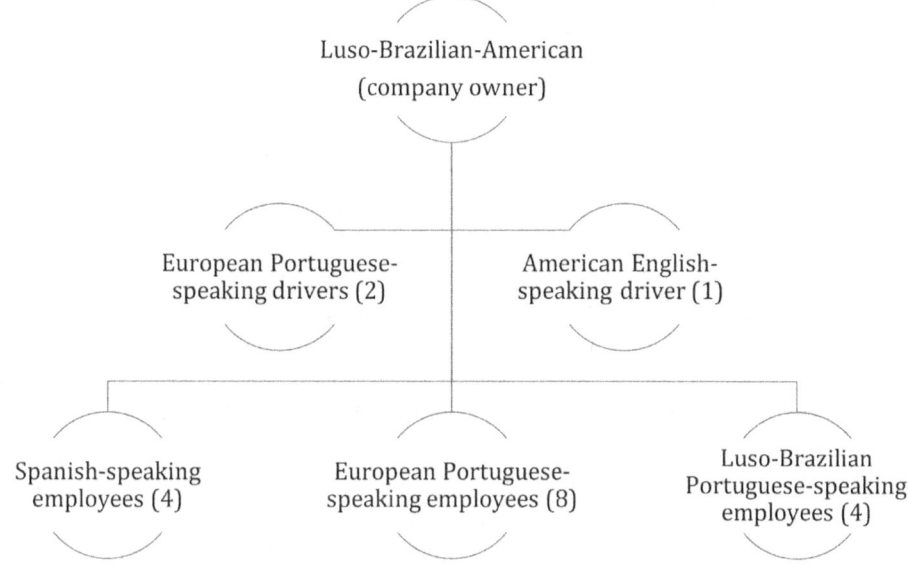

Figure 9.1 Shine's company hierarchy with Magda located at the top

employees (see Gonçalves and Schluter 2017 for a thorough discussion). Magda's preference for European Portuguese as the company-internal language has to do with her own L1 and her visions of the company's philosophy – which is to provide the best-quality service for her clients while maintaining loyal, diligent and respected employees – as well as the large supply of transnational domestic workers in the region (many of whom are residents of the Ironbound and Elizabeth, New Jersey).

3 LANGUAGE PROFICIENCY AND LANGUAGE POLICY AT SHINE

Shine's employees come from Portugal (10), Brazil (4), Ecuador (3) and Honduras (1). And while many of these women have lived in the US for considerable periods of time (ranging anywhere from 4–26 years), their levels of English proficiency range considerably, from non-existent to 'fluent', the latter meaning that they can understand and converse fairly easily on different topics in English, which was confirmed by Magda, several of Shine's employees and some of Shine's long-standing customers including Mrs Lo in Extract (1) below:

Extract (1)
Kellie: and how have you found their kind of English speaking abilities?

Mrs Lo: it totally varies
Anne: mhm
Mrs Lo: erm we have had some people who were absolutely fluent in English erm and other people who, had pretty much no English.

Indeed, many of Magda's employees are not proficient in English but have nevertheless been able to find and secure employment at Shine. The main reason for this has to do with Magda's ability to both linguistically and culturally broker between her Portuguese- and Spanish-speaking employees and her English-speaking clients. For Tse (1995: 485) 'language brokers facilitate communication between two linguistically and/or culturally different parties. Unlike formal interpreters and translators, brokers mediate, rather than merely transmit, information.' Because language brokers are considered mediators and, often, decision makers, they are equipped with metalinguistic awareness that is embedded within the ability to assess and act according to given situational contexts (Malakoff and Hakuta 1991). As the main mediator of Shine, Magda disseminates instructions and requests from her customers and translates them directly into Portuguese or Spanish in order for her employees to carry out the specified tasks within the homes they are responsible for cleaning. By functioning as Shine's main language broker, Magda attempts to reduce the need for direct, transactional communication between her employees and customers, thus mitigating and micro-managing the language contact situation and ensuing communication that might otherwise result between these individuals. Although Magda encourages interactional and thus communicative exchanges to build and maintain friendly customer-employee relationships, she discourages transactional communication, that is any communication having to do with the financial side of Shine due to her employees' limited English proficiency and the potential for any misunderstandings to occur. This becomes apparent in the following extract (2) in which Magda discusses the language policy designed for communication between her clients and her employees:

Extract (2)
Kellie: do you give them [the clients] explicit instructions . . . not to communicate with the cleaning ladies or?
Magda: no . . . I don't tell them, 'don't communicate', there, there is erm, erm, a paragraph [in the company's information booklet] that says, 'Do not leave a note because most of the cleaning ladies do not speak English so they may not understand and we really want to do a good job . . . if you leave a note, you leave it to me so then I can you know, tell the cleaning lady this, this and that and erm you know, there's no miscommunication in there [. . .] I tell some customers, 'If you leave a note for her, she's gonna take that note for me, so if you're asking her to do

something, it may not get done' [. . .] I mean the customers are told not to leave a note . . . but, but if they leave a note and some of them don't follow the rules you know?

Extract (2) refers to the seven-page document intended for clients which conveys details about the company's service and expectations for customers. Indeed, how clients should communicate via written means becomes especially important in order to avoid miscommunication. This extract also helps to show the role of language brokering in preserving a top-down communication structure in which Magda leaves little room for bottom-up input. As Magda explains in Extract (3), her language brokering between clients and employees removes extensive potential communication difficulties:

Extract (3)
Magda: If they [the customers] leave a note, erm [one of the cleaning ladies] will pick up the erm phone and say 'Well you know, I understand so much, so much but there's this that I don't understand' depending where it is you know sometimes I say, 'Well, spell it for me' you know? And she starts spelling and I can just you know pick up right away 'Oh ok, that's it' so I will give her the instructions, yeah.

In Extract (3), we get a glimpse into Magda's brokering practices as well as her willingness to assist her employees with deciphering clients' hand-written English messages, which according to Magda, could not be decoded by employees alone. Magda therefore functions as the company's main disseminator of instructions both during the preliminary planning process and in cases of last-minute changes or clarifications that cannot be communicated directly between the client and her employee as is exemplified in the scenario reconstructed above in (3).

As the company owner and primary language broker between her clients and employees, Magda is not only able to oversee any communication between the two groups, but she also attempts to maintain full control over it. The micro-management Magda engages in between her clients and employees means that her Portuguese- and Spanish-speaking employees do not actually need English in order to carry out their daily working duties. For many of Shine's employees, this lack of need diminishes their investment (Norton 2000) in English altogether and maintains some employees' preference for 'Magda-mediating' communication. Nevertheless, our other findings indicate that a number of instances of transactional employee-customer communication occur, in spite of Magda's attempts to have most communication of this type channelled through her. In fact, several of Shine's employees expressed a willingness and desire to learn and activate their English skills (however limited they were), while others, despite their English proficiency and creative deployment of linguistic and extra-linguistic resources, continued to measure their linguistic abilities against native speaker norms. The analysis that follows focuses on these different results and interactions, thus taking a closer look at individuals' descriptions of their communication in their local communities as well as at Shine.

4 COMMUNICATIVE PRACTICES

4.1 Communicative Practices in the Ironbound

As stated in section 2.1, the Ironbound, in Newark, New Jersey is a Portuguese- and Spanish-speaking community, where many of Shine's employees reside. In discussing the multilingual context and languages used there on a daily basis, Dona Aura, a long-time Shine employee and resident of the US for over twenty-five years, states the following:

> Extract (4)
> Dona Aura: Sim, lá em Newark é quase tudo, (XXX) praticamente é tudo português, português, espanhol, brasileiro ('yes, there in Newark, almost everything (XXX), practically everything is in Portuguese, Spanish, Brazilian')
> Kellie: então o seu dia-a-dia é mais o português? ('So, your day to day is more Portuguese?')
> Dona Aura: yeah, sempre o português, em casa, e tudo, é sempre português ('Yeah, always Portuguese, at home, everything, it's always Portuguese').

Whether at home or in restaurants or supermarkets, individuals' daily needs are met primarily in Portuguese. In fact, English in the Ironbound neighbourhood functions as an additional language of wider communication but is by no means compulsory for day-to-day requirements (cf Gonçalves 2012, 2015 for a thorough discussion).

The predominately European Portuguese, Spanish and Luso-Brazilian communicative practices carried out in the Ironbound (confirmed here by Dona Aura and other interviewees) resonate with the multilingual language practices found at Shine and its adherence to a European Portuguese language policy for company internal purposes. In these ways, Shine's employees, like Dona Aura, who are also residents of the Ironbound, do not necessarily require English for (a) their daily lives or (b) their workplace tasks.

4.2 Communicative Practices at Shine: A Case of Grassroots English

In our interview with Paloma, a European Portuguese employee, who had been living in the US for nearly a decade, she discusses her English proficiency skills with reference to her job at Shine:

Extract (5)
Kellie: então você acha que o teu nível de inglês é suficiente para o trabalho? ('and so do you think your English level is sufficient for the job?')
Paloma: não, não é no ('no it's not')
Kellie: não é? Por que? ('no it's not, why not?')
Paloma: por que pronto, por que as vezes a gente quer se falar mais coisas ou as mulheres às vezes querem nos falar a nós a gente não consegue (.) a gente pronto a gente hello, good morning ou bye- bye ou assim mas (.) o essencial mesmo não sabe e, quer e não consegue e (.) mas pronto, mas a gente pra mim acho que se a gente, souber falar o essencial por exemplo, hello, good morning, o mais importante, ser simpático pra mulheres pra falar (.) pronto o essencial, de ser educado assim ('because, well, because sometimes we want to be able to say more things or the women sometimes would like to say more to us and we aren't able to (.) we well we hello, good morning or bye-bye like that but the important things really we don't know it's, you want to but you're not able to, but but anyway for me I think if we're able to say the essentials for example, hello, good morning, the most important thing, is to speak nicely to the women (.) well the most important thing is to be polite

In this extract, Paloma admits that despite living in the US for over a decade, her English is not really adequate for the job. In explaining her situation and willingness to be able to actually converse more with clients, she continually makes use of the inclusive 'we' (*a gente*) to index that all of the domestic workers have a difficult time communicating with clients. Her comment also subtly suggests that domestic workers do not receive extensive or sufficient L2 input during their working hours in order to acquire the communicative skills that would allow them to use the target language with their English-speaking clients. Her use of code-switching, truncated repertoires or grassroots English within this particular extract, in which diverse lexical items such as *hello*, and fixed phatic communicative phrases like *good morning* and *bye-bye* are included in her talk, suggests that Paloma does indeed have a small inventory of English structures that are employed for specific communicative purposes, as in this case of greeting clients.

Within studies on code-switching, Matras (2009: 111) has referred to this as 'situations of superficial or minimal bilingualism' for individuals who have 'a rudimentary knowledge of another language'. Rudimentary knowledge of another language resonates well with Blommaert's notion of 'truncated repertoires' and a case where 'no one knows all of a language' (2010: 103). Blommaert, drawing on the work of Hymes (1996), maintains that 'there is nothing wrong with that phenomenon of partial competence: no one needs all the resources that a language potentially provides'. Moreover, he states that 'our 'real language' is very much a biographical given, the structure of which reflects our own histories and those of the communities in which we spent our lives' (ibid.). Indeed, the communities in which Paloma, Dona Aura and many other of Shine's employees spend much of their lives and free time are in the Ironbound. Coming back to Paloma's extract also highlights that within this specific workplace context and space, other Shine employees are also being exposed to particular registers and structures that are being used and repeated regularly (like greetings and salutations) with clients, which they have acquired in direct interactions. As such, many employees, similar to Paloma, are able to draw on their truncated and multilingual repertoires in order for their communicative goals to be met.

Another Shine employee who has acquired English informally and through direct interactions with clients is Anita, a Hispanophone from Honduras. Anita had been living in the US for six years and is one of Shine's few employees who expresses a strong preference for direct communication with clients exclusively in English. Because of the dominance of Spanish- and Portuguese-language services in her local neighbourhood and Shine's Portuguese-centric language policy, it would indeed be possible for her to carry out her daily routines and work with very limited English. As some clients' use of Spanish could potentially facilitate her communication with them, we asked her if she would prefer customers to address her in Spanish:

Extract (6)
Anita: [Prefiero] inglés para poder aprender (.) Si no nunca voy a aprender. si me dan la facilidad de tratar en español yo nunca voy a tratar entonces de hablar el inglés ('I prefer English to be able to learn (.) if not I will never learn, if they give me the possibility of trying in Spanish I will then never try to speak English')
Anne: Hay algunas que no hablan nada [de inglés] (.) Por qué piensa que usted es diferente? ('some of the women [employees] can't speak any English (.) Why do you think you are different?')
Anita: yo pienso de que el idioma inglés es muy importante en ese país [. . .] si usted quiereseguir adelante tiene que saber inglés porque el inglés le abre las puertas, este es el idioma de este país ('you have to know English because English opens doors. It is the language of this country').

In her response to our question, Anita positions herself as an enthusiastic language learner who considers interactions with customers as opportunities for English language learning and language practice from below, whereas using Spanish would stymie her progress. In fact, Anita values the potential for her workplace to serve as a site for the *situated learning* of English (Toohey 2000) from 'below' (Schneider 2016). In this way, Anita's workplace interactions with customers may be regarded similarly to practices learned within a specific community of practice à la Lave and Wenger (1991), which allow her to engage in situation-oriented negotiation of English language meaning as legitimate peripheral participation. Moreover, she aims to apply this acquired knowledge to situations possibly beyond the Shine client-employee domain.

In this extract, Anita deems English language proficiency to be 'very important' and to carry a high instrumental and symbolic value for its ability to 'open doors' to new opportunities and to move people 'ahead' in their upwardly mobile trajectory. This perspective stems from Anita's experiences with language use and practices in the situation-specific domain of employee-client interactions with that of the hegemonic ideology of English within US workplace domains in general. Anita's vision of learning English to improve her life chances and possibly compete in the job market resonates with what Terasawa (2016) has referred to as the 'English divide'. The English divide is characterised by exclusive elite society members who have the financial resources and access to learn English in the hope of attaining a high level of competence, which would then give them an edge in the job market over their less qualified colleagues who do not have the linguistic and symbolic capital to move ahead. Although the interview with Anita directly addresses English within the context of her specific clients' homes, her response points to the national scale of the US in general with her reference to and repeated use of 'this country'.

Similar to Anita, Bianca, a Portuguese employee who has lived in the US for twenty-three years and has worked for Magda for twenty-two of them, assesses her English language proficiency according to standard American norms and does not evaluate her English skills positively. Nevertheless, Magda has placed her in positions – assistant manager and acting manager when Magda is away – which require substantial communication and direct contact with clients. From our interview with Magda, we know that Bianca rarely needs to rely on Magda's language brokering help when interacting with clients; moreover, given Magda's emphasis on frequent and effective customer communication, it is clear that she would never place an employee who lacked sufficient communication skills in a customer service position. Within the context of her job Bianca frequently negotiates meaning successfully with anglophone interlocutors, but when in absolute doubt she sometimes relies on her own highly bilingual daughter (raised in the US since age one) for brokering assistance. As a result, Bianca positions herself as a limited English speaker because she thinks her communicative successes are solely connected to Shine-specific domains – as she states below:

Extract (7)
Bianca: [Os clientes] falam comigo [em inglês] e eu consigo entender, mas são aquelas coisas básicas que s[ão] dizem respeito ao cleaning service, não é? então eu . . . eu nesse assunto não estou assim tão ok se tu falas pra mim ah em ingles. ('[The customers] speak to me [in English] and I am able to understand, but they are basic things that are related to the cleaning service, you know? [. . .] And so I . . . I in this way am not so OK if you speak to me in English').

In Extract (7), Bianca refers to her ability 'to understand' Shine's anglophone clients. While it is clear that her receptive skills are both developed and advanced, she is not convinced that her actual active English language production skills are satisfactory for the task of extensive communication with clients. In fact, Bianca rates her competence as simple. In this way, she suggests that she can engage in interactional and rudimentary communication about her work and cleaning but lacks the ability to discuss other topics, either of a transactional nature (pertaining to the financial aspects of Shine) or a communicative/interactional nature, with clients. Bianca, thus, compares her English knowledge and use on all linguistic levels (from phonetic to pragmatic) with an idealised American standard to measure and self-assess her linguistic practices in the local-situational setting. As a result, Bianca finds her skills to be less than satisfactory, which is in direct opposition to how Magda, Jill (the anglophone driver) and several long-standing clients of Shine assessed Bianca's English competency and proficiency skills (see Gonçalves 2015 for a discussion).

Unlike perhaps other speakers of grassroots English, who have learned English informally and who may not necessarily be concerned with 'linguistic correctness' (Schneider 2016: 3) found at different levels, our results indicated that several of Shine's employees were concerned with linguistic correctness, especially Bianca. In fact, despite her rather negative self-assessment and native speaker target norm, Bianca manages to creatively deploy her linguistic resources when necessary in order for effective communication to occur. The following example of being creative with addressee forms is a case in point:

Extract (8)
Bianca: que eu devo falar, se eu for trabalhar na casa de uma senhora Americana como essa senhora é o nome dela, eu acho que devia chamar por Mrs Jones não é? ('I should speak, if I go to work in a home of an American woman like this woman Katie Jones, Katie Jones, it's her name, I think I should call her Mrs Jones right'?)

Kellie: mhm

Bianca: mas como eu fui habituada a chamar só Mrs Katie acho que não está bem, tá muito feio pra mim eu não me sinto confortável a chamar pra ela Mrs Katie nem como o marido chamar Mr Mike, eu, I não sinto eu sinto que está errado mas eu não sei falar de outra maneira ('but since I already got used to calling her Mrs Katie I think it's not good, it's very ugly for me I don't feel comfortable calling her Mrs Katie and not even with her husband saying Mr Mike I don't feel, I feel that it's wrong, but I don't know how to say it differently')

Kellie: então você fala Mrs Katie ou cê fala Mrs Jones? ('so do you say Mrs Katie or do you say Mrs Jones?')

Bianca: Mrs Katie Mrs Katie

Kellie: e ela importa? ('and does she mind?')

Bianca: até hoje nunca disse que se importava, mas eu acho que estou a fazer feio devia dizer Mrs Jones ('until today she hasn't said that she minds, but I think I'm doing something ugly, I should say Mrs Jones')

Kellie: cê podia também falar Mrs Jones ('you could also say Mrs Jones')

Bianca: mas já acho= ('but I already think')

Kellie: =por que você não fala Mrs Jones ('why don't you say Mrs Jones?')

Bianca: não sei se tá se está bem, pronunciado ('I don't know if it's, if it's pronounced well')

In this extract Bianca's English use of the addressee form *Mrs Katie* using her client's first name rather than the standard and perhaps even expected surname that follows can be regarded as an instance of a creative stylistic choice or a language learning strategy of avoidance. Bianca is well aware that the use of one's first name rather than one's surname to address someone formally is 'incorrect', but nevertheless continues to address this client in this way due to her potential mispronunciation of *Jones*. Indeed, the phonemes in both English and Portuguese are pronounced differently. In Standard English, the phoneme /dʒ/ is pronounced as a voiced palatal affricate, but it is pronounced as a post-aveolar stop in Portuguese and often considered an allophone of /d/ when used together with loanwords (Parkinson 1988). It appears therefore that Bianca is well aware of the actual phonological transfer from her L1 that would occur if she were to pronounce *Jones* with a voiced alveolar stop. Rather than risking a potential mispronunciation of a client's name, Bianca chooses to make use of her full linguistic repertoire or what Cook (1999) refers to as one's 'multicompetence' and be creative with her addressee terms. While Bianca's creative choice for addressing *Mrs Katie* may indeed be unexpected, it has been and continues to be accepted by the client herself, who, over the years has never attempted to 'correct' Bianca, thus adhering to Firth's (1996) well-known 'let it pass principle' within such communicative interactions. The 'let it pass principle' permits interlocutors, in this case Bianca and Mrs Jones, to overlook specific linguistic idiosyncracies and allows for variation and accommodation on a local level.

5 CONCLUSION

In this chapter, I have shown how English has been acquired and used from 'below' within a domestic labour and thus blue-collar workplace context in the US by examining the ethnographic data of a multilingual cleaning company and interviews conducted with Magda, the company owner, her migrant Portuguese- and Spanish-speaking employees, and English-speaking clients. Contrary to existing literature which emphasises English language proficiency for reasons of recruitment and social mobility especially within a US context, the results from this study indicate otherwise. In fact, this study has shown that a re-evaluation of more context-specific and local linguistic practices between individuals who do not share an L1 in order for effective communication to be achieved is worth pursuing in order to better understand the multiple and complex factors surrounding language acquisition and use by individuals who have acquired English in informal settings and in direct interactions rather than through formal higher educational contexts. Our findings suggest that 'traditional' models like De Swaan's (2001) hierarchy of languages are in need of a more nuanced analysis and one which is further in sync with contemporary times in the twenty-first-century expansion of English and possibly other languages as well. This also means, for example, acknowledging recent emerging theoretical frameworks which have discarded fixed and bounded notions of language and languages altogether in favour of much more fluid, semiotic resources and repertoires that individuals draw on for effective communication. Conclusions about the high communicative and thus economic value of English (and other languages) featured in De Swaan would therefore benefit from consideration of the communicative practices in smaller-scale contexts such as the household cleaning spaces of Shine discussed in this chapter.

Indeed, some of the ways in which Shine's employees are recruited and can advance within the company hierarchy have less to do with their English language proficiency than with their diligence, cleaning skills and obedience towards Magda, the company owner, who also functions as the main language broker and mediator between her migrant employees and anglophone clients. At Shine, employees are therefore not required to have any English proficiency at all for tasks relating to their work duties. In fact, they can and often do opt for Magda-mediated communication, as was seen with Paloma, whose English language repertoire was restricted to greetings and fixed phrases despite having resided in the US for over a decade. Paloma's lack of English proficiency stems from several factors. Firstly, she resides in the Ironbound neighborhood, which is Portuguese rather than English dominant and where Portuguese is imbued with high symbolic value and cultural capital despite the significance of English regionally, nationally and even globally. Secondly, cleaning homes is considered a language-marginal job, where domestic workers are often on their own and thus lack language contact and language input. When there is contact, and if Paloma cannot get by with the rudimentary English skills she has learned on the job, she is always able to rely on Magda as her language broker and mediator. These factors (and others which have not been touched upon in this chapter) affect her overall investment in English.

For individuals like Anita, however, acquiring English within a US national context regardless of where she resides is extremely important to her, exemplifying her high investment in English for instrumental purposes. The ability to acquire and strengthen her English competence and skills at work with English-speaking clients within a local-situational space is seen as advantageous and as a possible venue to secure upward mobility. Thus, Anita's language acquisition may be regarded as opportunistic, where she would not miss the chance to practise and improve her English in the hope one day of possibly securing a better job locally, regionally, nationally or even globally. This was a point made by Anita herself, who mentioned that if she learned English well enough, she just might be able to teach it to others in Honduras in the future.

With regard to Bianca, we saw that despite her negative evaluation of her English proficiency and skills, her limited English language resources have not blocked her upward mobility within Shine's company hierarchy. As we learned, Bianca's position as assistant manager, acting manager and driver are all positions of responsibility, earned through her hard work, diligent nature, loyalty to Magda and less so through her language competence, although this latter factor cannot be underestimated. While Bianca does not consider herself a fluent or even proficient speaker of English, we know from Magda, Jill and several of Shine's clients, and also experienced first-hand, that she is able to function in English when necessary and also quite well. In fact, Bianca is the epitome of what Pennycook (2014) might call a *resourceful speaker*. For Pennycook, an important evaluation criterion when measuring language ability has to do with speakers' resourcefulness (and thus creativity) in order for effective communication to be achieved. This is in line with the work of Canagarajah (2007), Blommaert (2010) and Schneider (2016), all of whom discuss the negotiation of meaning and the saliency of accommodation on the part of all interlocutors involved within a particular speech event of individuals who do not share a common L1. Indeed, this was the case with Bianca and the example shown regarding her creative deployment of using a first name, *Mrs Katie* rather than a surname, *Mrs Jones* so as not to mispronounce *Jones* and potentially also lose face. This linguistic resourcefulness of Bianca's was not only consistently done over the years but was also accepted and 'passed' by Mrs Katie herself, exemplifying this client's flexible and accommodating nature within this particular communicative event where speakers come from diverse ethnic, racial, socio-economic and linguistic backgrounds.

Investigating a blue-collar and domestic workplace context where English is acquired from below has shed light on the ways in which language repertoires are used and evaluated by transnational migrant domestic workers who are located at the lower end of the socio-economic scale and also largely under-represented within sociolinguistic studies. For Schneider (2016), one reason why scholarship on lower-class individuals has been neglected has to do with academic orientations to formal education strategies and the 'ultimate goal of guiding students to attain norm-oriented linguistic skills' (2016: 4). I could not agree more and have argued elsewhere (Gonçalves and Schluter 2017) that existing language barriers and trust concerns among researchers and participants are additional factors affecting the dearth of studies within such contexts. And while some scholars might claim that such factors are obvious and perhaps even self-evident, I would argue that by not exploring blue-collar workplaces and individuals located at the other end of the socio-economic scale, the work we are doing is ultimately epistemologically biased. By not taking account of the experiences of individuals who do not have formal higher education and lack access to and thus cannot afford (both time- and money-wise) to acquire or learn another language in traditional formal classroom settings, we are not only doing a disservice to less privileged and 'non-elite' society members, but to the field of sociolinguistics more generally.

ACKNOWLEDGEMENTS

This work was supported by the Research Council of Norway through its Centres of Excellence funding scheme, project number 223265. I would like to thank Palgrave Macmillan for permission to reproduce Extracts 4, 5 and 8 and Springer for permission to reproduce Extract 2 and Figure 9.1. I would also like to thank the editors, Christiane Meierkord and Edgar Schneider, for their valuable comments on earlier drafts of this chapter. All shortcomings are my own.

TRANSCRIPTION CONVENTIONS

= latched, overlapping talk
(.) pause in terms of millisecond
[. . .] information not included
[X] unintelligible information

NOTES

1. All names throughout this study are pseudonyms.
2. Westwood is not the real place name and has been changed along with individuals' proper names to protect individuals' and Shine's anonymity. Elizabeth, Newark and the Ironbound are the real place names.

REFERENCES

Arnold Denise and Joseph R. Bongiovi (2013), 'Precarious, informalizing, and flexible work: transforming concepts and understandings', *American Behavioral Scientist*, 57: 3, 289–308.

Auer, Peter (2007), 'The monolingual bias in bilingualism research, or: why bilingualism is (still) a challenge for linguistics', in Monica Heller (ed.), *Bilingualism: A Social Approach*, Houndmills: Palgrave, 319–39.

Block, David (2018), *Political Economy and Sociolinguistics: Neoliberalism, Inequality and Social Class*, London: Bloomsbury.

Blommaert, Jan (2010), *The Sociolinguistics of Globalization*, Cambridge: Cambridge University Press.

Campbell, Elizabeth and Luke E. Lassiter (2015), *Doing Ethnography Today: Theories, Methods, Exercises*, Malden, MA: Wiley Publishers.

Canagarajah, Suresh (2007), 'Lingua franca English, multilingual communities and language acquisition', *The Modern Language Journal*, 91, 923–39.

Canagarajah, Suresh (2011), 'Translanguaging in the classroom: emerging issues for research and pedagogy', in Li Wei (ed.), *Applied Linguistics Review 2*, New York: Mouton de Gruyter, 1–27.

Cook, Vivian (1999), 'Going beyond the native speaker in language teaching', *TESOL Quarterly*, 33: 2, 185–209.

Coupland, Nikolas (ed.) (2010), *The Handbook of Language and Globalization*, Oxford: Wiley-Blackwell Publishing.

Czarniawska, Barbara (2007), *Shadowing: and Other Techniques for Doing Fieldwork in Modern Societies*, Copenhagen: Copenhagen Business School Press.

De Houwer, Annick and Lourdes Ortega (eds) (2019), *The Cambridge Handbook of Bilingualism*, Cambridge: Cambridge University Press.

De Swaan, Abram (2001), *Words of the World: The Global Language System*, Cambridge and Malden, MA: Polity Press.

Firth, Allan (1996), 'The discursive accomplishment of normality. On "lingua franca" English and conversation analysis', *Journal of Pragmatics*, 26, 237–59.

Gonçalves, Kellie (2012), 'Semiotic landscapes and discourses of place within a Portuguese-speaking neighborhood', *Interdisciplinary Journal of Portuguese Diaspora Studies 1*, 71–99.

Gonçalves, Kellie (2015), 'The pedagogical implications of ELF in a domestic migrant workplace', in Hugo Bowles and Alessia Cogo (eds), *International Perspectives on English as a Lingua Franca*, New York: Palgrave Macmillan, 136–58.

Gonçalves, Kellie (2019), 'Young bilingual adults', in Annick De Houwer and Lourdes Ortega (eds), *The Cambridge Handbook of Bilingualism*, Cambridge: Cambridge University Press, 59–75.

Gonçalves, Kellie (2020), '"What the fuck is this for a language, this cannot be Deutsch?" Language ideologies, policies, and semiotic practices of a kitchen crew in a hotel restaurant', *Language Policy*.

Gonçalves, Kellie and Helen Kelly-Holmes (eds) (2021), *Language, Global Mobilities and Blue-collar Workplaces*, New York: Routledge.

Gonçalves, Kellie and Anne Schluter (2017), '"Please do not leave any notes for the cleaning lady, as many do not speak English fluently": policy, power and language brokering in a multilingual workplace', *Language Policy*, 16: 3, 241–65.

Gonçalves, Kellie and Anne Schluter (eds) (2020), 'Language, inequality and global care work: an introduction', *International Journal of the Sociology of Language*, 262, 1–15.

Heller, Monica (ed.) (2007), *Bilingualism: A Social Approach*, London: Palgrave Macmillan.

Heller, Monica, Sari Pietikäinen and Joan Pujolar (2018), *Critical Sociolinguistic Research Methods: Studying Language Issues That Matter*, New York: Routledge.

Holmes, Janet (2012), 'Discourse in the workplace', in Ken Hyland and Brian Paltridge (eds), *Continuum Companion to Discourse Analysis*, London: Continuum, 185–98.

Hymes, Dell (1996), *Ethnography, Linguistics, Narrative Inequality: Toward an Understanding of Voice*, Abingdon: Taylor and Francis.

Laitin, David, D. and Rob Reich (2003), 'A liberal democratic approach to language justice', in Will Kymlicka and Alan Patten (eds), *Language Rights and Political Theory*, Oxford: Oxford University Press, 80–104.

Lanza, Elizabeth (2008), 'Selecting individuals, groups and sites', in Li Wei and Melissa G. Moyer (eds), *Research Methods in Bilingualism and Multilingualism*, Malden, MA and Oxford: Blackwell Publishing, 73–87.

Lave, Jean and Etienne Wender (1991), *Situated Learning: Legitimate Peripheral Participation*, Cambridge: Cambridge University Press.

Lederer, Muriel (1979), *Blue-collar Jobs for Women*, New York: Dutton.

Lønsmann, Dorte and Kamilla Kraft (2017), 'Language in blue-collar workplaces', in Bernadette Vine (ed.), *The Routledge Handbook of Language in the Workplace*, New York: Routledge, 138–49.

McAll, Christopher (2003), 'Language dynamics in the bi- and multilingual workplace', in Robert Bayley and Sandra Schecter (eds), *Language Socialization in Bilingual and Multilingual Societies*, Bristol: Multilingual Matters, 235–50.

McDowell, Linda and Jane Dyson (2011), 'The other side of the knowledge economy: 'reproductive' employment and affective labours in Oxford', *Environment and Planning A*, 43, 2186–201.

Madison, D. Soyini (2012), *Critical Ethnography: Method, Ethic and Performance*, London: Sage.

Makoni, Sinfree and Alastair Pennycook (eds) (2006), *Disinventing and Reconstituting Languages*, Bristol: Multilingual Matters.

Malakoff, Marguerite and Kenji Hakuta (1991), 'Translation skill and metalinguistic awareness in bilinguals', in Ellen Bialystok (ed.), *Language Processing in Bilingual Children*, Cambridge, MA: Cambridge University Press, 141–66.

Martin-Jones, Marilyn and Deirdre Martin (eds) (2016), *Researching Multilingualism: Critical and Ethnographic Perspectives*, Abingdon: Taylor and Francis.

Matras, Yaron (2009), *Language Contact*, Cambridge: Cambridge University Press.

Meierkord, Christiane (2012), *Interactions across Englishes. Linguistic Choices in Local and International Contact Situations*, Cambridge: Cambridge University Press.

Newark City Data (2017), <http://www.city-data.com/city/Newark-New-Jersey.html> (last accessed September 2019).

Noblit, George, Susan Y. Flores and Enrique G. Murillo (eds) (2004), *Postcritical Ethnography: Reinscribing Critique*, New York: Hampton Press.

Norton, Bonny (2000), *Identity and Language Learning*, Harlow: Pearson Education Limited.

Novoa, Andre (2015), 'Mobile ethnography: emergence, techniques and its importance to Geography', *Human Geographies*, 9: 1, 97–107.

Papastergiadis, Nikos (2000), *The Turbulence of Migration: Globalization, Deterritorialization and Hybridity*, Oxford: Polity Press.

Parkinson, Stephen (1988), 'Portuguese', in Martin Harris and Nigel Vincent (eds), *The Romance Languages*, Oxford: Oxford University Press, 131–69.

Pennycook, Alastair (2010), *Language as a Local Practice*, Abingdon: Routledge.

Pennycook, Alastair (2014), 'Principled polycentrism and resourceful speakers', *The Journal of Asia TEFL*, 11: 4, 1–19.

Pennycook, Alastair (2016), 'Mobile times, mobile terms: the trans-super-poly metro movement', in Nikolas Coupland (ed.), *Sociolinguistics: Theoretical Debates*, Cambridge: Cambridge University Press, 201–16.

Schneider, Edgar, W. (2011), *English Around the World: An Introduction*, Cambridge: Cambridge University Press.

Schneider, Edgar W. (2016), 'Grassroots Englishes in tourism interactions', *English Today 127*, 32: 3, 2–10.

Schreier, Daniel and Marianne Hundt (eds) (2013), *English as a Contact Language*, Cambridge: Cambridge University Press.

Spolsky, Bernard (2009), *Language Management*, Cambridge: Cambridge University Press.

Strömmer, Maiju (2016), 'Affordances and constraints: second language learning in cleaning work', *Multilingua. Journal of Cross-Cultural and Interlanguage Communication*, 35: 6, 697–721.

Terasawa, Takunori (2016), 'Has socioeconomic development reduced the English divide? A statistical analysis of access to English skills in Japan', *Journal of Multilingual and Multicultural Development*, 38: 8, 1–15.

Thurlow, Crispin (ed.) (2020), *The Business of Words: Wordsmiths, Linguists and Other Language Workers*, New York: Routledge.

Toohey, Kelleen (2000), *Learning English at School: Identity, Social Relations, and Classroom Practice*, Clevedon: Multilingual Matters.

Tse, Lucy (1995), 'Language brokering among Latino adolescents: prevalence, attitudes, and school performance', *Hispanic Journal of Behavioral Sciences*, 17: 2, 180–93.

Zentella, Ana Celia (1997), *Growing up Bilingual: Puerto Rican Children in New York*, Oxford and Malden, MA: Blackwell.

Part III:
English in forced migration

CHAPTER 10

Language Use among Syrian Refugees in Germany

Guyanne Wilson

1 INTRODUCTION

At the start of 2018, as a result of the Syrian Civil War, some 13 million Syrians had been displaced. The majority of the displaced have resettled in other Middle Eastern countries, particularly Turkey (3.4 million people), Lebanon (1 million people) and Jordan (660,000 people) (Connor 2018). A sizable population of Syrian refugees[1] has also settled in Europe, and Germany, with 530,000 Syrian refugees in 2017, hosts the fifth largest Syrian refugee population worldwide. Syrians form the largest refugee population in Germany, accounting in 2019 for just over a quarter of all refugees in Germany (Bundesamt für Migration und Flüchtlinge 2019). The majority of the Syrian refugees have settled in the state of North Rhine Westphalia (NRW), in towns such as Essen, Bochum and Münster. Social and scholarly interest has focused primarily on the processing of asylum requests and the provision of social services, particularly health, education and housing, for refugees (for example Aumüller 2018). At the core of all of this is language; in order to process an application, receive medical attention or apply for housing, people must be able to communicate with one another. However, to date little research has been undertaken which looks at language use by Syrian refugees in Germany. This chapter examines language use among Syrian refugees in NRW. Specifically, it studies the role of English, particularly in comparison to Arabic and German, among Syrian refugees.

The next section discusses the role of English worldwide and in the Expanding Circle, before going on to discuss English as a lingua franca, particularly among refugees, and language use among refugees. This is followed by a description of the methodology, and an introduction to the participants. After this, the use of Arabic, English and German among refugees is explored.

2 BACKGROUND

2.1 Mutlilingualism and Languages in Contact

Multilingual language users can draw upon a number of linguistic resources. The notion of the linguistic repertoire, first developed by Gumperz (1965: 85) and defined as 'the totality of linguistic forms regularly employed within the community in the course of socially significant interaction', helps to conceptualise how these resources are organised. Earlier approaches to repertoire were concerned with the repertoire of the speech community as a whole, focusing on the languages and varieties that members of a speech community had available to them in their daily interactions. More recent work, however, understands repertoire as more dynamic, and language resources as mobile. Repertoire is considered at an individual level, and particular attention is given to individual linguistic biographies and how these shape the linguistic resources an individual has at their disposal (Busch 2017). Thus in Blommaert's (2010) analysis of an asylum application by a Rwandese male, the applicant's repertoire is understood as shaped by his migration history, and not determined by place of birth. This biographic focus on repertoire is useful for understanding the language use of refugees, who may go through many different countries before arriving at a final destination, and, while they may not become proficient speakers of all languages they encounter, may well pick up bits of languages before moving on. In this regard, Blommaert's notion of 'truncated repertoires', the idea that language use exists in 'various chunks and pieces of language that we deploy for specific tasks' (2010: 104), is also critical, since it gives credence to the bits of language that people have available to them.

For many speakers, English is an important element of their individual linguistic repertoire. Indeed, the increased mobility of people and their linguistic resources which has characterised globalisation has been accompanied by widespread adoption of English as a lingua franca (ELF). Jenkins (2009: 200) describes ELF as communicative situations in which English is the 'language of choice, among speakers who come from different linguacultural backgrounds'. Though these speakers typically come from Expanding Circle backgrounds (see below), ELF does not exclude communication with speakers from the Inner or Outer Circles (Jenkins 2009: 201). ELF interactions which occur in 'business, education (both school and university settings), tourism, politics, technology and the media' (Jenkins et al. 2011: 297) have been well documented. The nature of these contexts means that the data used in ELF research are often based on the language of proficient speakers of English (although see Schneider 2016 for an exception). The Vienna-Oxford corpus of English for example only contains conversations from 'fairly fluent ELF speakers' (Breiteneder et al. 2006: 164). However, it is not always the case that interlocutors in ELF exchanges are highly educated (Meierkord 2012: 19), or that they are fluent speakers of English, and English interactions involving this latter group of speakers are under-researched.

One reason for this is that such grassroots Englishes are diverse and difficult to define. Schneider provides a working definition of grassroots speakers of English as speakers who have 'learned English in direct interactions rather than through formal education, largely disregarding target variety orientations or concerns about linguistic correctness' (2016: 3). Thus, the notion of grassroots Englishes is linked to Blommaert's truncated repertoires in that the extent of English proficiency is limited to the context for which the bits of English are learned. For Meierkord (2012), English at the grassroots involves a range of everyday exchanges in which people may use English. In the German context, Meierkord proposes that interactions between Germans and immigrants who speak English as a second language but not German will take place in English (2012: 148) and could serve as an example of a grassroots interaction. By looking at language use in interactions between Germans and Syrian refugees, this chapter examines this claim for an important segment of the immigrant population.

While the status of English in Syria is yet to be documented, the language's status in Germany has been widely researched (see Hickey 2019). English is the most learned foreign language in German schools and the main language of academia and academic research, and it plays a central role in business and commerce, administration, government, politics and international trade (Hilgendorf 2007). Although Hilgendorf documents mixed attitudes towards English, she finds that Germans readily switch to English in conversation with English L1 speakers, even if the latter are proficient speakers of German. Ehrenreich's (2010) study of language use in one German multinational company shows that English is often the preferred language in international business interactions, even among multilingual colleagues at the German headquarters. The ability to speak English is seen as essential for those in managerial positions (p. 418). However, German is used in decision-making meetings in order to ensure 'maximum communicative effectiveness and avoid any BELF-induced [Business English as a Lingua Franca] loss of information' (Ehrenreich 2010: 425). In educational contexts, Kautzsch (2014) provides evidence for the change in the status of English as a foreign language in Germany to situations of increasing bilingualism, at least among educated speakers.

However, English, though a major lingua franca, is not the only lingua franca available. Bolton and Meierkord (2013) show that although English is used by immigrants in Sweden, particularly in everyday, informal contexts, it is eventually replaced by Swedish as the immigrants' proficiency in the host language improves. Even in English-speaking communities, English need not serve as a lingua franca. Altherr-Flores et al. (2018) describe how Chinese immigrants who otherwise spoke English or Cantonese spoke Mandarin while engaged in church activities at their Mandarin-speaking church in the United States. They also report on the use of Nepali and Spanish as a lingua franca among the Lhotshampa in the United States as a means of integrating themselves into their border-town community.

The competition between English and other languages described above requires a theoretical consideration of the relationship between English and other languages. De Swaan's global language system names English as the world's hypercentral language, 'the hub of the linguistic galaxy' and the 'language of global communication' (2001: 5). One tier below English are the supercentral languages, which serve to connect speakers of different languages (De Swaan 2001:5) and include Arabic, French, German, Russian and Spanish. De Swaan argues that when speakers of different supercentral languages encounter one another, the language in which they communicate will be English. The model thus predicts that conversations between Arabic-speaking refugees from Syria and German speakers would take place in English. With regard to relationships among varieties of English, Kachru's (1985) model arranges the Englishes spoken around the world into three circles: an Inner Circle where English is spoken as a first language; an Outer Circle, comprising countries in which English is spoken as a second language and often serves official functions; and an Expanding Circle, comprising countries where English is learned as a foreign language and serves no official functions. Both Syria and Germany belong to the Expanding Circle. However, as Bruthiaux (2003: 169) notes, proficiencies within and across Expanding Circle contexts can range from no knowledge of English to native-like fluency. This means that, in both Germany and Syria, there is likely to be variation in English language proficiency across speakers, despite co-membership in the Expanding Circle.

2.2 Language and Syrian Refugees

Although media representations of Syrians in Germany often present young professionals with a high proficiency in English (De Wit and Altbach 2016: 10), the proficiency in English among Syrians is varied. Education First's English Proficiency Index[2] 2018 ranks Syria as 76th out of 88 countries examined, with a very low level of proficiency. Syrian teachers of English in displaced persons' camps in Lebanon furthermore report that the level of English teaching and learning is not as high in Syria as it is in other Middle Eastern countries, such as Lebanon (Karam et al. 2017: 175). Nevertheless, English is seen as a vital resource among Syrian refugees. They view English as a lingua franca in which they can communicate with non-Arabic speakers, read international news and keep informed about the situation in Syria (Cinkara 2017: 199). English is seen as critical for educational success. The teachers in Karam et al.'s (2017) study stress the importance of English for Syrian students in Lebanon, where the languages of instruction are French and English. English's importance in education is also stressed by Cinkara's (2017) respondents, though her informants are Syrian university students in Turkey. Moreover, Steele (2017) advocates for the teaching of English to refugees in transit in Turkey arguing that many of them will eventually settle in countries in which more than half the population speaks English. Six of the countries which Steele lists as settlement destinations are officially English speaking: Australia, Canada, Ireland, New Zealand, the United Kingdom and the United States (Steele 2017: 41–2). The remaining nine countries (Belgium, Denmark, Finland, Germany, Luxembourg, Netherlands, Norway, Sweden, Switzerland) do not have English as an official language. However, Steele's argument seems rooted in an ELF ideology which supposes that, regardless of the language of the community, English will be an asset. Finally, English is seen as critical to material success, even within Syria where, as one of Cinkara's informants notes, English will be used for communication with the rest of the world once the civil war has ended (2017: 199).

Refugees may encounter English in interactions with immigration and other officials in their place of settlement. Edwards (2016) testifies to the presence of English in several spheres of Dutch official life. English exists both alongside and in place of Dutch in written and spoken government communications and in the armed forces, so refugees to the Netherlands might expect to be able to use English in official interactions. Despite regulations mandating the use of either Dutch or French in asylum interviews in Belgium, Maryns (2014, 2015) reports that English is often used either between immigration officers and interpreters hired to interpret the proceedings for the applicant, or between immigration officers and applicants. Given the proximity of Germany to the Netherlands and Belgium, it will be interesting to compare whether similar patterns of English language use in official public contexts exist.

Refugees also face pressure to learn the language of the host country. Acquisition of the host language is linked to economic success and is seen as a sign of positive integration, whether that language be Dutch (De Vroome and van Tubergen 2010), Turkish (Cinkara 2017; Steele 2017; Şimşek 2018) or German (Haug 2008 for Germany; Plutzar 2010 for Austria). Learning the host country language is necessary in order to gain access to social services such as health and education (Cinkara 2017: 197), for access to jobs, and as a social lubricant between refugees and the host community. However, access to host country languages is often difficult. Brücker et al. note that the majority of Syrian refugees in Germany arrive with no knowledge of German (2016: 8) but are motivated to learn the language. Their enthusiasm, however, is dampened by long waiting times and other bureaucratic issues that hinder access to the insufficient number of available courses. As an interim measure, many receive tuition from volunteers, learn via apps or YouTube videos, or hire private language teachers. However, as Şimşek notes, this final option is only available to those with sufficient economic resources (2018: 13). Thus, many refugees are barred from full participation in the host society because of their lack of ability in the language.

With the arrival of large numbers of Syrian refugees in Germany, particularly from 2015 onwards, scholarly attention has been given to their integration into German society, focusing on the integration of refugees outside of urban areas (Ritgen 2018), and on provisions made for refugees in terms of housing, language courses, childcare and education (Aumüller 2018). Each refugee in possession of a residence permit has the right to a place in an integration course, and several municipalities ensure that appropriate language courses are available at community colleges and/or through volunteer organisations (Aumüller 2018: 189). While due attention has been given to the practical aspects of language learning with regard to the provision of language courses, little is known about the actual language resources of the incoming refugees and how these resources are activated in their everyday lives.

This chapter addresses this gap by answering the following questions:

1. What is the linguistic repertoire of educated Syrian refugees resident in North Rhine Westphalia (NRW)?
2. In which domains are the various languages most employed?
3. What is the role of:
    a) Arabic
    b) English
    c) German
   in the lives of educated Syrian refugees in NRW?
4. What evidence is there for grassroots language use among Syrian refugees in NRW?

3 DATA AND METHODOLOGY

This chapter applies a qualitative, phenomenological approach to study language use among Syrian refugees in Germany. During the period March 2017 to May 2019, five semi-structured interviews were conducted with Syrian refugees resident in Bochum, Essen and Münster. The interviews were carried out either on the campus of the Ruhr University Bochum, or at the participants' homes. One of the refugee interviews was recorded with video and audio materials, but all other recordings were obtained on audio only. The duration of each interview ranged from 40–65 minutes, and each person was interviewed once. The interviews were carried out by the author[3] and focused on participants' language use in different domains. The interviews were conducted either in English or in German, though code-switching between the two languages occurred. The reliance on interview partners who were proficient in either English, or had at least a B1 level of German according to the Common European Framework of Reference, meant that people from Syria with limited proficiency in either of these languages were excluded, and thus that speakers who could truly be described as grassroots speakers of English are not represented. Indeed, as Carla, the social worker interviewed for this project, noted, proficiency in English and French was limited to Syrians of higher social classes. However, it could be argued that, at least briefly, the participants' status as refugees placed them in a lower socio-economic standing than they would have had in Syria. Among the participants in this study, Mr Rahal, a qualified engineer in Syria, was unable to find similar employment in Germany, and instead worked as a technician. Similarly, Amira, an English teacher, was unemployed for a long time and eventually retrained as a translator since her teaching qualifications were not accepted in Germany. Thus, relocation was accompanied by loss of socio-economic status, and so in the broadest sense these interviews can be considered uses of English at the grassroots.

In addition to interviews with refugees, eight stakeholders involved in the settlement and integration of refugees in Germany were interviewed. This group included professionals and volunteers. Three people were interviewed individually, but the remaining five, who together ran a joint project for refugees, were interviewed as a group. Thus, language use by Syrian refugees is addressed from the perspective both of the refugees and of the people with whom they frequently communicated. The stakeholder interviews were all video-recorded and lasted between 30 and 45 minutes. The interviews were transcribed orthographically and, where necessary, translated into English by the author. In the extracts that follow, only the English translations will be provided due to space constraints.

3.1 The Participants

In total, eight Syrian refugees were interviewed: four unmarried adults and one family of four. Amira, Mahdi, Nabil and Hassan[4] are unmarried adults from Syria. At the time of her interview in 2017, Amira was thirty-three years old and had been living in Germany for two years. She fled Syria, where she worked as a secondary school English teacher, in 2015, making the treacherous sea crossing with her sister, with whom she lived in Bochum.

Nabil also arrived in Germany in 2015, spending time in Thüringen before finally settling in Bochum, where he lived with his parents and younger sister. Nabil was unwilling to share details about issues not related to language and integration.

At the time of his interview in 2018 Mahdi was twenty-three years old. He fled Syria in 2015 with two of his uncles and lived with them in Marl before he relocated to Münster, where he was granted asylum by the university chaplain.

Mahdi was housed in a students' residence hall where he lived among some 100 university students.

Hassan had no family in Germany. At the time of his interview in 2019, Hassan, thirty, had been in Germany for three years and was enrolled as a student at the Ruhr University Bochum (RUB). He lived in a shared apartment with two German housemates.

The Rahal family arrived in Germany in 2013 when their daughters Tahira and Yara were five and two respectively. Prior to their arrival, Mr Rahal worked as an electrical engineer in Syria and Mrs Rahal, who had studied English Literature at university, also worked. The family first settled near Aachen but moved to Essen where Mrs Rahal's brother was studying medicine. They were later joined in Germany by Mrs Rahal's parents. At the time of the interview, Tahira, aged thirteen, was a pupil at a grammar school in Essen, while Yara, eight, attended primary school. Mrs Rahal worked as a social worker and Mr Rahal worked as a technician.

In addition to the refugees, several Germans engaged in work with refugees were also interviewed. Pater Paul is a German Jesuit priest who established a shared living community for male refugees in Essen. The household comprises eight men from different countries. At the time of the interview in 2017, the house's residents came from Guinea, Equatorial Guinea, Lebanon, Congo and Syria, and ranged in age from 17–68.

Carla is a social worker from Spain who had lived in Germany for four years at the time of her interview in 2017. She holds a master's degree in Migration Studies and worked for several years at a refugee camp in Essen.

Kathrine is a student reading English and Latin at the RUB. Kathrine's involvement with refugees came through a university project in which German students were paired with refugees.

The AK Fluechtlinge – Refugee Working Group – is a student group based in Münster. The group organised a language café for refugees, football games for adult refugees and games and stories for the children. Five members of the group were interviewed together and so, to avoid any confusion that could arise due to the number of names, this group of students will be referred to as AKF.

4 RESULTS: THE LANGUAGE REPERTOIRES OF SYRIAN REFUGEES

The Syrians interviewed were found to speak three main languages: Arabic, English and German. In addition to these, they had some knowledge of Kurdish, French, Turkish and Greek. The different languages and proficiencies reflected their individual biographies, highlighting, for instance, the route they had taken to Germany via Greece or Turkey. The German participants spoke German,

English, Spanish and, in some cases, French. This section explores the repertoires of the Syrian speakers.

4.1 Arabic

All of the Syrian adults interviewed speak Arabic as their first language. In contrast, none of those who work with the refugees either on a paid or volunteer basis speak Arabic. Arabic is reserved for interactions with other Syrians, be they family or friends, and with other Arabic speakers. This is seen in Extracts (1) and (2).

> Extract (1)
> Hassan: Arabic with the refugees who came with me [. . .] I speak Arabic with the people who speak Arabic.

> Extract (2)
> Nabil: Friends too. Yeah because we are living in Syria and all my neighbours uh Arabic, Arabs, Kurdish, Christian and we have the languages.

Arabic is important for interpersonal relationships and for eight-year-old Yara it is a source of frustration that she sometimes has difficulty expressing herself in the language, as developed in Extract (3).

> Extract (3)
> Mrs Rahal: When we are by granny and grandad. My parents don't speak so well and also don't understand [German] very well and because of that she tries to tell them something in German and then I say Yara, Arabic. Then she has to think about what the word is in Arabic [. . .] She's stronger in German.
> Interviewer: Would you like to speak Arabic better or is it okay for you?
> Yara: Well I go to Arabic school and I will definitely be happy when I can speak better Arabic later on.

Moreover, Arabic is an important part of Syrian identity. For this reason, both Rahal girls are enrolled in weekly Arabic classes. Extract (4) shows how Tahira and her parents are proud of her progress in the language.

> Extract (4)
> Tahira: I'm going to skip a class [. . .]
> Mrs Rahal: Tahira can speak good [Arabic]
> Mr Rahal: [Very very] good
> Mrs Rahal: High Arabic

4.2 English

All of the Syrians interviewed have some competence in English. Tahira and Yara learn English at their respective schools. The adults, however, all learned English in Syria via different routes and to different levels. In the first instance, English is acquired in school and is widely spoken especially among the younger generation, as Mahdi explains (Extract (5)).

> Extract (5)
> Mahdi: We actually as a younger generation we have all learned English like real good. Like we practise the language often. Also when we were in Syria we had this like, we were like this gaming society where like we sit and we start playing online games with other players, international players where English is the common language.

In addition to this, Mahdi and Hassan share that they received additional coaching in English, either from family members, or at private institutions, while both Amira and Mrs Rahal have obtained a bachelor's degree in English Literature.

The Germans, particularly the university students, also speak English to a high level and indeed one of them, Kathrine, was studying English. As a result, the common language between the two groups is English, especially during the early phases of the refugees' settlement in Germany. In this way, the use of English aligns with the predictions made by De Swaan's (2001) model since hypercentral English replaces the two supercentral languages (German and Arabic).

Eventually, however, English is often replaced by, or at least used alongside, German in interpersonal communication, as Amira (Extract (6)), Nabil (Extract (7)) and Hassan (Extract (8)) all highlight. However, as Mahdi's account (Extract 9) of his first night in student halls and in subsequent interactions with friends shows, this need not always be the case.

> Extract (6)
> Interviewer: Who do you speak English with?
> Amira: No one.
> Interviewer: Oh you don't speak English anymore?
> Amira: No well at the beginning when I was new in Germany I could only speak English. But now I'm trying to speak more German.

> Extract (7)
> Nabil: Because I didn't speak very good German I was more relaxed when I was speaking English. After that when I started to learn more German, I start now speak German and English together.

Extract (8)
Hassan: In the beginning I spoke English and then bit by bit my German got better and then I decided to speak German with people, so my German would be better.

Extract (9)
Mahdi: I went down and I start talking to Toby in English start getting to know him better. And then some other people join the group and we start I start talking with every other person. It was really interesting and I think a lot of people also wanted to try their English [. . .] I mean they had interest in who I am and why am I here but I think they also wanted to see how good in English they are [. . .] And I think some of them had a lot of fun speaking English to me and some of them until now, we speak English. Like we both know that I can speak German. We both know that if we speak German we can understand each other but we speak English.

English is an interim lingua franca, replaced by German as soon as the refugees can, but remaining important in instances of communication breakdowns and where complex ideas need to be discussed (Extract (10)).

Extract (10)
Kathrine: If we are having spontaneous communication problems so when we usually speak in German but then some words are missing and then we switch to English. Or also when it's when problems arise like with a contract which is just difficult to explain in German.

English is also present in different educational settings. Mr Rahal reports how the teachers at his daughters' pre-school would speak to him in English to help him understand what was needed. Although all of his classes are in German, Hassan shares that some of the literature for his master's programme is only available in English. He faces some difficulty reading the language, because his proficiency in English is not adequate to digest complex academic texts (Extract (11)).

Extract (11)
Hassan: I started a B2 English course last month, but I didn't complete it. There was too much to do.

In healthcare situations, English is used to varying degrees. Mr Rahal notes that at the pharmacy, younger pharmacists were willing to speak to him in English, but older pharmacists were reluctant. The children's paediatrician, however, was always willing to use English. In customer-centred interactions, such as at the bank, English is widely spoken since, as Hassan points out, it is in the service provider's interest to accommodate the customer.

The data reinforce Steele (2017) and Cinkara's (2017) assertions that English can serve as an adequate interim language among refugees and help them communicate with people in their destination countries. Indeed, it is often expected that interlocutors will be able to speak English and lack of proficiency in English can cause communication problems. Carla, the social worker, notes that while highly educated and economically advantaged Syrians are able to speak English and French, it is not the case that all arrivals from Syria are able to do so (even if all the participants in this study can; compare Şimşek 2018 above). The AKF members report that with one exception, the participants in their language café are unable to speak English, or at least sufficient English to facilitate communication.

Low English proficiency is not only an issue for Syrians. Pater Paul claims to know little English, speaking, as he calls it, 'broken English for broken people'. Mahdi reveals that the priest responsible for granting him this asylum also professed limited proficiency in English (Extract (12)), and the young church secretaries were also reluctant to use the language (Extract (13)).

Extract (12)
Mahdi: He doesn't trust himself that he could speak English and I couldn't speak German like nothing.

Extract (13)
Mahdi: Anja tried. But Vicki, no way. If you killed her she would never speak English.

Furthermore, all the Syrians interviewed report that, in their experience, government officials are reluctant to speak English (Extracts (14) and (15)). This offers a striking juxtaposition to the Netherlands, where English was reported to be present in official contexts (Edwards 2016).

Extract (14)
Mrs Rahal: In the immigration office, at the Job Centre, they always avoid speaking English [. . .] We spoke English with them at the beginning [. . .] and they were most of the time unfriendly when they heard that we spoke English. They would always say, we speak German here. The official language is German [. . .] It's different from person to person but one sees that with English you can't get far.

Extract (15)
Mahdi: They as an employee, they are not allowed to speak English with us [. . .] because they are not certified translators so if something happened

like a miscommunication between both of them I think then it would be a problem to say oh he said that in English.

Early visits to the immigration office take place in the company of an interpreter who mediates between the immigration officer and the refugee either in English or in Arabic, though, unlike the Belgian context reported in Maryns (2014, 2015), the participants all report the absence of an official interpreter from the state.[5]

Although English is often touted as a language whose mastery can lead to significant social and material opportunities, this hegemony of English is somewhat subdued in the German-speaking context, particularly in the public sphere. The belief in English's hegemony, however, can have negative repercussions for refugees who may have invested years in learning the language, with the expectation that they could use it anywhere. In Extracts (16) and (17), Mahdi tells the story of his two uncles, who speak poor German but very good English. They are unable to find jobs and he reports as follows:

Extract (16)
Mahdi: It's a big disappointment for them because now they are not able to use what they have learned their whole life.

Extract (17)
Mahdi: It's either they learned the wrong language or they are in the wrong country.

English does not give Mahdi's uncles the access to global society that it promised and, in spite of their proficiency in English, they are left on the peripheries, reinforcing Mrs Rahal's belief that with English 'you can't get far'. Together with Extract (14), these statements reaffirm previous findings which highlight the importance of learning the language of the host community for integration (cf. Haug 2008; Plutzar 2010; De Vroome and van Tubergen 2010). This will be explored in more detail in the section on German below.

In spite of this, the refugees still maintain the belief that English is an important language. Hassan notes that he wants to improve his English, but only after achieving the highest possible level of German. Similarly, Amira, who is completing training as an interpreter, is currently seeking opportunities to practise her English.

What becomes clear from these extracts is that the English spoken by the Syrian refugees interviewed here would not count as instances of grassroots English following Schneider's definition. All the participants learned English in a formal educational setting. Far more interesting is the fact that the refugees have little opportunity to use English. Except for interactions with German friends, English plays a relatively limited role in their lives. The insistence on the use of German at the immigration office provides a direct contrast to Maryns's (2015) findings with regard to the use of English in asylum applications in Belgium. Mahdi offers a plausible explanation for the avoidance of English in official contexts (Extract (15)), aligning himself with Ehrenreich's (2010) finding on German use in high-level meetings to avoid miscommunication. Regardless of the reasoning offered, both these situations limit the refugee's choice of language in the process. The reluctance of the secretaries (Extract (13)) to use English with Mahdi is counter to what Hilgendorf (2007) reports and contradicts the experiences of the Rahal family with the pharmacists. It could perhaps be accounted for by considering possible differences in the educational experiences of the secretaries and the pharmacists. However, since none of these people were interviewed, one can only speculate.

4.3 German

The third main language spoken among the Syrian refugees is German. German is viewed as necessary for survival, and all the participants interviewed were motivated to learn German, even before their arrival (Extract (18)).

> Extract (18)
> Mahdi: When I was in Syria, I learned two things in German: the numbers from one to twenty and how to say I'm sorry I cannot speak German, can you speak English.

Among the participants, Yara and Tahira have the highest German proficiency. Throughout the interview, Yara's family expresses their belief that Yara's first language is German. Yara confirms that people don't believe she is Syrian because her German is so good. The sisters claim to communicate with each other in a mixture of Arabic and German, but Yara later on admits that she uses mostly German with Tahira. At home, the family speaks to one another in Arabic, but when the girls are among friends, they speak German both to each other and to their friends, and in public spaces such as Yara's First Communion class, mother and daughter communicate with each other in German.

Yara's comments on her proficiency in German match the observations made by other participants. Nabil notes that his sister, who arrived in Germany speaking only Kurdish at the age of five, after less than a year at school not only mastered German but also prefers to communicate in the language at home. The members of AKF likewise comment that the children learn German quickly and become their 'little translators', mediating conversations between their parents and German speakers. Thus the youngest Syrians are an example of language shift in progress, as German has begun to replace Arabic as their main language for communication.

German proficiency among the adults interviewed is also high. Upon their arrival in Germany, Mrs Rahal enrolled in language courses and achieved C1 level within twelve months. Mr Rahal obtained B2 level, and at the time of the interview Mahdi was preparing for his C1 examination. At the time of their interviews, both Amira and Nabil were enrolled in German B1 courses, but subsequent to this Amira enrolled in B2 and C1 courses and at the time of writing was training to be an interpreter for German, Arabic and English. Hassan was enrolled in several B2–C1 level courses focusing on academic skills in German.

German is used in official and semi-official interactions. Appointments at the immigration offices are always carried out in German, even if the refugee is unable to speak the language. This was illustrated above in Extracts 14 and 15. German is also the language of contracts for day-to-day commodities such as housing, mobile phones and banks, even if customer support is available in English. Pater Paul conducts the initial interviews for residents in the house in German, and house notices and rosters are all in German. In spite of their advanced proficiency, however, the refugees all admit to facing difficulties in understanding the content of contracts and to signing them without being certain of what they were agreeing to.

Except for Hassan, who once had an Arabic-speaking doctor, and the Rahals, whose paediatrician speaks English, doctor's appointments take place in German. As a result, health and illness are a source of anxiety for refugees. In Extract (19) below, Hassan explains the linguistic preparations that must be undertaken before a doctor's visit. Carla also shared that, when possible, a translator is sent with the patient to the doctor.

> Extract (19)
> Hassan: I couldn't find an Arabic doctor so I had to go to a German doctor and I just spent two nights learning the words for this topic so that I could explain my problem to the doctor.

Once the Syrians' language proficiency allows it, German is also the language used with German-speaking friends, who are an important resource for language learning. Amira and Nabil lament the fact that, outside of their classes, they have limited opportunities for speaking German. In contrast, Hassan and Mahdi have more opportunities for interaction with German speakers. Hassan's housemates are both German, and through his university courses he interacts with many German speakers. Mahdi lives in student halls of residence and interacts with several German-speaking students. He is confident in his use of German and uses it not only in informal conversations but also on social media outlets like Facebook. He can also perform more complex spoken tasks, like speeches. He has, for example, preached the homily at Sunday mass at the student church. Moreover, his written proficiency in German is high. Although he is Muslim, Mahdi is a member of the church's parish council where he takes the minutes of meetings.

German, rather than English, is also used as a lingua franca for communication with refugees from diverse backgrounds. In a refugee camp, for example, Carla (Extract (20)) confirms:

Extract (20)
Carla: When they don't speak the same language, the same native language, they use German. So the few German words they learn in the time that they were here.

Here, we see an example not of grassroots English, but of grassroots German. Refugees in the camps do not yet have access to language courses, so any German they know is learned from interactions with camp workers or with volunteers who come to spend time at the camp.

German is viewed as necessary for successful integration, both by the refugees and by the professionals working with them. This is seen in Extract (21).

Extract (21)
Hassan: At the beginning [English] is okay. But if we are living in Germany permanently it is really a lot better to have a good knowledge of German because it makes life easier and we can better integrate ourselves in the society since [without] the German language in Germany, sometimes integration doesn't work very well.

Mrs Rahal shares this view, particularly with regard to her children's integration. She recounts an experience at Tahira's pre-school shortly after the family's arrival (Extract (22)):

Extract (22)
Mrs Rahal: Tahira couldn't understand a word of German and the teachers would say, 'Now close your eyes' and Tahira sat there and didn't react and I saw that and I really, really cried. That hurt me a lot that my daughter understood nothing. We didn't either. And I only looked at the other children and I wanted my daughter to do that too.

Furthermore, success in learning German is linked to perceived material benefits (Extract (23)). The adults are motivated to learn German as a means of continuing their studies at German universities or of obtaining high-paying jobs.

Extract (23)
Pater Paul: For his work as an engineer he needs to be able to speak German at a high level and therefore he studies and studies and studies and studies the language like a mad man so that he can pass his six-month probation period.

The refugees in this study align with those in Brücker et al.'s (2016) study in terms of their motivation to learn German, and with work by De Vroome and van Tubergen (2010) which found a link between refugees' ability in Dutch and their occupational status, with Dutch-speaking refugees earning more than those who spoke only limited Dutch.

4.4 Other Languages

Though the main languages spoken by the Syrian refugees are Arabic, English and German, they are not the only languages spoken. One of the young men, Nabil, also speaks Kurdish, but its use is limited to his immediate family. In addition, Mahdi and Amira both claim limited proficiency in French, which they learned at school, and Pater Paul reports that French is sometimes used as a lingua franca in the community where he lives, in communication involving refugees from Syria, Lebanon, Congo, Guinea and the other German priest in the house. Indeed, on visits to the house, the author's German utterances were often translated into French by residents of the house for one another. At the mosque, Mahdi reports that Turkish is often used alongside German.

In the refugee camps, the refugees come into contact with a milieu of languages. In Extract (24), Carla notes that, particularly among children:

Extract (24)
Carla: They would be talking in German but they were hearing words here and there and you see that suddenly the kid from Iraq is using Serbian words to explain something and the kid from Albania is trying to make fun and repeating words in Arabic.

This kind of code-mixing is not unique to interactions among children. Hassan, who had worked as a cook before resuming his studies, describes the languages used at work in Extract (25).

Extract (25)
Hassan: Arabic, English. A lot of different languages. Everything except German because they were all relatively new to Germany and couldn't speak any German.

These instances of borrowing can be viewed as grassroots multilingualism: truncated repertoires (Blommaert 2010) created for the purposes of work, play and prayer. In the case of the adults, they may involve, but are not limited to, English.

5 CONCLUSION

The findings above show how Syrian refugees' language repertoire has been affected by their biography (Busch 2017). Although Amira, in her interview, notes that in Syria people don't really know about German, German has been added to their repertoire due to the circumstances that forced them to leave their country and resettle in Germany. English, too, is particularly important in interpersonal communication with Germans, and in situations where refugees receive language support from German-speaking friends. However, though Kautzsch (2014) reports that English plays a greater role at all levels of education, including as a language of instruction, notions of spreading bilingualism, particularly regarding English use, seem to be limited to educational settings and not to other official contexts. Instead, the experiences of several informants and their relatives confirm Pennycook's assertion that the notion of English as an international language is more fantasy than it is fact (2004), and seem to suggest that notions of English's hypercentrality (De Swaan 2001) are restricted by what Blommaert et al. (2005) would term space – physical and temporal characteristics that regulate how communication takes place. Space has to do with environmental characteristics; in the first instance the physical environment of Germany, in which German is the official language, and where German is seen as essential for integration. More specifically, physical environment is restricted to NRW, and for many informants in this study to the Ruhr Valley. It may well be that Syrian refugees' experiences in other metropolitan areas differ linguistically from those reported here. Additionally, there is the historical space of the refugee crisis, where refugees, who are powerless, can also be rendered language-less, since communicative practices must be legitimised in each new space (Blommaert et al. 2005), and in the German space, ideologies of language integration render even English illegitimate, at least from an official standpoint. Because, as Blommaert et al. note, language use is a matter of social position rather than linguistic potential, the interviewees' low social position as refugees outweighs their competence in English, the world's most powerful linguistic currency, since 'the function and value of those repertoires and skills can change as the space of language contact changes' (Blommaert et al. 2005: 211). These findings show that theories purporting English's hypercentral status and the importance of ELF require a more nuanced understanding of how English interacts with other languages in different contexts.

Simultaneously, the findings in this study reinforce findings by Bolton and Meierkord (2013) since the refugees, like the immigrants to Sweden, shift from English to the host language and use it as a lingua franca. This highlights the need to consider the role of lingua francas other than English. With specific regard to grassroots Englishes, the author's lack of knowledge in Arabic meant that people whose competence in English and German is truly restricted could not be interviewed, and so grassroots English as it is more generally understood could not be explored in this chapter. However, all interviewees reported that Germans whose competence in English was low avoided speaking in English altogether, and could simultaneously evoke the hegemony of German in the German space, thus enabling the use of grassroots German. This does not mean that grassroots Englishes are never used among Syrian refugees, rather that interviews, in spite of the insight they give into language use, are not the best tool for eliciting this information. Indeed, the participants reported grassroots uses of English and German in refugee camps and among low-wage workers, so these may be settings in which more ethnographic work could be undertaken. Moreover, these uses signal something that has been overlooked in the study of grassroots Englishes: as part of truncated repertoires, grassroots Englishes exist alongside and in relation to other grassroots languages, but also alongside other more recognised language forms, such as ELF. Grassroots languages should thus be considered within the framework of the larger ELF complex and multilingualism as a whole.

NOTES

1. The definition of refugees, asylum seekers or internally displaced persons is continually debated. Since all of the people interviewed referred to themselves as refugees, this is the term that will be used throughout.
2. Though methodologically problematic, this index provides a basis for the comparison of English language proficiency around the world.
3. I am thankful to Timo Bothe for technical support provided during the interviews.
4. To protect the identity of the participants, pseudonyms are used throughout this work.
5. Although the BAMF says that refugees can request an interpreter, documented visits to the immigration offices in Essen during 2020 required individuals to bring their own interpreter. Alternatively, officials may ask for volunteer interpreters among those in the waiting area.

REFERENCES

Altherr-Flores, Jenna Ann, Dongchen Hou and Diao Wenhao (2018), 'Lingua francas beyond English: multilingual repertoires among immigrants in a southwestern US border town', *International Journal of Multilingualism*, 1–27.
Aumüller, Jutta (2018), 'Die kommunale Integration von Flüchtlingen', in Frank Gesemann and Roland Roth (eds), *Handbuch Lokale Integrationspolitik*, Wiesbaden: Springer, 173–98.
Blommaert, Jan (2010), *The Sociolinguistics of Globalization*, Cambridge: Cambridge University Press.
Blommaert, Jan, James Collins and Stef Slembrouck (2005), 'Spaces of multilingualism', *Language and Communication*, 25: 3, 197–216.
Bolton, Kingsley and Christiane Meierkord (2013), 'English in contemporary Sweden: perceptions, policies, and narrated practices', *Journal of Sociolinguistics*, 17: 1, 93–117.
Breiteneder, Angelika, Marie Louise Pitzl, Stefan Majewski and Theresa Klimpfinger (2006), 'VOICE recording-Methodological challenges in the compilation of a corpus of spoken ELF', *Nordic Journal of English Studies*, 5: 2, 161–87.
Brücker, Herbert, Nina Rother, Jürgen Schupp, Christian Babka von Gostomski, Axel Böhm, Tanja Fendel, Martin Friedrich, Marco Giesselmann, Yuliya Kosyakova, Martin Kroh and Simon Kühne (2016), 'Forced migration, arrival in Germany, and first steps toward integration', *DIW Economic Bulletin*, 6: 48, 541–56.
Bruthiaux, Paul (2003), 'Squaring the circles: issues in modeling English worldwide', *International Journal of Applied Linguistics*, 13: 2, 159–78.
Bundesamt für Migration und Flüchtlinge (2019), *Das Bundesamt in Zahlen 2018: Asyl, Migration und Integration*, Nürnberg: Bundesamt für Migration und Flüchtlinge.
Busch, Brigitta (2017), 'Expanding the notion of the linguistic repertoire: on the concept of Spracherleben – The lived experience of language', *Applied Linguistics*, 38: 3, 340–58.
Cinkara, Emrah (2017), 'The role of L+ Turkish and English learning in resilience: a case of Syrian students at Gaziantep University', *Dil ve Dilbilimi Çalışmaları Dergisi*, 13: 2, 190–203.
Connor, Phillip (2018), 'Most displaced Syrians are in the Middle East, and about a million are in Europe', *Facttank. Pew Research Centre*, <https://www.pewresearch.org/fact-tank/2018/01/29/where-displaced-syrians-have-resettled/> (last accessed 28 August 2019).
De Swaan, Abram (2001), *Words of the World. The Global Language System*, Cambridge: Polity.
De Vroome, Thomas and Frank van Tubergen (2010), 'The employment

experience of refugees in the Netherlands', *International Migration Review*, 44: 2, 376–403.
De Wit, Hans and Phillip Altbach (2016), 'The Syrian refugee crisis and higher education', *International Higher Education*, 84, 9–10.
Education First (2018), *English Proficiency Index. Education First*, <https://www.ef.com/wwen/epi/> (last accessed 30 September 2019).
Edwards, Alison (2016), *English in the Netherlands: Functions, Forms and Attitudes*, Amsterdam: Benjamins.
Ehrenreich, Susanne (2010), 'English as a business lingua franca in a German multinational corporation: meeting the challenge', *The Journal of Business Communication*, 47: 4, 408–31.
Gumperz, John J. (1965), 'Linguistic repertoires, grammars and second language instruction', *Languages and Linguistics*, 18, 81–90.
Haug, Sonja (2008), 'Sprachliche Integration von Migranten in Deutschland', Working Paper der Forschungsgruppe des Bundesamtes 14, Nürnberg: Bundesamt für Migration und Flüchtlinge.
Hickey, Raymond (ed.) (2019), *English in the German-speaking World*, Cambridge: Cambridge University Press.
Hilgendorf, Suzanne K. (2007), 'English in Germany: contact, spread and attitudes', *World Englishes*, 26: 2, 131–48.
Jenkins, Jennifer (2009), 'English as a lingua franca: interpretations and attitudes', *World Englishes*, 28: 2, 200–7.
Jenkins, Jennifer, Alessia Cogo and Martin Dewey (2011), 'Review of developments in research into English as a lingua franca', *Language Teaching*, 44: 3, 281–315.
Kachru, Braj B. (1985), 'Standards, codification and sociolinguistic realism: the English language in the outer circle', in Randolph Quirk and Henry G. Widdowson (eds), *English in the World: Teaching and Learning the Language and Literatures*, Cambridge: Cambridge University Press, 11–30.
Karam, Fares J., Amanda K. Kibler and Paul J. Yoder (2017), '"Because even us, Arabs, now speak English": Syrian refugee teachers' investment in English as a foreign language', *International Journal of Intercultural Relations*, 60, 169–82.
Kautzsch, Alexander (2014), 'English in Germany. Spreading bilingualism, retreating exonormative orientation and incipient nativization', in Sarah Buschfeld, Thomas Hoffmann, Magnus Huber and Alexander Kautzsch (eds), *The Evolution of Englishes: The Dynamic Model and Beyond*, Amsterdam: Benjamins, 203–27.
Maryns, Katrijn (2014), *The Asylum Speaker: Language in the Belgian Asylum Procedure*, London: Routledge.
Maryns, Katrijn (2015), 'The use of English as ad hoc institutional standard in the Belgian asylum interview', *Applied linguistics*, 38: 5, 737–58.
Meierkord, Christiane (2012), *Interactions across Englishes: Linguistic Choices in*

Local and International Contact Situations, Cambridge: Cambridge University Press.
Pennycook, Alistair (2004),' The myth of English as an international language', *English in Australia*, 139, 26–32.
Plutzar, Verena (2010), 'Sprache als "Schlüssel" zur Integration? Eine kritische Annäherung an die österreichische Sprachenpolitik im Kontext von Migration', in Herbert Langthaler (ed.), *Integration in Österreich: Sozialwissenschaftliche Befunde*, Innsbruck, Vienna, Bozen: Studien Verlag, 1–15.
Ritgen, Klaus (2018), 'Integration in ländlichen Räumen–die Rolle der Landkreise', in Frank Gesemann and Roland Roth (eds), *Handbuch lokale Integrationspolitik*, Wiesbaden: Springer, 407–31.
Schneider, Edgar W. (2016), 'Grassroots Englishes in tourism interactions', *English Today*, 32: 3, 2–10.
Şimşek, Doğuş (2018), 'Integration processes of Syrian refugees in Turkey: "class-based integration"', *Journal of Refugee Studies*, 1–18.
Steele, Timothy J. (2017), 'English language teaching to Syrian refugees in transit', *Online Journal of English Language Teaching*, 2: 1, 40–52.

CHAPTER 11

Uprooted Speakers' Grassroots English: Metalinguistic Perspectives of Asylum Seekers in Germany

Axel Bohmann

1 INTRODUCTION

A view of World Englishes (WE) at the grassroots, almost by definition, invites attention to metalinguistic questions in addition to structural description. Grassroots settings, as defined here in opposition to elite and institutional settings, involve difference in language forms and norms: minimally between local usage and an institutionally legitimised standard of English, but often involving a much wider range of ethnolinguistic resources. How linguistic differences are perceived, made sense of and mapped onto socially meaningful categories in such settings is an ethnographic question of relevance to the sociolinguistics of English in the globalised twenty-first century.

This chapter discusses metalinguistic accounts offered by residents of a preliminary reception centre (PRC) for asylum seekers in Southwestern Germany. The analysis traces how members of this highly transient, multilingual and multi-ethnic community construct the role of English in their communicative environment. I also pay attention to speakers' awareness of different kinds of English and the indexicalities associated with these.

The chapter demonstrates how speakers of heterogeneous ethnolinguistic backgrounds who co-inhabit a tightly confined space draw on histories, geographical trajectories and circulating ideologies in order to give structure to their complex communicative environments. Close attention to local metalinguistic accounts reveals how global relationships in the World System of Englishes (Mair 2013) are enlisted for situated interpretations. At times, these interpretations assume predictable forms; at others, innovative and surprising connections are drawn that rework the global system of Englishes into novel relationships at the local level. The study therefore highlights the dynamic interaction of global and local indexicalities in a transient, multilingual grassroots setting.

2 THEORETICAL BACKGROUND

The field of WE is currently undergoing a theoretical reorientation away from a relatively static, variety-centred perspective to an increasing focus on dynamic processes, language contact and mutual influence. Schneider (2007) was the first major contributor to incorporate these elements at a theoretical level. In recent years, the focus on identity, indexicality and linguistic plurality has been sharpened both from within the field (Schneider 2014; Mair 2013) and from without (Blommaert 2010). As long as WE research was, explicitly or implicitly, concerned with national (standard) varieties of English, description of these varieties and their linguistic features was the chief analytical enterprise. Their status as varieties was often taken for granted, as part of what constitutes a nation state. It is clear that much of the present-day dynamics involved in the global spread of English – from computer-mediated communication (for example Honkanen 2020) to super-diverse megacities (for example Heyd et al. 2019) to the discourses of global youth-cultural movements (for example Alim 2015) – exists below the radar of such a nationally restricted perspective. English in these contexts exists both below the national level in complexly structured communities of practice of various sizes, and above by virtue of the global flows of people, discourses and semiotic resources that are embedded in them.

The response to these new (or at least, newly perceived) phenomena cannot be simply expanding the list of 'Englishes' that exist in the world. As Mair (forthcoming) writes,

> [t]he full elaboration of national standard varieties of English for all successor states of the British Empire and the smaller number of former US colonial dependencies is not the natural end point in the sociolinguistic evolution of English in the postcolonial period.

I would add that any attempt to simply elaborate a finite list of varieties crucially misses the point. Any use of English, and grassroots usage in particular, is embedded in intricate ecologies where different linguistic forms and different orders of normativity come into play. Abstracting away from these contexts blinds the analytical view to some of the most productive and important processes currently involved in the dynamics of global English, such as the availability of resources from different varieties within the same communicative context and the openness of linguistic forms to conflicting interpretations.

How different normative contexts compete and clash with each other can be observed particularly clearly in the context of mobility. When speakers and linguistic resources travel, expectations, functions and associations that were self-evident in one context may become invalid or distorted in the next (Blommaert 2010). A sociolinguistics of mobility, therefore, faces the challenge of accounting for often unexpected linguistic and pragmatic effects. Doing so requires close attention to local contexts combined with a view towards systemic relationships beyond the strictly local, such as global differences in access to different forms of English and normative evaluation of these forms. This simultaneous focus on the immediately local and the systemic global aspects of English in the world is one of the major challenges in the field today.

In the study of WE, Mair's (2013) World System of Englishes offers a framework for explaining dynamic global relationships among varieties. This model stratifies standard and non-standard varieties according to 'demographic weight and ... transnational reach' (Mair 2013: 260) in order to account for global contact phenomena within English. Varieties are grouped on a central-peripheral cline, with Standard American English (AmE) as the hypercentral 'hub' variety. The model is less radical than some scholars (for example Pennycook 2007) deem necessary in that it retains the notion of 'variety'. However, there is a clear recognition that the ontological status of varieties is not that of unproblematic, empirically tangible entities. Rather, for many speakers, they act as cognitive realities which serve as models for their own linguistic behaviour as well as anchors for social categorisation. It is this importance from the emic perspective of speakers on the ground that Mair's model addresses first and foremost.

At a local, empirical level the study of transient multilingual communities (TMCs) affords insight into the interactional dynamics associated with mobility. Defined as 'social configurations where people from diverse sociocultural and linguistic backgrounds come together (physically or otherwise) for a limited period of time around a shared activity' (Mortensen and Hazel 2017: 256), TMCs are conceptual opposites of the traditional kinds of speech community on which most current notions of variety are based. Such speech communities are characterised by shared linguistic resources, evaluations and socio-pragmatic norms, whereas each of these elements requires negotiation in TMCs. This opposition to traditional community models makes TMCs productive sites for a re-evaluation of the global sociolinguistic dynamics of English.

Research on TMCs has been developed largely in the context of English as a lingua franca studies (Mortensen 2017; Pitzl 2018), where emphasis is placed on local creativity and communicative behaviour situated within its immediate interactional context. However, combining a TMC perspective with attention to more enduring, systemic linguistic-ideological relations is a promising approach in the context of WE. Early research on TMCs has highlighted the recontextualisation of existing semiotic resources (Goebel 2010). The link between such existing frames and their local contextualisation is made explicit in the concept of 'langscaping . . . where members explore and discover one another's linguistic repertoires and social-geographic trajectories and histories' (Hazel 2017: 317). In a longitudinal analysis of a series of video-recorded workplace interactions, Hazel (2017) traces how code choice norms develop as participants identify language-biographical commonalities among themselves. In the process, the range of linguistic resources available for in-group communication becomes both elaborated and situationally differentiated depending on specific speaker constellations. Thus, a langscape is not an empirical given, but is constructed through participants' negotiation of the histories, contexts and discourses of relevance to their locally situated interactions. Langscaping highlights interactional micro-context while at the same time directing attention towards wider contexts and sociolinguistic orders as reflected in speakers' lived experience.

In the present chapter, I discuss the discourse of members of a TMC of asylum seekers in Southwestern Germany. Recently, there has been a proliferation of research at the intersection of language and asylum mainly in two areas: discourse-analytical studies of how migrants are represented by various institutional actors such as popular media (for example Gabrielatos and Baker 2008) or state agencies (for example Blommaert 2009) on the one hand and analysis of communicative problems in high-stakes institutional encounters on the other (for example Jacquemet 2011; Maryns 2014). Comparatively little work exists on the everyday linguistic practices in asylum seekers' lived realities (but see Goglia 2009, and this volume; Wilson, this volume). In this contribution, I analyse sociolinguistic interviews with asylum seekers from West Africa in relation to how they construct the role of English in their communicative environment and how they draw on different kinds of English as social categorisation devices. The guiding question is how indexicalities at global, or at least supralocal scale levels become enlisted and recontextualised in a locally confined setting characterised by transience and ethnolinguistic diversity.

3 FIELD SITE

Participants in this study were residents at a PRC for asylum seekers in Southwestern Germany. At the time of the interviews, I had visited this centre once during an official open house event. Subsequently, however, I started offering a sports programme for residents on a voluntary basis. The analysis I present below, while focusing on the discourse in the interviews, also draws on ethnographic knowledge accumulated during my volunteer engagement, which comprised more than a year of weekly visits to the site.

PRCs exist across Germany and are designed to be the first official point of contact where newly arrived migrants apply for asylum, are registered into a centralised system, and receive accommodation until they are transferred to a more permanent residence (Bundesamt für Migration und Flüchtlinge 2019). Living conditions are characterised by limited space and a high amount of institutional regulation. At the time of the interviews, residents were living in large tents partitioned off into small personal quarters. Access to the site was tightly regulated, with ID checks for anybody entering or leaving. There were no cooking facilities; instead food was provided at scheduled meal times. The strict separation from the outside world and the regimentation of residents' quotidian activities render the centre a 'total institution . . . where a large number of like-situated individuals cut off from the wider society for an appreciable period of time together lead an enclosed formally administered round of life' (Goffman 1962: xiii).

It is difficult to make reliable statements about the number of residents and their background, as these are subject to short-term fluctuation and official numbers are not easy to come by. At the time of the interviews, the PRC accommodated between 200 and 300 persons, who were predominantly male and of African origin (Zimmermann 2018). Among the languages I have encountered regularly on site are English, German, French, Arabic, Kurdish, Fulah, Mandinka, Igbo and occasional Spanish and Italian. Staff and volunteers responded to this multilingual environment with pragmatic solutions, settling for whichever language most readily facilitated communication. I have noted staff-resident interactions in German, English, French and Arabic, including different varieties and combinations of any of these.

Every resident I talked to looked back on an extended trajectory of migration, the rough outline of which is similar in most cases: a lengthy and strenuous overland leg from the homeland to Libya, where most participants spent a long interval – anywhere between a few months and well over a year – awaiting passage across the Mediterranean Sea. The sea journey ended either in Spain or, in most cases, Italy. Many participants report spending another significant period of time in their European country of arrival, before ultimately moving on to Germany.

Participants' narratives of their journeys themselves, interesting as they are, are not the main focus of this chapter. What is important to note is that the interviewees did not simply migrate from their home country to Germany. The sociolinguistic dynamics of their lives involve more than a tension between the place of origin and their present location, encompassing the sociolinguistic footprints of prolonged movement through various sociolinguistic orders. I use the term 'sociolinguistic orders' to refer to contexts in which both the presence and the evaluation of different linguistic forms assume relatively stable, often at least in part officially regimented forms. Nation states, with their official language policies and institutional power to circumscribe communicative norms, are prime examples. However, sociolinguistic orders may exist at both more locally restricted scale levels (Blommaert 2010: 32–7) such as individual communities of practice, as well as more general ones such as the World System of Englishes. In the course of their linguistic biographies, participants in the present study have acquired both resources and normative frameworks that can be situated at a range of scale levels. Table 11.1 is a schematic representation of these multiple sociolinguistic scales.

Table 11.1 Locally relevant sociolinguistic orders at different scale levels

Scale level	Sociolinguistic order
Global	World Language System (De Swaan 2001)
Global	World System of Englishes (Mair 2013)
Regional/national	West African linguistic ecologies (Pidgin, Wolof, Mandinka, Edo, Igbo, etc.)
Regional/national	Migration trajectories (Arabic in Libya, Italian in Italy)
National	Monoglot ideology of the German nation state (Blommaert 2009)
Local	Norms and expectations in individual interactions

This table presents a sketch rather than a comprehensive enumeration of the different scale levels at play in interactions at the PRC. Whether and in what way each level is drawn upon by participants is an empirical question. What the sketch illustrates is the different levels to which orientation in interaction is possible in processes of norm negotiation and social categorisation.

Starting at the bottom, linguistic resources and the socio-pragmatic norms for their deployment need to be negotiated in situ in the context of local interactions. Many analyses focusing on transience emphasise this local level of norm emergence in the micro-diachrony of (repeated) interactions (Mortensen 2017; Pitzl 2018). In the present study, I adopt a slightly different perspective, tracing instead how the frames brought into play and reworked at the local level relate to more enduring sociolinguistic orders as represented in Table 11.1.

The next relevant level is that of the German nation state and its monoglot linguistic ideology. According to Blommaert, '[a] monoglot ideology makes time and space static, suggests a transcendent phenomenology for things that define the nation state, and presents them as natural, neutral, acontextual, and nondynamic: as facts of nature' (2009: 421). In regard to language, the context-free, neutral and normal ideal is the codified standard, as represented in reference grammars and testing regimes. In Germany, as in most European countries, knowledge of the abstractly formulated standard language becomes a yardstick by which to measure immigrants' ability and willingness to 'integrate' as well as a gatekeeping threshold for access to the labour market. Dialectal and other sociolinguistic variability is erased in the process. The pressure to live up to the monoglot ideal of German proficiency is frequently reinforced by institutional as well as volunteer actors. At the same time, access to German classes for the interviewees is limited to a few hours of volunteer-taught lessons on site. This fact, combined with the interviewees' having spent only a relatively short time in Germany, means that their German proficiency tends to be rudimentary. The sociolinguistic order at the German national scale level is therefore likely to be perceived as a source of pressure and linguistic insecurity.

Beyond the level of the nation state, two different kinds of scale are of further relevance. Firstly, participants have been socialised into linguistic ecologies in their countries of origin which encompass English as well as a range of local languages. Participants from Gambia have command of a local variety of English as well as their home language, often Mandinka. Awareness of a range of other local languages, such as Fula or Wolof, can also be assumed. Command of these differs significantly from individual to individual, but indexical associations with each language are likely predictable from the local West African context. Similar observations pertain for speakers from Cameroon and Nigeria, with the added dimension of French as an additional postcolonial language in the former case and the duality of Nigerian English (NigE) and Nigerian Pidgin (NigP) in the latter. When encountering other speakers from West Africa, regional linguistic resources and interpretive frames are likely to be activated both for negotiating communicative footing and for social categorisation.

The second supranational scale level relates to the sociolinguistic 'baggage' accrued during the migration trajectory. Of particular relevance here are Libya and Italy as relatively long-term stopovers for many participants. Inevitably, exposure to sociolinguistic realities in these places will have both contributed to the pool of resources at participants' disposal (if to varying degrees) as well as socialised them into the respective normative frameworks at play in the two countries. Such sociolinguistic knowledge may be drawn upon to emphasise shared experiences or potentially even to facilitate communication with interlocutors with whom no other lingua franca can be established. Exposure to Arabic in Libya also opens up avenues for communication with a range of speakers from the Arab world while at the same time carrying religious indexicalities. The Italian sociolinguistic situation, on the other hand, represents the first encounter with European linguistic ideologies and language-related institutional regulation.

Finally, at a global level, there is the World Language System (De Swaan 2001) as well as the World System of Englishes (Mair 2013). These do not represent contexts of linguistic socialisation so much as they can help explain more local processes of such socialisation. Participants' motivations to learn some languages rather than others as well as the associations they draw between forms of language and speaker groups may sometimes be best explained with reference to such global relationships.

The key question which the present chapter pursues is how participants draw on the different scale levels represented in Table 11.1 in order to make sense of their transient and volatile linguistic environment. In the face of transience and unstable and potentially clashing sociolinguistic norms, participants need to develop strategies for establishing stable frames of reference. As the analysis below will show, they do so with reference to both local contexts but importantly also to enduring indexicalities situated at the very global level of the World System of Englishes.

4 DATA AND METHOD

The analysis draws on seven hours of interviews conducted with two participants from Gambia, five from Nigeria and one from Cameroon. With the exception of two women from Nigeria, all participants are male speakers in their twenties. Participants have been living at the PRC for anywhere between a couple of days and six months at the time of recording. All of them have since been relocated to different residences or have been deported.

Contact was established through a 'broker' (Schilling-Estes 2007: 178), a linguist who at the time was employed at the PRC in a non-academic capacity. The interview was the first contact between the researcher and interviewees in all cases. All interviewees have acquired African varieties of English either in the context of formal schooling or as part of their linguistic socialisation in the home. Their native language backgrounds, command of German and knowledge of other foreign languages (such as Arabic, Italian, Spanish) vary from individual to individual.

The interview protocol followed a semi-formal design which encouraged active discussion at the expense of a strict content focus. Questions were language-biographical, targeting participants' linguistic repertoires, histories of acquisition, and present linguistic and communicative situation. The focus was generally on the roles of English and German but attention was paid to all languages mentioned by the participants. Unlike in a typical sociolinguistic interview, questions explicitly directed participants' attention to their own and others' language use and asked them to comment on and evaluate these practices. The result is recordings which are rich in metalinguistic commentary and lend themselves to analysis in terms of ideology and metapragmatic awareness. The material is less well suited for structural description; however, where such description is required for contextualising the interview content, the analysis will draw on the linguistic form of the material itself as well as ethnographic observations subsequently made during my volunteer work at the site.

I analyse the data from a content-oriented discourse analytical perspective with a specific focus on talk about language (Preston 1994). Attention is paid both to explicit metalinguistic commentary as well as to implicit contextualisation against participants' sociocultural frames of reference. Of particular interest are statements about participants' own and others' practices and the emergent dynamics of identification and differentiation resulting from these (Bucholtz and Hall 2005).

The transcription conventions for the extracts below follow a broad orthographic rendition, enriched with a small set of additional conventions (see the Appendix at the end of the chapter). Phonetic transcription was limited to cases where explicit attention is drawn to the phonetic shape of a word or phrase.

While the analysis draws on the full set of interviews in order to identify common patterns, the extracts given in the sections below represent statements from five of the eight participants. These speakers are coded as follows:

A: German linguist, male, age 34 years
E: Nigerian (Ogoni) asylum seeker, male, five months in Germany
I: Nigerian (Igbo) asylum seeker, male, four months in Germany
N: Gambian (Mandinka) asylum seeker, male, six months in Germany
O: Nigerian (Edo) asylum seeker, male, two months in Germany
R: Cameroonian asylum seeker (ethnicity unknown; English L1), male, four months in Germany

5 THE ROLE OF ENGLISH IN THE LOCAL LANGSCAPE

The first question to be settled in any interaction in the TMC under discussion is code choice. A reasonable hypothesis would be that speakers settle on the language that most readily facilitates communication, that is a shared West African language where possible, a shared lingua franca such as Nigerian Pidgin where no mutually shared local language is available, and, in cases where neither of the preceding is an option, English. In such an approach to code negotiation, a trade-off between individual competence and maximal overlap with interlocutors' repertoires needs to be considered. Given the diversity of linguistic backgrounds at the PRC, one might expect English to be a prominent resource for communication. On the other hand, given that participants have only spent limited time in Germany and have not had access to formal German language classes, the role of German might be assumed to be negligible. These expectations in relation to English and German, however, are not fully borne out by the interview data. For this reason, while the present section focuses on the role of English, attention to the way German is constructed as a competing vehicle of communication is required. The code negotiation process described by most participants is evidenced in Extract (1).

Extract (1)
(I, A)
A: in camp do y- would you say you speak mostly Igbo? mostly English? (.) mostly maybe even German?
I: mostly (1.2) because (.) almost English *Deutsch (German)* and so (0.8) depending the person you meet,
if I meet Igbo? we speak Igbo? if I meet Yoruba or Hausa we speak English or eh Pidgin if I meet like eh-eh (.) Frenches because I don't know how to speak French I will mix Germany small a bit.
(. . .)

        Sometimes Igbo? (.) we will eh speak e:h eh *DEUTSCH (German)*,
        (1.0) eh as training?
A: okay (.) with other Igbo speakers?
I: yes.

This speaker expresses a relatively straightforward process of code negotiation 'depending [on] the person you meet'. The first choice is that of his native language Igbo, which however is conditional upon interlocutors sharing his ethnolinguistic background. Much as would be the situation in Nigeria, the medium for communication with fellow Nigerians of different ethnicities becomes English or Pidgin. In contexts where none of these varieties serves as a feasible vehicle of communication, impromptu strategies need to be developed. Notably, there is a clearly perceived linguistic barrier in communication with speakers from French-speaking countries, who are constructed as a clearly distinct group, 'the Frenches'.

Less predictably, the interviewee also mentions the role of German in facilitating communication in otherwise linguistically difficult encounters. The participant has only spent four months in Germany without access to formal German classes. Elsewhere in the discussion he emphasises his difficulty with the language and demonstrates a command that is largely limited to formulaic expressions. All residents from French-speaking African countries I have encountered during my volunteer work at the PRC, on the other hand, were able to speak English at least at a level that enabled basic communication. It is, therefore, not unreasonable to suspect that the choice of German is motivated not only in terms of communicative ease. Across all interviews, participants frequently highlight the importance of German, which arguably reflects an awareness of the strong normative expectations imposed by Germany's official monoglot ideology. Extract (2) gives further evidence in this direction.

    Extract (2)
    (N, A)
    N: the people we are staying together,
        (0.8) li:ke our fellow Gambians or another part of c- another country like Guinea Senegalese you know,
        (1.0) when we are sitting together we don't try to speak maybe English or German you know we normally speak our local language so that make people to be suffer to learn how it is like *Deutsch (German)* you know.

The point of departure for this participant is not how interactional context motivates language choice, but how ethnolinguistic similarities influence what interactions take place to begin with. In the ethnolinguistically homogenous situations this participant constructs as the norm, the role of English and German is diminished in comparison with 'our local language'. Up to this point, the logic of the account is intuitive in terms of sheer communicative ease: one tends to interact more with people who share the same ethnic and linguistic background. However, the participant offers a critical evaluation of this practice, explaining how people 'suffer' from it in the long run by not learning German. Here again, the immediate need for German as a vehicle of communication is not readily apparent. Rather, a general acknowledgement of the symbolic value gained through knowledge of German in the wider sociolinguistic ecology of Germany can be inferred from this statement.

A more marginal, but not insignificant, role is reserved for languages acquired during the trajectory of migration. In the absence of otherwise shared linguistic common ground, speakers may resort to these resources, as the following statement demonstrates:

Extract (3)
(O, A)
O: many people have still=they just (.) they have still travelled to many places.
A: mhm
O: you understand,
Most of them they came from Italy.
A: mhm=mhm
O: so sometimes we speak Italy together=
A: =okay
O: yeah.
A: completely? [(.) or just a couple of words
O: [yes
yes the we just speak,
so sometimes we argue although we say we should stop=want to LEARN German.

In the part of the interview leading up to Extract (3), O has listed an impressive range of languages that circulate in the PRC: Igbo, Yoruba, English, Italian, German, French and Arabic. Responding to the question of whether he ever mixes these, he elaborates on the role of Italian enabling lingua franca communication by virtue of interlocutors' shared migration trajectory through Italy. Similarly to Extract (2), the excerpt ends with an opposition constructed between interactional practice and the participant's aspiration to use more German and increase his fluency in that language.

From the extracts discussed so far, it would seem that the status of English is rather less important than might be expected. On the one hand, where local

African languages can be taken as shared, these are clearly preferred over English. On the other hand, in the many situations where English would appear as a logical option for lingua franca communication, participants highlight the importance of German instead and occasionally also mention additional languages such as Italian. Yet, for the speakers discussed here, English takes on functions beyond simple communicative effectiveness. In a sociolinguistic environment where their command of German is under explicit scrutiny and found to be lacking, command of English can act as a source of pride and self affirmation.

> Extract (4)
> (E, A)
> E: I know that ah
>   (0.6) in ENGlish I'm perfectly.
>   (1.0) yeah (.) nothing come from English (.) I will pick.
>   (0.8) everything that come from English? (.) I held.
>   so (.) I'm not perfect in any other thing I'm doing but
>   (0.6) I know that within inside me (.) I speak English perfectly.
>
> Extract (5)
> (O, A)
> O: I never to (.) go to school.
> A: ok.
> O: BUT (.) I can speak good language=
> A: =mhm mhm s=
> O: =I can speak good language.
> A: mhm so did you learn English (.) uh (.5) just from the people you were
> O: no
> A: around? or
> O: no
> A: how did you learn English?
> O: (0.6) ah:: ah: is English is-is part of me,
> A: ok (.) mhm
> O: you understand?
>   (0.8) is no difficult language for me.

In both Extracts (4) and (5) English is discussed in connection to the participants' core sense of self ('within inside me' and 'is part of me'). In both cases, command of English is contrasted with other aspects of the speaker's identity that are felt in some way to be negative or inadequate. The contrast is explicit in E's statement 'I'm not perfect in any other thing I'm doing'. It is implied in O's statement that English is 'no difficult language for me', from which can be inferred difficulties with other languages. Thus, while the communicative utility of English is generally downplayed, it may provide a sense of stability that other languages cannot offer. Participants' native languages may be too limited in terms of the number of interactions they facilitate, whereas German is constructed as maximally difficult and foreign, if valuable, in all interviews.

To sum up the role of English in relation to other languages in the langscape constructed in the interviews, the language retains an important presence. However, in the accounts offered by the participants, this importance is cast not so much in terms of communicative utility, but rather in terms of identity and ethnolinguistic egalitarianism. Participants' ability to navigate different sociolinguistic scales can explain this pattern. In both a very concrete spatial as well as a more abstract, institutional-ideological sense, participants are restricted to the national scale level of Germany. They need to present their asylum case to German authorities and, as part of the process, are required to demonstrate their willingness and ability to integrate, in part through their command of German. English, as the hypercentral prestige language at the very hub of the World Language System, is not quite as valuable as one might expect since it is difficult for participants to transcend the local scale level. Its international prestige does have an effect locally. Yet, this effect is constructed in relation to identity rather than communication.

6 VARIATION WITHIN ENGLISH: LOCAL INTERPRETATIONS AND GLOBAL INDEXICALITIES

Up to this point, 'English' has been discussed as if it were a clearly identifiable, internally undifferentiated whole. This is indeed the predominant local perspective, doubtlessly reflecting much more widespread beliefs about the nature of language(s) in general. However, when directly asked about variation within English, participants demonstrate both a keen ear for fine-grained differences as well as a rich set of indexical associations connected to different kinds of English. The first point is evidenced at a phonetic level in Extract (6):

Extract (6)
(R, A)
R: Ghana (.) they want to call [blɔd] they will say [blaːd].
    (. . .)
    they want to call the [dɔktə] they say [dɔk]- [daːkta].
    (. . .)
    In Nigeria they want to call [tɛːtiː],
    (.8) [tɛːtiː] a figure?
A: oh [θɜɹdiː]?
R: yeah
    they wi- they will say [taːtiː].

These observations are quite accurate. Both Ghanaian English (GhE) and Ghanaian Pidgin English have a tendency to merge the BATH, TRAP and STRUT vowels. The phonetic target in all three vowels is commonly rendered as [a] (Huber 2004: 850). A different participant, E, mentions a very similar shibboleth, explaining that Ghanaian speakers pronounce the word *come* as [kɑːm]. This vowel feature therefore appears to reflect some degree of shared salience in identifying a speaker as Ghanaian.

In the case of Nigerian *thirty*, the realisation of the NURSE vowel as [aː] is also in line with available descriptions. In Hausa English, this vowel is categorically realised as [aː], whereas it may have a range of orthographically conditioned variants in Igbo and Yoruba English (Gut 2004: 820). While the most common of these in the case of *thirty* would be [e], realisations as [a] are found in words such as *perch* and *Sir*. Participant R's rendition, if not completely in line with fine-grained local variation, therefore, is not without a basis in actual usage.

Accuracy of the participant's perception and reproduction, however, is only part of the story. What is more relevant to the present context is that the excerpt evidences a clear awareness of linguistic difference that is directly connected to a speaker's national origin. Individual vowel variation is indexically linked to different varieties, and these varieties can be drawn upon as social categorisation devices. Linguistic difference, once perceived, is rarely taken as a neutral fact of life, but usually entails evaluative inequalities. This does not necessarily mean that one variety is unambiguously framed as 'better' or 'worse' than another; usually much more complex sets of indexicalities attach to such differences (Blommaert 2010). The following extract provides a surprisingly rich example of this kind of indexical proliferation:

Extract (7)
(E, A)
A: and would you say that at (.) the *Heim (centre)* ah where you live thaːt?
(0.8) all the different people there=I mean you have people I think from Guinea right?=from (.) [Gambia Cameroon other places
E: [Gambia
A: (0.5) uh (1.0) do you all communicate mostly in ENGlish? (.) or?
E: yeah=yeah we communicate most in English but ah,
in my *Heim (centre)* we have different type of (.9) tone of speaking English like ah the Gambia people they speak the way ah ah
(0.8) let me say the Jamaica people speak (.)
A: ok
E: you know with English yeah but ah
(.5) even the Ghanaian (.) the Ghanaian English is more more more clear (.) more than the Nigerians.

(1.0) we the Nigerians we speak (.) English different between the
Ghanaian and the Gambia.
so the Gambia people speak (.) like the JaMAIca while the
eh eh Ghana people speak the REAL English.
we the Nigerians we speak English but,
(0.6) we communicate with each other

Teasing apart the evaluative relationships among the three kinds of English mentioned in Extract (7) is not a straightforward task. The least ambiguous statements relate to GhE, which receives valuation as both 'clear' and 'the real English'. Such sentiments reflect established beliefs about GhE the origins of which are difficult to trace. The fact that, historically, Ghana was the West African country with 'the longest tutelage under British rule before independence' (Quarcoo 1994: 329) and that 'English continues to function as a sociolinguistic High language' (Huber 2004: 847) may offer partial explanations. Innocent Chiluwa (p.c.) also suspects a role of GhE L1 interference from Ewe phonology in promoting the notion of the variety being more 'clear'. Later in the interview Extract (7) is excerpted from, as well as elsewhere in the data, GhE is also referred to as 'the best'.

Compared to this general reverence towards GhE, participant E takes a more ambivalent stance towards his own group's use of English. NigE is characterised not directly through the use of evaluative adjectives, but in opposition to the purported clarity of GhE ('more clear (.) than the Nigerians'). The last sentence of the excerpt elaborates this position. The recognition that Nigerians speak English is immediately followed by the qualifying statement 'but (0.6) we communicate with each other'. This juxtaposition suggests that overt prestige is higher for GhE, but that Nigerian forms of English fulfil important functions as in-group markers. It is unclear here whether the kind of English under discussion is NigE or NigP, or whether the statement refers to both.

The most striking metalinguistic statement made in Extract (7) is the notion that Gambians speak English 'the way ... the Jamaica people speak'. This sentiment occurs twice in the excerpt, and the lexeme *Jamaica* receives emphatic stress the second time it is uttered. In terms of the linguistic histories and structural properties of Jamaican English (JamE) and Gambian English (GamE), there is little reason for such a connection to be drawn. However, two further participants make similar claims. Participant E's statement therefore is not simply an ad hoc, idiosyncratic notion, but appears to reflect a more generally shared linguistic belief. Nor is this belief limited to out-group descriptions. In the part of the interview leading up to Extract (8), participant N from Gambia has talked about asylum seekers from other African countries pretending to be from Gambia. He has explained that these can be told apart from genuine Gambians on the basis of their English, specifically mentioning that real Gambians 'like to speak like Jamaicans'.

> Extract (8)
> (N, A)
> A: do you do that too? (.) trying to=like
>   trying to speak like a Jamaican? [yeh man?
> N: [yeah [.] @yeah yeah@
> A: ok (.) can you (.5) DO that for me just for the=for the record I'd love to hear what it what that sounds like?
> N: like it's just like,
>   for example mba if you are talking to your friend like mba,
>   [bɔɪ] how are you doin' [ɪnɪʔ]
>   yeah?

Participant N claims as part of his repertoire a Jamaican-inspired variety of English that is constructed as shared with many of his compatriots. His performance of this register relies on the vocative [bɔɪ], the invariant tag question [ɪnɪʔ], and potentially a tenser realisation of the GOOSE vowel than in the rest of the interview. None of these features can unambiguously be related to JamE on structural grounds. A JamE realisation of *boy* would be [bwaɪ], with an inserted glide before the vowel and a lower onset of the diphthong. The tag question *innit?* is commonly associated with colloquial British English (BrE). There is a phonetically and pragmatically similar expression [iːnɔː] in JamE. Yet, as with [bwaɪ], if this expression did indeed serve as a model for N's performance, the phonetic realisation is slightly inaccurate. There is also a pragmatic misfit in that both BrE *innit?* and JamE *ino* commonly follow statements and not questions such as is the case here. The result is a stretch of discourse whose structural proximity to any variety on the Jamaican post-creole continuum is dubitable at best.

In the absence of clear linguistic evidence, what accounts for the pervasiveness of the connection many participants draw between GamE and JamE? An obvious answer is the circulation of Reggae music and/or Rastafarian ideology, both of which enjoy popularity among Gambians (Ebere and Charles-Ebere 2018). In the stretch of the interview following Extract (8), participant N highlights the connection many Jamaican dancehall and reggae musicians have to his home country, claiming that they own residential compounds there. He also lists several influential Jamaican artists whose concerts he attended in Gambia, such as Morgan Heritage, Sizzla and Luciano. The conviction of this participant as well as others that there is a connection between JamE and GamE, therefore, seems to be based largely on the perceived cultural similarity of the two countries and specifically many Gambians' eagerness to adopt Jamaican cultural practices.

Even in the absence of clear linguistic similarities, such group perceptions may be enough to establish as cognitively real the notion of a certain variety. This process bears similarity to the discursive construction of Pittsburghese documented extensively by Johnstone (2013, among others), although in the present case, interesting transnational contact phenomena further complicate the picture.

Finally, participants are not only confronted with other West African speakers of English. In many quotidian interactions with Germans, English assumes the role of the only feasible lingua franca. Residents at the PRC are consequently required to position their own English against that of their German interlocutors. Neither employees at the PRC nor Germans working for state institutions typically have received English instruction beyond the high school level. Against this backdrop, the metalinguistic statements offered by several participants about Germans' English are worth discussing.

Extract (9)
(I, A)
A: I know Germans speak English very differently from how Nigerians speak English,
I: yes (.) but (.) Germany English,
A: mhm
I: is is (.7) is normal.
A: okay.
I: than Nigerian.
A: mhm.
I: is pure English.
A: aha okay @
I: [understand
A: [so you are saying the Germans [speak better English?
I: [yes
   yeah is better English.

Extract (10)
(O, A)
O: oh you know (.) whe:n=whe:n=whe:n German (.) person speak (.) language,
   (0.4) the tongues?
   (.) the way you speak it will different that person that came from Nigeria.
A: mhm mhm.
O: with person that (.) eh that=eh German person if he speak he speak like person that came from eh: (.6) eh eh United States.

In both Extracts (9) and (10), Germans are credited with speaking a prestigious variety of English. Participant I in Extract (9) directly compares Germans' and Nigerians' English and finds the former to be 'normal', 'pure' and 'better' in comparison. In Extract (10), the valuation is expressed more indirectly, by likening Germans' English to the global prestige variety AmE. Interestingly, this connection is established on physiological grounds, referring to the different 'tongues'. From a linguistic standpoint, these sentiments are as disheartening as they are inaccurate, yet they find expression in several interviews. They can be regarded as a lingering effect of colonial ideology, according to which the language of white colonisers was elevated as the only valid way of speaking. Such a perspective divides the linguistic world not primarily according to descriptive linguistic facts but according to speaker groups closely linked to skin colour. Once the difference between these groups is accepted as given, linguistic differences between them are highlighted, potentially even invented, and any internal differentiation is erased (Irvine and Gal 2000). The notion that Germans speak English like Americans, as a general statement, certainly requires erasure of a good deal of evidence to the contrary. It should also be emphasised that this notion is not universally shared by all participants. Other speakers clearly recognise that Germans have difficulties speaking English and construct themselves as more proficient speakers.

7 DISCUSSION AND CONCLUSION: HISTORIES, GEOGRAPHIES, AND GLOBAL FLOWS WITHIN LOCAL CONFINES

The PRC is an intensely local site, physically marked off from the outside world by means of fences and ID checks. It is an intensely diverse place in terms of the ethnicities, linguistic repertoires and personal histories of the people that populate it. Finally, it is an environment in which transient social constellations are the norm and communication requires ad hoc norm negotiation and problem-solving strategies.

In such a context, it would be tempting to focus on very local interactional processes and their short-term temporalities. Productive as such a perspective would be, it is important not to lose sight of the more persistent sociolinguistic orders that are drawn upon in such locally specific processes. It is the combination of systemically global relations and their momentary actualisation which will help account for the new patterns emerging in settings such as the PRC. The notion of langscaping has helped combine these two perspectives within one framework.

The analysis has demonstrated that participants draw on personal histories and geographic contexts as well as less tangible, circulating discourses in order to map out their langscape at the PRC. In many cases, the effects appear predictable, such as when code choice is based on what is maximally shared across interactants' ethnolinguistic backgrounds. However, a number of findings do not have this level of prima facie plausibility. Participants' insistence on their use of German even for in-group communication is one of these, as is the widespread notion that Gambian speakers somehow sound Jamaican. Reference to shared repertoires and communicative effectiveness does little to explain these patterns. Instead, normative orders beyond the narrow context of individual interactions need to be considered. In the case of German, the institutional power of the state's monoglot ideology (Blommaert 2009) is of particular relevance. The case of Gambians' purported linguistic Jamaican-ness is more complicated. The global influence of reggae/dancehall music and Rastafarian thought, its adoption and adaption within Gambia, as well as other Africans' awareness of these processes need to be taken into account. In other words, attention is required to transcultural flows (Pennycook 2007) of pop-cultural discourse and their localisation at a national scale level, as well as a wider, regional West African scale level.

Restricting the view to varieties of English, and at the risk of oversimplifying complex and contested interpretations of the local langscape, a sketch of how different ways of speaking are locally indexicalised reads as follows: GhE is associated with clarity and correctness, potentially linked to BrE. NigE receives little overt prestige but is constructed as a source of in-group identity. GamE gets indexically linked to the supercentral non-standard variety JamC. Finally, the way Germans speak English is likened to AmE, presumably on the basis of skin colour and a local prestige differential between Africans and Germans. Consequently, in this very local context in which none of the more central varieties in the World System of Englishes (AmE, BrE, JamC) is part of anyone's natural repertoire, they all come into play as social categorisation devices. In this process of re-indexicalisation, new sociolinguistic links and expectations are formulated.

While such local indexical processes are worthy of study in their own right, many in the field of WE will be interested primarily in their long-term influence on the structure of and relationships between varieties of English. The present chapter cannot offer conclusive answers to such questions. More sustained work and more data on grassroots contexts like the one under discussion here are needed. At the University of Freiburg, a DFG funded project[1] is currently under way to achieve just that. The present contribution demonstrates that established frames of 'nation – speech community – variety' are not sufficient to capture the full range of the sociolinguistic dynamics involved in such situations, and it points to the relevant sociolinguistic orders that need to be taken into account to achieve a more realistic analytical picture.

APPENDIX: TRANSCRIPTION CONVENTIONS

.	sentence-final intonation
,	non-final intonation
?	question intonation
(.)	short pause
(.3)	timed pause
wor-	sharp termination
wo:rd	lengthening of sound preceding colon
foreign (translation)	non-English word followed by an English translation in parentheses
word=word	no discernible pause between words or intonation units
A: word= B: =word	no discernible pause between turns
WORD	increased volume
°word°	beginning and end of quieter speech
@	laughter

NOTE

1. 1652/12-1 'West African Englishes on the Move: New Forms of English as a Lingua Franca (ELF) in Germany'; PI: Christian Mair.

REFERENCES

Alim, H. Samy (2015), 'Hip hop nation language: localization and globalization', in Sonja L. Lanehart (ed.), *The Oxford Handbook of African American Language*, New York: Oxford University Press, 850–62.

Blommaert, Jan (2009), 'Language, asylum, and the national order', *Current Anthropology*, 50: 4, 415–41.

Blommaert, Jan (2010), *The Sociolinguistics of Globalization*, Cambridge: Cambridge University Press.

Bucholtz, Mary and Kira Hall (2005), 'Identity and interaction: a sociocultural linguistic approach', *Discourse Studies*, 7: 4–5, 585–614.

Bundesamt für Migration und Flüchtlinge (2019), 'Ankunftszentren und AnkER-Einrichtungen', *Asyl und Flüchtlingsschutz*, 14 November, <https://www.bamf.de/DE/Themen/AsylFluechtlingsschutz/Ankunftszentren/ankunftszentren-node.html> (last accessed 22 January 2020).

Ebere, Charles and Evan Charles-Ebere (2018), 'Bumster subculture and Rastafari identity in The Gambia: the search for survival and social mobility among marginalised male youth', *Bangladesh e-Journal of Sociology*, 15: 1, 134–47.

Gabrielatos, Costas and Paul Baker (2008), 'Fleeing, sneaking, flooding: a corpus analysis of discursive constructions of refugees and asylum seekers in the UK Press 1996–2005', *Journal of English Linguistics*, 36: 1, 5–38.

Goebel, Zane (2010), 'Identity and social conduct in a transient multilingual setting', *Language in Society*, 39: 2, 203–40.

Goffman, Erving (1962), *Asylums: Essays on the Social Situation of Mental Patients and Other Inmates*, Chicago: Aldine.

Goglia, Francesco (2009), 'Communicative strategies in the Italian of Igbo-Nigerian immigrants in Italy: a contact-linguistic approach', *Sprachtypologie und Universalienforschung*, 62: 3, 224–40.

Gut, Ulrike B. (2004), 'Nigerian English: phonology', in Edgar W. Schneider, Kate Burridge, Bernd Kortmann, Rajend Mesthrie and Clive Upton (eds), *A Handbook of Varieties of English: A Multimedia Reference Tool*. Vol. 1: *Phonology*, Berlin and New York: Mouton de Gruyter, 813–30.

Hazel, Spencer (2017), 'Mapping the langscape: developing multilingual norms in a transient project community', *Journal of Linguistic Anthropology*, 27: 3, 308–25.

Heyd, Theresa, Ferdinand von Mengden and Britta Schneider (eds) (2019), *The Sociolinguistic Economy of Berlin: Cosmopolitan Perspectives on Language, Diversity and Social Space*, Boston and Berlin: Mouton de Gruyter.

Honkanen, Mirka (2020), *World Englishes on the Web: The Nigerian Diaspora in the United States*, Amsterdam: John Benjamins.

Huber, Magnus (2004), 'Ghanaian English: phonology', in Edgar W. Schneider, Kate Burridge, Bernd Kortmann, Rajend Mesthrie and Clive Upton (eds), *A Handbook of Varieties of English: A Multimedia Reference Tool*. Vol. 1: *Phonology*, Berlin and New York: Mouton de Gruyter, 842–65.

Irvine, Judith T. and Susan Gal (2000), 'Language ideology and linguistic differentiation', in Paul V. Kroskrity (ed.), *Regimes of Language: Ideologies, Polities, and Identities*, Santa Fe, NM: School of American Research Press, 35–84.

Jacquemet, Marco (2011), 'Crosstalk 2.0: asylum and communicative breakdowns', *Text & Talk*, 31: 4, 475–98.

Johnstone, Barbara (2013), *Speaking Pittsburghese: The Story of a Dialect*, Oxford: Oxford University Press.

Mair, Christian (2013), 'The World System of Englishes: accounting for the transnational importance of mobile and mediated vernaculars', *English World-Wide*, 34: 3, 253–78.

Mair, Christian (forthcoming), 'World Englishes: from methodological nationalism to a global perspective', in Theresa Heyd and Britta Schneider (eds), *The Bloomsbury Handbook of World Englishes*, Oxford: Bloomsbury.

Maryns, Katrijn (2014), 'The interdiscursive construction of irresponsibility as a defence strategy in the Belgian Assize Court', *Language & Communication*, 36: 1, 25–36.

Mortensen, Janus (2017), 'Transient multilingual communities as a field of investigation: challenges and opportunities', *Journal of Linguistic Anthropology*, 27: 3, 271–88.

Mortensen, Janus and Spencer Hazel (2017), 'Lending bureaucracy voice: negotiating English in institutional encounters', in Markku Filppula, Juhani Klemola, Anna Mauranen and Svetlana Vetchinnikova (eds), *Changing English: Global and Local Perspectives*, Berlin and New York: Mouton de Gruyter, 255–76.

Pennycook, Alastair (2007), *Global Englishes and Transcultural Flows*, London and New York: Routledge.

Pitzl, Marie-Luise (2018), 'Transient international groups (TIGs): exploring the group and development dimension of ELF', *Journal of English as a Lingua Franca*, 7: 1, 25–58.

Preston, Dennis R. (1994), 'Content-oriented discourse analysis and folk linguistics', *Language Sciences*, 16: 2, 285–331.

Quarcoo, Emmanuel (1994), 'The English language as a modern Ghanaian artifact', *Journal of Black Studies*, 24: 3, 329–43.

Schilling-Estes, Natalie (2007), 'Sociolinguistic fieldwork', in Robert Bayley and Ceil Lucas (eds), *Sociolinguistic Variation: Theories, Methods, and Applications*, Cambridge: Cambridge University Press, 165–89.

Schneider, Edgar W. (2007), *Postcolonial English: Varieties Around the World*, Cambridge: Cambridge University Press.

Schneider, Edgar W. (2014), 'New reflections on the evolutionary dynamics of world Englishes', *World Englishes*, 33: 1, 9–32.

Swaan, Abram de (2001), *Words of the World: The Global Language System*, Cambridge: Polity.

Zimmermann, Frank (2018), 'Das erste Wohnhaus der künftigen LEA wird eröffnet', *Badische Zeitung*, Freiburg, 20 April 2018.

CHAPTER 12

Onward Migration from Italy to the UK: Reshaped Linguistic Repertoires and the Role of English

Francesco Goglia

1 INTRODUCTION

In the last thirty years, the number of immigrants in Italy has rapidly increased. In 2003 immigrants numbered around one and a half million; by January 2015 their number had increased to more than five million (Caritas Migrantes 2015).

In recent years, newly naturalised citizens have left Italy to move to another European country. According to Italian national statistics (Istat 2019), out of 669,000 non-EU citizens who naturalised between 2012 and 2017 around 42,000 have moved abroad. This phenomenon is not unique to Italy, but is part of a larger process of onward migration within the EU which sees individuals or entire families of non-EU origin who initially settled and naturalised in one EU country (either as refugees or economic migrants) migrate to another one. The key factor in this kind of migration is the citizenship of an EU country which also provides freedom of movement and the possibility of relocating to another country. In the last decade, a growing literature within migration studies has investigated this phenomenon and has highlighted several general socio-economic push and pull factors that trigger onward migration. Among others, these include: the desire to move to a country with a large co-ethnic and co-religious community, discrimination, job and career opportunities, transnational links with friends and family, welfare benefits, better educational opportunities for the second generation, and less bureaucracy in the UK than in Continental Europe (Lindley and van Hear 2007; van Liempt 2011; Ahrens et al. 2016; Kelly and Hedman 2016; Mas Giralt 2017; Della Puppa 2018; Della Puppa and King 2018; McGarrigle and Ascensão 2018; Ramos 2018).

There are no comprehensive studies so far on multilingualism and the complex linguistic repertoires of migrants who have migrated onward. Families which migrate onward often decide to do so after a substantial length of life, sometimes decades, in another EU country, and the second generation are in most cases born in that country or arrived at a very young age. Participants in this study have migrated to the UK with their families (or some members) and belong to the category that Ahrens et al. (2016) label as 'family movers', whose motivation to migrate is to improve the future of the second generation.

Furthermore, existing studies on onward migration have only hinted at the second generation of onward-migrant families (Ahrens et al. 2016; Della Puppa and King 2018), identifying the children's future as one of the main pull factors for the families' decision to migrate onward. However, more research is needed on how families, and in particular members of the second generation, re-prioritise their use of the languages in their linguistic repertoires or how they cope with the challenge of maintaining both their heritage language(s) and the language(s) of the other EU country.

The aim of this chapter is to discuss how the second generation of onward-migrating families from Italy to the UK view the English language and the role they assign to it in their linguistic repertoires. Drawing on qualitative interviews conducted in the UK, the chapter analyses grassroots discourses to understand the role of English as a trigger factor to migrate onward in terms of linguistic capital, what attitudes participants hold towards the language and whether these attitudes are based on common ideologies within the family, the country of origin, or Italy. In the next section, I will provide a brief overview of the main theoretical concepts that underpin this discussion, in particular the concepts of linguistic repertoire, ideology and capital. I will then review current studies on the role of English in the linguistic repertoire of immigrants in Italy and onward migrants. The methodology section will be followed by the findings of this study.

2 THEORETICAL FRAMEWORK AND KEY CONCEPTS

The literature on multilingualism in immigrant communities or for individual migrants is vast, but it tends to focus on retention and use of the language of the country of origin and acquisition of the language of the country of arrival. However, contemporary migration is more and more transnational, and individuals may move several times to several countries in their lifetime or sustain multiple engagements between the country of origin and subsequent destinations. Onward migration within the EU falls into this kind of 'multi-step' migration. More recent sociolinguistic research has emphasised the transnational nature of contemporary migration and the importance of looking at individual migrants' trajectories in order to highlight effects on migrants' linguistic repertoires and identities in the host destination (Blommaert 2010; Blommaert and Dong 2010; Pauwels 2016; Tovares and Kamwangamalu 2017). Because onward migration within the EU is a new phenomenon, there are no comprehensive studies on multilingualism and language maintenance among migrants who have migrated onward. Drawing on Blommaert and Backus (2013), I will use the notion of linguistic repertoire as the totality of linguistic-semiotic resources that individuals have gathered throughout their lives. A list of the languages spoken by individual migrants does not provide the full picture of their multilingualism, as speakers may not have the same competence in all languages or may have a linguistic competence based on specific domains or activities (Blommaert et al. 2005).

From a sociolinguistic perspective, onward-migrating families have an enriched linguistic repertoire that includes the language(s) of the country of origin of the parents – which I will refer to as heritage languages – and the language(s) of the previous EU country of residence. Life in the third country requires them to reorganise their linguistic repertoires and their language use, both within and outside the family domain. These individuals' experiences of migration and linguistic repertoires are more complex than those of migrants arriving directly from outside Europe, in a one-step migration. Furthermore, migrants have to reshape their linguistic resources according to the host country they are in and their use of languages or attitudes towards them is indexical of language ideologies in the country. A concept which is very useful in the case of onward migration is linguistic capital, as part of Bourdieu's cultural capital (1986). For Bourdieu, knowledge of languages and education represent cultural capital that can provide power and access to resources to citizens in a given society. The value of cultural capital varies according to societies and ideologies. A very simple example is the value of the official national language in any EU country to gain access to the job market.

In Italy for example, immigrants are required to speak Italian and any knowledge of English is not necessary. Even when there is a need for English, very often immigrants from English-speaking countries are not hired because their education credentials are not recognised in Italy and if their variety of English diverges from British English or American English their proficiency is looked down upon. For example, many English-speaking immigrants from West Africa, despite holding high school certificates or university degrees from their countries, and being fluent in their varieties of English, cannot use this cultural capital in Italy (Goglia 2015).

3 IMMIGRANTS' RESHAPED LINGUISTIC REPERTOIRES IN ITALY AND THE ROLE OF ENGLISH

Many immigrants arrive in Italy with already complex linguistic repertoires, including local languages and more widely used national languages in their country of origin. In the case of former British colonies, linguistic repertoires may also include a variety of English and an English-based pidgin (or creole).

This is the case, for example, for Ghanaians (Ghanaian English and Ghanaian Pidgin) or Nigerians (Nigerian English and Nigerian Pidgin English). Although not focusing on English, several studies on immigrants' multilingualism in Italy have already provided insights on immigrants' use of their variety of English and their attitudes towards English as an international language (Goglia 2011, 2015; Guerini 2017; Mazzaferro 2017; Chini and Andorno 2018). These studies have revealed with empirical data how the English language, as an immigrant language, is maintained or used in the form of code-switching in communicative interactions even in Italy, a country in the Expanding Circle where the use of English is very restricted. In her study on Ghanaian immigrants in Bergamo, Guerini (2017) found that her participants perceived English to be the most prestigious language that provides linguistic capital for economic advancement both in Ghana and abroad (p. 231). Mazzaferro (2017) discussed the presence of English in the linguistic repertoire of the Filipino community in Turin from the perspective of translanguaging. He showed how in interactions within the family, speakers draw on all linguistic resources in their repertoire, among these their knowledge of English for effective communication.

English may also be useful in communication with Italians or other English-speaking immigrants. In my study on Igbo-Nigerians in Padua, most participants revealed that they often used English with Italians who can speak English or English and Pidgin English for inter-ethnic communication with Nigerians of different ethnic groups and other English-speaking migrants, such as Ghanaians or Cameroonians (Goglia 2015).

4 ONWARD-MIGRATING FAMILIES' REPERTOIRE AND THE ROLE OF ENGLISH

Onward-migrating families from Italy have a very complex linguistic repertoire. Parents usually speak their heritage language(s), and they may have some knowledge of a variety of English spoken in their country of origin. Once in Italy they had to learn Italian and, depending on the region in which they resided, they may have some knowledge of an Italian dialect.[1] During the period of their stay in Italy, there has been little or no chance to learn or improve their English, as their new life and work in Italy required only Italian or Italian dialects in pretty much all communicative domains. Occasionally some knowledge of English may be used to communicate with Italians who speak it or with other English-speaking immigrants. However, in Italy, English is not as useful as in Northern European countries, as the case of immigrants in Sweden discussed in Meierkord (2012: 149). As for members of the second generation born in Italy, they speak Italian as their first language. They may have learnt the heritage language(s) from their parents and may have some knowledge of Italian dialects, often used by Italian youngsters in the form of code-switching in conversation with peers. They may also have learnt English or other foreign languages at school like all Italian students. When these families migrate onwards to the UK, English is added to their linguistic repertoire. Parents learn it informally again as they did with Italian, while their children join the educational system and soon replace Italian with English as the language used in education and public domains. For example, European-Somalis in the UK add English to their already complex linguistic repertoires, with for example Dutch or Danish (depending on where they were onward-migrating from), Somali and Arabic, and any other language they may have learnt (Valentine et al. 2009).

Studies on EU onward migration, although not focusing on sociolinguistic issues, have touched upon the English language and a British education as pull factors for the choice of the UK as a preferred destination. In her study on Dutch-Somalis (of refugee origin) migrating onward from the Netherlands to the UK, van Liempt (2011: 259) reported that parents wanted their children to be fluent in English and get British degrees which they regarded as more recognised. A similar attitude towards English and a British education is echoed in Ahrens et al. (2016: 91), who found that several German-Nigerian and Swedish-Iranian parents had even sent their children to British international schools to study English for their future to take advantage of transnational ties in other countries. In their research on Italian-Bangladeshis who migrated to London, Della Puppa and King (2018) found that parents were concerned that their children could not be educated in English in the Italian educational system, a language they regarded as key capital for the future career of their children both in Bangladesh and anywhere in the world. The aim of this chapter is to add a sociolinguistic perspective to the research on onward migration. The research questions guiding my analysis are as follows:

1. What is the role of English in the linguistic repertoires of onward-migrating families in Italy?
2. What attitudes do parents and children have towards English (and a British education)?
3. How are the linguistic repertoires of onward-migrating families reshaped in the UK?

5 METHODOLOGY AND PARTICIPANTS

The data discussed in this chapter are part of a larger ongoing project, funded by the Leverhulme Trust, which investigates multilingualism, language maintenance and shift, and language attitudes among the second generation of families who migrated onward from Italy to the UK.

The participants in this project are all the second generation of onward-migrant families, aged between 18 and 26, who have migrated from Italy in the last eight years. Participants were recruited through personal contacts and using the snowball technique among university students at British universities. No particular ethnic community was preferred, the key criterion was their experience of onward migration from Italy. I first informally introduced myself and informed participants about this project. At a later stage they were asked to sign an ethics consent letter and complete a short survey, which aimed to collect sociolinguistic information on the languages they and the members of their families spoke, their attitudes towards these languages, their language use with interlocutors of different generations, and how their language practices changed when they relocated to the UK. On completion of the survey, I interviewed participants, using the survey answers as a starting point, to obtain clarifications and further expansion on important points. These semi-structured interviews were intended to develop into more spontaneous informal conversations on the participants' experience of life in Italy and migration to the UK. The interviews made participants reflect on important issues such as their views on language maintenance, their identity and the challenges they had to face when they migrated to the UK. The interviews were conducted mainly in English, although some participants preferred Italian. The interviews lasted between thirty and sixty minutes, were audio-recorded and took place either in public places, such as cafés at the universities or via Skype if a meeting in person could not be arranged. The data collection is ongoing, but so far twenty-six participants have been interviewed. In this chapter, I will report on findings on the use of English and attitudes towards this language.

The approach taken in this study sees the interview as a type of communicative interaction in which the content is locally constructed by both the interviewer and the interviewee (Pavlenko 2007; De Fina 2011; De Fina and Perrino 2011). With this approach the presence of the interviewer is not seen as a disturbance to obtaining natural data, but rather as participating together with the interviewee in the communicative interaction. The object of this study is indeed the way participants present their use of languages and reflect on it during the interaction with the interviewer. Participants in this study were generally keen on taking part in the study. Not only were they often pleasantly surprised by a researcher taking an interest in their experience of migration and multilingualism, but they were also very willing to share their ideas and the challenges they had faced in terms of language learning and identity. My role as an Italian interviewer in this study has actually triggered reflections and storytelling that otherwise would have remained undetected (cf. De Fina 2011).

6 LINGUISTIC REPERTOIRES PRIOR TO ONWARD MIGRATION

In this section, I will discuss some extracts from my participants' interviews in which they talk about the role that English held in their linguistic repertoires in Italy, the role that it played in the family decision to migrate onward and the actual use in the UK. A number of themes have emerged related to English in the interviews: English in the linguistic repertoire of parents in Italy, English in the linguistic repertoire of the second generation (participants) in Italy, English and a British education as a pull factor for onward migration, and English in the reshaped linguistic repertoires in the UK. I am aware that participants belong to different ethnolinguistic groups and may have had different trajectories; for this reason all extracts are contextualised with key information on the linguistic repertoires and life trajectories of the specific participants. In the extracts below, all participant names are pseudonyms. I have provided the hyphenated nationality and when relevant the ethnic group in brackets as this is important in order to have a clear idea of the family linguistic repertoire. When interviews were conducted in Italian, I provide only the English translation of the extracts.

6.1 English in the Linguistic Repertoire of Parents in Italy

The language policy in Italy makes Italian the dominant language in all aspects of public life. The parents of the participants in this study migrated to Italy from Commonwealth countries in the 1990s. In most cases, Italy was not the preferred destination, but was just an available destination for economic migrants to migrate to Europe. For this reason and because there are no previous colonial links with most immigrants' countries (except for some migrants from Ethiopia, Somalia and Eritrea), the first generation of immigrants has had to face the challenge of learning the Italian language. Not all immigrants coming from Commonwealth countries could speak a variety of English when they arrived in Italy.

In some cases, participants reported on their parents having little or no knowledge of English when they were in Italy. In the following extract, Neha, a female Italian-Indian (Punjabi) who migrated with her family in 2014, talks about her parents' knowledge of English before moving to England:

Extract (1)
[. . .][2] my parents learnt English, really basic level, when they were in India at school, but when they moved to Italy, they completely forgot English because they only spoke Italian and Punjabi.

Neha belongs to an Indian Punjabi family. She explains that English was not part of the linguistic repertoire of the family in Italy and her parents' limited initial knowledge of English faded away during their life in Italy. Her parents retained Punjabi as a family language and prioritised the use of Italian for their new life in Italy. Neha herself is a Punjabi speaker and studied English only when she started secondary school in Italy. Prior to their onward migration, English was not part of the family's linguistic repertoire.

Another interesting case is that of Ajoba, a female Italian-Ghanaian who came to the UK with her family six years prior to the interview. She speaks Italian and learnt English at school in Italy. However, she feels she cannot speak Twi (the most widely spoken Ghanaian language) very well, a language she learnt from her parents, and reveals that she can speak a bit of Veneto dialect (spoken in the north-east of Italy). In the following extract, while talking about the languages used in the family at the time of the interview in England, Ajoba explains that she had to speak in Twi (which she calls 'Ghanaian'[3]) with her mother because she is not fluent in Italian, while with her father and her brother she speaks Italian. Ajoba's perception of her mother's knowledge of Italian and English is very negative; she almost hyperbolically says that during her stay in Italy her mother 'did not learn Italian' and 'she does not even speak English'.

> Extract (2)
> I speak Italian with my father and my eldest brother and sometimes I speak Twi with my mother [. . .] because my mother did not learn Italian when she was in Italy and every time she speaks Ghanaian with my father [. . .] she does not even speak English, only Ghanaian.

The parents of the participants in this study are both from the same ethnolinguistic groups. In such endogamous families, parents tend to speak their heritage language among themselves and in some cases with their children. In Ajoba's experience, Twi is key for communication with her mother, who holds it as her preferred code, since she does not speak Italian and English. Evidence from other interviews also confirms that the use and maintenance of Twi among Ghanaians in the diaspora is rather high, as opposed to Ghanaian English. Twi is also used in Ghanaian Pentecostal churches and is taught to the second generation.

While the use of the heritage language among parents is reported by all participants, not all participants report on their own active use of these languages as in the case of Ajoba. In Extract (3), Adeyemi, a female Italian-Nigerian (Yoruba), who was born in Italy and migrated to the UK ten years prior the interview, described her parents' use of the heritage language within the family. Both her parents can speak Yoruba and Nigerian English.

> Extract (3)
> My parents speak Yoruba and me and my sisters can understand, but can't speak it, so they speak it around us, but because we can understand them,

but we can't speak it back to them, we are just answering in Italian or English, either one of them.

Adeyemi's family language policy prioritised the use of Italian and Nigerian English over Yoruba, and therefore Adeyemi only has a passive knowledge of her parents' language ('we can understand them, but we can't speak it back to them'). The maintenance of the heritage language in these families is part of the individual family's language policy and is also the individual speaker's choice (Spolsky 2012). The use of English at home depends on the parents' level of proficiency and the deliberate choice to prioritise its use over the heritage language. Previous research on Igbo-Nigerians in Italy found that parents, educated in English until high school or university level, did not teach Igbo to their children even though the Igbo language is a very important marker of Igbo identity. The parents preferred to speak English and Italian, which were perceived as more useful for the future career of the second generation (Goglia 2015).

6.2 English in the Linguistic Repertoire of the Second Generation in Italy

Oluchi is a male Italian-Nigerian (Igbo) who arrived in the UK in 2010. His parents migrated to Italy in the 1990s, and after obtaining Italian citizenship they took the decision to move to the UK in 2006. Oluchi stayed back with family friends to finish high school and then joined his family in 2010. When the family were in Italy, they used to speak Italian at home, with the parents speaking Igbo between themselves. English was also used together with some Pidgin English, but Oluchi focused on learning English only when in secondary school. However, as many participants in this study stressed, the English they learnt at school did not prepare them to face the challenge of communicating and studying in the UK.

> Extract (4)
> [...] the problem is, as you know very well, the way English is taught in Italy, I knew how to say, for example gutter in five different ways, but I could not speak English with someone my age, it is a bit that English that you study Geoffrey Chaucer, but then you cannot hold a conversation in English [...]

Oluchi believes that in the Italian educational system's curriculum the focus is more on the rules of the language, for example nuances of the lexicon ('gutter in five different ways') and the literature ('Geoffrey Chaucer') rather than on practising the language for actual communication. Oluchi's parents' language policy was to prioritise the knowledge of Italian for their children. Although they are both educated and fluent in Nigerian English, they have not actively taught English or Igbo to their children. Oluchi remarked on having a passive knowledge of Igbo elsewhere in the interview since it was used by his parents at home.

A similar choice to prioritise Italian within the family was taken by Efua's family. Efua is a female Italian-Ghanaian who arrived in the UK on her own in 2016; some members of her family are still living in Italy and others have migrated onward to Germany. Efua was born in Ghana and migrated to Italy to join her family when she was only seven years old. When she arrived in Italy she could speak English and Twi. Guerini (2017) also found that some Ghanaian immigrants in Bergamo leave their children in Ghana in their early years to make sure they learn English and Twi (p. 232). In the following excerpt Efua talks about the use of languages in her family in Italy:

Extract (5)
... at home I have never spoken English, maybe I used to listen to English and American songs because I liked them, but at home in particular I used to speak Italian very often, but at home we mainly spoke Italian because when I arrived my father wanted me to learn Italian properly, so at home we only spoke Italian, later when I learnt Italian we spoke the dialect that we speak at home, but English very rarely also because our English is not the proper English, it is like 50 per cent English and 50 per cent dialect. I know families that used to also speak English at home, but it is very rare.

When Efua joined her family in Italy, her father prioritised the use of Italian in the family to make sure Efua learnt Italian. Later, they used what Efua calls 'the dialect that we speak at home', namely the Twi language. Efua observed that they did not speak English and goes on to explain that their English is 'not proper English'. Her comments reflect a generalised Italian/European ideology that does not consider prestigious African varieties of English. Efua also adds that 'it is like 50 per cent English and 50 per cent dialect', referring to an unmarked mode of speaking in African countries in which the African language(s) are mixed with varieties of African English (cf. Goglia 2011, 2018; Guerini 2017; Mazzaferro 2017). It is important to note that in the extract she refers to Twi as a 'dialect' to stress that Twi is a more local Ghanaian language as opposed to English, which is more pan-Ghanaian and also an international language. The label 'dialect' is the same one that Italians assign to their regional languages, although just like Twi in Ghana these are languages and not dialects. Efua's statement shows her understanding of the parallels between the Ghanaian and the Italian linguistic repertoires (cf. Goglia 2018: 716).

This deliberate family policy to prioritise the use of Italian in Italy triggered a language shift towards Italian. The fact that there were no active efforts to teach English to their children and a preference for using the Italian language in the family reveals that onward migration was not planned earlier and was only contemplated when the family naturalised. Other participants in the study report having similar language policies and of having learnt English only at school even if their parents are English speakers (cf. Adeyemi's family language policy in Extract (2). An exception is a female Italian-Sri Lankan (Tamil) participant who reported using only Tamil within the family and no English, but her parents sent her to private English tuition for many years. This choice was not linked to the future onward migration move, but to a previous plan to relocate to Canada. Ahrens et al. (2016: 91), discussing the studies of Swedish-Iranians and German-Nigerians migrating onward to the UK, found that several parents had sent their children to British international schools to learn English while still living in Sweden and Germany, to provide them with a future transnational education and career.

7 ENGLISH AND A BRITISH EDUCATION AS PULL FACTORS TO ONWARD MIGRATION

All participants in this study mentioned the English language and the British education system as the main pull factors for the family's decision to leave Italy, among them Tariq, a male Italian-Bangladeshi, who migrated onward to the UK with his family in 2010. His father was made redundant because of the economic crisis that hit Italy in 2008. In Extract (6), he explains that the family decided to move to allow him to be educated in the UK.

Extract (6)
the main reason to migrate to England was my education because . . . honestly, I would say that education in England is much better than in Italy [. . .] for example I do not think it would have been easy to go to the university here if I had just arrived from Italy [. . .] if I had done my high school in Italy.

Tariq's statements reproduce the ideology of the prestige of British education. His positive attitude towards a British education is based on his family ideology and the more generally positive attitude in Bangladesh towards British education and institutions (cf. Della Puppa 2018). He arrived in the UK when he was twelve, without any knowledge of English. Elsewhere in the interview, he told me how children of Italian-Bangladeshi families who migrate onward to the UK speak Italian at the beginning, since they cannot speak English. In the extract, Tariq seems to acknowledge that leaving Italy at a young age was vital to gather knowledge of the English language and to be able to access the British university system. In Extract (7), recalling his family's decision to move to the UK,

Tariq explains the opportunities that proficiency in English as an international language can offer ('many doors will be open') as opposed to the limitations of a more local language such as Italian. This reference to English as linguistic capital refers to a language ideology in Tariq's family pre-migration and clearly to opportunities available to young students such as Tariq (the second generation), but not to his parents. The value of English as linguistic capital is enhanced also due to the use of English in high domains in Bangladesh as a result of British colonialism; as Tariq says, 'Bangladesh was a British colony, so English is well recognised there' (cf. Della Puppa 2018).

> Extract (7)
> ... once you know English, many doors will be open, it is one of the most spoken languages in the world, much more than Italian. Also, Bangladesh was a British colony, so English is well recognised there.

It must be noted that this language ideology which assigns international English a high prestige had been dormant in these families when they settled in Italy, where Italian was the dominant language for the second generation's future careers. Gaining Italian citizenship also provided an opportunity for the family to choose to migrate onward. While living in Italy, these families were undergoing a language shift towards Italian. English added no major extra value to their daily life in Italy. Participants in this study enact in different ways their parents' positive attitudes towards English as an international language that can give access to better career prospects in their countries. The limitations of the Italian language and the Italian educational system in terms of future career prospects are perceived clearly by both parents and children (cf. Ahrens et al. 2016; Della Puppa 2018). Knowledge of English is regarded as vital for the future of the second generation. Although some participants view the Italian educational system as satisfactory, they nevertheless believe that it does not ensure a secure future. We must remember that in the last ten years unemployment among young people in Italy has been very high and career prospects are declining.

8 RESHAPED LINGUISTIC REPERTOIRES AFTER ONWARD MIGRATION

The choice of onward migration typically comes after both parents and children have spent many years living in Italy. For all families in this study, their new destination is the UK, where English is the dominant language. As we have seen in previous sections, families gave priority to the use of Italian in Italy and no conscious decision to study English was taken prior to the decision to migrate onward. Extract (8) is from the interview with Neha, who I introduced earlier. In the following extract, she talks about her parents' perceived knowledge of English after moving to England:

Extract (8)
When we moved to England, it was difficult because they did not feel comfortable with the language and even now they do not feel comfortable with the language, in fact my father, when he needs help like paperwork, always calls me and my brother [. . .] because he still uses more Italian and Punjabi, he finds it difficult to express himself in English, he really cannot, he does not speak it.

When they migrated to England, Neha enrolled in a college for two years to learn English in preparation for university. However, for her parents, she stressed 'it was difficult' because of their limited knowledge of English ('they do not feel comfortable with the language'). In Italy, Neha's parents spoke Punjabi among themselves and Italian outside the family and community domain. Neha stresses how, in the UK, she and her brother need to help their father with the English language as he still 'uses more Italian and Punjabi'. In Neha's family, both Punjabi and Italian are maintained within the family. The case study of Neha's family exemplifies very well the reshaped use of Italian in the linguistic repertoires of onward-migrating families. With onward migration, Italian is still used within the family and co-exists with the heritage language.

In Extract (9), Oluchi, a male Italian-Nigerian (Igbo) who was introduced in section 6.1, reflects on how his family language practices have changed after re-migrating to England.

Extract (9)
With us they speak Italian and among themselves they have always spoken Igbo [. . .] there is no difference between Italy and England . . . it is quite strange within our family it is like we had never left Italy based on what we do and how we speak, but when we are outside it is completely different.

Talking about his parents' use of Igbo between themselves, he stresses that 'there is no difference between Italy and England' as they keep using Igbo the way they used to do in Italy. He then goes on to realise that the family behave ('what we do and how we speak') as if 'we had never left Italy'. Language-wise, this family replicates the linguistic practices they had in Italy: the heritage language is used between the parents while Italian is used for intergenerational communication and among siblings. The maintenance of Italian is a result of this family language policy and linked to their identity as Italian-Nigerians. In public life, Oluchi says, 'it is completely different', as the required language is English.

9 CONCLUSION

In this chapter, I have discussed the role of English in the linguistic repertoires of families of third nationals who after obtaining Italian citizenship decide to migrate onward from Italy to the UK. This is a relatively new migration process that has not been investigated thoroughly so far from a sociolinguistic point of view.

The first research question concerned the role of English in the linguistic repertoires of these families. In the interviews, participants to this study, the second generation, provided a wide range of insights on their perception of the family's use of English in Italy and in the UK. When they were living in Italy, parents tended to prioritise the use of Italian for their children's future in the country and maintained their heritage languages for communication among themselves. Parents' use of English varied according to their level of education in their country of origin and was often mixed with the other family languages (cf. Guerini 2017; Mazzaferro 2017; Goglia 2018). The second generation's first language is Italian, and they learnt English through the Italian school system. Depending on the family language policy, they also had some knowledge of their heritage language, in most cases a passive knowledge of the language.

The second research question concerned parents' and children's attitudes towards English and British education. In the interviews, participants enact positive ideologies regarding English as linguistic capital and reveal that the family's decision to migrate onward was taken to provide them with a prestigious British education and a better future career. This is in line with other studies on onward migration which, in spite of not focusing on these families' linguistic repertoires, have identified the English language and a British education as two of the main pull factors that trigger the onward migration (Ahrens et al. 2016; Della Puppa and King 2018). Because the possibility to re-migrate within the EU only comes with citizenship and the family did not plan this second move, parents did not put any effort into maintaining English within the family or into making sure that their children learnt it. Even if all parents in this study are originally from countries that belong to the Outer Circle, where English has been adopted as a second language for intra-national use and holds high prestige, contrary to other immigration trajectories there was no active effort to maintain English within the family. With the possibility to migrate onward, parents' dormant ideologies of the opportunities offered by English as an international language and the prestige of English in their countries of origin reactivated.

The third research question focused on how the linguistic repertoires of onward-migrating families are shaped in the UK. All the participants talked to me about their initial struggle with the English language at the beginning of their time in the UK. They had to learn English quickly in order to cope with the challenges of a new school system. Onward migration to the UK re-prioritises the languages in the linguistic repertoires of both parents and children. Italian is no longer the most important language. A language shift towards English is possible again, after a period dominated by the Italian language. The investment of relocation is for the future of the second generation as the parents' own knowledge of English remains limited, giving them access to low-income jobs only. Parents continue to use their heritage languages in the family, together with Italian that is now also devalued to the status of a family language.

NOTES

1. The so-called Italian dialects are regional languages which, as Italian (Tuscan), derived from Vulgar Latin, but today they are not official nor fully standardised. Depending on the region, some dialects are still widely used in everyday communication and are very likely to be part of the immigrants' linguistic repertoire (Goglia 2018).
2. In all extracts '[. . .]' refers to the presence of more dialogue which was not reproduced because it was not relevant for the discussion, while '. . .' refers to a brief pause by the speaker.
3. The second generation often refers to the language of the country of origin of their parents with the nationality adjective, for example Ghanaian to refer to Twi or Nigerian to refer to Yoruba or Igbo. This is, in my opinion, a simplification of the linguistic repertoire of the country of origin in communications with Italians.

REFERENCES

Ahrens, Jill, Melissa Kelly and Ilse van Liempt (2016), 'Free movement? The onward migration of EU citizens born in Somalia, Iran, and Nigeria', *Population, Space and Place*, 22, 84–98.

Blommaert, Jan (2010), *The Sociolinguistics of Globalization*, Cambridge: Cambridge University Press.

Blommaert, Jan and Ad Backus (2013), 'Superdiverse repertoires and the individual', in Ingrid de Saint-Georges and Jean-Jacques Weber (eds), *Multilingualism and Multimodality: Current Challenges for Educational Studies*, Rotterdam: Sense, 11–30.

Blommaert, Jan and Jie Dong (2010), 'Language and movement in space', in Nikolas Coupland (ed.), *The Handbook of Language and Globalization*, Malden, MA: Wiley-Blackwell, 366–85.

Blommaert, Jan, James Collins and Stef Slembrouk (2005), 'Spaces of multilingualism', *Language and Communication*, 25, 197–216.

Bordieu, Pierre (1986), *Questions de Sociologies*, Paris: Les Éditions de Minuit.
Caritas Migrantes (2015), 'XXV Rapporto Immigrazione 2015', <https://www.migrantes.it/wp-content/uploads/sites/50/2019/05/Sintesi.pdf> (last accessed 30 January 2020).
Chini, Marina and Cecilia Andorno (eds) (2018), *Repertori e usi linguistici nell'immigrazione. Un'indagine sui minori alloglotti, dieci anni dopo*, Milan: FrancoAngeli.
De Fina, Anna (2011), 'Researcher and informant roles in narrative interactions: constructions of belonging and foreign-ness', *Language in Society*, 40, 27–38.
De Fina, Anna and Sabina Perrino (2011), 'Introduction: interviews vs. "natural" contexts: a false dilemma', *Language in Society*, 40, 1–11.
Della Puppa, Francesco (2018), 'Nuovi italiani attraverso l'Europa. Cittadini globali, stratificazioni civiche e percorsi di mobilità sociale in tempi di crisi', *Sociologia italiana*, 12, 95–119.
Della Puppa, Francesco and Russell King (2018), 'The new "twice migrants": motivations, experiences and disillusionments of Italian-Bangladeshis relocating to London', *Journal of Ethnic and Migration Studies*, 45, 1–17.
Goglia, Francesco (2011), 'Code-switching among Igbo-Nigerian immigrants in Padua (Italy)', in Eric Anchimbe and Stephen A. Mforten (eds), *Postcolonial Linguistic Voices: Identity Choices and Representations*, Berlin: Mouton de Gruyter, 323–42.
Goglia, Francesco (2015), 'Multilingual immigrants and language maintenance: the case of the Igbo-Nigerian community in Padua', in S. Gesuato and M. Busa (eds), *Lingue e contesti: studi in onore di Alberto M. Mioni*, Padova: CLEUP, 701–10.
Goglia, Francesco (2018), 'Code-switching and immigrant communities in Italy', in Wendy Ayres-Bennett and Janice Carruthers (eds), *Manual of Romance Sociolinguistics*, Berlin: Mouton de Gruyter, 702–23.
Guerini, Federica (2017), 'English and the Ghanaian diaspora in Northern Italy', in Cecilia Boggio and Alessandro Molino (eds), *English in Italy. Linguistic, Educational and Professional Challenges*, Milan: FrancoAngeli, 223–36.
Istat (2019), 'Indagine conoscitiva in materia di politiche dell'immigrazione, diritto d'asilo e gestione dei flussi migratori', <https://www.istat.it/it/files/2019/09/Istat_Audizione_I_Commissione_18sett19.pdf> (last accessed 30 January 2020).
Kelly, Melissa and Lina Hedman (2016), 'Between opportunity and constraint: understanding the onward migration of highly educated Iranian refugees from Sweden', *International Migration and Integration*, 17, 649–67.
Lindley, Anna and Nicholas van Hear (2007), 'New Europeans on the move: a preliminary review on the onward migration of refugees within the European Union', COMPAS Working Paper 57 (WP-07-57), Oxford: COMPAS.
McGarrigle, Jennifer and Eduardo Ascensão (2018), 'Emplaced mobilities:

Lisbon as a translocality in the migration journeys of Punjabi Sikhs to Europe', *Journal of Ethnic and Migration Studies*, 44: 5, 809–28.

Mas Giralt, Rosa (2017), 'Onward migration as coping strategy? Latin Americans moving from Spain to the UK post-2008', *Population, Space and Place*, 23: 3, published online 11 March 2016.

Mazzaferro, Gerardo (2017), 'The relocation of English(es) in migratory contexts: the case of the Filipino community in Turin (Italy)', in Cecilia Boggio and Alessandro Molino (eds), *English in Italy. Linguistic, Educational and Professional Challenges*, Milan: FrancoAngeli, 237–50.

Meierkord, Christiane (2012), *Interactions across Englishes. Linguistic Choices in Local and International Contact Situations*, Cambridge: Cambridge University Press.

Pauwels, Anne (2016), *Language Maintenance and Shift*, Cambridge: Cambridge University Press.

Pavlenko, Anita (2007), 'Autobiographical narratives as data in applied linguistics', *Applied Linguistics*, 28: 2, 163–88.

Ramos, Cristina (2018), 'Onward migration from Spain to London in times of crisis: the importance of life-course junctures in secondary migration', *Journal of Ethnic and Migration Studies*, 44: 11, 1841–57.

Spolsky, Bernard (2012), 'Family language policy – the critical domain', *The International Journal of Multilingual and Multicultural Development*, 33: 1, 3–11.

Tovares, Alla V. and Nkonko M. Kamwangamalu (2017), 'Migration trajectories: implications for language proficiencies and identities', in Suresh Canagarajah (ed.), *The Routledge Handbook of Migration and Language*, London and New York: Routledge, 207–27.

Valentine Gill, Deborah Sporton and Katrine Bang Nielsen (2009), 'Identities and belonging: a study of Somali refugee and asylum seekers living in the UK and Denmark', *Environment and Planning D: Society and Space*, 27: 2, 234–50.

van Liempt, Ilse (2011), 'Young Dutch Somalis in the UK: citizenship, identities and belonging in a transnational triangle', *Mobilities*, 6: 4, 569–83.

Index

access to English
   in South Africa 95–7
   in Uganda 97–100
accommodation, 14, 144, 147–8, 162
acrolect, 13, 50–6, 61, 63–5, 97
agreement *see* concord
American English (AmE), 33, 123, 235, 250–1
angloversals, 135
Apartheid, 94–6
Arabic, 143–6, 148, 162, 167, 171–2, 174–9, 181, 211, 214, 218–19
article usage, 94, 107, 134–5
artistic representation of language, 115–16
asylum seekers, 15–16, 211–12, 215, 217, 222, 224, 229, 233, 236, 241, 245, 247
authenticity of language usage, 116, 127, 136

Bahrain, 14, 143–5, 149–50
Bangladesh, 15, 165–6, 168–71, 173–7, 179–81
Bantu, 51, 54, 56, 62–4
boda boda ('motor cycle taxi') driver(s), 50, 54, 62
Bollywood, 118
British education, 265–8
British English (BrE), 2–3, 55, 64–5, 180, 248, 251
'broken English', 33, 117, 222

capital, English as linguistic, 257, 265–8
China, English in, 7
code negotiation, 241
code-mixing, 188, 227, 264
code-switching, 4, 16, 107, 109, 148, 197, 258–9
colonial ideology, 250

commodification, 79
communication accommodation theory *see* accommodation
communicative competence, 72
communicative effectiveness, 27
communicative needs, 109
Complex Dynamic Systems, 26, 35
complexity, of utterances, 130
conceptual metaphors, 118
concord, lack of, 53, 55–6, 103–5, 110
   subject-verb, 103–4, 107
copula, omission, 132–3, 135
corpus, 128, 133, 191, 212
count nouns versus non-count nouns *see* mass nouns
creoles, 7, 11, 17, 94, 103, 107, 135–6
Critical Discourse Analysis (CDA), 115, 118–19
cross-linguistic influence, 31
cultural capital, 257

Dalit, 118
determiner usage, 104, 107, 134
diffidence, 62–3
disadvantage, 91–3, 95
domestic workers, 7, 9, 15, 168–9, 173–5, 178–9, 186–7, 189–90, 192–3, 197, 202–4

economic migration, 165–71, 177–82, 261
   low- and semi-skilled, 165, 169
   social and psychological costs, 167, 178
ELF *see* English as a Lingua Franca
elitist English, 1, 6, 58, 118

endonormative stabilization, 107
English
  as a Foreign Language (EFL), 7, 23, 25, 29–30, 32, 34, 41
  as a Lingua Franca (ELF), 1–3, 6, 10, 12, 16–17, 25, 38, 40, 49–50, 71, 74, 94–5, 98, 143, 145, 167, 211–15, 220–1, 228–9, 235, 249
  as a Native Language (ENL), 7, 23, 25, 29–30, 32, 34, 41
  as a Second Language (ESL), 2, 5, 7, 11, 23, 25, 145
  as cultural capital, 167
  for Specific Purposes (ESP), 40
English Language Complex, 1, 2, 11, 16, 35
English Vinglish, 118
ENL see English as a Native Language
ESL see English as a Second Language
ESP see English for Specific Purposes
ethical research considerations, 166, 170, 182
ethnography, 13, 15, 59, 70, 100, 166, 170, 190, 229, 233, 236, 240
ethnolinguistic, 62, 232, 236, 242, 245, 261–2
Expanding Circle, 3, 5–7, 25, 29–30, 32, 34, 65, 211–14, 258
extra- and intraterritorial forces, 35

Facebook, 37–8, 225
first language acquisition, 9, 135
first language transfer, 94
food and language, 127
formal acquisition of English, 91

Gambian English, 247–8, 251
German, 15, 16, 213–15, 218, 224–9
Ghanaian English, 246–7, 251, 258
Ghanaian Pidgin English, 258
Global South, 165–6
globalization, 9, 12, 24–5, 36, 39, 42, 70–2, 186, 188, 212
grassroots,
  contexts, 11–12, 28, 251
  English(es), 2–17, 23–7, 31, 33–6, 38, 41–2, 49–50, 52–61, 63–5, 70–1, 75, 85–6, 91–2, 110, 115, 117–18, 127–36, 143, 151, 165–7, 169, 178–82, 186, 188–9, 190–1, 197–200, 213, 217, 223, 226, 229
  German, 226
  identity, 77, 79, 219, 234, 244–5, 251

multilingualism, 4, 24, 26, 27, 36, 39, 42, 71, 117, 228–9
  notion, 3–5, 7–12, 70, 73, 86

habitual, 103–4, 110
Heidelberger Forschungsprojekt Pidgin-Deutsch, 93
heritage language(s), 16, 256–8, 262
holophrases, 135
hybrid English *see* mixed codes
hypercentral language, 1, 13, 187, 214, 220, 228, 235, 245

ideologies of language, 14, 23, 115–18, 120, 233, 238–40, 242, 245, 248, 250–1, 256–7, 264–6, 268
Igbo, 237–8, 241–3, 246, 258, 263–4
immigrants, 16, 93, 168, 213, 229, 238, 255–8, 261
incomplete sentences, 9, 28–31, 41, 117, 129–32
indexicality, 16, 49, 53, 231, 233–4, 236, 239, 245–6, 251, 257
Indian English, 1, 3, 5, 13–14, 36, 110, 118–19, 136
'indirect rule' policy, 5
inequality, 170, 179, 181
inflection, lack of, 133–5
informal input, 93, 95
instrumental motivation, 8–9, 26, 28, 38, 78–80, 117, 166, 189, 199, 203
integration, 215–17, 223, 226, 228
Interactions across Englishes, 27, 34, 42, 56, 109, 213
intercultural communication, 14, 144–7, 149, 162
interrogation, 94, 134–5, 168
interview, 39–41, 75, 81–2, 88, 149, 170–5, 177–8, 180–1, 197, 199, 216–18, 224–5, 228, 240–1, 243, 247–8, 260, 262, 264–5, 267
Italian, 16, 257
  dialect, 258

Jamaican
  Creole, 17, 116, 248, 251
  cultural practices, 248
  English, 17, 64, 247–8
  linguistic impact, 64, 251

Kiswahili, 75, 78–9, 98
Korea, English in, 7, 33, 117, 168

L1 *see* first language acquisition
langscaping, 235–6, 245, 250–1
language acquisition, 12, 24, 28, 35, 40, 72, 75, 95, 106, 110, 127, 131, 202–3; *see also* first language acquisition, Second Language Acquisition (SLA)
language attitudes, 6, 10, 13–14, 16, 50, 60, 109, 115, 117, 119–20, 136, 166, 170, 213, 256–60, 266, 268
language maintenance, 256, 259–60, 262–3, 267
language shift, 31, 147, 224–5, 259, 264, 266, 269
learnability, 93
learner English, 135, 220, 223; *see also* English as a Foreign language (EFL)
learning trajectories, 71, 81, 85
left dislocation *see* topicalisation
lingua franca, 1, 23, 24, 49–50, 146–7, 168, 179, 226–7, 229, 239, 241, 243–4
 communication, 25, 34, 243
 contexts, 34
 conversation(s), 23
 English *see* English as a Lingua Franca (ELF)
 features, 42
linguistic repertoire *see* repertoire
literary language / dialect, 116
low-skilled / semi-skilled, 166, 169, 181–2
Luganda, 62–3

Macaulay's 'Minute', 5
Mandarin, 1, 213
mass nouns, pluralisation of, 55
mean utterance length (MLU) *see* utterance length
media language, 116–17, 136
methodological research considerations, 166, 179–82
Middle East, 165–6, 168–72, 179, 181, 211, 214
migrant workers, 15
 social and psychological costs, 167, 179, 181, 190, 203, 212, 234–5
missing syntactic constituents, 132
mixed codes, 3, 8, 12, 36, 94, 188, 227
mobility, 3, 12, 70–1, 126, 174, 187

multilingualism, 4, 12, 15, 24, 26–7, 36, 39–42, 71, 75, 86, 117, 186, 188, 191, 196, 202, 212, 228–9, 255–60
multimodality, 120, 122, 123, 127

narratives, 58–9, 61, 166–7, 170–1, 179, 181, 237
natural language acquisition, 8, 28, 72, 93, 128, 135
negation, 108, 134–5
Nigerian English, 17, 239, 247, 251, 258, 262–4
Nigerian Pidgin English, 17, 239, 247, 258
Nilotic, 51, 55, 57
non-count nouns *see* mass nouns
non-postcolonial contexts, 23, 34
non-standard syntax, 132
norms, 13–14, 33, 35, 49, 64, 144, 162, 196, 199–200, 204, 232, 234–5, 237–9, 250–1

observer's paradox, 116
onward migration, 255–71
order of L2 acquisition, 135
Outer Circle, 3, 5–7, 49, 64–5, 165, 212, 214, 268
overgeneralisation, 28, 31, 94

paratactic syntax, 132, 135
past tense marking, 104, 107–8, 110, 134
pidgins, 2, 7, 11, 17, 94, 103, 104, 107, 135, 136
Portuguese, 15, 186, 191–4, 196–200, 203
postcolonial contexts, 23, 34
post-variety approach, 3
power, 3, 5, 8, 64, 71, 96, 119, 124, 147–9, 168, 170, 177, 178–80, 182, 228, 237, 251
pragmatics, 120
preposition usage, 31, 53, 59, 103, 107–9
progressive usage, 55, 64, 93, 103–5, 108, 110
pronoun usage, 28, 30, 94, 103, 105, 108, 134–5
protectorates, 49, 91, 97–8
Punjabi, 261–2, 267

question formation *see* interrogation

reduced constructions, 132
reduplication, 94, 104–5, 107–8, 110
remittance (recipient countries), 165–6, 169
repertoire, linguistic, 36, 40–1, 71, 186, 201, 212, 216, 218, 228, 235, 240, 250, 255–9, 261–2, 264, 267–9
 of parents, 261
 reshaped, 259, 266–7

scale level, 238–9, 245, 251
second generation migrants, 256
Second Language Acquisition, 12, 14, 24, 31, 117, 72, 93, 94, 127–8, 135, 136
   mechanisms, 28
self-correction, 105–10
settlers, 5, 91, 94–5, 98, 100–1, 109–10
simplification, 8–9, 28, 31, 39, 52, 117
social semiotics, 120
socio-economic status, 91
sociolinguistic order, 238
sociolinguistics of mobility, 234
South Africa, 11, 13, 14, 17, 91–3, 95–8, 100–5, 107–10
Spanish, 1, 15, 186, 191, 192, 194, 196, 198, 214
speech vs. writing, 116
Sridevi, 118, 126, 136
structural nativisation, 107, 109
subject omission, 133
subordination, 9, 132
super-diversity, 71, 85

Tamil, 3, 128, 265
Tanzania, 73–4, 78–9, 83–5
target language, 7, 10, 27, 93, 197, 200, 213, 246
teachability, 93

topicalisation, 55, 64
tourism, 8–9, 11, 13, 26, 31, 34, 39–40, 70, 74–6, 79–81, 86, 148, 212
transient multilingual communities, 233, 235–6, 241
translanguaging, 8, 27, 36, 94, 188, 258
transnational migration, 187, 204, 256
truncated repertoires, 188, 197–8, 212–13, 228–9
Twi, 3, 128, 262

Uganda, 13, 14, 49–66, 91, 93, 97–101, 105–10
United Nations, 6
utterance length, 129
   MLU (mean length of utterance), 131

vendor(s), 9, 50–1, 57–8, 62

World Englishes, 1–3, 10–2, 17, 23, 25–7, 29, 32–3, 35, 38, 42–3, 64, 70, 115, 119, 135–6, 143, 187, 233–5
World System of Englishes, 233, 235, 237–9, 251

YouTube, 115–16, 215

Zanzibar, 13, 70–1, 73–88
zero copula *see* copula, omission

EU representative:
Easy Access System Europe
Mustamäe tee 50, 10621 Tallinn, Estonia
Gpsr.requests@easproject.com

www.ingramcontent.com/pod-product-compliance
Lightning Source LLC
Chambersburg PA
CBHW081417230426
43668CB00016B/2269